THE DESIGN AND CONDUCT
OF MEANINGFUL EXPERIMENTS
INVOLVING HUMAN PARTICIPANTS

The Design and Conduct of Meaningful Experiments Involving Human Participants

25 Scientific Principles

R. Barker Bausell, PhD

OXFORD
UNIVERSITY PRESS

OXFORD

UNIVERSITY PRESS

Oxford University Press is a department of the University of
Oxford. It furthers the University's objective of excellence in research,
scholarship, and education by publishing worldwide.

Oxford   New York
Auckland   Cape Town   Dar es Salaam   Hong Kong   Karachi
Kuala Lumpur   Madrid   Melbourne   Mexico City   Nairobi
New Delhi   Shanghai   Taipei   Toronto

With offices in
Argentina   Austria   Brazil   Chile   Czech Republic   France   Greece
Guatemala   Hungary   Italy   Japan   Poland   Portugal   Singapore
South Korea   Switzerland   Thailand   Turkey   Ukraine   Vietnam

Oxford is a registered trademark of Oxford University Press
in the UK and certain other countries.

Published in the United States of America by
Oxford University Press
198 Madison Avenue, New York, NY 10016

© Oxford University Press 2015

Library of Congress Cataloging-in-Publication Data
Bausell, R. Barker, 1942–
The design and conduct of meaningful experiments
involving human participants : 25 scientific principles / R. Barker Bausell, Ph.D.
pages cm
Includes index.
ISBN 978-0-19-938523-2 (pbk. : alk. paper)
1. Human experimentation in medicine.   2. Human experimentation in psychology.
3. Experimental design. 4. Research—Methodology.   I. Title.
R853.H8B39 2015
174.2′8—dc23
2014026013

To Rebecca Barker Bausell, MD

CONTENTS

ACKNOWLEDGMENTS

I would like to thank Rebecca and Jesse Bausell for their help in preparing many of the book's figures. I also thank former dean, Janet Allan, and current dean, Jane Kirschling, University of Maryland School of Nursing, for providing continuing access to the University of Maryland library facilities. At Oxford University Press I greatly benefited from the services of Emily Perry, senior production editor, and Jerri Hurlbutt, copyeditor. And finally, I would like to acknowledge my editor, Abby Gross, for her unwavering support and for her belief in the importance of this project.

INTRODUCTION

The Design and Conduct of Meaningful Experiments Involving Human Participants discusses a family of methods essential for prospective behavioral, educational, psychological, social, and health experimentation involving humans. Experiments of this nature employ a unique scientific methodology involving the purposeful introduction of interventions for the sole purpose of observing their effect on discrete, measurable outcomes in real time. While such experiments are conceptually simplistic, they involve synthetic processes requiring both considerable knowledge and experience to perform correctly.

Controlled human experimentation was almost unknown a century ago, but it has since grown into a global industry with an estimated 75 new trials published daily in medicine alone (Bastian, Glasziou, & Chalmers, 2010). Given the astronomical cost of this scientific effort combined across *all* disciplines, both in terms of monetary value and human effort, a major purpose of this book is to suggest methods for maximizing the yield of these individual experiments—a consideration becoming increasingly important as we enter an era of increasingly limited resources. A related objective is to suggest strategies for increasing the methodological rigor with which such experiments are both designed and conducted. As such, the book does not deal with statistical issues in any depth—nor is it keyed to any single academic discipline. The same design principles, challenges, options, and issues apply to all *prospective* human experiments which involve (a) the administration of an intervention, (b) the collection of data relevant to the hypothesized effects of that intervention, and (c) the statistical analysis of those data to ascertain if the generated effects are consonant with those hypothesized.

On one level experimental research involving human participants is a rather specialized scientific enterprise that is conducive only to certain fields (e.g., psychology, education, political science, sociology, medicine, health promotion, nursing, social work) and, therefore, at first glance the book's subject matter may appear somewhat restrictive. However, prospective experimentation comprises the *only* viable option for generating definitive causal inferences regarding some of the most important questions facing scientists and clinicians—questions that tend to be highly specific and answerable via a simple "yes" or "no," such as:

1. Does vitamin C prevent breast cancer?
2. Does class size affect elementary school students' learning of mathematical concepts?

3. Does cognitive behavioral psychotherapy reduce depression?
4. Is moderate exercise more effective than bed rest in increasing mobility following surgery?
5. Does acupuncture reduce pain due to osteoarthritis of the knee?

Without question the exclusion of methods employed by all research *not* involving human participants eliminates many extremely important scientific endeavors, including some of the most striking *experiments* in the history of science such as (a) Arthur Eddington's 1919 trip to a remote African island to test a key prediction emanating from the theory of general relativity and (b) all laboratory work not involving bringing human research subjects into the building. However, human experimentation deals with issues and discrete procedures not relevant to other types of research employing animals, chemical reactions, tissues, cellular material, industrial production, or natural forces. Most obviously, the investigation of educational, behavioral, psychological, medical, and social issues requires an assiduous consideration of the potential risks and benefits of the research itself to participants and the society that supports it. This book extends this incontrovertible principle into something a bit less obvious (and for which there will be less than universal professional consensus), however, and that is the assumption that the applied human science should be held to another overriding ethical standard—namely the expectation that human experimentation should have the *potential* for meaningfully contributing to the quality of human life.

Meaningfulness is a difficult attribute to both define and judge in any context, but especially in science. Regardless of definitions, disciplines, and orientations, however, there is no disagreement that all scientific work of the nature just described requires

1. An understanding and acceptance of the governing ethical and cultural principles of the society of scientists, and
2. The acquisition of the educational prerequisites (and cultivatable attributes) necessary for both the pursuit of a successful scientific career and the conduct of meaningful experiments involving human participants.

To begin the process of facilitating the acquisition of these prerequisites, the first section of this book involves an introduction to the experimental process itself. The first chapter is dedicated to introducing 6 of an eventual 25 experimental principles considered to be prerequisites to becoming the type of scientist capable of designing and conducting meaningful experiments. Of equal importance, perhaps, the types of issues addressable (and not addressable) by prospective experiments involving human participants are delineated.

The second chapter makes the point, via a parable involving a hypothetical arthritis sufferer and her physician, that the conduct of experiments is hardly an exclusively scientific province. We all conduct experiments in our everyday lives, and we all make important causal inferences based on them as part of our evolved human job description. Navigating the web of challenging logical and psychological impediments associated with making *complex* causal inferences, however, has necessitated the creation of experimental science and has itself become one important key to our performance as *Homo sapiens*.

Chapter Three introduces the concept of experimental design by way of a fictitious experiment performed by our arthritis patient's physician, Dr. Jones. The crucial role played by an a priori hypothesis in the design process, as well as its importance in facilitating the evaluation of the concept of experimental *meaningfulness*, is examined through the lens of investigators' initial motivations for performing their experiments.

The fourth chapter extends the discussion of the experimental design process via a consideration of 10 impediments that prevent valid causal conclusions resulting from the most rudimentary (and commonly employed) formal experimental strategy: the single group, pretest-posttest design. The identity and mechanism of action of these artifacts, many of which were articulated a half-century ago in a classic research text (*Experimental and Quasi-Experimental Designs for Research* by Donald T. Campbell and Julian C. Stanley, 1966), are discussed.

The second section deal with those randomized experimental designs most crucial to research involving humans. Chapter Five introduces the two key foundational strategies on which these designs rest: the use of control (or comparison) groups and the randomization of participants to groups. Types and functions of five different control/comparison group genres are elucidated.

The sixth chapter begins the discussion of the design of multiple group experiments via the advantages of randomized vs. nonrandomized strategies. Five acceptable randomized, two unacceptable nonrandomized, and a hybrid design are presented. The advantages of the randomized over their nonrandomized counterpart are illustrated in terms of the 10 previously introduced experimental artifacts plus six new ones unique to multigroup studies.

A variety of factorial and repeated measures designs are then introduced in Chapters Seven and Eight—some commonly employed, some less commonly so, but each constituting a desirable component of every investigator's repertoire. All are capable of improving the informational yield and sensitivity of an experiment.

The third section deals with maximizing the sensitivity of the designs presented in Chapters Five through Eight as well as their proper implementation. Chapter Nine discusses a key component of design *sensitivity*—statistical power—poorly understood even by many successful practicing investigators. And since a well-designed (and sensitive) but carelessly conducted experiment is worthless, the generic behaviors, considerations, and processes involved in conducting experiments are outlined in Chapter Ten.

The fourth and final section begins with a consideration of issues surrounding the generalizability of research findings (Chapter Eleven), while the next chapter (Twelve) is given over to the introduction of three somewhat unique experimental paradigms (program evaluation, single-case experiments, and quality improvement studies) along with a number of designs specific to these research genres. The thirteenth chapter deals with everyone's least favorite (and therefore often most avoided) topic—bias and misconduct in the conduct and reporting of experimental findings. The book ends with a brief epilogue detailing the author's hopes and aspirations for his readers, along with a few final pieces of advice. An instructor's manual with suggestions for (a) class activities, (b) discussion topics, and (c) sample items designed to facilitate student understanding of the concepts presented in the text is available on a companion website www.oup.com/us/experimentaldesign.

Throughout the text, a concerted effort is made to foster a *deep* understanding of the "why" of the concepts presented, hopefully facilitated by (a) examples from the empirical literatures and (b) the aforementioned experimental principles designed to aid the reader in the pursuit of a meaningful, sustained scientific career. For to quote Jonas Salk, who surely qualifies as someone who did meaningful work: "The reward for work well done is the opportunity to do more."

REFERENCES

Bastian, H., Glasziou, P., & Chalmers, I. (2010). Seventy-five trials and eleven systematic reviews a day: How will we ever keep up? *PLoS Med*, *7*(9), e1000326. doi:10.1371/journal.pmed.1000326

Campbell, D.T., & Stanley, J.C. (1966). *Experimental and quasi-experimental designs for research.* Chicago: Rand McNally.

PART I

INTRODUCTION TO THE EXPERIMENTAL PROCESS

CHAPTER 1

CONDUCTING MEANINGFUL EXPERIMENTS

Prerequisites and Purposes

While the subject matter of this book involves designing and conducting experiments in the behavioral, educational, psychological, social, and health disciplines, it is important to keep in mind that this endeavor is only a small (but integral) part of the massive human enterprise we refer to as *science*. Science itself is comprised of a plethora of discrete disciplines, subdisciplines, and specialties employing a mind-boggling diversity of methods, objectives, philosophies, and approaches including observational, descriptive, correlational, and computer simulation designs. Yet all scientists are members of a single society possessing its own culture and basic mores. So the first step required for membership in this society and of becoming a scientist is to understand, accept, and, finally, be acculturated into this community.

This chapter therefore lists a number of principles that are prerequisites for the successful completion of this acculturation process along with some developable *attributes* that will prove helpful in the pursuit of a meaningful scientific career involving the conduct of experiments on humans.

THE PREEMINENT CULTURAL PRINCIPLE FOR SCIENTISTS IN GENERAL

> **PRINCIPLE #1: Do not contemplate a scientific career if you are not prepared to be absolutely, uncompromisingly, unfashionably honest and transparent.**

Scientific progress, indeed the scientific process itself, is integrally dependent upon the integrity of its practitioners. Professional honesty refers not only to the avoidance of complete fabrications, such as painting fake skin grafts on mice (Hixson, 1976) or reporting the results of identical twin studies for nonexistent children (Wade, 1976). Also included are the avoidance of small untruths and seemingly minor omissions, such as failing to mention minor glitches in a final research report that may have occurred during the course of an experiment, or changing one's hypothesis after a study's completion to fit the obtained results.

Reporting mistakes, identifying incidental findings as such, and simply being as transparent as possible regarding the conduct of one's work seldom result in serious professional setbacks. Instead, scientists who possess the courage to tell the entire truth and be totally transparent regarding their work are much more likely to reap long-term reputational benefits that more than compensate for any short-term setbacks. Scientists must also possess the discipline to recognize their personal biases and avoid the temptation to extend the implications of their experiments beyond the scope of their data. Those not capable of this sort of uncompromising (sometimes ridiculed) degree of honesty should consider more lucrative fields such as public relations or investment banking where, as compared to a scientific career, they can easily double their salaries and drive high-end imported cars.

BENEFICIAL, CULTIVATABLE SCIENTIFIC ATTRIBUTES

While perhaps not meriting the status of a "principle," there are a number of attributes that are quite useful for a scientist to possess. Among these are the following:

A methodical approach to one's work: Viewing the confirmation of one's own unique, previously unknown scientific discovery for the first time, no matter how small or specialized, can be one of life's most exhilarating experiences. Conducting the work resulting in it, however, can be simultaneously nerve wracking and tedious, involving a series of discrete, often repetitive behaviors, any one of which—if improperly performed—can torpedo the entire enterprise. It is therefore crucial for an investigator to possess the patience to check and recheck each step of the scientific process, as well as constantly evaluate the wisdom of one's procedural decisions, both a priori and emergent.

Learning from one's mistakes: No matter how methodical we try to be, mistakes (great and small) will inevitably occur—sometimes through lack of experience, sometimes through our own carelessness or that of our collaborators. While this may sound bromidic, these errors should be treated as valuable learning experiences which, once learned, should be freely acknowledged and never allowed to occur again.

Valuing intrinsic rewards for one's achievements: One motivation for hard work comes from the external rewards available to scientists. Scientists, especially later in their careers, probably appreciate money and professional advancement as much as anyone. In general, however, science is not as good a career choice as investment banking, administration, or plumbing for anyone for whom money or power are prime motivators. Instead, what scientists tend to treasure more are (a) the personal sense of accomplishment that accompanies their work, (b) the professional *status* this work eventually engenders among their colleagues, and (c) the opportunity to receive personal credit for their accomplishments.

Curiosity about everything even tangentially related to one's field of endeavor: While gaining recognition among one's peers is an understandable and even laudable goal, in the final analysis the accomplishments that a scientist looks back on with the greatest personal satisfaction involve the act of discovery (which, from the perspective of this book, often involves supplying a definitive answer to an unresolved question via a well-conceived, well-executed experiment). And while such discoveries can occur by accident, far more often they are due to hard work, competence gained from experience, and a scientific attribute for which we have no better word in English than *curiosity*. Everyone is endowed with a certain degree of this attribute, and it is enhanced by the habit of constantly searching for the solution to unsolved problems.

Being skeptical (and thereby open-minded): Perhaps more important even than curiosity is a cultivatable, often irritating, tendency to refuse to accept what passes for "common knowledge" as fact (or "obvious truths") as *the* truth. Good scientists tend to have specially developed antennae for detecting such lead-ins as "experts say" or "research says" or "the literature says" or "everyone knows."

Skepticism, while disappointingly rare, generally tends to be almost nonexistent (for both scientists and non-scientists) when evaluating one's own firmly held beliefs. It is much more common to be skeptical of others' views, but it is equally important to question one's own views and to recognize when we are just plain *wrong*.

Paradoxically, skepticism is also closely related to *open-mindedness*. All scientists, whether aware of it or not, operate within the confines of some sort of paradigm or theory. While desirable, since our disciplines' commonly accepted theories have usually gained acceptability *because* they have proved useful in generating confirmable hypotheses, the history of science suggests that these same constructions will eventually prove to be either incorrect or incomplete. It is therefore important to routinely acknowledge—from a personal and intellectual perspective—that slavish, unquestioning adherence to these generally accepted constructions may occasionally (a) blind us to alternate ways of viewing our discipline, (b) restrict us in the questions we might otherwise choose to investigate, or (c) make it more difficult for us to identify alternative explanations for our research results.

Open-mindedness is not a particularly pervasive scientific virtue, but it is cultivatable and therefore deserves the status of our second principle—partly because its absence can so easily lead to something that must be avoided at all cost—investigator *bias* (to which a later chapter is dedicated).

> **PRINCIPLE #2: Always be skeptical, but attempt to personally cultivate being open-minded.**

While all of the preceding attributes and principles are equally relevant to all types of scientific research, let's now turn our attention to experimental research involving human participants, beginning with a pair of unnecessary attributes relevant to *this* endeavor, followed by a few somewhat specialized prerequisites for its successful accomplishment.

UNNECESSARY (BUT NICE) ATTRIBUTES

1. *Mathematical aptitude*: With the advent of extremely easy-to-use point-and-click statistical packages, a working knowledge of multivariable calculus or differential equations is completely unnecessary for the successful conduct of human experimentation.

It is far more important to develop a conceptual understanding of concepts such as (a) probability as it relates to the normal curve, (b) variability in individual participant outcomes as they relate to experimental error, (c) statistical significance as it relates to both experimental error and the systematic difference between experimental groups, (d) randomness, and (f) correlation.

2. *Genius*: Geniuses are rare. Being extremely gifted isn't even as big an advantage in conducting an experiment as being methodical, developing a deep understanding of the procedural steps involved in experimental design (which constitutes the majority of the subject matter of this book), and being unafraid of hard work. Lacking genius will undoubtedly preclude anyone from developing an alternative to the theory of general relativity, but this book is concerned with designing and conducting experiments involving humans—not understanding elemental physical forces or the meaning of life.

PREREQUISITES FOR CONDUCTING EXPERIMENTS INVOLVING HUMAN PARTICIPANTS

Research training, especially with respect to hands-on experimental experiences and familiarization with the relevant cumulative experimental findings in one's specific field, provided by some of the behavioral, educational, and health disciplines sometimes appears to be less intense than that offered by many of their biological and physical counterparts. While there is no hard evidence for this generalization (and the following principle may be bromidic or even insulting to some), it is offered anyway for the sake of comprehensiveness.

> **PRINCIPLE #3: Do not contemplate independently conducting an experiment until you have mastered your general field and its experimental underpinnings.**

Experiments are not performed in a vacuum. Knowing *how* to design an experiment is a necessary, but far from sufficient, condition for actually doing so. Scientists must *understand* their fields as well as the basic paradigms underlying them. They are not required to accept existing theories and paradigms, but they must be thoroughly familiar with them.

From a practical perspective, then, if a beginning researcher has what he or she considers a most excellent idea for an experiment but is not thoroughly versed in the discipline encompassing it, the experiment should not be conducted. And unfortunately, there are few shortcuts to mastering one's discipline other than the tried-and-true steps of (a) enrolling in a good graduate program, (b) taking good courses, and (c) studying good textbooks.

Also unfortunately, even that isn't enough. One should also be familiar with the experimental literature in one's field—substantively (i.e., findings), methodologically (i.e., approaches and designs employed), and stylistically (i.e., the often subtle language conventions characterizing different disciplines, the mastery of which is an unwritten requirement for publication in their peer-reviewed journals). There are many ways to jump-start this type of knowledge, including participation in journal clubs, reading (or participating in) relevant meta-analytic and narrative literature reviews, monitoring the top journals in one's field, or simply reading as many published experimental reports as possible *while keeping an annotated bibliography of everything read*. For studies that appear to have no obviously unique features or merit, simply cutting and pasting the published abstract along with the reference will suffice. Bibliographic software (e.g., EndNote) greatly facilitates this process, the fruits of which can grow to encyclopedic proportions in time.

There is also something to be said for mastering as much of the empirical (not only experimental) research conducted in one's parent discipline (and not only in one's specific area of interest) as possible. The present author's research mentor (with whom he continues to be in contact four decades later) had a relatively unique method of acquiring such a perspective when he (the mentor) was a graduate student. Trained as an educational psychologist, he made periodic trips to the library to read the abstracts of all articles published in that discipline's premiere journal (*Journal of Educational Psychology*) back to its inception. And, of course, for those abstracts that seemed especially interesting he read the entire article.

Being young with a good memory, this gave him an excellent feel for both his field and its experimental basis. A strategy such as this would be considerably more convenient today since almost everything is online, as would the essential task of keeping abreast of new developments in one's area. As a mid-career research methodologist, your present author once found himself in need of updating his command of that multidisciplinary field's voluminous literature and over the course of a couple of years compiled a 2,660-entry annotated bibliography of journal articles and books that served him well for another decade (Bausell, 1991).

PRINCIPLE #4: Do not contemplate conducting research whose primary purpose is to change the way clinicians practice their professions unless you are an experienced clinician yourself or have an active co-investigator who is.

More concretely, no one should conduct an experiment dedicated to improving teaching practices within the public schools if they are not thoroughly familiar with both teaching and schools. The same applies to professional or therapeutic practices of any sort. At a minimum, collaborating with a practicing, experienced clinician when an experiment is to be conducted in a clinical setting, but especially if the purpose of the experiment is to impact clinical practice, improves the probability that the results will have a degree of clinical *relevance*. (The flip side to this coin also holds: A clinician should likewise not attempt to conduct research without benefit of collaboration with an experienced investigator.)

As will be discussed later, the results of a single experiment of any sort have little or no chance of exerting any immediately measurable real-world impact. Specific clinical practices, regardless of discipline, are affected by many other factors (e.g., costs, staffing, time constraints, institutional resistance to change, practitioner preferences, political realities, and ethical orientations). The end result is that experimental evidence often seems to wind up being ignored. And even when an experiment does attract interest outside of the scientific community, the public's memory span for research results may be even briefer than Andy Warhol's oft-quoted 15-minute prediction.

Yet, as a society we do seem to evolve slowly, learn from our past mistakes, and apply previously discovered scientific findings to help ameliorate real-world problems—just not as quickly as most of us would like. It therefore helps for inexperienced investigators to keep in mind that their primary job description involves performing work to further *their* chosen science rather than to affect immediate changes in the world—which is not to say that anyone in education, health, or the behavioral sciences should conduct experiments without considering their potential applicability to society. This consideration, after all, is at the heart of conducting *meaningful* experiments. It also doesn't mean that it isn't scientists' obligation to point out the real-world applicability of their work to all relevant parties who will listen. After all, hope springs eternal only if it is nurtured, and the hope that our scientific labors will ultimately have the potential to make the world a better place in which to live can be a powerful, enduring, and often frustrating motivator.

PRINCIPLE #5: Conduct your first research forays under the tutelage of an experienced, principled mentor.

A book such as this (if indeed there are any) may succeed in teaching the general principles of conducting experiments, but the only truly effective way to learn *how* to design, and especially how to conduct, an experiment is to actually do so. But without question, no one should attempt to conduct their first experiment *alone*.

For students, acceptance of this advice is pretty much mandated by most university-based institutional review boards (IRBs) requirements that an experimental protocol be either submitted or endorsed by a faculty member. This is a reasonable policy, because any trial designed or conducted by an unsupervised neophyte, even if low risk, will almost surely wind up wasting participants' time.

The best method of locating such a mentor is to either get a job working on an experimental project or to volunteer to do so. Most doctoral programs provide such opportunities through research assistantships or research rotations, but finding an experienced, principled mentor who has students' best interests at heart may require several trials and several errors. Since this process also involves hands-on experience conducting research, however, the search itself can greatly facilitate one's scientific learning curve.

Before undertaking such a search it is important to keep in mind that mentoring is a time-consuming, long-term, and potentially low-reward role for someone whose most valuable (and scarcest) asset is their *time*. It is therefore incumbent upon potential mentees to impress everyone with whom they work with their conscientiousness, commitment, low maintenance, and *drive*. It is also helpful to remember that the mentor–mentee relationship is bidirectional. Just as the mentee will rely on his or her mentor's help and reputation, it is possible that some day these roles will be reversed. A truly effective and principled mentor is like a professional parent: never a competitor but someone who takes enormous pride in the mentee's accomplishments.

WHAT PROSPECTIVE HUMAN EXPERIMENTS CAN AND CANNOT ACCOMPLISH

Although everyone has a basic understanding of what prospective experimentation entails, it may be worthwhile to review some of the basic purposes for which experiments are conducted in the behavioral, health, and educational sciences. First and foremost, all experiments are designed to facilitate the generation of a *causal* inference. Generically this is done by setting up a carefully controlled environment in which the environmental conditions can be altered systematically for two or more groups of participants. If one group changes substantive more on a prespecified outcome than the other, then (assuming everything was done properly) the investigator is permitted to infer that it is the altered experimental conditions that *caused* the observed change. If no differential change is observed on the outcome of interest, then the investigator would be permitted to conclude that the carefully altered conditions did not affect the outcome (always assuming that the experiment was properly designed and conducted).

With this said, it is important to realize that, while we can labor to eliminate all of the possible alternative explanations for a hypothesized finding (which is far easier to do in, say, animal laboratories than real-world human trials), few if any experiments are 100% definitive based on their own merits.

Experimental science, therefore, owes more of its success to the process of eliminating alternative explanations for phenomena than it does to *generating* their causal mechanisms (i.e., "inventing the intervention"). Penicillin, the general theory of relativity, or a new mousetrap might be tested (or evaluated) via an experiment, but considerable scientific effort precedes all experiments—whether occurring in a laboratory, a genius' mind, a skeptical examination of previous theory, or a thorough consideration of previously published experiments. Discoveries and inventions tend to be more the province of theoreticians, engineers, careful observers, or theory-generated (or otherwise inspired) trial and error than controlled trials. Experiments come later, after sufficiently plausible groundwork has been laid.

An experiment accomplishes two objectives, whether involving the controlled manipulation of a phenomenon or the observation of one under unique conditions:

1. It ascertains whether an effect or phenomenon actually occurs as predicted (e.g., pain reduction following acupuncture or light bending in the presence of gravity), and
2. It eliminates as many alternative explanations for an experimental result as possible (e.g., by including a placebo control group or measuring the degree of light distortion to see how closely it corresponded to the mathematical model).

In experimentation involving humans, the first objective is judged by probability levels emanating from statistical analyses of the collected data. The second objective is facilitated by employing appropriate experimental designs and implementing them with extreme care (which again constitutes the bulk of the subject matter of this book).

Amazingly, however, this conceptually simplistic process and its restricted range of results (e.g., the intervention was probabilistically superior, not superior, or was actually inferior to a comparison group of some sort) can serve a multitude of important scientific functions. There are also a multitude of different (and probably equally defensible) ways to categorize both experiments and experimental functions. In general, an attempt will be made to avoid categorizations and definitions in this book because they are seldom either mutually exclusive or particularly helpful. Also, the design and acculturation principles discussed are applicable to almost all types of experiments and experimental purposes involving human participants.

With that said, however, it may still be helpful to list nine of the more important functions of experimentation, the first two of which could serve as overarching experimentation genres (theory testing and efficacy determination) for those who prefer such categorizations:

1.   Testing a theory (i.e., an experiment *primarily* concerned with testing the validity of a theoretical prediction by empirically illustrating the existence of a phenomenon/effect and/or elucidating its etiology—or the conditions under which it occurs),
2.   Determining the efficacy of a previously untested (or inadequately tested) treatment, practice, strategy, or procedure under more controlled conditions,
3.   Improving the efficacy (e.g., by increasing the dose) of an intervention,
4.   Comparing the efficacy of two (or more) interventions,
5.   Replicating a previous finding,
6.   Determining how far a previous finding can be generalized (e.g., to other settings, populations, and conditions),
7.   Translating an important observational finding into an experimental (therefore causal) one,
8.   Answering a new question generated by a previous finding, and
9.   Challenging (or confirming) conventional knowledge (or practice).

Synopses of published examples will be provided of these functions throughout the book, most of which will be more clinically than theoretically oriented. Let's begin, however, with a rather complex, exemplary theoretical study (the first function) which also manages to be relevant to seven of the remaining eight functions. (This study also involves a number of procedural mainstays that will be discussed in detail later [i.e., *randomization, counterbalancing, and blocking*] and is presented at this point primarily to illustrate the types of inferences a well-conceived, well-designed, and well-executed experiment is capable of generating.) This study also very nicely empirically demonstrates the existence of an experimental artifact, the placebo effect, thereby providing a rationale for its assiduous control in certain types of research.

AN EXAMPLE OF DEMONSTRATING THE EXISTENCE AND ETIOLOGY OF A PHENOMENON (AS WELL AS ACCOMPLISHING SEVERAL OTHER OBJECTIVES)

An Analysis of Factors that Contribute to the Magnitude of Placebo Analgesia in an Experimental Paradigm (1999)

Donald Price, Irving Kirsch, Ann Duff, Guy Montgomery, and Sarah Nicholls

This experiment appeared in the journal *Pain* almost two decades ago. The first author, Donald Price, is a recognized pain expert and has published some very insightful technical books on the subject (Price, 1988; Price & Bushnell, 2004), but there are also books on alien abduction written by "recognized experts," so authority doesn't constitute scientific evidence.

The experiment was designed to (a) demonstrate the existence of a placebo effect and (b) elucidate some of the conditions involved in the phenomenon's occurrence. The participants were college students (the heavy lifters of nonclinical experimentation) and were told by the experimenter (appropriately dressed in a white lab coat) that the study for which they had just volunteered was designed to evaluate "a new, topical, local anesthetic...for its pain-reducing effects." They were told the drug's name was Trivaricaine, which had been proved effective in relieving pain. In actuality the "drug" was really a placebo that, in the authors' words, "was a mixture of iodine, oil of thyme, and water that produced a brownish, medicinal smelling effect when applied topically. This placebo concoction was placed in two medicine bottles labeled "Trivaricaine A" (or "Trivaricaine B"): "Approved for research purposes only." A third bottle contained only water and was creatively labeled "C."

After the students were familiarized with the equipment and the pain intensities to be used, they were assessed for their pain thresholds, and then the meat of the experiment began. (By necessity the description of this experiment has been condensed as much as possible, but suffice it to say that this "familiarization" was more elaborate than many entire experiments. Adequate training and familiarization of participants with the experimental environment is often a crucial component of a laboratory experiment such as this.)

Three areas on the participants' forearms were marked via labels "A," "B," and "C," with the locations of the labels rotated randomly from person to person. (We'll discuss the term *random* in more detail later, but it is a key aspect of all experimentation. In this instance it was used to avoid confounding anything—such as potential differences in sensitivity at different areas of the forearm—with the experimental conditions.) The investigators then informed the participants "that bottle C was a control wetting solution (which pretty adequately describes water) and that bottles A and B contained different strengths of the local analgesic Trivaricaine, which of course was patently untrue. So in effect, what we have is three experimental "conditions" (or interventions) consisting of (a) a strong placebo (strong only because the participants were told that it was a strong analgesic), (b) a weak placebo, and (c) no placebo (or no treatment at all).

Note that this strategy of exposing participants to all of the experimental conditions is a bit different from most trials in which different participants are randomly assigned to treatment groups. As will be discussed in Chapter Eight, this practice is referred to as a within-subjects or repeated measures (as opposed to a between-subjects) design and is feasible only when the treatments do not interfere or influence one another. When the strategy is feasible, however, it permits considerably greater experimental (and statistical) control than a design in which different participants are assigned different procedures.

After the students had been thoroughly familiarized with the drill, everyone was administered the pain *suggested* by the "medication's" description. The "strong analgesia" location on each person's arm received the mildest (least painful) temperature setting, the "weak analgesia" location received a considerably more uncomfortable setting, and the final location (at which point patients were told that were they receiving no pain medication at all, only the "wetting solution") received the most intensive painful stimulus of all.

What the investigators were attempting to do here was to create a *placebo effect* by *reinforcing* what the participants had been told *would* happen. None of the medications had any pain-relieving capabilities at all, but of course, the participants didn't know that. When the students were told they were receiving a strong medication, a carefully calibrated thermal stimulus of less magnitude was introduced than was the case when they were told they were receiving a weak medication. When the participants were told they were receiving no medication at all, the strongest thermal stimulus of all was administered, which had been previously demonstrated not to result in any skin damage or leave any discoloration. (While all experiments require pilot work, one such as this entails a great deal of preliminary work.)

The participants thus experienced exactly what they expected to experience based on what they were told to expect. And the pain "relief" they experienced wasn't due to their imaginations; it was quite real (even though it was a function of the investigators' deceptive manipulation of their thermal machine, not the fake medications).

So what we have here is a classical conditioning experience, very similar to Pavlov's dogs, except that instead of getting food, Price's participants received noxious stimuli. Then, once the investigators could be sure that their participants had been conditioned to believe in the effectiveness of the fake medications and would expect considerable pain relief from the strong placebo, the stage was set to find out if these expectations themselves could actually influence the amount of pain the students actually *experienced*.

To do this, Price and colleagues told participants they would receive some additional heat applications to each area treated by one of the three "medications." So naturally, everyone knew exactly what to expect, because they had already experienced these "medicinal" effects. This time around, however, precisely the *same* amount of pain was administered at each medication site. The amount of actual pain relief due to the medications was the same as well, which was *zero*.

The results, using the standard 11-point (0–10) visual analog scale (see Figure 2.1 in Chapter Two) used in hospitals and drug research, are presented in Figure 1.1 for both the pain actually experienced (labeled as "pain reality") and the conditioning placebo phase (the second column of points labeled "conditioning placebo effect," where the actual pain administered was the same for all three forearm areas). Naturally, a major difference between the three conditions in the "pain reality" results would be expected because participants really were administered different amounts of pain. But who would have expected there to be a difference in the second set of points representing the pain-conditioning phase, since there really weren't any differences in the amount of pain administered? Unless, of course, such a person suspected there might be such a phenomenon as an expectancy effect for pain (which happens to fit one of the definitions of a placebo effect).

Note that while the differences among the three experimental "treatments" in pain experienced following conditioning were not as great as the differences reported in the first phase (pain reality), these conditioned differences were in the expected direction and were statistically significant. (Note also that there were other results and hypotheses tested by this study, such as ascertaining if the

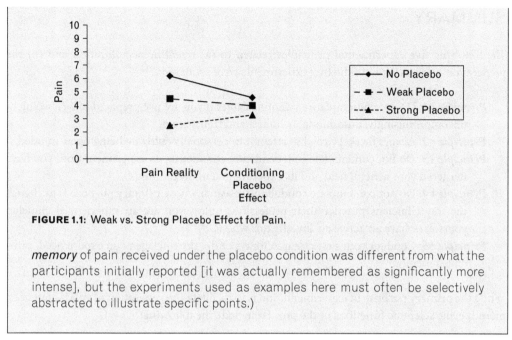

FIGURE 1.1: Weak vs. Strong Placebo Effect for Pain.

memory of pain received under the placebo condition was different from what the participants initially reported [it was actually remembered as significantly more intense], but the experiments used as examples here must often be selectively abstracted to illustrate specific points.)

While admittedly rather complex, this experiment was presented as the book's first example to illustrate a number of points. First, it is often possible to demonstrate the existence of a hypothesized phenomenon (in this case the placebo effect) and some of the conditions under which it occurs via an experiment design. Second, scientific experiments facilitate the control of extraneous factors (especially in a laboratory setting such as this) that "real-world" experiences and observations do not. And finally, and perhaps most importantly, every experiment leaves and creates many unanswered questions—the answers to which can only be supplied by additional experimentation (e.g., would the same effect accrue for an outcome other than pain, or are there alternative explanations for these results other than the placebo effect?).

Of course, most scientific experiments are neither as complex nor as well controlled as this example by Price and colleagues. In fact, the most minimalist definition possible of a prospective experiment might be:

> *An activity in which (a) an intervention is administered, (b) data are collected, and (c) the results are formally analyzed to ascertain the effects of the intervention.*

Naturally, this definition leaves out numerous recommended steps in the experimental process (e.g., measurements taken prior to the intervention, the use of randomized control groups and myriad other procedural strategies whose explication constitutes the bulk of this book), but it is a definition that succinctly covers most types of experiments from a teacher trying out a new strategy for teaching reading on her class to the Salk polio vaccine trials. It is also considerably more inclusive than many behavioral, educational, psychological, social, and health researchers would feel comfortable with, but it serves our purposes here by allowing us to examine the myriad difficulties associated with the generation of acceptable causal inferences based on experimentation. For we are all experimenters in our everyday lives, as illustrated by the experiences of one Mrs. Smith—to whom the entirety of the next chapter is devoted.

SUMMARY

The following five experimental principles related to (a) scientific acculturation and (b) the preparation necessary for conducting experiments were proffered:

Principle #1: Do not contemplate a scientific career if you are not prepared to be absolutely, uncompromisingly, unfashionably honest and transparent.

Principle #2: Always be skeptical, but attempt to personally cultivate being open-minded.

Principle #3: Do not contemplate independently conducting an experiment until you have mastered your general field and its experimental underpinnings.

Principle #4: Do not contemplate conducting research whose primary purpose is to change the way clinicians practice their professions unless you are an experienced clinician yourself or have an active co-investigator who is.

Principle #5: Conduct your first research forays under the tutelage of an experienced, principled mentor.

While the primary purpose of experimentation is to facilitate the generation of valid inferences, more specific scientific functions of the process include the following:

1. Testing a theory (i.e., an experiment *primarily* concerned with testing the validity of a theoretical prediction by empirically illustrating the existence of a phenomenon and/or elucidating its etiology or the conditions under which it occurs),
2. Determining the efficacy of an intervention (i.e., treatment, practice, strategy, procedure) by eliminating as many alternative explanations for this occurrence as possible,
3. Improving the efficacy (e.g., by increasing the dose) of an intervention,
4. Comparing the efficacy of two (or more) interventions,
5. Replicating a previous finding,
6. Determining how far a previous finding can be generalized (e.g., to other settings, populations, and conditions),
7. Translating an important observational finding into an experimental (therefore causal) one,
8. Answering a new question generated by a previous finding, and
9. Challenging (or confirming) conventional knowledge (or practice).

REFERENCES

Bausell, R.B. (1991). *Advanced research methodology: An annotated guide to sources*. Metuchen, NJ: Scarecrow Press.

Hixson, J.R. (1976). *The patchwork mouse*. Boston: Anchor Press.

Price, D.D., Kirsch, I., Duff, A., et al. (1999). An analysis of factors that contribute to the magnitude of placebo analgesia in an experimental paradigm. *Pain, 83,* 147–56.

Price, D.D. (1988). *Psychological and neural mechanisms of pain*. New York: Raven Press.

Price, D.D., & Bushnell, M.C. (Eds.) (2004). *Psychological methods of pain control: Basic science and clinical perspectives*. Seattle: International Association for the Study of Pain.

Wade, N. (1976). IQ and heredity: Suspicion of fraud beclouds classic experiment. *Science, 194,* 916–19.

CAUSAL INFERENCES AND THE STRANGE (BUT FICTITIOUS) CASE OF MRS. SMITH

O ver the millennia, making causal inferences has become part of our job description as *Homo sapiens*. Or, as Michael Shermer (2002) so eloquently put it, we have by necessity "evolved to be skilled, pattern-seeking, causal-finding creatures. Those who were best at finding patterns (standing upwind of game animals is bad for the hunt, cow manure is good for the crops) left behind the most offspring. We are their descendants" (p. xxiv).

Despite their importance to our survival and quality of life, however, our species isn't naturally very adept at making certain types of inferences under certain conditions. Being adaptable animals, we have developed a number of strategies and processes to improve our accuracy in this regard. Before considering these in any detail, however, let's examine (a) the types of inferences that are most problematic for us and (b) some of the natural impediments that make them even more so.

DIFFICULT CAUSAL INFERENCES

Like most tasks, some causal inferences are more difficult to make than others. Fortunately for us, our ancestors became quite adroit at making the most important and simplest ones: inferences involving outcomes that immediately, inevitably, uniquely, and powerfully follow the intervention. A classic example is a child learning to avoid a flame by touching it—purposefully (i.e., experimentally) or inadvertently.

Other causal inferences are considerably more difficult to make when the *outcome* does not immediately and inevitably follow the introduction of the *intervention*. As an example, take the seemingly simple and straightforward scenario involving an individual who experiences pain and visits a clinician who prescribed an intervention (let's say acupuncture) to relieve it. Here, at least eight disconnections between the cause and effect exist:

1.   The consequence (pain relief) may not inevitably occur as a result of the action (sometimes the intervention "works" and sometimes it doesn't).
2.   The consequence may not appear immediately but may do so later.
3.   The consequence is not predicted by a strong scientific theory or at least is not intuitively connected with the action (e.g., for some people it is counterintuitive that needles inserted somewhere completely dissociated with the location of the pain would relieve that pain by blocking the flow of chi—a so far unmeasured physical force—flowing through meridians in the body—so far a previously undetected physiological network).
4.   The consequence can occur in the absence of any action on the part of its recipient (the natural history of many symptoms is that they wax and wane or completely disappear with time and sometimes even incurable conditions inexplicably go into remission).
5.   The consequence may occur as a result of some other co-occurring action (such as ingestion of alcohol or an-over-the-counter analgesic).
6.   The consequence is not absolute but rather is measured in terms of a subtle gradient.
7.   The consequence has a large subjective component, or may even be psychosomatic.
8.   The consequence occurs for some individuals but not others, or occurs more strongly or consistently for some than for others.

Causal conclusions generated under such conditions are sometimes called *efficacy inferences* (i.e., the intervention "worked" because it cured the disease, relieved its symptoms, or affected some other psychological or educational outcome). Labels such as this are too limiting, however, because this genre of inference is also used to (a) determine if a given phenomenon actually occurs or is nothing more than a chimera, (b) hypothesize *why,* or *how,* a phenomenon occurs, (c) discover the necessary conditions (*when, where,* and *what* needs to be present) for this occurrence, (d) *create* new (or better) interventions, and so forth.

Regardless of their purpose, each of the eight disconnects listed here conspires to make such inferences completely unreliable when they are based primarily on human *experience*. Not because people are unobservant, but because so many alternative explanations exist for uncontrolled observations.

Still, in the absence of any alternative, human experience has served us reasonably well. Perhaps partly because of our development of more elaborate means of communication than any other species (which allows us to utilize the experiences of others in addition to our own). Our *need* for explanation (and its handmaiden, control) is so pervasive, however, that in the absence of anything better we have also become authority-respecting, and superstition-creating, animals.

Thus, while these eight inferential disconnects are problematic in their own right, they are supplemented by an entire family of omnipresent logical, statistical, and psychological impediments to arriving at valid inferences. These impediments, which will also be referred to as inferential or experimental artifacts, are as much a part of our physical and social environment as the air we breathe—the recognition of which undoubtedly contributed to the birth of an alternative inferential tool: formal scientific experimentation.

Consequently, this chapter will briefly examine a precursor to scientific experimentation that comprises a major component of our role as an inference-making species: the conduct of experiments on ourselves in our personal and professional lives. These uncontrolled, one-person experiments (not to be confused with the controlled single-case designs, discussed in Chapter Twelve) are especially useful for illustrating many of the natural impediments to valid causal inferences. It is the very existence and virulence of such impediments, in fact, that may have contributed to the development of science itself.

THE STRANGE (BUT FICTITIOUS) CASE OF MRS. SMITH

Since we've already mentioned acupuncture as a scientifically counterintuitive form of medical treatment, let us imagine a scenario in which an elderly woman (Mrs. Smith) had been troubled by recurrent knee pain due to osteoarthritis for several years. During much of that time, she had been under the treatment of the same trusted internist, Dr. Jones, during which he had prescribed a number of analgesics. They initially worked but eventually resulted in gastrointestinal symptoms almost as uncomfortable as her arthritis pain itself.

Over time, Mrs. Smith began to politely express a degree of dissatisfaction with her physician's conventional pharmaceutical treatments. Dr. Jones, in turn, had become so disheartened by his inability to relieve his patients' very real pain (without substituting equally deleterious symptoms) that he finally decided to give up his summer vacation to attend a continuing education workshop designed to teach physicians how to administer acupuncture—an ancient Chinese medical procedure.

So it came to pass, on her first appointment after his return that, when Mrs. Smith asked her physician once again if there wasn't *something* out there that he could use to help her, Dr. Jones was ready. He told her that, while he was not a huge fan of integrative medicine (previously known sequentially as snake oil, unconventional, alternative, complementary, and complementary and alternative medicine), acupuncture had been successfully used to relieve pain for thousands of years in Asia and that of all the integrative therapies it was deemed to be the most credible one by legitimate physicians (Berman, Bausell, & Lee, 2002). He also told her that while he could not guarantee that it would help her, in his professional judgment he *believed* that it could (and he could guarantee that it would be safe). He also admitted that he didn't know how many treatments would be required before she experienced any significant relief, but again he *believed* it would take only a few sessions. (Being a compassionate and responsible physician, he certainly wouldn't have offered to administer it to her if *he* had not personally believed in the therapy's efficacy.)

Mrs. Smith knew that Dr. Jones had her best interests at heart, knew that he was a competent, caring physician, and knew that he had *successfully* treated her for many different conditions over the past 20 years. She therefore thanked him and said she would consider it and get back with him.

Being a technologically savvy 75-year-old, she went home and immediately visited several acupuncture treatment sites on the Internet that breathlessly reported success for an astonishingly wide range of medical conditions. The sites also assured their potential customers that medical research had unequivocally proved that acupuncture was an effective, safe, and economically prudent treatment option, thereby reinforcing Dr. Jones's recommendation.

After several days, as her pain continued to escalate, Mrs. Smith called her physician's office and scheduled an acupuncture session for the next day, after a bit of cajoling of his long-time receptionist, with whom she was on a first-name basis. What both Mrs. Smith and Dr. Jones had now done, though neither conceptualized it in these terms, was *to design an experiment to produce a causal inference*. Dr. Jones was functioning as the investigator, Mrs. Smith as the participant. The purpose of Mrs. Smith's and Dr. Jones's experiment was to change what in scientific terms is called an *outcome* (or *dependent*) variable, by *introducing* an *intervention*.

But alas, unbeknownst to the two of them, an ancient *evil* also lurked in the background here: a collection of impediments seemingly purposefully and diabolically designed to ensure the production of an *invalid* causal inference. While there are a number of these impediments (or *artifacts*) which will be discussed throughout this book, for the present let's simply examine only two that would more than suffice to invalidate *any* conclusions Mrs. Smith makes regarding her treatment experience.

Natural history (also called *maturation* in fields other than health and medicine): By definition, outcome variables *change* over time, sometimes randomly, sometimes via a natural pattern of their own, sometimes as a function of our actions (or even imagination), sometimes due to unknown external or internal factors, such as an underlying disease or psychological condition. Mrs. Smith happened to be afflicted with a presently incurable, slowly degenerative disease which fortunately wasn't life threatening but whose primary symptom (pain) tends to wax and wane over time.

Pain is an interesting outcome variable (not untypical of some in common use in other disciplines), in the sense that it is difficult to measure "objectively" (i.e., physiologically or observationally), hence clinicians and researchers must rely on participant self-reports. Myriad procedures exist to measure pain, with the most frequently employed scale ranging from 0 (the complete absence of pain) to 10 (unbearable pain) on what is called a *visual analog scale* (Figure 2.1).

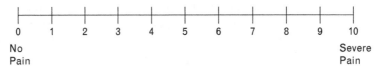

FIGURE 2.1: Typical Visual Analog Scale.

Let's assume, therefore, that the typical osteoarthritis patient's pain follows something approximating the admittedly oversimplified pattern depicted in Figure 2.2. In Mrs. Smith's case, since she

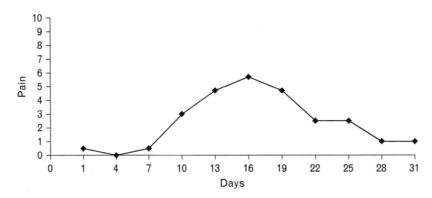

FIGURE 2.2: Natural History (Mrs. Smith's Pain, in this Case).

was able to finagle a prompt appointment when her pain was especially problematic, she would most likely have received her first acupuncture treatment somewhere near her Day 16 apex.

Now let's make a bold and unconventional assumption and assume that acupuncture is a physiologically totally inert medical "treatment." Based on this premise, let's consider the following question (which could serve as the research question this little experiment was designed to answer): What effect will acupuncture have on Mrs. Smith's pain?

☐ (a) Mrs. Smith's pain will be the same after the 2 weeks of acupuncture as it was before treatment.
☐ (b) Mrs. Smith's pain will increase slightly.
☐ (c) Mrs. Smith's pain will decrease dramatically.

The answer lies in two valuable pieces of prior information to which we are privy: (1) that acupuncture does not affect osteoarthritis pain *in and of itself* and (2) that Figure 2.2 depicts the natural history of osteoarthritis pain. If only the first piece of information were available, Option a might be a reasonable answer. However, since we know that arthritis pain waxes and wanes and that Mrs. Smith received her treatment when it was waxing, Figure 2.3 depicts the more likely outcome.

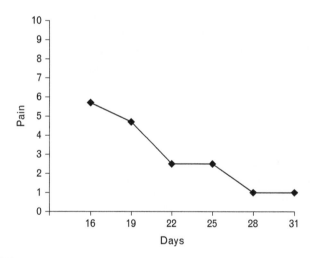

FIGURE 2.3: Natural History Masquerading as an Analgesic Effect.

Thus, since the intervention was introduced at or around Day 16, the answer to this admittedly trick question is therefore c. Mrs. Smith pain would have begun to decrease dramatically in the days immediate following the advent of her acupuncture treatments whether the treatment was effective or not.

However, since Mrs. Smith was privy to none of this information, how could she consider her treatment anything other than a rousing success? Figure 2.3 is a perfect example of why the logical fallacy *post hoc, ergo propter hoc* (after this, therefore because of this), inextricably ingrained in all of us, serves as an impediment to generating valid, complex inferences.

Unfortunately, there are a plethora of other artifacts always lurking in the background to confound any inference based on the *post hoc, ergo propter hoc* principle. These impediments function especially virulently for those actions that immediately, inevitably, and exclusively precede a consequence. It almost seems unfair that one of these artifacts involve Mrs. Smith's own *body* conspiring to confound her judgment. But such an artifact, know at least since Hippocrates' time, does indeed exist—as was so creatively demonstrated by Professor Price and his colleagues' experiment presented in the last chapter.

The placebo effect: The placebo effect is defined as an actual therapeutic response to an inert or irrelevant substance or procedure occurring in patients who believe they are receiving an effective treatment. Its etiology is based on classical conditioning (think Pavlov's dogs), although it occurs most strongly (but not exclusively) in symptoms such as pain or depression, which involve a degree of subjectivity. Strictly speaking, the placebo effect involves a physiological response to an intervention independent of that intervention's mechanism of action or absence thereof. In the case of pain, the brain can be induced to release endogenous opioids (which actually do have a biological analgesic action) in the presence of an expectation of benefit (again, often based on past conditioning). A placebo effect can therefore occur in addition to an effective analgesic's effects or in place of a completely ineffective intervention. It is a complex and fascinating phenomenon to which a considerable amount of scientific effort has been devoted (for overviews, see Price, 1988; Harrington, 1997; or Price & Bushnell, 2004) and whose effects can be differentiated from "imagined" or "psychosomatic" responses only through careful experimentation.

For present purposes it is enough to introduce the placebo effect as both a physiological and an inferential threat that is (a) more transitory than most therapeutic effects and (b) incapable of curing any known disease in its own right (although it is capable of temporarily relieving some of its symptoms). In Mrs. Smith's and Dr. Jones's completely uncontrolled "experiment," it constitutes an especially virulent threat to making a valid assessment of the intervention's efficacy, since it possesses an additive effect over and above that of natural history artifact (see Figure 2.4).

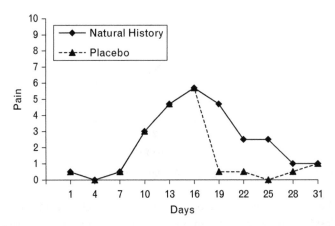

FIGURE 2.4: The Placebo Effect Added to a Natural History Effect.

Some additional (very human) logical artifacts: Added to natural history and the placebo effect, which are not restricted to humans incidentally, are a set of purely *psychological* or *personality*-related impediments to logical thought, critical thinking, and inferential ability in general, such as:

- A reluctance to admit when we are wrong (cognitive dissonance). The simple act of paying for a therapy increases both compliance with it and our perceptions of its value.

- A reluctance to abandon our beliefs or our opinions, even in the presence of contradictory evidence.
- A tendency to ignore experiences (or evidence) that contradict our beliefs and accept (or remember) those experiences that confirm them.
- Simple optimism or a belief that health outcomes are completely under our control (referred to as an internal locus of control).
- Respect for authority.
- A *National Enquirer* approach to life, or a propensity or need to believe the absurd.
- A conspiracy-oriented view of the world ("they" just don't want us to know the truth).

While these *attributes* are capable of clouding our judgment and preventing us from making valid inferences, they are not *experimental* artifacts, as are natural history and the placebo effect. Instead, they are quintessentially psychological and personality attributes that all of us (scientists and non-scientists alike) share to various degrees and, as such, are quite capable of influencing the interpretation and acceptance of even the most pristinely designed and conducted experiment. Part of our job description as scientists, therefore, resides in moderating these tendencies in our own work, which is certainly easier said than done. And their avoidance occurs only through vigilance and self-awareness.

SAME EXPERIMENT, DIFFERENT PERSPECTIVE: THE EQUALLY STRANGE (BUT STILL UNTRUE) CASE OF DR. JONES

Returning to our little natural experiment, let's consider Dr. Jones's response to its results. (We'll discuss institutional and societal natural experiments as they apply to program evaluation in more detail in Chapter Twelve.) We know he wasn't a conspirator here since he didn't purposefully set the scene for "tricking" Mrs. Smiths' brain into releasing endogenous opioids. We also know he didn't have a profit motive.

Instead, he was actually engaged in designing and conducting his *own* little single-case experiment, as do all clinicians (be they physicians, psychologists, teachers, or therapists) each time they try out any sort of treatment variation. But unfortunately, professionals' clinical experiences often constitute an exceedingly imperfect basis for judging the efficacy of their experiments. For in addition to the same psychological and personality impediments to logical thinking bedeviling their patients (indeed, all humans), sometimes the very nature of their professional roles can be problematic. In the case of physicians or therapists some of these include the following:

- A tendency to be influenced by the very placebo effects they either consciously or unconsciously elicit in their clients by the forcefulness of their recommendations (often based on a laudatory desire to relieve patient anxiety, give them a sense of expectancy or hope, or both),
- A tendency of patients to sometimes not frankly discuss a lack of improvement with their clinicians, because they do not want to hurt their feelings or risk angering them,

- The difficulties involved in keeping careful records of every patient outcome resulting from every patient visit,
- Selective memory (or a natural tendency to remember events that correspond to one's original beliefs), and
- Attrition, when dissatisfied patients vote with their feet and do not return for treatment, resulting in clinicians receiving more positive than negative feedback.

Naturally, Dr. Jones was understandably heartened by the results of his little experiment, based on Mrs. Smith's initial reported pain reduction after the first few days of treatment. Not surprisingly, he offered the treatment to other patients and found that it "worked" for some but not for others, and that the results were occasionally equivocal one way or the other. Because Dr. Jones was a charter member of the species *Homo sapiens*, however, he concluded that, overall, his acupuncture treatments were effective—partly because he (a) desperately wanted to help his patients and actually received far more positive than negative reports from them, (b) tended to recall the positive reports more poignantly than he did the negative ones (some of which were often tempered by politeness and even patient-supplied rationalizations for why the intervention might not have worked for them), and (c) experienced a degree of cognitive dissonance from giving up his richly deserved vacation in the Caribbean for a 2-week stay in a Des Moines *Holiday Inn Express* in order to attend the acupuncture workshop (the tuition for which was almost as expensive as his planned vacation).

The point here is that personal experience (even experience based on observations made by thoughtful, highly educated individuals) is an insufficient medium for making complex inferences. There are simply too many uncontrolled conditions accompanying those experiences, not to mention co-occurring events, that constitute plausible alternative explanations to the more natural inference that "the intervention did it." Likewise, clinical settings, in the absence of adequate research strategies, constitute very poorly controlled environments that are ripe with such co-occurring events—especially since systematic records (at least in a readably analyzable form) are seldom kept of patients, their treatments, and their outcomes.

Unfortunately, poorly designed experiments involving multiple participants offer little more protection against these inferential impediments than do uncontrolled clinical experience. This unfortunate fact is perhaps best illustrated by the continuing, less propitious adventures of the good Dr. Jones's experiences in designing a more formal (but still inferentially far from satisfactory) experiment, as detailed in Chapter Three.

SUMMARY

The primary purposes of the brief, very human scenario introduced in this chapter were to (a) illustrate that, as a species, we constantly engage in experimentation is our everyday lives and (b) introduce two inferential artifacts applicable to the design of informal and scientific experimentation:

Natural history (or maturation), which is defined as a tendency for some outcome variables to *change* over time, irrespective of the introduction of an intervention, and

The placebo effect, which is defined as a therapeutic response to an inert substance or irrelevant procedure occurring in individuals who believe they are receiving an effective treatment.

A number of seemingly built-in (or conditioned) psychological impediments were also discussed which conspire to make primitive experiments such as that performed by Mrs. Smith and Dr. Jones exceedingly poor foundations on which to base complex causal inferences—especially those in which the consequence does not immediately and inevitably follow the action—including

1. Cognitive dissonance,
2. The personal importance we place on our beliefs,
3. A tendency to ignore evidence that contradicts those beliefs,
4. A highly developed internal locus of control,
5. Respect for authority, and
6. A propensity to believe the absurd.

By implication, these artifacts (and psychological impediments), to which many scientists are also susceptible, require the design and conduct of more rigorous experiments than the one presented in this chapter.

REFERENCES

Berman, B.M., Bausell, R.B., & Lee, W-L. (2002). Use and referral patterns for 22 complementary and alternative medical therapies by members of the American College of Rheumatology: Results of a national survey. *Archives of Internal Medicine, 162,* 766–70.

Harrington, A. (Ed.). (1997). *The placebo effect: An interdisciplinary exploration.* Cambridge, MA: Harvard University Press.

Price, D.D. (1988). *Psychological and neural mechanisms of pain.* New York: Raven Press.

Price, D.D., & Bushnell, M.C. (Eds.) (2004). *Psychological methods of pain control: Basic science and clinical perspectives.* Seattle: International Association for the Study of Pain.

Shermer, M. (2002). *Why people believe weird things: Pseudoscience, superstition and other confusions of our time.* New York: Henry Holt.

CHAPTER 3

INTRODUCTION TO THE DESIGN OF MEANINGFUL EXPERIMENTS VIA THE CONTINUING ADVENTURES OF DR. JONES

As an adjunct faculty member of the local medical school who sometimes gave guest lectures and allowed first-year medical students to practice their interview skills on some of his patients, Dr. Jones was invited to give a presentation at the department of internal medicine's weekly brown-bag colloquium that was based on a case report he had recently published. It will probably come as no surprise that the subject of both the case study and Dr. Jones's talk involved his successful treatment of Mrs. Smith's osteoarthritis pain.

Case reports (or case studies), incidentally, constitute the most frequently published genre of articles in medicine, with almost 60,000 published in the year 2007 alone (Bastian, Glasziou, & Chalmers, 2010), but they are also quite common in practice-oriented journals in many other disciplines as well. In medicine they normally consist of a single clinical case that describes the medical condition with which the patient presents, its unusual clinical characteristics, the course of treatment prescribed, and the outcome of that treatment. Usually retrospective in nature and often accompanied by little more data than is routinely present in patient charts, they bear a striking similarity to our hypothetical scenario involving Mrs. Smith (i.e., possessing a complete lack of control for such inferential artifacts as natural history and the placebo effect). In general, however, they appear to be quite popular among clinicians, have at least one refereed journal devoted exclusively to the genre (*Clinical Case Studies*), and routinely appear in many of medicine's most prestigious journals.

In the course of Dr. Jones's understandably enthusiastic descriptions of his clinical success with Mrs. Jones, he was questioned by a characteristically boorish biostatistician who leveled a number of criticisms regarding his conclusions. Most of these objections took the form of complaints about clinicians such as Dr. Jones who presented their clinical experiences (in the absence of any real data) as actually constituting evidence of efficacy. Dr. Jones for his part was shocked by the woman's ignorance regarding the revered status case studies enjoy in clinical medicine and patiently tried to explain that he had been invited to share his *clinical* experiences with the group, not to discuss research. She in turn accused him of presenting a completely non-evidence-based case ballyhooing the efficacy of an intervention possessing no plausible biological mechanism of action.

Later that afternoon, over cocktails, while discussing the unreasonableness of the biostatistician with a fellow physician (a former classmate and now associate professor of internal medicine, who had invited Dr. Jones to present in the first place), the professor suggested that the two of them conduct their own experiment to prove that this non-physician didn't know what she was talking about—an experiment that would, once and for all, demonstrate how effective acupuncture was in reducing pain. He, the ex-classmate, proposed that they design the study together and then he, as a member of the faculty, would shepherd the proposal through the university's institutional review board (IRB) himself. (IRBs are committees originally set up to protect research participants, but now typically evaluate experimental design issues as well.)

Dr. Jones readily agreed, and the two of them had completed an outline of the basic design on their iPads by the time they had finished their third martini. But before viewing the fruits of their labors, let's first discuss the basic steps involved in the design of an experiment.

A Brief Introduction to Institutional Review Boards (IRBs)

IRBs are governmentally initiated institutional responses to 20th-century events that clearly mandated the need for a formal organized approach to protect human subjects from medical clinical research abuses over and above the dependence on the simple good will of physician investigators. Without question the most egregious examples of this need were provided by Nazi physician "investigators," examples of which the present author doesn't wish to detail here. Following World War II, a number of these physicians were brought before the now famous military tribunal in the German city of Nuremberg to answer for war crimes—primarily against (but not restricted to) citizens of Jewish descent. As a result of these trials, the 10-point Nuremberg Code was published detailing conditions required by permissible research that included dicta we now take for granted, such as (a) the risk should not exceed the benefit (further elucidated by the Declaration of Helsinki), (b) the topic should be for the benefit of society (which fits our definition of meaningfulness here), and (c) research subjects have the right to be informed about risks involved in participation and to withdraw from an experiment of their own volition, among others. (See William Schneider's brief, readable history of IRBs, at http://www.iupui.edu/~histwhs/G504.dir/irbhist.html.)

Although they couldn't quite compete with the Nazis' cruelty, American medical researchers registered their share of abuses as well. The most infamous was the Tuskegee Syphilis Study, which began in 1932, with the identification of hundreds of poor, uneducated black males in Alabama suffering from syphilis. The subjects were not told about their disease and were denied treatment for four decades, ending in 1972.

Unfortunately, the Tuskegee study was hardly an isolated incident; others usually involved vulnerable populations, especially prisoners who were experimentally exposed to a number of dangerous substances, with one set of investigators (Hodges, Baker, Hood, et al., 1969; Hodges, Hood, Canham, et al., 1971) even inducing scurvy in two *separate* studies even though everything we need to know about this particular disease has been known for centuries. (Ironically, the Nazi doctors tried at Nuremberg argued that their abuses were no greater than those conducted in the name of research in American prisons—see Reiter [2009] for a thorough (and thoroughly depressing) review of this genre of research.) By the 1960s awareness of the potential of ethical abuses in medical research was increasing, facilitated by events such as (a) the Declaration of Helsinki (which built upon the earlier Nuremberg Code), (b) an influential article by Henry Beecher (1966) detailing ethical problems with a selection of medical research articles, and, most importantly, (c) a 1966 edict by the U.S. Public Health Service that no new grants or continuation applications for existing ones would be funded without evidence of a peer review conducted by the parent institution regarding the ethics of the work proposed for funding.

While purely clinical medical research is not within our purview here, today all universities and other institutions receiving federal monies must have a formal peer review process in place, not just for medical research but for all types of research involving human participants. In universities, these committees are staffed by faculty conversant with research processes, and institutions such as the National Institutes of Health (NIH) occasionally conduct audits to ensure compliance with federal regulations. (Commercial IRBs exist for institutions too small to have their own IRB or for whom an internal IRB would not be appropriate, and research involving animals has its own oversight by a Committee on Animal Research and Ethics [CARE].)

Certain types of research are exempt from review (e.g., anonymous surveys and some kinds of educational research), but typically investigators must formally apply to their IRBs for such an exemption. Also, as the process has evolved, the scope of IRB reviews has expanded to consider issues such as judging the methodological soundness of the study procedures, the proposed sample size, protection of the participant confidentiality, and data integrity.

THE DESIGN OF EXPERIMENTS

Typically, experiments consist of controlled environments in which an intervention is introduced to participants in order to observe its effects on a specified outcome. The decisions regarding the procedures and strategies by which this is accomplished are referred to as the experimental *design*. The end product of these decisions (and the skill with which they are implemented) involves a test of a deceptively simple causal inference: The intervention *caused* changes in the outcome or it did not.

The totality of the design process can be visualized as a series of 10 discrete decisions. The order in which these decisions are completed is unimportant because the process of making them is both fluid and iterative (fluid because many decisions must typically be revisited, refined, and revised several times; iterative because each decisional change often necessitates changes in both prior and subsequent decisions).

These 10 multifaceted decisions, buttressed by considerable supplementary information, must be specified in a written proposal submitted to an IRB before any contact with potential participants can take place. Some version of each decision will similarly need to be described in the "methods" or "procedures" section of any publication resulting from the completed project.

The 10 decisions are formulated as questions in the following list, not in their order of importance (all are crucial) or the order in which they are made (which varies from study to study), but approximately in the order in which an IRB might request their answers.

1. What are the research aims, purposes, and/or research hypotheses?
2. What will the intervention(s) consist of and in what dose(s)/duration(s)?
3. What will the outcome(s) of the intervention(s) be, and (if more than one is employed) which will be the primary outcome (known in Dr. Jones's discipline as the *primary endpoint*)?
4. What types of participants will be recruited, how will they be recruited, and how much will they be told about the experiment at recruitment?
5. How, by whom, how often, and under what conditions will the outcome(s) be assessed?
6. To what will the intervention be compared (e.g., participant changes from baseline, a control group, or an alternative treatment of some sort)?
7. If it is one of the latter options, how will it be determined which participants receive which treatments (e.g., will they be randomized to groups, and if so, how)?
8. Will participants and/or experimental staff be prevented from knowing the identity of the treatment (or comparison group) to which they have been assigned (referred to as single or double "blinded" in some circles)?
9. How will the results be statistically analyzed?
10. Now many participants will be recruited? (This is determined by a statistical process discussed in Chapter Nine called a sample size [or power] analysis and is partially determined by the answers to questions 2, 3, 6, and 9.)

Definitional Interlude: The Two Usages of *Design*

Before proceeding, it is worth noting that there are two usages of the word *design*. One is derived from the verb *to design* and is pretty well encompassed by the 10-point decision process just presented. The other usage of the word is affixed to the *name* given to the resulting "product" or "experimental architecture" (enumerated in subsequent chapters, such as the *randomized pretest-posttest control group design* or a *single-group pretest-posttest design*), which is primarily determined by the answers to the sixth and seventh questions (the type of comparison group or strategy employed, and how participants will be assigned to both the intervention and its comparison).

THE DESIGN OF DR. JONES AND COLLEAGUE'S EXPERIMENT

In designing their experiment, Dr. Jones and his colleague (both of whom had received the same amount of research training in medical school—none) were forced to explicitly answer all 10 of these questions along with a few others required by the IRB before they received permission to contact potential participants, such as:

1. The risks and benefits of participation in the experiment,
2. Actions they would take in case adverse events occurred,
3. How confidentiality and the integrity of the data would be preserved,
4. How missing data would be handled (i.e., for participants who dropped out of the experiment), and
5. The exact wording of the informed consent agreement.

They were also asked for something they considered patently obvious and unnecessary: the primary aim or purpose of their study. Obvious and unnecessary, because they had begun the design process in the local tavern with a clear consensus on their experimental purpose and communicated it with unequivocal clarity in their IRB application, via the following statement:

> The purpose of this study is to demonstrate the effectiveness of acupuncture.

A call to an IRB official resulted in some suggested additions to this statement, such as "to assess," "osteoarthritis of the knee," and "analgesic efficacy." The application was resubmitted, and this time, following what our eager investigators considered an arduous process of back and forth communication with the IRB official over additional information and clarifications, final approval was received for their answers to the 10 design questions listed earlier:

1. *Aims, study purpose, and/or hypotheses*: Variability exists in IRB, funding agency, peer-reviewed journal, and biostatistics/research methodology instructor preferences with respect to whether formal hypotheses, specific aims, or general purposes are used to succinctly describe the experimental intent. Let us presume that Dr. Jones and his colleague opted to describe the study in terms of its overall purpose, which was revised as follows: "to assess the efficacy of acupuncture in reducing pain due to osteoarthritis."
2. *Intervention*: Based on a classic textbook on traditional Chinese medicine that was recommended in Dr. Jones's summer course, it was decided that all participants would receive six 20-minute treatments involving 12 needles placed at traditional points over a 2-week period.
3. *Outcome variable*: The primary endpoint would be the amount of pain reduction reported on the 10 cm visual analog scale (VAS) between the baseline and the 2-week end-of-treatment (EOT) assessments.

4. *Participant recruitment and informed consent*: Based on Dr. Jones's clinical experience, only participants similar to Mrs. Smith would be recruited who had been diagnosed with osteoarthritis of the knee and were experiencing pain of at least 3.5 cm on a 10.0 cm VAS. (The IRB insisted they define pain operationally in order to limit subjectivity in choosing participants, as well as give a quite detailed list of exclusion criteria [e.g., prohibited comorbidities such as bleeding disorders, and insufficient fluency in English to prevent comprehension of the informed consent agreement], all of which might be listed under a heading called "exclusion/inclusion criteria".) The investigators felt they had nothing to hide so, as part of informed consent, potential participants were told that acupuncture was a promising low-risk and ancient treatment for many varieties of pain. The informed consent agreement also specified exactly what would be required of participants in terms of attendance to receive treatments and assessment sessions. (Required assurances were also included, such as participant rights regarding the ability to withdraw from the study at any time without any treatment repercussions.) Recruitment would consist of Dr. Jones informing his qualifying patients of the opportunity to participate and his colleague posting an announcement thereof (the exact wording of which had to approved by the IRB) in the university's rheumatology clinic as well in the parking building's elevators.

5. *Data collection*: Supplementary demographic and clinical data would be collected immediately following informed consent via a questionnaire filled out by the participants in Dr. Jones's office, where the acupuncture treatment was also administered, and given to his secretary. The baseline and EOT VAS, along with some supplementary information regarding medication, treatment, and lifestyle changes during the past 2 weeks, would be collected by a work study student (assigned by the department chair to Dr. Jones's colleague) at baseline and EOT. More specific information was also requested regarding how confidentiality of participants would be assured, the exact timing of the assessments, and the procedures taken to protect the integrity of the data.

6. *Comparison to assess intervention effect*: For simplicity's sake, no comparison group would be used. (To make the study more clinically relevant, patients were allowed to continue on their usual medications.) The investigators reasoned that the efficacy of acupuncture would be demonstrated if their participants' pain was significantly reduced between baseline and EOT.

7. *Participant assignment to groups*: Since all participants would receive the intervention, no decision was required here.

8. *Participant/staff blinding*: Again, since all participants would receive the same treatment, no blinding was possible.

9. *Statistical analysis*: A paired *t*-test (also called a *t*-test for dependent samples) was specified on the basis of a published study the investigators found employing a similar design.

10. *Sample size justification*: As part of the IRB application the two investigators were forced to specify and justify the number of participants who would be recruited for the trial. They correspondingly employed an online sample size calculator and

incorrectly determined that 10 participants would be sufficient to provide them with an 80% chance of detecting a statistically significant difference between the baseline and EOT pain assessments if the intervention was effective.

The skeleton of this design is diagrammatically presented in Figure 3.1.

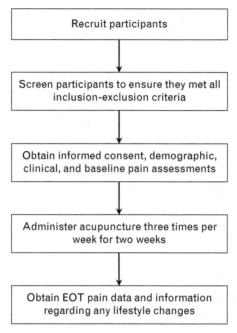

FIGURE 3.1: Abbreviated Flowchart.

A Note on Regulatory Issues and IRBs

So much variability exists with respect to interdisciplinary and inter-institutional differences in IRB requirements and regulatory requirements that this book does not cover these issues in detail. Thus, while a medical example was used in this instance (clinical experiments in medicine are probably the most stringently regulated of any discipline and would require considerably more detail than mentioned here, such as how adverse events would be monitored, evaluated, and reported, or how osteoarthritis would be documented), most of the points summarized here possess analogs in other disciplines. For example, a psychology experiment involving undergraduates might have no participation risks above the possibility of a paper cut, but a liberal arts IRB would still require assurances in this regard, as well as assurances that students' status in a class would not be affected by their refusal to participate or their subsequent decision to withdraw from the experiment prior to its completion. Likewise, an educational experiment conducted in the public schools would have quite different informed consent policies (e.g., might or might not require individual parental consent).

Before continuing our story, two key issues should be discussed. The first involves the formulation of the study hypothesis. The second involves how a hypothesis can be used to make an initial a priori judgment regarding the potential meaningfulness of the final experimental results.

THE FORMULATION OF THE EXPERIMENTAL HYPOTHESIS

While stylistic opinions differ on whether a discrete hypothesis is required in a research report or proposal, there is no such flexibility in the experimental design process. For design purposes a hypothesis is always preferable because of its utility in enabling the investigator (and anyone else with a professional interest in the study) to (a) evaluate the appropriateness of the experimental design in its entirety and (b) judge the experiment's potential meaningfulness. Perhaps even more importantly, however, a properly stated hypothesis forces an investigator to come to terms with exactly what a proposed experiment is capable of producing, which is simply a confirmation of (or failure to) confirm that hypothesis.

As might be expected, different preferred formats exist for hypotheses both between and within disciplines. Some prefer research questions instead of declarative sentences, and some prefer null hypotheses (which are stated in terms of "no differences" even when the investigator hopes and predicts that there "will be a difference") over directional ones. And as with most stylistic conventions, none are sacrosanct.

Today the majority of modern investigators appear to prefer the convention known as research hypotheses, which involve a simple declarative sentence stating the results expected to be obtained from an experiment. (If one's discipline, research committee, or the journal to which the final report will be submitted prefers another format, then by all means that preference should be honored. The end result will be the same, as will the relevance of everything that follows.)

A hypothesis is neither more nor less than an operational definition of a study's purpose. In a single declarative sentence it is capable of communicating cursory information about the five following crucial components involved in the experiment:

1. The identity of the intervention, including its duration and/or dose,
2. What the intervention is to be compared to,
3. The primary outcome variable/endpoint employed in this comparison (as well as the primary time of the comparison if different from the intervention duration),
4. A two- or three-word description of the types of participants to be used, and
5. The expected results.

Armed with this single-sentence distillation, another scientist should be able to glean the essentials of what an experiment will entail (or entailed). (And, of course, so could a peer reviewer for an IRB, a journal, or a funding agency.) More importantly for our purposes here, however, writing such a sentence is capable of providing its *author* with a visceral understanding of basically what will and will not accrue from the experiment once conducted—which leads to the following experimental principle:

> PRINCIPLE #6: **Always translate your proposed experiment into one or more formal, written hypotheses.**

One of the most appealing characteristics of the hypothesis-testing process (buttressed by the statistical conventions governing the treatment of experimental data) is the complete absence of equivocation. If an experiment is properly designed, conducted, and analyzed, there are no "maybes" regarding the results of a hypothesis test. There may be, and often are, disagreements regarding the scientific *interpretation* of the results, but the decision regarding the hypothesis itself is dichotomous (accepted or rejected, confirmed or not confirmed, supported or not supported, true or false, or whatever the relevant discipline's preferred language). This definitive, dichotomous characteristic automatically contraindicates wordings such as "the best way" or "good" or "to determine why." In other words, *an experiment deals only in discrete comparisons,* not value judgments or keys to the meaning of life.

In way of illustration, let's consider Dr. Jones's final statement of purpose (after some prompting by the IRB reviewers), "to determine the analgesic efficacy of acupuncture for osteoarthritis of the knee." This statement would not qualify as a hypothesis as defined here since it left out some important pieces of information, including the study design, the types of participants to be used, the experiment's duration, and the predicted results. Such information could easily be distilled into a single sentence, however, as witnessed by the following revision:

> Patients with osteoarthritis of the knee receiving six traditional Chinese acupuncture treatments over a 2-week period will report significantly less pain at the end of treatment than at baseline.

This sentence contains the requisite information necessary (a) to communicate to others the essence of what the experiment is about and (b) to serve as a reminder to the investigators themselves of the limited scope of the study to which they are about to devote so much energy, resources, and aspirations. Specifically:

1. *The identity of the intervention and its duration*: Acupuncture administered for 2 weeks. In addition, the type of acupuncture (traditional Chinese as opposed to, say, traditional Ayurvedic or modern medical) to be employed and its "dosage" (six sessions).
2. *The comparison*: A simple pre-post (or baseline-EOT) contrast involving the same participants. (Alternately, the name given to the discipline's design itself could replace this phrase, such as a single-group pretest-posttest design, as discussed later in the chapter.)
3. *The primary outcome variable*: Pain, or if more detail was desired, "a visual analog pain scale."
4. *Type of participants*: Patients with osteoarthritis of the knee. Additional information might include an age range if specified by the study's exclusion/inclusion criteria (such as "patients over 65 years of age with osteoarthritis of the knee") or even the minimum degree of pain required (or adjectives such as "moderate to severe" pain).
5. *Expected results*: Participants will report less pain at the end of the experiment than at the beginning. (While "statistical significance" [discussed briefly in Chapter Four] is implied in a hypothesis such as this, it can be explicitly stated if desired: "will report statistically significant less pain at $p \leq .05$ after 2 weeks than reported at baseline.")

Considerable additional detail required for evaluating the appropriateness of each of these five components would be presented in the methods section of either a study proposal or final journal article, but a single sentence can obviously communicate a great deal of crucial information about an experiment. Such a sentence also serves as a written record of the authors' original intent as well as a basis for evaluating (a) whether the experiment is worth conducting (many, if not most, published studies aren't) or (b) the degree to which the final results are likely to fulfill the investigator's motivations for conducting the experiment (even more don't qualify here).

EVALUATING THE MEANINGFULNESS OF A HYPOTHESIS

The importance of the outcome variable: Given that our objective here is the design and conduct of *meaningful* experiments, it follows that the choice of the *outcome* specified in the study hypothesis must constitute a key component of that process. In research involving human participants, it is difficult to imagine how an experiment (ergo the hypothesis it is designed to test) can be judged to be meaningful if it does not employ an outcome variable that is not directly related to the quality of human life. A trivial outcome variable ensures a trivial experiment, a trivial hypothesis, and a trivial result.

Of course, one investigator's triviality may be another's epiphany, but at the very least the contribution of a study's primary endpoint to someone's health, happiness, or quality of life should be seriously considered during the design process. If more beginning investigators evaluated their outcomes from this perspective, there would surely be fewer future experiments conducted involving attitudes toward this or that (or indeed a large proportion of *all* self-reported questionnaires).

At the very least, however, a primary experimental endpoint should be evaluated with respect to its investigator's estimation of its impact on the human condition. If an investigator does not consider a proposed outcome to constitute an individual or societal *good* in its own right (or if it has not been proximally *related* to one [see Chapter Nine] by credible empirical research), then serious consideration should be given to selecting a different outcome variable. (Convenience, ease of collection, and/or the fact that a variable has been used in previous research do not constitute sufficient reasons for selection.)

It is difficult to provide interdisciplinary guidelines for choosing meaningful outcomes. A generic approach, however, is to delineate the key rationale for a discipline's or specialty's existence and then select only outcomes that reflect those purposes (or are *empirically* related to those purposes no more than once or twice removed).

This single criterion will drastically reduce the number of acceptable outcome variables in any discipline. As an example, in experimentation conducted in the elementary school, the quintessentially meaningful outcome variable is learning. Learning, however, occurs *only* in the presence of instruction, broadly defined to include direct instruction by the classroom teacher, homework assignments, or any type of relevant experiences provided in the home or elsewhere. The most important variable directly relevant to instruction is time-on-task (also similarly broadly defined) and can therefore be conceptualized as either a substitute (but still meaningful) outcome variable or a potentially effective component of an experimental intervention.

After that, most of the constructs that *appear* to be related to learning aren't or haven't been causally linked to either it *or* time-on-task, which (according to the criteria presented earlier) disqualifies them as meaningful experimental outcome variables for schooling's learning objectives. Motivation, for example, which theoretically comes in different varieties (e.g., intrinsic vs. extrinsic, and can supposedly be assessed via self-reported questionnaires) may itself be a causal function of other variables, such as the student's home learning environment or even past schooling learning success. Establishing such links can be determined nonexperimentally by sophisticated modeling approaches, but if motivation or the method by which it is measured isn't *causally* (and strongly) related to learning or time-on-task (but is likely to be caused by other nonmanipulative variables such as the home environment), then it does not constitute a meaningful outcome variable for the learning objectives of schooling. Nor are most affective-attitudinal self-report variables in education (and perhaps numerous other disciplines as well).

Of course, each empirical discipline has its own theories and therefore its own definitions of meaningfulness. Time may eventually sort the wheat from the chaff, but this isn't assured by any means, and a beginning investigator's ultimate success in conducting meaningful experiments may well depend on his or her *personal* sorting ability, which will largely depend on the utility of the guiding theories he or she chooses.

The importance of developing a viable, meaningful intervention: Obviously, if the outcome is a key component of experimental meaningfulness, the intervention designed to affect it is equally important, although more difficult to evaluate since its effect on the former won't be known until after the experiment is conducted. Setting this uncertainty aside (after all, determining the intervention's effect is the primary purpose of experimentation), by far the most difficult part of the design process is the choice of a viable intervention: whether it is done by (a) choosing an existing experiment to replicate, (b) testing a new application for an existing intervention, (c) enhancing an existing intervention, or (d) developing a completely original one.

A prerequisite for an intervention to be meaningful is a sound theoretical (or practical) rationale for its potential to produce a nontautological effect (positive or negative) on a meaningful outcome. The term *nontautological* is used to indicate an effect that (a) is *not* painfully obvious (such as one that is completely subsumed by an accepted scientific theory, such as ascertaining if teaching children in a certain way will produce learning [all relevant instruction, regardless of method, results in learning]), (b) does *not* constitute an unneeded replication of a thoroughly documented scientific or clinical finding, and (c) is evaluated by a sufficiently controlled design employing an appropriate comparison group (as will be discussed in detail in Chapter Five).

Strategies for developing potentially viable and meaningful interventions include the following:

Familiarizing oneself with the systematic/meta-analytic reviews in one's discipline. Collecting and reading as many of these as possible (and there will be a lot of them) can provide ideas for interventions and avoid duplicative research. Their reference lists are also excellent sources of important and relevant trials.

Identifying a theoretical or empirical rationale for why an intervention should produce a hypothesized effect. Seat-of-the-pants intuition is not an adequate rationale for designing and testing an intervention. If the intuition becomes an obsession, at the very least search for a rationale in the literature and comply with two future experimental principles: #7 (solicit professional feedback) and #23 (always conduct at least one pilot study—in this instance, preferably a very small one).

Keeping abreast of published trials by continuously reviewing the tables of contents of the primary journals in one's area with an eye toward identifying

1.   Correctable design glitches that might change the results of an intervention's evaluation.
2.   Questions that are specifically created by the trials themselves.
3.   Suggestions by the investigators for additional needed work (many such suggestions will be nonspecific, such as "more research is needed…" although occasionally something

interesting will be proposed). If the latter, contacting the investigator(s) constitutes a professional courtesy and might result in additional useful information and perhaps even a useful collaboration.

4.   Methods by which unsuccessful interventions could be strengthened to produce stronger effects (although many published experiments will have achieved statistical significance due to publication bias—see Chapter Thirteen).

5.   Alternative explanations for experimental results that potentially could render a significant effect nonsignificant or (preferably) vice-versa.

Additionally, of the nine scientific functions addressable by experimental research presented in the first chapter, only four do not actually require the development of a novel intervention (since they involve working with previously developed ones):

1.   Replicating a previous experimental finding (because the intervention will obviously have already been developed),

2.   Determining how far a previous finding can be generalized (e.g., to other settings, populations, and conditions)

3.   Improving the efficacy of an existing intervention (e.g., by adding more components to it or increasing its dose), and

4.   Comparing the efficacy of two (or more) interventions that haven't been previously compared (if both interventions have been previously developed).

The remaining five not only require the creation of a new intervention but also provide the rationale and hints for developing them (although, as always, considerable creativity and pilot work are normally required to create the final product):

1.   Determining the efficacy of a previously untested treatment, practice, strategy, or procedure under controlled conditions,

2.   Theory testing (by illustrating the existence of a phenomenon/effect and/or elucidating its etiology [or the conditions under which it occurs]),

3.   Translating an observational finding into an experimental one,

4.   Challenging (or confirming) conventional knowledge, and

5.   Answering a new question generated by a previous finding.

The importance of visualizing experimental results: Once the outcome and intervention have been finalized, the next step in the evaluation of meaningfulness involves visualization of the actual effect the latter is likely to have on the former. Three steps are involved here: (a) listing all the possible experimental outcomes, (b) assessing the probability of each, and (c) visualizing the hypothesized effect in terms of the actual numeric value likely to be produced. Let's illustrate this process via Dr. Jones's single-group comparison acupuncture study.

Listing the possible experimental outcomes: In a single-group, pretest-posttest group design such as Dr. Jones's trial, there are three and only three possibilities:

1.   Reported pain decreases from baseline to EOT,

2.   Reported pain increases from baseline to EOT, and

3.   There is no difference between pain reported at the baseline and EOT assessments.

Estimating the probability of each experimental outcome: Since all experimental outcomes are not equally likely to occur, discrete probabilities for each possible outcome should be estimated at the design stage. When summed, they should add up to 1.00, since individual probabilities always range from 0.00 to 1.00, and these particular probabilities are mutually exclusive.

Once done, if the likelihood of obtaining statistical significance in the predicted direction is extremely low, then the risks and benefits of proceeding should be weighed. (As will be discussed later, it is considerably more difficult to get a negative result accepted for publication than a positive one, even though the former may constitute an equally important *scientific* contribution.) If the probability of one outcome is estimated to be 1.00, on the other hand, then the experiment may be tautological in nature and not worth conducting.

While it is usually not possible to *accurately* assess the probability of the various result options for of any worthwhile experiment a priori, experienced investigators routinely (if unconsciously) assess the likelihood of obtaining a particular finding. It therefore behooves novices to conduct this exercise at the design stage even if their estimates are not likely to be overly accurate.

Unfortunately, no generic advice exists for increasing the accuracy of these predictions other than to (a) become thoroughly familiar with the related empirical literature (i.e., Principle #3) and (b) solicit as much help from more experienced researchers as possible. Also unfortunately, the number of *possible* experimental outcomes increases with the complexity of many of the designs that will be presented in subsequent chapters—but, if anything, this fact of experimental life only increases the importance of predicting their likelihoods—which is important enough to merit its own principle:

> **PRINCIPLE #7: Once the hypothesis is formulated, delineate all of the possible experimental outcomes, attempt to assess the probability of each of their occurrences, and *attempt to visualize the actual numerical outcome likely to accrue if the hypothesis is supported.***

The italicized portion of this dictum is perhaps its most important component and constitutes the next step in the evaluative process.

Visualizing the numeric value of the hypothesized effect: The necessity of hypothesizing an effect size, to estimate an experiment's optimal sample size, will be discussed later—but that is not what is being called for here. To evaluate the potential meaningfulness of the experiment as a whole, what is being suggested is that investigators estimate the most likely result in terms of the outcome variable's actual metric.

At first glance this may appear absurd at best and demented at worst. How can anyone visualize the descriptive statistics that will appear in the results section of the final research report? And if they could, what validity would such a "guess" have?

The answer to the first question is that hints are available in the research literature from experiments that employ the identical outcome variable to that of the proposed study. (Descriptive statistics will be available from some of these studies and hopefully from all of the experimental ones.) The answer to the second question is that there may be very little precision associated with such "guesses," but correctly predicting the final numerical results isn't all that important. The purpose of this exercise is to facilitate the assessment of the potential meaningfulness of the proposed experiment *regardless of whether* its hypothesized results occur or not.

Thus, if an investigator chooses to employ a Likert-type 10-item, 5-point scale (e.g., each item is accompanied by anchors from strongly disagree [1] to strongly agree [5]) as the outcome variable (e.g., to assess whether or not the intervention resulted in improved attitudes toward something), that investigator knows that the final result (assuming a single-group design such as Dr. Jones employed) will consist of two means: one at baseline and one at the end of treatment (EOT). Assuming that the 10 items are summed to produce a total score, our investigator also knows that the resulting two numbers will range in value somewhere between 10.0 and 50.0.

Assuming that the scale had been used previously, the investigator might also find that similar participants scored on average around 40.0. (If the scale hadn't been used previously it probably shouldn't be used as the primary experimental outcome variable unless considerable nonexperimental research had confirmed its utility.) Thus, perhaps our investigator might guess that the final results would look like those in Table 3.1.

Table 3.1: Hypothesized Results for an Experiment Employing an Attitudinal Outcome Variable.

Baseline	EOT
40.0	42.5

And Table 3.1 is exactly what this experiment will produce: two numbers, undoubtedly not these exact two numbers, but two numbers nevertheless.

Of course, in an actual statistical analysis the software will produce subsidiary information such as standard deviations, confidence intervals, and the p-value associated with the difference between these two means. But basically this little table reflects what a single-group baseline-EOT (or pretest-posttest) experiment will produce.

So what purpose does such an a priori prediction regarding what might (or could) result from an experiment serve? It allows investigators to look at their projected results and ask themselves a simple question:

So what?

Or, more expansively:

How might these results eventually be used to improve someone's quality of life or advance a scientific field?

Or, more specifically:

Does this 2.5 (40.0–42.5) difference have any intrinsic meaning? Will it help anyone? Change anything?

If a meaningful outcome variable (e.g., pain or depression for a continuous scale, or mortality or graduation *rates* for a dichotomous one) were to be chosen in the first place, then the answer (and the question), of course, would be moot. Or alternately, for those prospective investigators of a bit less idealistic and considerably more pragmatic bent, the question might be amended to:

Will these projected results satisfy my personal motivation for conducting the experiment?

And to answer that question, the investigator must perform a bit of introspection buttressed by a consideration of what is reasonable to expect from the conduct of an experiment involving human participants. Before taking on this final evaluation of experimental meaningfulness, however, let's examine another key element in the evaluative process.

The importance of soliciting professional feedback: While it may be possible for a theoretician to work alone, evaluating the potential meaningfulness of an experiment should not be done in isolation, at least early in one's career. Presumably, everyone contemplating the conduct of an experiment has a professional network of some sort with whom ideas and strategies can be discussed, but at some point it is wise to solicit *formal* professional feedback on one's hypothesis and the experimental design selected to test it.

The optimal point in the design process to solicit this feedback is difficult to specify, since each experiment is unique in its conceptual development. Many institutions require pre-IRB reviews, which can be quite helpful, but they are often more keyed to evaluating (and potentially improving) the experiment's basic purpose and design than its *meaningfulness*. It is probably optimal, therefore, to seek professional opinions regarding meaningfulness both fairly early in the design process and again near the end, once the final step involving assessing one's personal and professional motivations for conducting the experiment has been completed. The investigator soliciting this type of advice is, of course, under no obligation to accept it. But unaccepted advice can still be quite helpful later when writing the final journal article, by anticipating a potential peer reviewer's similar objection. (Such advice can also be helpful at the design stage, by adding a variable or a measure to vitiate an anticipated criticism.)

There are also no rules regarding who should be consulted, although if the prospective investigator (a) is a graduate student with an advisor, (2) needs to use another investigator's resources, and/or (3) has access to a mentor, the initial choice or choices at least are obvious. (These individuals can also be helpful in suggesting other individuals to contact as well.) Some settings also provide opportunities for investigators to present their proposals at brown-bag colloquia, journal clubs, or similar forums. Regardless of the identities of the individuals from whom help is solicited or the form it takes, the process itself is important enough to deserve the status of our eighth experimental principle:

PRINCIPLE #8: Always solicit as much professional feedback on your hypothesis, design, and rationale as possible prior to conducting an experiment.

In support of this principle, it is wise to purposefully maintain and expand one's network of professional contacts over time. And unlike most of our experimental principles, this one possesses both upsides and a few downsides. Potential disadvantages include the difficulty of obtaining honest, unbiased assessments of one's ideas due to reviewers' (a) limited time, (b) reluctance to be frank (even, or perhaps especially, if they secretly consider the proposal to be demented), (c) professional jealousy, (d) lack of expertise, and/or (e) lack of interest in providing feedback to others. The primary potential advantage (which outweighs all of the downsides) involves the very real possibility that someone will suggest something important that the investigator hasn't considered—perhaps a design wrinkle, a secondary hypothesis, a superior way to measure a variable, a potential confound, some needed pilot work, or even (heaven forbid) that the experiment has already been conducted.

Soliciting professional feedback also involves certain expectations on the part the solicitor:

1. Being specific regarding the type of feedback desired. For example, should the reviewer concentrate on the design, the hypothesis, the importance of the study, its likelihood of success, and/or any relevant studies they know of?

2. Supplying reviewers with the information (and only the information) they need to provide the necessary feedback. (For example, if additional relevant studies are desired, the reviewer should be supplied with a bibliography of the relevant work the prospective investigator is already aware of.)

3. Being gracious in the presence of negative or useless comments and thanking the reviewers for their efforts (and if it is delivered in person, avoiding betraying any emotions regarding negative comments delivered). In the long run, negative comments are often more useful than positive ones anyway.

4. Reciprocating the favor by reviewing others' proposals when requested.

Which leads us to the final, partly introspective step (and partly reality check) in evaluating the potential meaningfulness of a proposed experiment.

The importance of examining one's professional and personal motivations and aspirations for conducting an experiment: There are almost certainly more disparate *motivations* for conducting an experiment than there are functions that experiments involving human participants are capable of fulfilling. Some of these motivations are justifiable and some are merely understandable. Some are unacceptable and some are simply not within the capability of an experiment to fulfill. In all cases, however, an introspective consideration of one's personal motivations can impact the design of an experiment and help determine whether it is worth conducting at all, which is perhaps the quintessential definition of experimental meaningfulness. Let's consider a few of the justifiable scientific (hence, meaningful) motivations first (which not coincidentally are all variations on the scientific functions addressable by experimentation listed in the first chapter):

To test a theory (or elucidate the cause of a phenomenon): Disciplines differ with respect to what their practitioners mean when they refer to "theory," with the more successful sciences (e.g., physics, neuroscience) usually meaning something considerably more discrete and specific than their social, educational, and behavioral counterparts. In general, however, all theories (regardless of discipline) have (or should have) the core purpose of explaining the cause or "why" of *something*.

This is nowhere more clearly and eloquently explained than in an influential *Science Magazine* essay written a half-century ago by J.R. Platt, in which he explored the question of why some fields progress much more rapidly than others (the laggards being the behavioral and psychological sciences). Written in 1964 (an ancient era as present-day scientists keep time), Professor Platt chose molecular biology and high-energy physics as case studies, arguing that it was the systematic application of inductive (or strong) inference dating back to Francis Bacon that characterizes these fields and accounts for these disciplines' progress. In his words:

Strong inference consists of applying the following steps to every problem in science, formally and explicitly and regularly:

(1) Devising alternative hypotheses;

(2) Devising a crucial experiment (or several of them), with alternative possible outcomes, each of which will, as nearly as possible, exclude one or more of the hypotheses;

(3) Carrying out the experiment so as to get a clean result;

(1′) Recycling the procedure, making subhypotheses or sequential hypotheses to refine the possibilities that remain; and so on. (p. 347)

In this vein, the author suggests that the essence of scientific thought resides in two questions asked of anyone (including oneself) who either (a) puts forth a theory ("But sir, what experiment could *dis*prove your hypothesis?") or (b) describes a proposed (or completed) experimental study ("But sir, what hypothesis does your experiment *dis*prove?").

These questions encapsulate the essence of science. They also constitute an excellent method to evaluate the meaningfulness of an experimental hypothesis.

With that said, it is important to realize that no single experiment or series of experiments is likely to definitively "*dis*prove" (and certainly will not dismiss) any widely held theory. This is perhaps best illustrated by the physicist James Clerk Maxwell—preceding, but greatly admired by, Albert Einstein—who is quoted by Klotz (1980) as describing the process of conversion from one theory to another as just a bit short of instantaneous in one of his lectures:

> There are two theories of the nature of light, the corpuscle theory and the wave theory; we used to believe in the corpuscle theory; now we believe in the wave theory because all who believed in the corpuscle theory have died. (p. 175)

To find out something that has never been known before: This objective is both vague and elusive, but the present author would be the last person to discourage anyone from trying to achieve it. He had the great fortune of documenting the existence of two phenomena for the first time under controlled conditions. And while there probably weren't more than a dozen individuals anywhere (all schooling researchers) who were even vaguely interested in them, it was a unique and very special experience that, as of this writing, is fresh nearly four decades later.

Of course, it could be argued that all of our hypotheses are unique in their own way, but in truth most experiments uncover only minute granules of knowledge (if that). Few discover or document the existence of either a completely new phenomenon or a suspected one. Science does, however, sometimes afford us the opportunity and the tools to *look* where none have had the capability (or the ingenuity) for looking before.

To create something capable of improving the human condition: Some may argue that this is the province of art (for aesthetic creations) or engineering (for utilitarian ones), but as an experimental motivation it doesn't refer to stunning paintings or superior mousetraps. Instead it refers to a relatively rare genre of endeavor (common in the successful sciences, uncommon in the others) that incorporates past scientific findings into the creation of a program or product whose efficacy will then be evaluated via controlled experimentation. Effective vaccines, drugs, health promotion programs, psychological counseling approaches, and computerized tutoring programs are all examples of how this motivation can be accomplished via experimentation involving human participants.

Replicating another experiment considered important enough to deserve confirmation: A replication of a published experiment isn't sexy and often doesn't appeal to reviewers or journal editors. Replication does constitute an important part of the scientific enterprise, however, and it possesses the tactical advantage that the trial is already designed and the original results are already known. It may still be wise to include at least one substantive change in the design that would not affect the new experiment's status as a replication (i.e., would not be used as an alternative explanation if the original effect failed to be replicated). Possibilities in this regard include the addition of (a) a second outcome that might be of interest (and which theoretically should be affected by the intervention), (b) a second independent variable (e.g., a blocking variable to assess a potential aptitude by treatment interaction [not recommended in educational research given their rarity]), (c) an additional intervention which logically could be compared to the original (or combined with it to potentially make it more effective), (d) a variant of the intervention, such as a more or less intensive dose (but included in addition to the original to preserve the replication), (e) a follow-up interval (if not included in the published trial), or (f) a strategy to test an alternative explanation for the original results.

While permission from the original investigators is not required to replicate their experiments, there are two excellent reasons to contact them. First, it is a professional courtesy and will most likely be taken as a compliment implying that the original work was considered important enough to replicate (assuming that the original study was completely and transparently reported). Second, and more importantly, it is often possible to obtain useful information about the original experiment, including access to some of their unpublished materials that may save considerable time and labor.

Depending on the degree of help received, an offer might be made to the previous investigator regarding a co-authorship on any accruing paper. (As mentioned earlier, the more contacts, colleagues, and collaborators developed early in one's career, the better.)

Guidelines for choosing a study to replicate (and possibly extend slightly in one of the ways just suggested above) are difficult to provide. An obvious criterion is that the original experiment is considered to be scientifically significant. (A second opinion here would be helpful, as well as checking the original's post-publication citation count.)

Redesigning (as opposed to replicating) a previously published experiment considered to have produced erroneous results: This one can be relatively problematic, although it can constitute a viable choice if the original experimental results were (a) counterintuitive, (b) theoretically unexplainable (at least by one's personal operative paradigm), or (c) appeared to possess an obvious glitch in its design or conduct that, if corrected, would produce a different result. To constitute a viable reason for redesign, the identified methodological glitch would need to be capable of producing either a false positive or false negative result. There is really no way of estimating the probability of this occurrence, unless the glitch emanated from the experiment employed (a) a too small sample size (as discussed in Chapter Nine) for suspected false negative results or (b) an inappropriate control group (discussed in Chapter Five). Both scenarios may require a bit of expert help in evaluating.

A negative study can constitute a better choice for a redesign, since a positive result will be easier to publish if the original investigators' results proved incorrect. Setting out to demonstrate that an intervention does not work is problematic (see the discussion on non-inferiority designs in Chapter Nine as one example). Other problems include the following: (a) journal reviewers and research consumers must be convinced that the replication was methodologically superior to the original; (b) negative results are more difficult in general to publish because of publication bias; (c) journal reviewers and their editors are often reluctant to publish replications in general: and (d) for those in the early stages of their careers, the original investigators may have more credibility (unless the new investigator assembles an experienced team).

Example of a Redesigned Experiment from the Present Author's Youth

In an early 1970s study, a well-known educational researcher failed in a series of attempts to validate a measure of teacher effectiveness based on student learning. This individual, later elected president of the American Educational Research Association, compared the learning produced by experienced, school of education–trained teachers with housewives, electricians, and auto mechanics (Popham, 1971) and found that the untrained, noncredentialed, inexperienced individuals produced the same amount of student learning as their converses.

The author, Professor James Popham, was far too savvy (scientifically and politically) to conclude that perhaps, just perhaps, the training provided by the colleges of education of those days did not impact the amount students learned in the public schools, but implications for teacher training institutions seemed clear to one education doctoral student at the time, who immediately set out to demonstrate that the original experiments were *incorrect*.

Without going into excruciating details about the redesign, the young man talked his advisor into recruiting undergraduate elementary education students who had not yet received any methods instruction or teaching experience and arranged to compare them to a group of experienced, credentialed elementary teachers. A 2-week mathematics unit to which the elementary students had not been exposed was developed, and both groups of teachers taught the units for the same amount of time to comparable students.

To both investigators' surprise, the redesigned study came up with the same negative finding as the original larger and better funded experiment (Moody & Bausell, 1971). Still finding this difficult to believe, the graduate student and his compliant advisor (by then a collaborator) performed a redesign of their original redesign (Bausell, Moody, & Walzl, 1973) and came up with the same result.

Decades later, these two experiments, along with many others conducted by the same doctoral student, were influential in the formulation of an exceedingly parsimonious theory of school learning (Bausell, 2010—for which Professor Popham wrote a flattering comment for the book cover). Of course, the end result was that all of this effort wound up being ignored (both Popham's original experiments and their redesigned ones), but this is the nature of educational research, where everything winds up being ignored and the discipline itself appears to be imprisoned in an endless, ever-repeating loop.

In the more successful empirical disciplines, replication (of which redesigns are a subset) of obviously important experimental results (or results that enjoy widespread media attention) constitute an important mechanism of scientific advance. There are simply too many components of the experimental process that go wrong (including investigator bias and fraud, as discussed in Chapter Thirteen) for the results of a single study (think cold fusion or the reputed claims for cures over the years for still largely incurable diseases) to be widely implemented without independent replication. This task, however, is normally reserved for established, well-funded investigators—not novices, such as the present author was for his first replication (which could also have been better designed).

To change an ineffective (or to demonstrate a more effective) professional practice: Every profession engages in both ineffective and non-evidenced-based clinical practices. As with other cherished beliefs, the results of a single experiment are seldom sufficient to change firmly entrenched behaviors.

And per previous counsel (Principle #4), experiments involving changes in clinical practice should not be attempted by investigators without significant clinical experience (or significant input from a clinically experienced member of the investigative team). Otherwise, it is simply too easy to overlook something relevant in the construction of the intervention and especially the comparison group (e.g., using an atypical setting for a usual practice control).

To experimentally test a previous nonexperimental research finding: The story of documenting the association between smoking and lung cancer is well known and constitutes an example of an important and extremely meaningful relationship that is almost impossible to translate into an experimental investigation involving human participants. (Even the investigators of the Tuskegee Syphilis Study might have objected to randomly assigning their black participants to either smoke or not to smoke in order to observe the mortality differences between the two groups (http://en.wikipedia.org/wiki/Tuskegee_syphilis_experiment). Well, perhaps *they* wouldn't, but ethical concerns aside, such a study would have taken decades to conduct, given the length of time required by tobacco smoke to produce lung cancer. (Of course, experimental animal studies could have been, and were, conducted to document the effect.)

What isn't so well known, however, is that a number of prominent research methodologists, statisticians, and scientists of the era adamantly rejected the association on methodological grounds. These researchers included (a) Sir Ronald Fisher, a prominent biologist and inventor of the analysis of variance; (b) Joseph Berkson, a physician and prominent statistician who made major contributions to the very statistical procedures that were used in making the smoking–cancer association; and (c) Hans Eysenck, one of the most prominent psychologists of the 20th century, a protégé and defender of Cyril Burt.

Berkson, incidentally, continued his opposition even after the U.S. Surgeon General's (some would say belated) report on the topic in 1964 (*Smoking and Health: Report of the Advisory Committee to the Surgeon General of the United States*)**,** and Eysenck received funding from the tobacco industry. Fisher unfortunately passed away 2 years before the Surgeon General's report was published, so we have no way of knowing if he would have eventually changed his mind.

Vandenbroucke (1989), in summing up these individuals' actions (in an article entitled "Those Who Were Wrong"), perhaps too kindly concluded that "although humanity progresses as science progresses, the path of progress is often only clear in retrospect." More to our point here he summed up the difficulties of judging the validity of evidence, based on methodological quality:

> Maybe, at the cutting edge of research, as new discoveries are being made, we ought to give up all hope of deciding by methodological principles which scientific statements will ultimately prove to be right and which will not.

As mentioned earlier, experimental research constitutes a minority of the research involving humans, partly because so many of our societal and personal issues are subject to manipulation. Milgram (1963), for example, studied obedience under contrived circumstances that nevertheless were capable of inducing unjustifiable psychological stress in its participants that (one hopes) would not be allowed by a 21st-century IRB. We can study the correlates and possible predisposing factors associated with violence, but we can't ethically manipulate them or purposefully induce any other illegal behaviors. We can analyze existing data on the social, educational, and financial correlates of childhood neglect, abuse, and poverty, but we can't manipulate poverty itself.

Fortunately, for out purposes here, however, many independent variables employed in correlational research are not as difficult to manipulate as these examples. And while some causal (i.e., independent) variables may appear to be next to impossible to translate to an experimentally intervention, a little creativity often provides the means to do so. One example involves the following (certainly creative) experimental translation of previous correlational evidence which strongly suggested that playing video games was negatively correlated with extra school academic pursuits and therefore probably with student achievement as well (e.g., Schmidt & Vandewater, 2008). Hopefully, this example will also illustrate that experimental research, besides being intellectually challenging, can actually be *fun*. (This experiment is also an example of the merger of two designs discussed in later chapters: [a] the randomized covariate-posttest control group and [b] the randomized delayed intervention design.)

RESEARCH EXAMPLE OF TRANSLATING A CORRELATIONAL FINDING TO AN EXPERIMENT

Effects of Video-Game Ownership on Young Boys' Academic and Behavioral Functioning: A Randomized, Controlled Study (2010)

R. Weis and B.C. Cerankosky

Citing a number of correlation studies that had found a negative relationship between academic achievement and time spent playing video games, the authors argued that this relationship deserved to be examined via an experimental approach because of the weaknesses inherent in all nonexperimental studies.

Despite nonexperimental evidence suggesting that the excessive playing of video games was related to lower test scores, most correlational evidence possesses a "chicken vs. egg" alternative explanation. In this case, for example, how do we know that the finding showing that boys who spend more time playing video games tend to do worse in school is causal in nature? Or what direction the causation manifests itself? Perhaps the video-game devotees spend more time in these activities *because* they do not do well in school and feel that studying doesn't have any payoff for them. Or perhaps children who spend inordinate amounts of time playing video games have poor adult models in their homes who, for one reason or another, don't supervise their children's completion of homework or require them to engage in academic activities during their free time.

The authors buttressed their rationale for the experiment via the plausible theory explaining why a causal negative relationship *should* exist between the two variables of interest: namely that the time spent playing video games *displaces* the time available for academic pursuits, such as reading or completing homework. (And, as previously discussed, there is no better documented, experimental, or correlational relationship in education than the relationship between time-on-task and learning.) Specifically, the investigators argued that the most defensible method of determining the etiology of the game playing–student achievement relationship was to randomly assign some students to play more video games than others. But how could such a feat be accomplished ethically or practically? The answer, as mentioned, was quite creative.

Design: The most obvious and perhaps most ethically defensible approach would be to begin with students who already play video games and somehow limit the amount of time half of them were allowed to do so. But while the removal of an already occurring behavior or intervention is a time honored and often effective approach, it was contraindicated in this case for two reasons:

1. First it would be difficult to ensure compliance because the investigators would need to convince someone (most likely parents) to limit the amount of time the games would be made available. Some parents undoubtedly would (and some would not) comply, thereby "watering down" the intervention.
2. Second, by using students whose video-playing behaviors had already become ingrained (i.e., were already fully addicted), limiting these behaviors might induce resentment and not necessarily result in their (a) picking up a book and reading or (b) completing homework assignments more conscientiously (or suddenly engaging in self-study).

So the approach these researchers chose was to identify elementary school children who did not currently own a gaming system and provide half of them with one. This, they reasoned, would result in the children who received the *opportunity* to spend more time playing video games actually availing themselves of that opportunity, while the children who did not receive said opportunity would have no reason or mechanism to increase their gaming time. And since the identity of those who received this opportunity and who did not would be decided randomly, the group who received the gaming systems and those who did not would be approximately equivalent with respect both to time spent playing games prior to the study as well as their academic achievement.

But a question arises as to whether such an intervention is ethical, since the experimenters suspected that spending increased time playing video games is detrimental. To at least partially address this issue (and perhaps to get the protocol through their IRB) the researchers added an inclusion criterion involving selecting only families in which the parents reported that they did not own a gaming system but were planning to purchase one for their children. Another, even more essential nod to ethics, was the provision of age-appropriate video games to be provided with the system, since there is also some evidence that playing violent video games may result in negative affect and behavior on the part of their players.

But, as will be discussed in the next chapter, equally crucial decisions arose in composing the control group. It is not sufficient to simply assign students and their families to not receive the video system because they might (a) feel slighted, (b) be less likely to comply with the experimental protocol, and (c) even to drop out of the trial. To prevent such occurrences the investigators chose to also provide control families with a gaming system, but to delay its presentation until the experiment was over (a 4-month interval) in order to (a) incentivize the continued involvement of the control group (since if any of its members chose to drop out of the study they would not receive the reward) and (b) avoid resentful

demoralization of the participants due to receiving nothing of value from participation in the experiment.

An attempt was made to reduce the sensitizing effects of the experiment on
parents by telling them that the purpose of the study was to study the effects of
video games on boys' development and thereby (theoretically) de-emphasizing the
educational focus of the study. Whether this masking approach was successful
is questionable, but it is consonant with good research practice. Whether teachers knew the identity of experimental vs. control students was not reported, even
though such knowledge is always problematic in studies involving potentially subjective outcomes.

Results: Students who received the video-game intervention scored significantly lower on reading and writing at the end of 4 months than their control
counterparts who had not yet received the games. (There were no differences on
math scores.) Experimental students played video games approximately 30 minutes more per day than control students (39.4 vs. 9.3 minutes). (Control students,
while not owning video games, were not prohibited from playing them in other students' homes.) On four teacher-reported subscales, one (school-related problems)
was significantly higher for the experimental students. There were no statistically
significant parental-reported behavioral differences between the two groups.

A pervasive problem with this and almost all experiments involves the need to structure the
"natural" environment to a certain extent in order to clearly differentiate between the intervention and comparison groups. This results in a question of whether an effect occurring in the
more artificial environment would also occur in the natural setting to which the experiment
aspires to model.

These issues are discussed in more detail in Chapter Eleven, under the general topic of external validity (or the more idiosyncratic dichotomy of science designed to demonstrate "what
is" vs. "what could be"). At the very least, however, when experiments such as this video-game
experiment produce similar results to large-scale correlational studies, considerable credibility
is afforded to the bottom-line inference emanating from both genres.

SOME UNDERSTANDABLE (BUT NONMEANINGFUL) MOTIVATIONS FOR CONDUCTING AN EXPERIMENT

The necessity of starting someplace: Everyone does, and Principle #5 (conducting one's first
experiment under the tutelage of an experienced, principled mentor) provides cursory advice
on how to do so. So let's file this one under the "understandable" category, because we all do have
to gain experience somewhere.

To pad one's vitae: This one is deemed understandable because academic scientists do need
to be cognizant of their publication count for promotion and funding considerations. However,
designing and conducting an experiment is a labor-intensive endeavor that may result in
"only" a single publication. Experiments also usually require considerable time and labor of its

participants, so it is preferable to obtain what one considers an adequate number of publications from other sources rather than conducting trivial experiments. Examples include the following:

1.   Collaborations on meta-analyses and other empirical projects,
2.   Collaboration on experiments that other investigators initiate (such as a mentor or colleague),
3.   Secondary analyses of existing databases, or
4.   Methods-based articles.

The more empirical skills (e.g., statistical, analytic, graphical, assessment, article retrieving, systematic reviews, database creation) one develops, the more frequently publishing opportunities will arise. And in the long run, these additional skills will most likely improve an investigator's experimental work as well.

SOME UNJUSTIFIABLE MOTIVATIONS

Wouldn't it be interesting? It seldom is. In the early phase of designing a study it is not uncommon to hear someone (seldom an experienced investigator) suggest an additional outcome variable or even a second experimental group constituting some variant of the intervention prefaced with this timeworn phrase.

"Interesting" is neither a design nor a scientific term. It is too idiosyncratic, for the simple reason that what is interesting to one individual is likely to be completely irrelevant (or trivial) to another. ("Interesting" effects also seldom turn out to be "statistically significant" ones.) Adding questionnaires or collecting information to facilitate secondary (including subgroup) analyses seldom results in anything of scientific interest (or even of idiosyncratic interest to *anyone*). When they do, they are quite likely to be nonreplicable because of their post hoc nature (often colloquially called a "fishing expedition" in research), which drastically increases the chances of finding spurious statistically significant results. We'll refer to such results as Type I errors in Chapter Nine, but for present purposes it is sufficient to say that even when the computer output designates a subgroup analysis (i.e., a nonhypothesized finding) as statistically significant, it probably isn't, which gives rise to our ninth principle:

> **PRINCIPLE #9:   Always explicitly designate nonhypothesized subgroup analyses and secondary analyses employing outcome variables other than the primary outcome as such when reporting the results of an experiment. (When reading a published report, put little or no credence in a nonreplicated subgroup analysis or experimental effects involving multiple secondary outcome variables.)**

For a general critique of the problems associated with subgroup analyses, see Wang, Lagakos, Ware, et al. (2007). For a specific example of the methodological artifacts attending one form of the practice in education (i.e., aptitude-by-treatment interactions, which are seldom identified and even less frequently replicated, see Bracht [1970] or Gufstafsson [1978]).

To become rich and/or famous: Forget both of these. Becoming rich is more likely than becoming famous if you do succeed in building a better mousetrap, but the evaluation of its efficacy would have much less to do with its success than with clever marketing (which is by implication prohibited by Principle #1). As for fame, in this celebrity-worshiping society even Andy Warhol's 15-minute rule isn't realistic for most of us in science.

There are exceptions to all generalizations, however, so some improbable aspirations may be realized, and some that may seem inappropriate may still result in an excellent experiment. The bottom line of this final step in the evaluation of meaningfulness (the importance of examining one's professional and personal motivations and aspirations), like the ones that preceded it, are not absolute guarantees that anyone's experiment *will prove* meaningful. It, and each of the others, is only a worthwhile step that has the capability of increasing the probability of success. With that disclaimer, therefore, our 10th experimental principle is offered:

> **PRINCIPLE #10: Once a final hypothesis has been decided on, attempt to honestly assess your primary motivations (or aspirations) for conducting the experiment.**

BUT WHAT DOES ALL OF THIS HAVE TO DO WITH DR. JONES'S EXPERIMENT?

After all, Dr. Jones selected an undeniably meaningful outcome variable (pain reduction), and his study might still have passed the meaningfulness criteria presented in this chapter (although he could have been faulted for not having mastered the experimental underpinnings [Principle #3] on which his intervention rested [which indicates that acupuncture is no more effective than a placebo]). Unfortunately, even strict adherence to all of the experimental principles and advice tendered so far would not qualify his study as serious science. Many additional, extremely nefarious *experimental* artifacts remain that demand more control than Dr. Jones's single-group design permits—artifacts that if not prevented or controlled automatically prohibit any experiment from supporting a scientific inference or even qualifying as an actual scientific endeavor.

That, however, is the subject matter of Chapter Four.

SUMMARY

The crucially important and often perhaps unavoidably subjective concept of experimental meaningfulness is introduced within the context of the design process itself, which includes 10 basic decisions—the first three of which are the most relevant for evaluating the meaningfulness of a study. These decisions are

1. The hypothesis (or hypotheses) to be tested.
2. The intervention to be employed.

3. The outcome that will be used to determine the intervention's effect(s).
4. The types of participants to be recruited, the manner in which they are recruited, and how much they will told about the experiment at recruitment.
5. How, by whom, how often, and under what conditions the outcome(s) will be assessed.
6. To what the intervention will be compared (e.g., participant changes from baseline, a control group, or an alternative treatment of some sort).
7. If different experimental conditions are employed, how membership in them will be determined (e.g., whether randomized to groups and, if so, the manner in which it will be accomplished).
8. Whether participants and/or experimental staff will know the identity of the treatment (or comparison group) to which individuals have been assigned.
9. The statistical procedures by which the data will be analyzed.
10. The number of participants who will be recruited.

The hypothesis itself is a single declarative sentence which serves as an operational description of the entire experiment and is therefore crucial to evaluating the meaningfulness of the entire enterprise. It consists of five crucial elements:

1. The identity of the intervention and its duration,
2. The comparison of interest (e.g., a before–after assessment of the outcome or an intervention vs. control group contrast),
3. The primary outcome variable,
4. The type of participants used, and
5. The expected results.

Specific suggestions for determining the meaningfulness of a hypothesis include (a) ascertaining whether the primary outcome is empirically related to the quality of human life, (b) establishing the importance of (and approaches to) the development of viable interventions, (c) visualizing the most likely results to accrue from an experiment, and (d) examining one's motives for conducting the experiment.

Toward these ends, the following five experimental principles were added to our growing collection:

Principle #6: Always translate a proposed experiment into one or more formal, written hypotheses.

Principle #7: Once the hypothesis is formulated, delineate all of the possible experimental outcomes, attempt to assess the probability of each of their occurrences, and *attempt to visualize the actual numerical outcome likely to accrue if the hypothesis is supported.*

Principle #8: Always solicit as much professional feedback on your hypothesis, design, and rationale as possible prior to conducting an experiment.

Principle #9: Always explicitly designate nonhypothesized subgroup analyses and secondary analyses employing outcome variables other than the primary outcome as such when reporting the results of an experiment. (When reading a published report, put little or no credence in a nonreplicated subgroup analysis or experimental effects involving multiple secondary outcome variables.)

Principle #10: Once a final hypothesis has been decided on, attempt to honestly assess your primary motivations (or aspirations) for conducting the experiment.

REFERENCES

Bastian, H., Glasziou, P., & Chalmers, I. (2010). Seventy-five trials and eleven systematic reviews a day: How will we ever keep up? *PLoS Med, 7*(9), e1000326.

Bausell, R.B. (2010). *Too simple to fail: A case for educational change.* New York: Oxford University Press.

Bausell, R.B., Moody, W.B., & Walzl, R.N. (1973). A factorial study of tutoring versus classroom instruction. *American Education Research Journal, 10,* 591–7.

Beecher, H.K. (1966). Ethics and clinical research. *New England Journal of Medicine, 274,* 1354–60.

Bracht, G.H. (1970). Experimental factors related to aptitude-by-treatment interactions. *Review of Educational Research, 40,* 627–45.

Gufstafsson, J-E. (1978). A note on class effects in aptitude × treatment interactions. *Journal of Educational Psychology, 70,* 142–6.

Hodges, R.E., Baker, E.M., Hood, J., et al. (1969). Experimental scurvy in man. *The American Journal of Clinical Nutrition, 22,* 535–538.

Hodges, R.E., Hood, J., Canham, J.E., et al. (1971). Clinical manifestations of ascorbic acid deficiency in man. *The American Journal of Clinical Nutrition, 24,* 432–443.

Klotz, I.M. (1980). The N-Ray affair. *Scientific American, 241,* 168–75.

Milgram, S. (1963). Behavioral study of obedience. *Journal of Abnormal and Social Psychology, 67,* 371–8.

Moody, W.B., & Bausell, R.B. (1971). The effect of teacher experience on student achievement, transfer, and retention. Presented at the 1971 meeting of the American Educational Research Association, New York.

Platt, J.R. (1964). Strong inference. *Science, 146,* 347–53.

Popham, W. J. (1971). Performance tests of teaching proficiency: Rationale, development, and validation. *American Educational Research Journal, 8,* 105–17.

Reiter, K. (2009). Experimentation on prisoners: Persistent dilemmas in rights and regulations. *California Law Review, 97,* 501–66.

Schmidt, M.E., & Vandewater, E.A. (2008). Media and attention, cognition, and school achievement. *The Future of Children, 18,* 63–85.

Vandenbroucke, J.P. (1989). Those who were wrong. *American Journal of Epidemiology, 130,* 3–5.

Wang, R., Lagakos, S.W., Ware, J.H., et al. (2007). Statistics in medicine—reporting of subgroup analyses in clinical trials. *New England Journal of Medicine, 357,* 2189–94.

Weis, R., & Cerankosky, B.C. (2010). Effects of video-game ownership on young boys' academic and behavioral functioning: A randomized, controlled study. Psychological Science, 21, 463–70.

WHY POORLY DESIGNED EXPERIMENTS ARE INADEQUATE FOR MAKING COMPLEX INFERENCES

The Single-Group Pretest-Posttest Design (or the Unfortunate Conclusion of Dr. Jones's Foray into the World of Science)

D r. Jones and his colleague had no doubt that their participants' pain would decrease as a result of the acupuncture. And, if no concurrent changes in the participants' medications or other circumstances occurred during this time period, the investigators felt they would then be in possession of nearly indisputable evidence for the analgesic efficacy of acupuncture. Or at the very least, they would have the necessary evidence to allow Dr. Jones to serve his boorish critic an ample helping of crow at his next colloquium presentation.

He would, after all, now have hard data from multiple patients collected under standardized conditions to supplement his previous clinical experiences. If the study was properly conducted it would also surely prove what he already *knew* to be true—that acupuncture was a viable nonpharmaceutical alternative (if not the long-sought panacea) for decreasing osteoarthritis pain.

Fortuitously, the experiment itself went off with only a few very minor glitches and following the final treatment of the final participant, Dr. Jones had his colleague's work study student enter the data into a spreadsheet. To his absolute delight he found that 8 of 10 participants had experienced at least some pain relief following introduction of the intervention (see Table 4.1).

Table 4.1: Hypothetical Data for Dr. Jones's Experiment.

Participant	Baseline Pain	EOT Pain	EOT–Baseline Difference
1	3.50	2.50	−1.00
2	3.60	1.90	−1.70
3	3.70	5.10	+1.40
4	3.70	2.90	−0.80
5	4.00	3.30	−0.70
6	4.50	5.00	+0.50
7	6.10	5.10	−1.00
8	6.70	4.60	−2.10
9	7.10	6.40	−0.70
10	7.10	5.90	−1.20
Average	5.00	4.27	−0.73

Dr. Jones's friend and colleague then called in a favor from another (less boorish) biostatistician who agreed to analyze the data for them and to write a sentence or two describing the results in exchange for an authorship on the final paper. Several weeks later, following six clicks of his mouse and the 7 minutes it took him to write a sentence summarizing the results, the two budding scientists received their answer:

As determined by a paired t-test ($t = 2.28$ [9], $p = .049$), the participants' pain significantly declined from baseline following 4 weeks of acupuncture treatment.

Statistical Interlude: The Meaning of Statistical Significance

Since the purpose of an experiment is to test a hypothesized causal relationship between the intervention and the outcome variable, some sort of objective basis is needed on which to determine whether the hypothesis should be accepted or rejected. While investigators originally employed descriptive statistics and made their case on the basis of the direction and perceived magnitude of any obtained differences, it soon became obvious that something a bit more objective was needed. Sir Ronald Fisher (1935), an extremely influential statistician, geneticist, inventor of analysis of variance, and author of a seminal textbook on experimental design (*The Design of Experiments*), rose to the occasion and suggested that scientists adopt a probability level (also called an alpha level) based on the distribution of whatever inferential statistic was used to analyze their data.

The alpha level he suggested was .05, which is interpreted as "differences of the magnitude of those obtained in the experiment [that] would occur by chance alone no more than five percent of the time." This convention was generally accepted, with any results obtained equal to (or below) .05 being declared statistically significant and any above that value declared not statistically significant. The obtained probability (called the *p*-value), which like all probabilities ranges between 0 and 1.0, was based on the distribution of the particular statistic employed (in Dr. Jones's case, the *t*-test, whose distribution is identical to that of an analysis of variance, which Sir Ronald Fisher invented, involving two groups as well as several other statistical procedures). The *p*-value obtained in an experiment such as this is dependent on a number of factors: (a) the homogeneity of the sample, (b) the number of participants used, (c) the size of the mean difference, and (in the case of the paired *t*-test) (d) the correlation between the baseline and end-of-treatment (EOT) assessments.

Academics have been debating the merits of this convention ever since it was suggested, some advocating reliance on confidence intervals, effect sizes, or both. In truth, however, the "statistical significance" concept is so firmly entrenched that it is unlikely to disappear anytime soon, thus most investigators simply use the convention mandated by the journal to which they plan to submit their results and do not concern themselves with its propriety.

The statistical significance concept, while not without drawbacks, is not an unreasonable strategy and apparently works quite well as long as everyone avoids reading more into the concept of statistical significance than it deserves—keeping in mind that statistical significance is simply a probability level based on a theoretical statistical distribution and does *not* indicate that the differences obtained (a) are "real," (b) possess any practical or clinical importance, (c) would replicate 19 times out of a hundred (i.e., $1.00 - 05 = 0.95 = 19/20$), *or* (d) (as in the case of Dr. Jones's experiment) indicate a defensible causal inference. Two related concepts, *statistical power* (the probability of obtaining statistical significance for a given experiment when its hypothesis is correct) and *beta* or *Type II error* (the probability of not obtaining statistical significance under the same conditions), will be discussed in more detail in Chapter Nine.

Needless to say, Dr. Jones was ecstatic at the biostatistician's blessing, so he formally applied to present the results of his study at his professional organization's next annual conference and the paper was accepted. Both he and his colleague felt very good about their results and prepared for the redemptive approbation of their peers.

Rather than continue this story (which, like many academic parables, has somewhat less than a completely satisfying conclusion), let's examine the design flaws (or inferential threats) that contribute to making these results considerably less than scientifically definitive. (We'll ignore the small number of participants since an actual trial would use more.)

First, however, in the spirit of fairness, let's acknowledge what is superior about the data emanating from an experiment such as this as compared to Dr. Jones's professional experience (on which his ill-fated initial colloquium was based). Six features come to mind immediately:

1. The consequences (pain) of the action (acupuncture) were measured systematically, recorded, and subjected to a formal statistical analysis. True, Dr. Jones must still rely on his patients' self-reports, but there are no viable alternatives for measuring pain. Also, the use of a well-researched, standardized instrument such as a visual analog scale

provides (a) a degree of social and professional distance between participants and care-givers, (b) control of individual differences in verbal expression, and (c) documented numerical results to replace the investigator's verbal descriptions.

2. Multiple participants were used, which helped to rule out the possibility that the result-ing inference was based on a single aberrant case.

3. Many of the experimental participants (i.e., those recruited via the clinic and through flyers posted in the elevator) did not share a personal-clinical history with Dr. Jones to the degree that Mrs. Smith did, therefore reducing the likelihood that any positive results would be due to politeness or fear of reprisal. The strategy of using someone other than the clinician administering the intervention to collect the pain assessments also helped in this regard (as did the assurance of confidentiality of all responses mandated by the IRB).

4. Unlike the spontaneous, unstructured, and often retrospective nature of clinical treat-ment, the experiment was prospectively planned and conducted. In order to obtain per-mission to even approach patients the investigators were required to produce a written document explicitly detailing their procedures. They were further required to report any deviations from this protocol to the IRB, as well as apply for permission to institute any changes to it.

5. Data (also self-reported) were collected on any co-occurring events capable of influencing pain in addition to (or instead of) the intervention. If none occurred, then at least some evidence for ruling out *one* alternative explanation for the results would be provided.

6. The changes depicted in Table 4.1 were most likely not a chance occurrence. In fact, there was only a 4.9% chance of this as determined by the biostatistician's analysis of the data. By scientific (or at least statistical) convention, therefore, Dr. Jones and his col-league were permitted to conclude that their participants probably did actually experi-ence a decline in pain from baseline to EOT.

Unfortunately, no existing scientific conventions permitted their conclusion that the intervention *caused* the changes observed in the outcome variable. There are, on the other hand, numerous epistemological reasons prohibiting such inferences based on the experi-ment's rudimentary (some, including the present author, would say *primitive*) *experimental design*.

The research design employed by Dr. Jones and his colleague is called different names in different disciplines, but here we will call it a *single-group pretest-posttest design*. The "single-group" part of the label indicates that no control or comparison group existed, such as a separate group of participants who do not receive the intervention. (This epistemological weakness is sometimes sanitized by referring to the strategy as "using the same people to serve as their own controls.")

Diagrammatically, this exceedingly simple (and primitive) design can be depicted as in Figure 4.1.

FIGURE 4.1: Single-Group Pretest-Posttest Design.

While this architecture does possess a few advantages over something like a single cli-nician–client encounter, this does not imply that the single-group pretest-posttest design qualifies as a serious *scientific* strategy. It does not. To illustrate why, let us re-examine Dr. Jones's initial foray into empirical research with an eye toward identifying any impediments to inferring, based on his results depicted in Table 4.1, that "acupuncture *caused* or *resulted in* or *was responsible for* the observed reduction in his experimental participants' pain perception."

We've mentioned natural history and the placebo effects as potential factors that prohibited Mrs. Smith's personal experiment from producing an ironclad inference. As it happens, these two phenomena are equally deleterious for experimental inferences as well, especially the design chosen by Dr. Jones and his colleague. Natural history and the placebo effect are examples of what are called "experimental artifacts," "experimental confounds," "confounding factors," or "threats to the *internal validity* of an experiment," the latter of which is concerned with a seemingly very simple question:

Was the inference resulting from the experiment (i.e., the intervention was responsible for the observed changes in the outcome variable or the lack thereof) correct, or were those results due to the presence of some sort of procedural or logical error in the experimental design (or its implementation)?

Regardless of what they are called, these procedural glitches—some of which are obvious, some counterintuitive—can all be conceptualized (and globally defined) as *anything* that could potentially (a) be mistaken for, (b) inflate, (c) deflate, or (d) disguise a true experimental effect.

Let us therefore re-examine natural history and the placebo effect (which potentially bedeviled Mrs. Smith's causal conclusion) from the perspective of Dr. Jones' experimental results before introducing some other equally nefarious scientific impediments.

EXPERIMENTAL ARTIFACT #1: NATURAL HISTORY OR MATURATION

In Mrs. Smith's case we know (from Figure 2.2) she received her acupuncture treatment when her pain—which waxed and waned over time—was at its height. (If she had received her treatment at its lowest point she might well have concluded that acupuncture *increased* her arthritic pain.)

Unfortunately, similar conditions could have operated for the volunteers in Dr. Jones' clinical trial. They were, after all, *permitted* to participate *only* when they were experiencing a significant amount of pain (at least a 3.5 on the VAS), which was a completely reasonable strategy. (It makes no sense to administer an intervention to participants who won't benefit from it, such as a weight loss experiment involving participants who aren't overweight.) Thus, to the extent that the natural history of Mrs. Smith's osteoarthritis pain constituted a reasonable depiction of people suffering from osteoarthritis of the knee in general, wouldn't such people be more likely to commit the necessary time and effort involved in participating in an experiment when their pain was progressively bothering them more than usual? In other words, this artifact *can* occur (or its potential for occurring can exist) as easily for a group of people as for a single individual.

Thus, while admittedly exaggerated, Figure 4.2 might also grossly characterize the effects of natural history on Dr. Jones' experiment if he were to have recruited 10 Mrs. Smith–type participants.

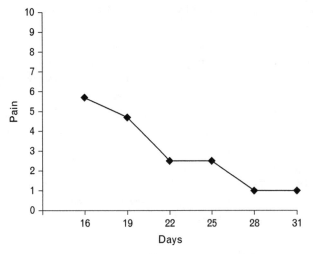

FIGURE 4.2 Natural History Masquerading as an Analgesic Effect in a Single-Group Pretest-Posttest Design

Amelioration: When participants with a propensity to change on the outcome variable in the absence of any intervention are used in a single-group pretest-posttest design, there is very little that can be done to control these effects. The most effective strategy is to reduce their likelihood by keeping the duration of the experiment as brief as possible. This, however, must be balanced with scientific concerns such as providing the intervention with sufficient time to exert its maximum influence. (Thus, if Dr. Jones had reason to believe his therapy could be effective after only a session or two, natural history [or its threat] could have been greatly reduced.)

However, occasionally the natural history/maturation artifact occurs in unanticipated ways. For example, since the majority of osteoarthritis patients are relatively elderly, they will share a tendency to change as a function of their age. This might in turn manifest itself in physical discomfort while sitting in a waiting room or lying on an examination bench for an extended period of time. Or, more realistically, children participating in a year-long longitudinal study may well change "naturally" (or "mature") over the experimental interval, irrespective of (or in addition to) any intervention introduced during that time.

EXPERIMENTAL ARTIFACT #2:
THE PLACEBO EFFECT

The same logic holds for the placebo effect. If it can occur for one person, it can occur for 10. Most people who volunteer to participate in an acupuncture trial undoubtedly either believe (or hope) the therapy has the potential to help them. These expectations may be conditioned in different ways for different participants (e.g., by testimonials from acquaintances, the media, Internet ads that likely will pop up when a potential participants seeks information on the therapy, or even the informed consent agreement), and they may be further reinforced by the acupuncturist's demeanor or even the ritualistic accessorized practices accompanying the therapy.

Thus the classic conditions for eliciting a placebo effect are present in experimental settings, just as they are in clinical ones. Whether these conditions produce as dramatic effects in the former as the latter is not known, but what is known is strong placebo effects can be reliably elicited in experimental settings, as was illustrated by the Price, Kirsch, Duff, et al. (1999) example presented in Chapter One.

Amelioration: Many experimental outcomes (e.g., learning, mortality, weight loss, prevention of diseases) are not subject to placebo effects. For those that are (e.g., pain, depression, tremors) or plausibly could be, the only way to *prevent* a placebo effect is to actively attempt to dispel expectancy effects (and therefore hopefulness), which might well result in no one volunteering for the experiment (not to mention raising the ire of IRB reviewers). This leaves controlling for a placebo effect as the only viable option, and the only way to do that is to use a placebo control group of some sort, which is obviously impossible in a single-group pretest-posttest design.

So far we've mentioned two inferential artifacts that may or may not operate in a single-group pretest-posttest design. Unfortunately, there are numerous others, the first of which *inevitably* occurs under certain rather common conditions.

EXPERIMENTAL ARTIFACT #3: REGRESSION TO THE MEAN

This artifact's etiology is statistical in nature, is rather counterintuitive, and has been recognized by researchers for well over a century (Galton, 1886). It is called *regression to the mean*, and it is a phenomenon that is independent of expectations (as is required for the placebo effect) or naturally occurring outcome changes due to participant characteristics (as are natural history or maturation effects).

Regression to the mean is an unusual artifact because it *always* occurs with mathematical predictability whenever the outcome variable (be it pain, memory, learning, or attitudes toward widgets) is measured with a significant degree of *error* twice. From a design prospective, however, regression to the mean is problematic only when participants are selected for an experiment *because* they exhibit more extreme scores (either high or low) on that outcome variable than those of the population from which they are drawn.

This phrase "selected…*because* they exhibit more extreme scores… than those of the population from which they are drawn" is important, because even though Dr. Jones's participants certainly had more extreme scores than those of the general population, a problematic regression-to-the-mean effect would occur only if his participants had more extreme scores than was typical of patients with osteoarthritis of the knee (or perhaps more precisely, more extreme than was typical for *them*).

When applied to an individual's score, the phenomenon can be conceptualized as occurring when that individual's baseline score happened to be more extreme than is typical for that *person*. Hence regression to the mean would be extremely difficult to tease out of a natural history effect, as hypothetically depicted in Figure 4.2. There is really no need to distinguish between the two, however, since they can operate independently of (or in conjunction with) one another—thus both need to be either avoided or controlled.

Statistical Interlude: Random Measurement Error and Regression to the Mean

Anytime a group of reasonably normally distributed (think bell-shaped curve) individuals are measured, the resulting scores involve a degree of error. This error is by necessity either higher than is "typical" for some individuals (positive error) or, for an approximately *equal number* of people, lower (negative error) than it "should be" or is typical for *them*. (An individual's "typical" score might be conceptualized as the mean score that would result from that individual being measured innumerable times under varying circumstances.) Thus, not only do a sample's actual scores (i.e., the ones actually obtained on the measurement instrument) usually approximate a normal distribution (if the sample is large enough), but so do those of the actual scores' two components: a systematic component (which we'll henceforth refer to as "true" scores, in keeping with classical measurement theory) and a "random," error component, which is normally of smaller magnitude than the true component.

Now, let's suppose a group of individuals known to be relatively representative of a population of interest was measured on an experimental outcome (think pain) and then two subgroups were selected from them: the 25% of individuals who achieved the highest scores and the 25% who scored the lowest. Obviously, these two subgroups would differ dramatically on the outcome variable because they were selected on the basis of their differences. (The two sets of scores would, however, possess equivalent proportions of "true/consistent" and "random/error" components.)

Not so obviously, perhaps, although the two subgroups did not differ with respect to their overall error rates, they would differ with respect to their *proportions* of positive and negative random error components—both from each other and from that of the total group. Just as the top 25% subgroup contained higher actual scores than those of its bottom 25% counterpart, it would also contain a higher proportion of positively biased error. (The opposite, of course, is true of the lowest scoring quarter.) The error is still random, but its direction, unlike the distribution within the total group, is now *unequally* distributed between the two extreme groups.

Now, consider what would happen to this positively and negatively biased error when the group is remeasured, as occurs in a single-group pretest-posttest design, for this is key to the etiology of the concept of regression to the mean. Since error is by definition random, the same individuals will not possess the same degree of error (or the same direction in which that error occurred) upon remeasurement. Some who had a positive component the first time will have a negative component the second time and vice versa. These changes in directional bias would have had no practical effect had the original total group been remeasured (assuming they were representative of the relevant population), since the first and second measurements would contain the same proportions of positive and negative error. (The overall changes effect would have resulted in a complete washout, with the average score for the first assessment being, for all practical purposes, almost identical to the mean of the second assessment, assuming nothing substantively intervened between measurements.)

However, this is not true for the remeasurement means of the two extreme groups that were selected, *because* they were different from one another (i.e., the highest scoring 25% and the lowest scoring 25%) and from the population of which they were both a part. Since the initially positive group had *more* positively than negatively biased error, this distribution will be completed reshuffled the second time around like a deck of cards, with the new distribution being somewhere near a 50-50 positive/negative breakdown. This in turn would result in the mean score for the second measurement being lower than occurred on the first measurement for this initially high-scoring group. (And, as always, the opposite pattern will accrue for the lowest group—their mean for the second assessment will be *higher* than that obtained on the first.)

This, then, is the counterintuitive crux of the regression-to-the-mean phenomenon. It can masquerade as an intervention effect, and it can even result in spurious statistical significance in a single-group pretest-posttest design when the intervention itself had no effect at all, making regression to the mean an especially potentially virulent inferential artifact. Regression to the mean is also unique among the artifacts discussed in this chapter, however, because its magnitude can be estimated via a relatively simple formula if the correlation between the two assessments is known (Weeks, 2007).

Amelioration: While regression to the mean cannot be prevented in a single-group pretest-posttest design when participants are selected for a study based on their extreme scores on the outcome variable, it can be dissipated by employing multiple baseline (pretest) assessments. Since the vast majority of the regression-to-the-mean effect occurs between the first and second baseline assessments, using only the second baseline assessment in the data analysis largely dissipates the effect prior to the EOT assessment. (Of course, as will be discussed shortly, the artifact can be controlled by the presence of an appropriate comparison group to which "extreme" participants are randomly assigned.)

EXPERIMENTAL ARTIFACT #4:
THE REPEATED TESTING ARTIFACT

It is a bit perverse to mention this particular artifact immediately after suggesting multiple baselines as a means of ameliorating regression to the mean, but such are the vicissitudes and perversities of experimental design. Repeated testing, like regression to the mean, is not intuitively obvious, and its direction is also quite predictable. Unlike regression to the mean, however, it does not emanate from selecting participants based on extreme scores on the outcome variable. It is also not a particularly powerful effect and normally, by itself, would not be expected to invalidate the results of most experiments. But since it can occur in addition to other artifacts, it must be considered—especially in single-group designs.

The repeated testing artifact occurs only for certain types of outcomes and not all of those. It is perhaps best viewed as a sort of practice effect in which participants score higher (or in a more socially desirable manner) on the second administration of a cognitive (e.g., knowledge), affective (e.g., attitudinal or personality), or self-reported behavioral (e.g., dietary or sexual practices) measure than they do on their first experience with the measure.

Its occurrence on knowledge tests is probably explained by respondents either (a) remembering the mistakes made the first time they take the test and correcting them on the second administration (e.g., by looking up the correct answers or discussing items with other test takers) or (b) being less likely to make random errors on the second testing because of familiarity with the testing format. In the case of measures with clearly socially acceptable answers to the individual items, the effect may be due to participants being more cognizant of the test's intent after the first administration. (Respondents may then change their original answers in order to appear less deviant or to give investigators the responses they think are desired.)

Amelioration: It is worth repeating that this is not a strong effect and does not operate for all participants or all types of self-report outcomes. There is, for example, no evidence for the occurrence of a repeated testing artifact for self-reported VAS pain scales as was used in the Price et al. placebo study in Chapter One.

Assuring participants of the confidentiality of their responses and reminding them how important honest responses are to the validity of the experiment could theoretically help ameliorate any tendencies toward providing socially acceptable responses (or misguided attempts to please the investigators).

Note that a related artifact called *pretest sensitization* (Campbell & Stanley, 1966) is not included here, along with a design (the Solomon four-group design) specifically created to control for it (Solomon, 1949), because of the lack of evidence that the effect itself exists with any degree of frequency. (Pretest sensitization involves the possibility that the act of taking a pretest will heighten intervention participants' awareness of an unusually reactive intervention and thereby produce a false positive result).

EXPERIMENTAL ARTIFACT #5: INSTRUMENTATION CHANGES

Instrumentation is defined as changes occurring between the baseline and EOT in the actual measurement instrument or the procedures for administering or collecting data therefrom. It is an obvious and easily avoided experimental artifact, but is still one that beginning investigators should be aware of.

As an absurd example, if two completely different questionnaires were used to assess the outcome variable at baseline vs. EOT there would be no basis on which to evaluate the effect of the intervention in a single-group experiment since the instruments' differences would be perfectly confounded with the experimental comparison. (As will be discussed later, this isn't necessarily true for multigroup experiments where the baseline measure can be used as a covariate for the EOT assessment.) More subtle examples include (a) different research assistants collecting the data using different instructions and (b) employing different data collection procedures or formats (e.g., collecting the baseline assessment via a paper-and-pencil questionnaire and the EOT assessment by telephone). It is doubtful that *all* of these latter discrepancies would produce large effects, but there is no reason this artifact should be allowed to occur in experimental practice.

Amelioration: Everything that can be standardized in the assessment process should be. Identical formats, instruments, data collection settings, laboratories (if relevant), and instructions given to participants should be employed. Obviously, staff turnover is always a possibility; employing standardized data collection training procedures (including scripts) should prevent personnel changes from being problematic.

EXPERIMENTAL ARTIFACT #6: VOLUNTEERISM

The vast majority of experimental research requires informed consent on the part of either the participants or their guardians. This in turn ensures that experimental participants often differ from non-volunteers (e.g., ECRI Health Technology Assessment Information Service, 2002; Lovato, Hill, Hertert, et al., 1997; Wilhelmsen, Ljungberg, Wedel, & Werko, 1976) on factors such as the following:

1. Altruistic motivations (e.g., hoping to contribute something positive to the human good by advancing science),
2. Financial need (in those instances in which participants are paid for their time and effort),
3. Greater propensities for risk-taking behavior,
4. Having fewer demands on their time (e.g., job and family responsibilities), and/or
5. Feeling especially desperate regarding the course of their disease (in clinical research).

In addition, participants often volunteer on the basis of (a) the perceived benefits of the intervention (which are typically described in recruitment materials), (b) participation benefits (e.g., free health care and/or monitoring during the course of the study, monetary compensation, course credit), and/or (c) interest in the topic area. (It is difficult to imagine many people volunteering to receive an intervention they considered worthless or to undergo an invasive procedure if they are not compensated sufficiently for doing so.)

The very act of volunteering may even trigger certain psychological or personal artifacts such as cognitive dissonance, which in turn could be sufficient to induce participants to convince themselves that they improved as a function of the experience (not to mention the inconvenience the participation entailed). The presence of such concomitant factors might even influence participants to be more likely to comply with the experimental protocol or change their responses on self-reported outcomes (e.g., intent to change, attitudes, health-related quality of life) than would (or will) occur when an intervention is made available in a nonexperimental setting.

Amelioration: There is very little that can be done to avoid this type of effect in a single-group pretest-posttest design other than to (a) be as inclusive as possible in recruitment efforts, (b) avoid creating expectancy effects in participants, and (c) avoid self-reported outcome variables, when possible. The direction these effects take (when they exist) can be unpredictable but probably tends toward producing false positive results (i.e., masquerade as an intervention effect).

EXPERIMENTAL ARTIFACT #7:
EXTRANEOUS EXTERNAL EVENTS (AKA HISTORY)

While not always the most plausible inferential threat to a single-group pretest-posttest design, it is always possible that some extraneous event occurred concomitantly with the intervention capable of either (a) independently affecting participant outcomes or (b) influencing participants' reaction to (or compliance with) the intervention. In Dr. Jones's experiment, examples might be (a) an influential media event dealing with acupuncture, (b) a persuasive advertisement campaign for a new analgesic that convinced some participants to try it during the experimental interval (and thus provide some benefit over and above acupuncture's placebo effect), or (c) unseasonably warm weather following the baseline assessment that might have had a salutary effect on participants' arthritic knee pain independent of the intervention.

This artifact differs from natural history in the sense that it is not a function of participants' conditions or personal characteristics but is extraneous to them. Like natural history, however, it is quite capable of producing either false positive or false negative results.

Amelioration: Generally speaking, the briefer the duration of the experiment, the less likely problematic extraneous external events are to occur. Also, since the *possibility* of this artifact's occurrence is more problematic than the *probability* of it (which cannot be determined), focused data collected from participants concerning any known occurrence of potential confounding events are always indicated. Assuming that no such occurrence was observed or reported, *some* reassurance (at least to investigators, if not to research consumers) is provided that any outcome changes that did or did not occur were not due to specific co-occurring extraneous events. (One problem with the single-group pretest-posttest design is that it permits a sort of guilt-by-suspicion mentality due to its inability to *control* for the possibility of this and other artifacts.)

EXPERIMENTAL ARTIFACT #8: DEMAND CHARACTERISTICS (OR THE "GOOD-SUBJECT" PHENOMENON)

This artifact occurs primarily for noncognitive (e.g., affective) self-reported outcome variables and is somewhat of a catchall category. It is similar to the "repeated testing artifact" with respect to the propensity to encourage socially acceptable behavior but is more general in nature.

These effects could occur in Dr. Jones's study if participants felt a need to reward the good doctor for his sincere efforts to relieve their arthritis pain or, alternately, by participants adjusting their pain ratings at the end of the experiment based on what they perceived the study staff's aspirations were for the study (perhaps even unconsciously communicated by the latter). It is not unheard of for research assistants (e.g., Dr. Jones's work study student) to feel pressure to produce salutary results and hence to provide subliminal (or less subtle) hints to participants regarding hoped-for results.

A few experiments have even been conducted that are designed to elicit such effects, the most famous of which is detailed in Rosenthal and Jacobson's (1968) book, *Pygmalion in the Classroom*. The authors describe an experiment in which teacher expectancies were manipulated by informing them of the identity of certain students in their class who were classified as "late bloomers" via the administration of an intelligence test. (The "late blooming" designation was, of course, bogus, with the targeted students being selected randomly within each classroom.) At the end of the year these students achieved significantly higher test scores than their "non-late-blooming" counterparts, leading to the conclusion that expectancy effects can influence behavior in important ways. Other studies detailed what these teacher behaviors entailed (Brophy, 1983, Rosenthal, 1994), although the jury remains out concerning the strength (and even the existence) of the Pygmalion effect itself, based on methodological concerns (Thorndike, 1969).

Amelioration: These expectancy (or self-fulfilling prophesy) effects can be avoided to a certain extent by carefully training research assistants in the data collection protocol. Also, investigators should avoid conveying any sense of urgency with respect to the desired experimental outcomes to either participants *or* research assistants. (Even if an investigator desperately hopes for positive results, he or she should adopt the persona of a dispassionate seeker of *truth*.)

Usually it is not necessary to reveal the explicit research hypothesis anyway, only the general question that the experiment is designed to answer. It is also unwise (and often not particularly meaningful) to couple extremely transparent interventions with self-reported affective outcomes.

EXPERIMENTAL ARTIFACT #9:
HAWTHORNE-LIKE EFFECTS

Most of us behave differently when we know we are being watched, and participating in an experiment involves some very intensive watching. This was aptly illustrated over two decades ago by an experiment in which participants' hand-washing behaviors were observed and recorded in public bathrooms via two different conditions: when they knew they were being observed vs. clandestine observation (Munger & Harris, 1989). The results were quite dramatic: Participants aware of being observed were almost twice as likely to wash their hands (77% vs. 39%).

An even more famous instance of this phenomenon (at least from the perspective of the history of science) occurred in a series of industrial experiments in which the very act of observing and measuring workers' productivity reputably caused them to increase their output. Dubbed the Hawthorne effect after the Western Electric Company plant (Hawthorne Works) in which the study occurred, this phenomenon soon came to represent a tendency for experimental participants to behave differently when they know they are in a trial (even though there are serious questions as to whether the effect actually occurred in the original, poorly designed Hawthorne experiments, which involved studying the effect of lighting changes on worker productivity [Franke & Kaul, 1978]).

The Hawthorne effect can be conceptualized as a special instance of the previous category (demand characteristics), since trial participants sometimes not only behave differently knowing they have an audience, but they can also have a tendency to provide investigators with the results presumed to be desired. In compliance research, for example, this tendency can involve experimental participants behaving more sensibly, such as by taking their prescribed medications more conscientiously (or at least reporting that they do).

Amelioration: It is difficult to assign a probability tvo how likely these Hawthorne and Hawthorne-like reactivity effects are to occur in any given experiment. The original Hawthorne Works experiments involved an uncontrolled single-group pretest-posttest design, so, not surprisingly, more controlled studies have failed to document their existence in other arenas (e.g., Adair, Sharpe, & Huynh, 1989). It is worth repeating, however, that appearances can be almost as harmful to scientific credibility as reality, hence the best preventive strategy is to specifically design the experimental intervention and procedures to be as unobtrusive as possible.

Since experimental scenarios (such as the hand-washing experiment just described) not requiring informed consent are extremely rare, participants will usually be aware that they are being observed or studied. Investigators should nevertheless make the participation experience as naturalistic and low key as possible and always avoid communicating their hypotheses and desired results.

Although the avoidance of exceedingly transparent (or reactive) interventions and investigator aspirations have been mentioned as ameliorating factors in several of the preceding artifacts, this advice is important enough to be elevated to the status of an experimental principle:

PRINCIPLE #11: Avoid interventions whose relationship to self-reported (or reactive observational) outcome variables are potentially obvious to participants.

As an example, conducting an experiment in which the intervention involves reading a passage extolling the virtues of ethnic diversity immediately followed by an attitudinal scale designed to measure bigotry is a bit on the reactive side and invites participants to provide politically correct results. (Alternately, so does an intervention consisting of contrasting different scenarios designed to change or predict a self-reported outcome.) Granted, this principle might significantly reduce the amount of psychological experiments currently being conducted with college students, but the meaningfulness of such research is highly questionable anyway. In other words, would society be greatly disadvantaged by the disappearance of such experiments?

Since trivia will probably be with us always, perhaps a more general, and practical, piece of advice should be added to our growing pantheon of experimental principles:

PRINCIPLE #12: To the extent permitted ethically and scientifically, communicate as little as possible to participants and research staff about the specific purpose and hypothesized results of an experiment.

At first glance, this principle might seem to be designed to undermine the informed consent process, but that is not its intent. Research participants have an ironclad right to know everything required of them as a function of volunteering for a study, what the risks and benefits of it are, what the intervention globally consists of (e.g., acupuncture, an online educational module), and a very general description of the research topic (e.g., investigating "strategies for reducing pain" or "methods for increasing learning"). Participants do not, on the other hand, need to know the investigators' aspirations for the study, their hypotheses, or even the relationships being studied.

Opinions vary on this topic, and since IRBs are composed of people with opinions, so too will institutional research policies vary to a certain extent. An ethical principle that is not a matter of opinion, however, is that scientists bear the same responsibility for protecting their clients' (i.e., participants') interests and well-being as do clinicians for their clients. And this responsibility to participants includes the following:

1. Never physically endangering them unless the direct benefits outweigh the risks, which is a judgment investigators are not qualified to make. Some degree of physical risk is inevitable in medical research, but it is not justifiable in most other disciplines.
2. Never subjecting them to any sort of emotional or psychological distress. Such research simply should not be conducted at all (e.g., the Milgram [1963] experiments).
3. Never embarrassing them in any way. If this constitutes an important area of study in a discipline, choose another discipline.
4. Always protecting their dignity and freedom of choice, including the uncontested freedom to leave an experiment at any time of their own choosing, regardless of reason, without repercussions of any sort.
5. Always ensuring confidentiality regarding any data collected or events occurring within the experimental setting (with the exception of certain legally mandated exceptions such as evidence of child abuse).
6. Always treating them as you would wish to be treated (or as you would wish your children or your aging parents to be treated).

EXPERIMENTAL ARTIFACT #10: EXPERIMENTAL ATTRITION

The final inferential artifact to be discussed in relation to the single-group pretest-posttest design is potentially the most serious. It is a rare experiment spanning any substantial amount of time that does not lose some of its participants. And when substantial attrition does occur, it constitutes a serious threat to the validity of any experiment, especially those employing single-group designs.

The reasons for attrition can be varied, but when it occurs there is always the possibility that dropouts are systematically different from those who persevere. More problematically, this difference may be related to the benefit (or lack thereof) accruing from the intervention.

Since Dr. Jones's experiment was completely hypothetical, none of his participants withdrew from the study over the 2-week interval employed. But if *any* of the participants except #3 and #6 in Table 4.1 had dropped out of the study (perhaps because they were satisfied with the relief they had received), then the overall results would not have been statistically significant. On the other hand, if *either* participant #3 or #6 dropped out because he or she did not believe the intervention was working or for any number of other reasons, the *p*-values would have been even more impressive (dropping from .049 to .004 and .028, respectively).

Unlike many of the artifacts that have been (and will be) discussed in this book, experimental attrition is an equal-opportunity offender that has the potential to invalidate *any* experimental design. Its perniciousness resides in the fact that there is no way to definitively determine how participants would have changed on the outcome variable had they remained in the experiment, hence the only truly satisfactorily method of dealing with the problem is prevention. A single-group design is especially disadvantaged when participants are not available for EOT assessment, because of the lack of a control group. (In a controlled study the attrition *rates* can at least be compared to one another.)

Of course, it is always possible to compare participants statistically who dropped out with those who did not on whatever information was available at baseline (e.g., baseline outcome values, demographics). It is even possible to statistically model what participants' outcomes would have been had they remained in the study, but few scientists take such projections seriously, at least in single-group designs. Even if no substantive differences exist on any measurable variable between those who complete the experiment and those who do not, there is no guarantee that the two groups were not systematically different on the key concern of interest: propensity to *change* on the outcome variable (or to benefit or be harmed by the intervention). And, unfortunately, we have no way to ever measure what "*might* have happened."

The good news is that if attrition is reasonably low (anything above 20% probably invalidates an experiment), then dropouts do not constitute a major validity threat if a reasonably large effect is obtained. And in the absence of attrition (such as Dr. Jones's hypothetical study), the artifact can be completely discounted.

Amelioration: Strategies for minimizing experimental attrition (which, as always, must defer to scientific issues) include the following:

1. Keeping the experimental interval as brief as scientifically appropriate.
2. Minimizing the demands placed on participants to the maximum extent possible.

3. Always specifying an a priori primary endpoint (i.e., primary outcome *and* the point in time at which it should register the largest intervention effect).

4. Obtaining multiple methods for contacting participants and keeping in touch with them throughout the trial (for those experiments that span any length of time).

5. Establishing as much rapport with participants from enrollment to the end of the trial as possible.

6. Emphasizing the importance of completing the trial to participants at enrollment and suggesting that it is more harmful to leave early than not to enroll in the first place.

7. Reimbursing participants for their time and expenses to the maximum extent permitted by the study budget and the IRB (e.g., structuring payments in an ascending manner so that participants will receive a substantive bonus for completion of the study as well as incentivizing data collection over the entire study interval).

8. Having an IRB-approved backup data collection plan in place for obtaining key assessments from dropouts.

9. When attrition does occur, ascertaining participants' reasons for dropping out (including anything that might be done to prevent its occurrence in future studies).

10. Despite their limitations, always conducting an intent-to-treat analysis that includes strategies such as persuading dropouts to engage in the final outcome assessment and/or modeling admittedly imperfect data imputation strategies. (Any discrepancies between these analyses and the results for participants who completed the trial should be mentioned in the final research report.)

And with attrition, we end the 10 inferential artifacts most problematic for the single-group pretest-posttest design. Hopefully, this discussion has illustrated the need for far more experimental control in investigating cause and effect than this intuitively appealing strategy is capable of providing. And while the single-group pretest-posttest design is superior in many ways to a case study involving a single participant (and is perhaps adequate for experiments involving outcome variables impervious to all known interventions such as the cure of a completely intractable disease), this design simply suffers from too many inferential threats to make it a viable scientific strategy.

What is obviously needed, therefore, is a more robust experimental approach. Toward this end, two extremely powerful strategies (the addition of control/comparison groups and randomization) will be introduced in Chapter Five.

SUMMARY

Ten experimental artifacts (also variously conceptualized as "experimental confounds," "confounding factors," and/or "threats to the internal validity of an experiment") were discussed from the perspective of the single-group pretest-posttest design. Natural history and the placebo effect were introduced earlier as artifacts capable of invalidating the causal inferences we all make in our everyday life. But, if anything, they are even more debilitating in poorly controlled experiments, where they possess the potential of (a) being mistaken for, (b) inflating, (c) deflating, or (d) disguising a true experimental effect. Most are extremely difficult to control in a single-group pretest-posttest design, although a number of strategies were presented that under certain circumstances can help ameliorate or prevent these artifacts' deleterious effects.

These 10 potential threats (along with the eight which follow in subsequent chapters) should either be memorized or converted to a checklist, to enable the evaluation of the quality of individual experiments and the propriety of their experimental designs. The 10 artifacts introduced to this point are as follows:

> *Experimental Artifact #1*: **Natural history or maturation**: a tendency for participants' outcome values to change over the experimental interval as a function of their physical or mental conditions, time, or development.
>
> *Experimental Artifact #2*: **The placebo effect**: a therapeutic response to an inert or irrelevant substance or procedure occurring in participants who *believe* they are receiving an effective treatment.
>
> *Experimental Artifact #3*: **Regression to the mean**: a statistical tendency for participants selected on the basis of extreme values on the outcome variable to exhibit less extreme scores when remeasured.
>
> *Experimental Artifact #4*: **Repeated testing**: a tendency for participants to exhibit higher (or more socially acceptable) scores the second time they are administered certain types of outcome measures, resulting from familiarity with the measures themselves (e.g., by correcting their initial mistakes or becoming aware of the intent of the questionnaire).
>
> *Experimental Artifact #5*: **Instrumentation changes during the course of an experiment**: changes on an outcome variable attributable to changes in the format of the measure itself (or the manner in which it is administered).
>
> *Experimental Artifact #6*: **Volunteerism**: a tendency for the participants who volunteered to take part in an experiment to possess a greater or lesser propensity to change on the outcome variable than those who declined to do so.
>
> *Experimental Artifact #7*: **Extraneous external events (aka history)**: the potential for an event external to the experimental setting to occur during the course of the experiment capable of independently influencing responses on the outcome variable.
>
> *Experimental Artifact #8*: **Demand characteristics (or the "good-subject" phenomenon)**: a tendency for participants to provide the investigator with desirable (or socially acceptable) outcomes following the intervention.
>
> *Experimental Artifact #9*: **The Hawthorne (or reactivity) effect**: a tendency for participants to behave differently as a function of being in an experiment or being observed.
>
> *Experimental Artifact #10*: **Experimental attrition**: the possibility that participants who withdraw from experiments may have changed more or less on the outcome variable (or would have so changed had they not withdrawn) than those who remain.

Based on the etiology of several of these inferential artifacts (and the need to prevent or control them), two additional experimental principles were introduced:

> *Principle #11*: Avoid interventions whose relationship to self-reported (or reactive observational) outcome variables are potentially obvious to participants.

Principle #12: To the extent permitted ethically and scientifically, communicate as little as possible to participants and research staff about the specific purpose and hypothesized results of an experiment.

REFERENCES

Adair, J.G., Sharpe, D., & Huynh, C-L. (1989). Hawthorn control procedures in educational experiments: A reconsideration of their use and effectiveness. *Review of Educational Research, 59*, 215–28.

Brophy, J.E. (1983). Research on the self-fulfilling prophecy and teacher expectations. *Journal of Educational Psychology, 75*, 631–61.

Campbell, D.T., & Stanley, J.C. (1966). *Experimental and quasi-experimental designs for research.* Chicago: Rand McNally.

ECRI. (2002). ECRI Evidence Report: Patients' reasons for participation in clinical trials and effect of trial participation on patient outcomes. Retrieved from https://www.ecri.org/Documents/Clinical_Trials_Patient_Guide_Evidence_Report.pdf

Fisher, R.A. (1935). *The design of experiments.* London: Hafner.

Franke, R.H., & Kaul, J.D. (1978). The Hawthorne experiments: First statistical interpretation. *American Sociological Review, 43*, 623–43.

Galton F. (1886). Regression toward mediocrity in hereditary stature. *Journal of the Anthropological Institute of Great Britain and Ireland, 15*, 246–63.

Lovato, L.C., Hill, K., Hertert, S., et al. (1997). Recruitment for controlled clinical trials: Literature summary and annotated bibliography. *Controlled Clinical Trials, 18*, 328–52.

Milgram, S. (1963). Behavioral study of obedience. *Journal of Abnormal and Social Psychology, 67*, 371–8.

Munger, K., & Harris, S.J. (1989). Effects of an observer on hand washing in public restroom. *Perceptual and Motor Skills, 69*, 733–5.

Price, D.D., Kirsch, I., Duff, A., et al. (1999). An analysis of factors that contribute to the magnitude of placebo analgesia in an experimental paradigm, *Pain, 83*, 147–56.

Rosenthal, R. (1994). Interpersonal expectancy effects: A 30-year perspective. *Current Directions in Psychological Science, 3*, 176–9.

Rosenthal, R., & Jacobson, L. (1968). *Pygmalion in the classroom.* New York: Holt, Rinehart & Winston.

Solomon, R.L. (1949). An extension of the control group design. *Psychological Bulletin, 46*, 137–50.

Thorndike, R.L. (1969). But you have to know how to tell time. *American Educational Research Journal, 6*, 692.

Weeks, DL. (2007). The regression effect as a neglected source of bias in non-randomized intervention trials and systematic reviews of observational studies. *Evaluation & the Health Professions, 30*, 142–60.

Wilhelmsen, L., Ljungberg, S., Wedel, H., & Werko, L. (1976). A comparison between participants and non-participants in a primary preventive trial. *Journal of Chronic Disease, 29*, 331–9.

PART II

EXPERIMENTAL DESIGNS
FOR RESEARCH
INVOLVING HUMANS

C H A P T E R 5

ENTER THE CONTROL GROUP AND
A *DEUS EX MACHINA*

H opefully, the last chapter has indicated a need for more robust designs in experimental
research than the single-group pretest-posttest (which is little more than an imposter).
Basically, the key to any experiment is a *comparison* of some sort, and the robustness of
this comparison determines the confidence to be had in the inference the experiment is
designed to permit.

Without such a comparison an experiment is not an experiment. And while the rudimentary
single-group design just discussed does permit contrasting participants' outcome values *before
and after* the introduction of an intervention, the plethora of accompanying inferential artifacts
renders the results only marginally better than useless. Fortunately, our scientific predecessors
have left us with an extremely powerful alternative: the use of separate *groups* of participants to
serve as a basis of comparison for the intervention(s) of interest. One of the first and most famous
experiments to employ this innovation occurred aboard a ship over two and a half centuries ago.

AN EARLY (AND FAMOUS) EXAMPLE OF
AN EXPERIMENT INVOLVING SEPARATE
CONTROL/COMPARISON GROUPS

The Lind Scurvy Trial (1753)

James Lind

Operating under an incorrect theory regarding the mechanism of action of a disease called scurvy, James Lind, a ship physician in the Royal Navy, designed an
experiment in 1747 involving the assignment of 12 scurvy-afflicted sailors to six
separate groups: the ingestion of (1) cider, (2) a sulfuric acid compound (Lind

believed that scurvy was caused by bodily decay and could thus be cured by acid), (3) vinegar, (4) seawater, (5) a spicy paste of some sort washed down with barley water, and (6) two oranges and a lemon (since citrus fruit had been long advocated as a cure for scurvy).

The unique aspect of this experiment involved the existence of multiple comparison groups *run under carefully controlled conditions* (i.e., all six groups were run concurrently using identical environments, diets other than the substances tested, and medical treatments). Naturally, two participants per group precluded any sort of meaningful statistical analysis of the results, which was just as well since none were as yet available.

Nevertheless, the results were sufficiently dramatic (one sailor receiving the vitamin C–rich citrus intervention was apparently cured and the other was able to return to work) to indicate to the investigator that the citric-fruit group was superior to the other substances involved (which fortuitously either contained no vitamin C or minimal amounts thereof).

Lind published his results 6 years later (Lind, 1753) and was promptly ignored. Gradually, however, his finding was adopted—facilitated by another ship-based study in which a daily dose of two-thirds of an ounce of lemon juice reportedly resulted in a complete absence of the disease for the entire crew during a 23-week naval voyage.

Interestingly, this latter experiment involved a single-group design, which can produce useful results for addressing certain types of extremely rare inferences— namely those in which the outcome never occurs in the absence of the tested intervention and/or inevitably occurs following its introduction.

THE LOGIC OF A CONTROL/COMPARISON GROUP

Today, almost all scientists agree that successful experiments (i.e., those capable of definitively documenting a complex causal relationship between the introduction of an intervention and concurrent changes in an outcome) require something possessing more epistemological rigor than is afforded by a simple "before–after" comparison involving the same participants—something more similar, in other words, to the design employed by Dr. Lind than the one employed by Dr. Jones: a separate group (or groups) of participants who receive either nothing at all or something quite different from the intervention of interest.

When this second group (for present expository purposes let's simply assume only one is used) receives nothing capable of affecting the outcome variable (except one or more of the 10 inferential artifacts introduced in the previous chapter), it is referred to as a *control* group; when it consists of a potentially active condition (such as a second intervention), we will refer to it here as a *comparison* group.

The logic of this strategy, practically unknown before James Lind's time, is simplicity itself:

1. If *everything* can be held constant (or controlled) in the two groups, *except* the fact that the participants in one group are administered the intervention and their counterparts in the control (or comparison) are not, and

2. If both groups are assessed on the same outcome variable during the same time period (recalling that the treatment of participants in both groups is identical except for access to the intervention), then

3. Any improvement observed in the intervention group over and above that observed for the control/comparison group on the outcome variable at the end of the experiment can be attributed to intervention (pending the determination of statistical significance).

While this logic would appear to be impeccable on the surface, being privy to Dr. Jones's travails suggests that there may a slip or two "twixt the cup and the lip." In Dr. Lind's study something very, very important was not held constant or controlled: There was no assurance that the individuals assigned to the six groups did not differ from one another in some crucial way that could affect the outcome. True, he apparently did an admirable job of controlling for extraneous factors by ensuring that the sailors received exactly the same treatment and diets other than the six interventions, but how do we know these individuals did not initially differ from one another in some important way, such as the severity of their illness?

Fortunately, at least with respect to the history of science, this experiment was designed to address an inference considerably less complex than Dr. Jones's acupuncture trial. Specifically, Dr. Lind did not need to contend with the majority of the eight characteristics defining complex causal inferences: his outcome (the cure of scurvy) (a) inevitably resulted from the same intervention (sufficient vitamin C from some source), (b) did *not* occur in the absence of the intervention (e.g., the natural history of scurvy consists of death in the complete absence of vitamin C), (c) could not result from other co-occurring interventions (at least none present on board an 18th-century naval ship), (d) was absolute and not measured on a gradient (the sailors were or were not cured), (e) did not possess a subjective component (the sailors weren't asked to rate how they felt), and (f) effectively occurred for everyone receiving the intervention.

However, it is probably a safe guess that no reader of this book will ever conduct an experiment possessing all six of these inferential characteristics. And if someone did, they would still be wise to take steps to avoid our 11th experimental artifact.

EXPERIMENTAL ARTIFACT #11: SELECTION

In the parlance of experimental design, *selection* is defined as the possibility that the experimental groups initially contain participants with different propensities to change on the outcome (or to be differentially responsive to the intervention[s]). It is not applicable to single-group experiments such as Dr. Jones's study, and selection is potentially more pernicious than all 10 of the experimental artifacts discussed in Chapter Four, partly because there is often no way to predict which (if any) participants have a differential potential to change over the course of an experiment. Added to this problem is our inability to predict the direction of this artifact, which means that selection can result (assuming a two-group study) in either false positive results (when participants with a greater propensity to change in the hypothesized direction on the outcome variable are assigned to the intervention group) or false negative results (when the same scenario exists for the control group).

At first glance, selection would appear easily avoidable by simply (a) locating two groups with similar outcome values who met the inclusion criteria, (b) introducing the intervention to one and not the other, and then (c) readministering the outcome variable to both. Unfortunately, while this strategy is methodologically superior to the single-group pretest-posttest design, it does not dispel the *possibility* that the experimental groups will be initially nonequivalent on one or more key factors. And like many of the 10 experimental artifacts previously discussed, it is the *potential* of occurrence (i.e., nonequivalence on the groups' propensities to change in the future or in response to external—often unknown—factors) that is so damning here.

In arenas other than science it would usually be considered unfair that critics of an experiment are not required to produce evidence for initial nonequivalence in order to dismiss its findings. In science, however, it is incumbent upon the investigator to prove his or her "innocence"—which is rather difficult, since there would appear to be no possible way to ensure that two (or more) groups are equivalent on *unknown* factors.

Fortunately, the "invention" of the control group was followed by an equally propitious advance a century and a half or so later—an innovation that turned out to be the experimental design equivalent of a *deus ex machina* whose crowning achievement turned out to be the prevention of our 11th experimental artifact. (For those unfamiliar with Greek drama, this term was used as a ruse employed by playwrights who had painted themselves into a corner with their plots and thus had to extricate themselves by lowering an actor representing a god down onto the stage to tie up the loose ends.)

RANDOMIZATION

Called *randomization* or *random assignment*, this strategy came into full scientific use only during the 20th century to solve the Catch 22–like conundrum of controlling for unknown and unknowable potential initial differences between the participants assigned to experimental groups. (A conundrum because how could anyone ever reasonably assume that the logical prerequisite for use of a control group had been met [i.e., that there were no preexisting initial between group differences on any relevant factors] when we are always ignorant of the identity of most of these factors?)

The answer turned out to be extremely simple, if counterintuitive. Why not embrace our ignorance and randomly assign participants to groups? Since by definition a random event (a) cannot be predicted, (b) has no associated cause, and (c) is correlated with *nothing*, our ignorance of which causal variables need to be controlled experimentally wouldn't matter. Said another way, if we could find a way to ensure that there was *nothing* systematic in the way participants were assigned to groups, the possibility of biased selection could be largely eliminated.

And thus was a major methodological breakthrough in science achieved, metaphorically by throwing up our hands, closing our eyes, and taking a leap of faith by trusting in random choice. Initially, this process was performed disparately and informally by flipping a coin, mixing up names of participants written on slips of paper and drawing them from a proverbial hat, or using tables of random numbers found in the appendices of statistics textbooks. As time went on, however, the process became more formalized and involved assigning identification numbers to participants and using computers to select which individuals would be assigned to which groups.

Myriad types of randomization and procedures for implementing them exist, depending on the design of the trial. Two of these procedures will be discussed later in this chapter, while others will be introduced subsequently along with their parent designs. For our purposes here, however, *random assignment* is defined as a process that ensures that each participant has an equal chance of being assigned to each experimental group as compared to all other participants.

Note that this definition does not imply that any given participant (e.g., Participant #001) has an equal chance of being assigned to the intervention as opposed to the control group. Rather, it means that Participant #001 has exactly the same chance of being assigned to the intervention group as any other participant (e.g., Participant #002). (Thus, if a study involved an unequal allocation ratio, such as 2:1, for example, this would mean that twice as many participants would be assigned to one group [usually the one easiest or cheapest to run] as to the other. Thus *both* Participant #001 and #002 would be twice as likely to be assigned to the former [66.66%] as to the latter [33.33%], but they both, along with all other participants, would still have the same probability of being assigned to any single condition.)

This, in turn, means that the only way that the experimental groups can differ initially (i.e., before anything is differentially done to them) is by chance alone. Group assignment is not under the control of any human, or other systematic factor, therefore bias (inadvertent or purposeful) does not enter the equation.

Nothing is perfect, of course, so random assignment does not *guarantee* initial equivalence between experimental groups. Since group assignment is decided randomly, there is always the possibility of *random* differences occurring. And random events are, by definition, beyond our control.

The probability of a random event biasing an experiment's randomization process is quite small, however, especially if the number of participants involved is reasonably large (say, 20 per group or more). This probability is further reduced by the fact that initial differences between intervention and comparison groups are not important unless they are related to (a) the outcome variable, (b) propensity to change thereon, or (c) differential responsiveness to the intervention. Since such factors constitute only a tiny minority of all of the possible ways in which the groups could potentially differ, the probability of a chance occurrence (which is low to begin with) involving one of these variables is small (but not impossible). The bottom line, however, is that *if* investigators (a) randomly assign participants to groups, (b) do so properly, (c) employ reasonable sample sizes, (d) describe the process, and (e) test its effectiveness on key variables, then—*by unwritten convention*—*research consumers (critics and advocates) generally assume that the selection artifact was not operative in the study in question.*

This, in turn, constitutes the justification for our 13th principle:

PRINCIPLE #13: When conducting an experiment, always use at least one control or comparison group and (for designs using different participants in the study groups) always randomly assign participants to all experimental conditions.

Randomization strategies: Part of the reason the randomization process has become increasingly formalized over time, especially in the conduct of *clinical* trials, is the necessity of limiting the omnipresent possibility of bias as the financial and career stakes for these experiments continue to grow. What follows, therefore, is a list of suggestions for complying with these conventions. At present, some disciplines will consider them unnecessary, but in reality they are not particularly labor intensive and appear to be in the process of spreading to all areas involving human experimentation.

1. Always use a computer to assign group membership. This involves first giving each individual a numerical ID number and placing the number–name link in a secure password-protected file (or in a locked cabinet, such as the one containing the original signed informed consent agreements). Most software packages have a random-assignment option and random-assignment calculators are available online (e.g., http://www.randomizer.org/form.htm). (Other informal approximations of random assignment [e.g., assigning odd numbers to one group and even numbers to another or simply flipping a coin] would probably result in initial equivalence between groups, but are also likely to result in an automatic rejection from some journals.)

2. When possible, use the same person throughout the recruitment process to perform the randomization. A biostatistician or research methodologist is a good choice if one is part of the research team. If not, someone who is likely to remain with the project should be assigned the task and properly trained.

3. Take steps to ensure the integrity of the assignment by employing sealed opaque envelopes with ID numbers on the outside and assigned group membership plus ID on the inside for experiments in which participants must be assigned as they become available. This is done to prevent tampering with or subverting the assignment process.

4. In general, adopt a "need to know" approach with the group assignment results. The fewer individuals who know the identity of participants' group memberships the better. (The individual assigned to collect data should always be blinded, when possible.)

5. Report the randomization process employed briefly in the methods section of the final article submitted for publication. This can be as brief as "participants were randomly assigned to the experimental and control group via a computer program," depending on the conventions of the targeted journal.

6. Test the effectiveness of the randomization process by computing inferential between-group statistics (e.g., chi-square for categorical variables, and t-tests and analyses of variance for continuous ones) on all key baseline and demographic variables. Report the results in the final report via a sentence or two and a table, if indicated.

Certain experimental designs require specialized allocation procedures that will be discussed when those designs are introduced. Other strategies, such as adaptive designs (e.g., Chow & Chang, 2006; Chow, Chang, & Pong, 2005), which adjust the group allocation based on accruing results (and hence require periodic statistical analysis of the results) will not be discussed here because of their rarity and limited applicability.

In general, it is desirable to assign equal numbers of participants to groups unless an a priori decision is made to do otherwise. Confusion exists in some circles regarding whether random assignment can be constrained to produce groups of exactly equal numbers. (Using an unconstrained randomization process for a total sample size of, say, 40 would be unlikely to produce two groups of *exactly* 20 participants each.)

However, there is no reason why a computer cannot be instructed to randomly assign equal numbers of participants to each group or any desired participant-to-group ratio. This will in no way violate our definition of random assignment as a process *ensuring that each participant has an equal chance of being assigned to each experimental group as compared to all other participants.* With this in mind, let's consider three types of random assignment for three separate scenarios:

1. *Scenario 1*: All participants are available at the beginning of the experiment and are run at approximately the same time. Here, all that is required is that the randomization software perform an equal allocation to the groups involved, with the constraint that equal numbers of participants are assigned to them.

2. *Scenario 2*: Participants are assigned to groups as they become available. The recommended method of randomization here involves creating small blocks of participants (the number of which is evenly divisible by the number of groups) and then assigning group membership within each block. This strategy accomplishes two objectives: (1) ensuring that the number of participants assigned to a group is effectively equal and (2) ensuring that relatively equal numbers of participants are assigned to each group over the course of the experiment, thereby controlling for temporal effects. (See Procedural Interlude: Random Assignment Using Blocks of Participants, for a description of the mechanics involved in this process.)

3. *Scenario 3*: An a priori hypothesis is made involving a variable known to be related to the dependent variable or suspected to be differentially responsive to the intervention. As an example, suppose that it was deemed important to assess whether or not an intervention was as effective for one gender as for another. The first step in the randomization process would be to determine whether or not equal numbers of males and females would be recruited for the experiment. (Equal numbers are preferable but not necessary if one group is more difficult to recruit.) The second step would then involve randomly assigning males and females separately to groups (for Scenario 1) or to groups *within blocks* (for Scenario 2). This process becomes slightly more complicated (and hence requires block-to-block adjustments) for Scenario 2 but not burdensomely so.

Procedural Interlude: Random Assignment Using Blocks of Participants

When it is not possible to run the entire sample simultaneously and it is desirable to (a) ensure equal allocation of participants to groups *and* (b) control for differential temporal effects (e.g., the intervention being administered more consistently at the end of an experiment because of a practice effect for study personnel), it is often preferable to randomly assign participants within blocks.

To further avoid the possibility of unauthorized treatment or experimental staff from determining the identity of group membership, it is also recommended that different block sizes be employed (two is sufficient).

The number of blocks used must be evenly divisible by the number of groups (e.g., blocks of 2 and 4 for two-group studies: blocks of 3 and 6 for three-group studies), and then the order in which these blocks will be employed is randomly assigned. Thus, for any experiment using blocked assignment, a two-tier randomization procedure will be used.

To illustrate, let's assume a two-group experiment with a projected sample size of 20 participants per group. Since the identity of all participants is usually not known prior to a trial, this process might occur as follows:

1. The number and size of blocks to be employed would be chosen. Assuming the use of two equal numbers of block sizes, six blocks of two participants and six blocks of four participants would be used with four left over [i.e., 40 = (6 × 4) + (6 × 2) R 4]. Since four participants are left over, either two blocks of size 2 participants or one block of size 4 should be randomly selected for the final four participants. Let's assume the former, thereby creating a total of 14 blocks, 6 of size 4 and 8 of size 2.

2. The order in which the blocks are to be employed is then randomly assigned. Thus, in our particular example, this process might result in the following assignment:

Block Order	Block Size
1	2
2	4
3	4
4	2
5	2
6	4
7	4
8	4
9	2
10	2
11	2
12	4
13	2
14	2

3. Participants are then randomly assigned within blocks (beginning with Block 1 and ending with Block 14) as they become available. This can be done before recruitment because numbers are assigned, not names, and these numbers will correspond exactly to the order in which participants become available and are run. Thus ID#s 1 and 2 would comprise Block 1; ID#s 2, 3, 4, and 5 would be assigned to Block 2; and ID#s 39 and 40 to Block 14. Then within Block 1, ID#1 might wind up being randomly assigned to the control group and, by default, ID#2 would be administered the intervention. Two participants in Block 2 (perhaps #3 and #5) might be randomly assigned to the intervention, while #4 and #6 would fall into the control group, and so forth.

4. This process is continued until participants have been randomly assigned to all 14 blocks.

Admittedly, this is a rather elaborate procedure, but it (a) is not difficult to implement, (b) ensures equal numbers of participants within the two experimental groups, and (c) makes it next to impossible for anyone to break the randomization code, short of industrial espionage. The process itself can be described in the final research report succinctly: "To facilitate masking of participant allocation, a two-stepped blocked assignment process was employed in which (a) the order of 14 block sizes of 2 and 4 were first randomly assigned and (b) participants were then randomly assigned within each block to intervention or control conditions as they became available."

A LITTLE MORE ON THE LOGIC OF CONTROL/COMPARISON GROUPS

It will be recalled that we earlier defined a control group as an experimental condition containing no substantive constituent (excluding inferential artifacts such as a placebo effect) that would be expected to causally affect the primary outcome variable. A comparison group, by contrast, was defined as possessing a potentially active component causally related to the outcome variable but which is either (a) completely independent of the intervention or (b) demonstrably different from the intervention in some definable way. Before discussing different types of control and comparison groups and the distinctions between them, however, it will be helpful to consider the basic theory governing the use of experimental control in general. This, in turn, will be done using Dr. Jones's hypothetical single-group data presented earlier.

How control/comparison groups work: To this point, prevention was given a heavy emphasis in the discussions of how to ameliorate experimental artifacts in a single-group pretest-posttest design. Unfortunately, many artifacts are extremely difficult to prevent (e.g., regression to the mean and the placebo effect), while others (e.g., extraneous external events, demand characteristics) may occur unbeknownst to investigators. And that is where control/comparison groups prove so useful and essential, by taking a completely different tack to ameliorating these artifacts' effects.

As their name suggests, control groups provide a mechanism for *controlling* spurious effects by *allowing* them to occur, capturing them via the use of a comparable group of participants who do not receive the condition of interest, and *deducting* the resulting outcome changes from the intervention effects.

In way of illustration, let's consider the single-group pretest-posttest design employed by Dr. Jones. As discussed earlier, the intervention effect was clearly represented by the difference between the posttest (end of treatment; EOT) and the pretest (baseline), or -0.73, on the 11-point visual analog scale (VAS) in Dr. Jones's experiment, which was determined to be statistically significant [$t = 2.28$ (9), $p = 0.049$]:

	Average Pain at Baseline	Average Pain at EOT	Difference
Intervention Group	5.00	4.27	−0.73

Now, let's pretend for a moment that Dr. Jones had been able to magically delete the actual effects of regression to the mean and the placebo effect from his single-group study. Let's further assume that regression to the mean turned out to constitute 15% of his original difference while the placebo effect accounted for 35% of it, for a total of 50%. (These are obviously hypothetical estimates since the overall baseline–EOT change in a single-group pretest-posttest design is often considerably greater than the 14.6% [−0.73/5.00] posited here.)

	Baseline Pain	Placebo Effect	Regression Effect	EOT Pain	Difference
Intervention Group	5.00	−0.255	−0.11	4.635	−0.365

Now, not surprisingly, the same paired sample t-test computed on these results indicates that the baseline-to-EOT difference is no longer statistically significant [$t = 1.13$ (9), $p = .284$].

However, since there is no magical incantation to delete experimental artifacts from a single-group study, Dr. Jones's only option would have been to employ a placebo control group to capture the effects of these two artifacts, which would then be "subtracting" out, by comparing the acupuncture experimental group's outcome with the placebo control group's outcome in the final statistical analysis.

Let's illustrate how this is done via the original hypothetical data (Table 4.1) coupled with an appropriate placebo control group (Table 5.1).

Table 5.1: Dr. Jones's Original Results vs. Placebo Control Group.

Intervention Group

Participant	Baseline Pain	EOT Pain	EOT–Baseline Difference
#1	3.50	2.50	−1.00
#2	3.60	1.90	−1.70
#3	3.70	5.10	+1.40
#4	3.70	2.90	−0.80
#5	4.00	3.30	−0.70
#6	4.50	5.00	+0.50
#7	6.10	5.10	−1.00
#8	6.70	4.60	−2.10
#9	7.10	6.40	−0.70
#10	7.10	5.90	−1.20
Average	**5.00**	**4.27**	**−0.73**

Control Group

Participant	Baseline Pain	EOT Δ – Placebo	EOT Δ –Regression To the Mean	EOT Pain	EOT–Baseline Difference
#11	3.50	−0.35	−0.15	3.00	−0.50
#12	3.60	−0.60	−0.26	2.75	−0.85

(Continued)

Table 5.1: (Continued)

Participant	Baseline Pain	EOT Δ – Placebo	EOT Δ –Regression To the Mean	EOT Pain	EOT–Baseline Difference
#13	3.70	0.49	0.21	4.40	+0.70
#14	3.70	−0.28	−0.12	3.30	−0.40
#15	4.00	−0.25	−0.11	3.65	−.035
#16	4.50	0.18	0.08	4.75	+0.25
#17	6.10	−0.35	−0.15	5.60	−0.50
#18	6.70	−0.74	−0.32	5.65	−1.05
#19	7.10	−0.24	−0.10	6.75	−0.35
#20	7.10	−0.42	−0.18	6.50	−0.60
Average	5.000	−.255	−.110	4.635	−0.365

Note: The intervention group contained placebo, regression to the mean, and possibly other extraneous effects; the placebo control group, being randomly assigned, also contain placebo and regression-to-the-mean effects.

In this scenario we now have two *groups* of participants: one (the intervention group) that received acupuncture (and would be subject to both a placebo and a regression-to-the-mean effect) and one (the control group) that received a *fake acupuncture* procedure (and would therefore also be subject to a placebo and a regression-to-the mean effect). As mentioned earlier, since the original pain reduction was reduced from −0.73 to −0.365, a statistical analysis performed on the new data (this time employing an independent sample's t-test comparing the two group's baseline-to-EOT changes in pain) would produce statistically nonsignificant results $[t = 0.81 \ (18), p = 0.431]$ along with the inference that acupuncture was *not* effective in reducing osteoarthritis pain. (Other analyses, perhaps preferable to this one, could have been conducted on these data, such as a repeated measures analysis of variance or an analysis of covariance, but all would have produced comparable, nearly identical, results.)

While these are completely hypothetical data, they hopefully represent what a control group is *capable* of doing: absorbing (or capturing) at least *some* of the effects of confounding variables which are then "subtracted" out of the intervention vs. control comparison. And this is the basic underlying logic of using control groups. They are by no means perfect (e.g., participants often correctly guess which group they are in, thereby resulting in a smaller placebo effect for the placebo control group than for the intervention group), but they constitute by far the best control strategy we have in our experimental arsenal. And, combined with randomization, they are especially effective in preventing *selection*.

Since experiments using control groups allow the majority of the confounding-effects to be "subtracted out" of the final intervention effect, they inevitably result in smaller intervention effects than do single-group experiments. Thus, as illustrated in Table 5.2, Dr. Jones's single-group design (and completely fabricated data) resulted in a comparison of 5.00 vs. 4.27 and thus an efficacy estimate of −0.73. The addition of a control group in effect reduced this efficacy estimate by half $[(−0.730) − (−0.365) = −0.365]$.

Table 5.2: Dr. Jones's Results with a Control Group Assuming a
Regression-to-the Mean Effect.

	Average Pain at Baseline	Average Pain at EOT	Difference
Intervention Group ($N = 10$)	5.000	4.270	−0.730
Control Group ($N = 10$)	5.000	4.635	−0.365

EXPLAINABLE VS. UNEXPLAINABLE VARIATIONS IN OUTCOME VALUES IN A TWO-GROUP EXPERIMENT

A reasonable question regarding the hypothetical data accruing from Dr. Jones's hypothetical experiment might be as follows:

> Why can't we assume that the −0.365 figure (remaining for the intervention group's results after the control group's results are subtracted out) actually represents the effects of acupuncture and thus make *p*-values and statistical significance irrelevant?

The easy answer is that we *could*, if (and only if) we could assume the experiment was properly designed and conducted. But since there is no such thing as a perfectly controlled experiment, it is important to put this assumption in perspective.

First, a villain lurks within every experiment, called *measurement error*. So far we've discussed this culprit in terms of regression to the mean, but nothing is measured without error, and the measurement of humans is especially error laden because of their large individual differences with one another. That and the fact that most of their attributes are easily affected by temporal, day-to-day (and in some cases minute-to-minute) fluctuations.

Then, for every experiment in which participants are randomly assigned to groups, another culprit lurks, called *sampling error*, which is due to the absolute impossibility of constructing two or more groups of humans with exactly the same propensity to change on any given outcome over time or to react exactly the same to the same experimental conditions. For as miraculous as it is, randomization can only be assumed to ensure that experimental groups *usually* do not differ *substantively* on any key variables before the experiment commences—not that the experimental groups will be composed of *identical* participants. For even if the groups possess exactly the same baseline measurements on the outcome variable as occurred for our simulated data (which is vanishingly improbable), they would not necessarily possess exactly the same outcome *values* because humans differ so dramatically from one another, both in response to being measured and in unpredictable fluctuations in the construct being measured.

Fortunately, both measurement and sampling error can be assumed to be random in nature, and randomness is easier to deal with in experiments because, being nondirectional, it can be neutralized in the statistical analysis process by increasing the number of observations. Unfortunately, there is an even more significant genre of error that simply represents human variations (genetic, behavioral, and experiential) that we cannot explain and which may be nonrandom (i.e., directional). It is therefore more useful to categorize individual differences that occur in outcome changes over the course of an experiment that are *explainable* based on the experimental design vs. those that are *unexplainable* (since we truly don't know what component of an outcome change is due to random chance and what is actually caused by a factor of which we are simply unaware).

To visualize the difference between these two types of individual differences, Table 5.3 reframes our two-group results solely in terms of absolute changes between their self-reported baseline and EOT pain.

Table 5.3: The Two-Group, Hypothetical Experiment Reframed with Baseline–EOT Differences.

Intervention Participants	Baseline–EOT Δ's	Control Participants	Baseline–EOT Δ's
#1	−1.00	#11	−0.50
#2	−1.70	#12	−0.85
#3	+1.40	#13	+0.70
#4	−0.80	#14	−0.40
#5	−0.70	#15	−.035
#6	+0.50	#16	+0.25
#7	−1.00	#17	−0.50
#8	−2.10	#18	−1.05
#9	−0.70	#19	−0.35
#10	−1.20	#20	−0.60
Means	−0.73		−0.365

Given that error or unknown influences are present in every measurement we take, we have to assume that all 20 of the difference scores recorded in Table 5.3 (as well as the two means based on them) have some unexplainable components associated with them. Some may be random, some systematic, but we can't separate the non-error component from the error component of each of these scores unless we are privy to additional relevant information on each participant. What we can do, however, is separate what is explainable in terms of the experimental design employed and what is unexplainable *if (and only if) we can assume the experiment was properly designed and conducted.* (A key purpose of some of the more sophisticated designs presented later in the book is to apportion as much of the unexplained category into the explained component as possible.)

In our present two-group design, however, let's look at what we *can* explain. We can explain why the intervention group's mean of −0.73 is different from the control group's mean of −0.365. How? We did something different to all 10 of the intervention participants than we did to the 10 control participants. So, on average, we can explain why the intervention participants reported a greater reduction in pain than did their control participants. If the acupuncturist inadvertently "tipped off" the control participants to the fact that they were receiving a fake treatment instead of the real thing, our explanation might be incorrect regarding what we could explain here, but let's assume that we knew the experiment was correctly performed.

Next, let's look at what we can't explain about the numbers in Table 5.3. Why, for example, is there such a discrepancy between the baseline and EOT pain reports of Participant #3 and Participant #4? They both reported identical baseline pain intensity (3.7 on a 10-point VAS), they both received the same amount of acupuncture, and they both suffered from osteoarthritis of the knee. Participant #3's pain actually increased over time, however, while #4 reported a sizeable reduction in it. We could, of course, always speculate regarding the reason(s) for this discrepancy (e.g., #3 might have had a more advanced case of arthritis but was at a different point in her or his pain cycle at baseline than #4, participant #3 might have twisted a knee the day before the EOT assessment, and so forth), but given the information available to us, we simply do not know why #4 and #3 differ so dramatically.

Outcome variations among participants *within* each of the experimental groups are therefore designated as *unexplainable* variation, while outcome differences *between* the groups are considered *explainable* variation. Or, from a statistical perspective, within-group variation is also designated as *error*, while between-group variation is designated as *systematic*. Also, from a statistical analytic perspective, the independent sample's *t*-test performed on these data reported earlier actually contrasted the size of the explainable with its unexplainable counterpart (taking the sample size into consideration) and thereby derived the *p*-value of 0.431, which by Sir Ronald Fisher's convention indicates that the systematic variation attributable to acupuncture in this particular experiment was due to chance (i.e., was due to error or unexplainable sources). Or, visualized from another perspective, the systematic variation (what we can explain) was greater than the nonsystematic variation (that we can't explain).

One of the many beauties of some of the more sophisticated experimental designs presented in the next few chapters involves their ability to partition outcome scores into ever more explainable categories, resulting in smaller proportions of unexplainable components. (However, the logic of these designs, as well as the more complex statistical procedures required for the analysis of their data, remains identical to that of the hypothetical example just discussed.) Following the presentation of these designs, Chapter Nine will describe how increasing the number of experimental participants (among other strategies) can also serve to increase the ratio of what we can explain about the results of an experiment and what we cannot.

The role of control/comparison groups in explaining outcome variations: Obviously, the presence of randomly assigned control/comparison groups is integral to maximizing explainable (and minimizing unexplainable) variations in outcomes. When we think of or read about experiments, however, we tend to think solely in terms of the randomized interventions employed and minimize the importance of their control/comparison groups.

From a methodological and interpretive perspective, however, the type of control/comparison group employed is absolutely crucial. But equally crucial is the manner in which the control group/comparison group is procedurally constructed, because selection of the proper genre thereof is only the first step in the process. For just as the intervention must be thoughtfully and explicitly operationalized, so too must its control group.

True, a randomized control group in which participants receive no treatment at all is capable of controlling the majority of the artifacts listed to this point (the placebo effect being an exception). Randomization to any sort of control/comparison group is capable of vitiating *selection*, the only experimental artifact (and an extremely pernicious one) discussed to this point which is applicable *only* to designs using two or more groups. Unfortunately, there are a few more.

Thus, before enumerating the general types and functions of control/comparison groups, we will need to consider another, equally potentially pernicious, experimental artifact applicable only to multiple-group studies. Unfortunately, this one is immune to the effects of randomization, but (fortunately) not to the manner in which the control group is constructed.

EXPERIMENTAL ARTIFACT #12: DIFFERENTIAL ATTRITION

Differential attrition occurs when different proportions of participants withdraw from experimental groups, which is a largely preventable occurrence that potentially results in either false positive or false negative results.

Nondifferential attrition (Experimental Artifact #10) itself is less problematic in multigroup experiments than in single-group designs *if* all intervention and comparison groups witness approximately equal proportions of withdrawals. However, high attrition (e.g., >20%) is quite capable of invalidating any experiment, single- or multigroup. And participants dropping out of a study because of displeasure with their group assignment constitute a potentially disastrous internal validity threat. And since the potential that something occurred for a given reason is almost impossible to assess after that "something" has occurred, prevention is by far the best remedy. (Differential attrition therefore becomes an artifact like selection that bestows guilt by suspicion even if exactly the same number of participants drop out of each group.) Of course, if attrition itself does not occur, then obviously differential attrition doesn't either.

To illustrate how participants' reasons for attrition might differ between groups, among other possibilities individuals in the intervention group could drop out because they

1. Realized the intervention was not "helping" them,
2. Felt they had received all of the intervention benefits and therefore saw no reason to continue,
3. Experienced noxious side effects, or
4. Considered the intervention a waste of time.

Participants could drop out of the control group, on the other hand, because they

1. Realized (and resented the fact) that they were receiving nothing of benefit,
2. Decided to seek an alternative treatment for their worsening symptoms, and/or
3. Gleaned the purpose of the experiment and decided to seek the intervention from other sources.

Amelioration: Everything listed in the previous chapter dealing with minimizing experimental attrition applies here as well. Again, if no one withdraws prematurely from the study, obviously there is no *differential* attrition. These strategies are important enough to repeat here, however, along with a few others that will be discussed in more detail shortly:

1. Keeping the experimental interval as brief as scientifically appropriate.
2. Minimizing the demands placed on participants to the maximum extent possible.
3. Obtaining multiple methods for contacting participants.
4. Establishing as much rapport with participants from enrollment to the end of the trial as possible.

5. Emphasizing the importance of completing the trial to participants at enrollment and suggesting that it is more harmful to leave early than not to enroll in the first place.
6. If attrition does occur, having an IRB-approved backup data collection plan in place for obtaining key assessments from dropouts.
7. Reimbursing participants for their time and expenses to the maximum extent permitted by the study budget and the IRB. (Structuring payments in an ascending manner in such a way as to incentivize data being collected over the entire study interval is helpful.)
8. Making the control/comparison groups as attractive as possible.
9. Promising to make the intervention available to control/comparison participants at the end of the experiment.
10. When attrition does occur, conducting an intent-to-treat analysis and/or employing data imputation strategies.

Differential attrition *rates* are, of course, simple to detect. Ascertaining if these differential rates are caused by participants dropping out of the experimental conditions because of some unique characteristic of (or reaction to) one of the conditions is more problematic, but potentially identifiable via an exit interview, as advocated by the following experimental principle:

PRINCIPLE #14: Whenever possible, conduct a post-experimental "exit" interview to ascertain information on undetected protocol violations, guesses regarding group assignment (when applicable), reactions to experimental procedures (e.g., noncompliance with them), and reasons for withdrawal.

This information can be collected via a brief questionnaire or telephone interview administered to both participants completing the study and those dropping out of it. It should be kept as brief as possible with an eye toward (a) suggesting procedural improvements for the next experiment, (b) discovering untoward procedural and external events that may have been unknown to the investigator, and (c) providing hints for alternative explanations for experimental results not controlled by the design employed.

In addition to simply asking participants why they withdrew from an experiment, good research practice requires an empirical examination of the correlates of attrition—both for the trial as a whole and for the experimental conditions individually. While sample sizes usually preclude the obtainment of statistical significance in these analyses, participants who drop out of the study should be contrasted to those who do not with respect to baseline outcome scores and other relevant variables such as covariates and clinical information. In addition, an intent-to-treat analysis and data imputation procedures should be modeled because once participants are randomized they are officially "in" the experiment and any data collected from them should be analyzed as such. Hence, if at all possible, participants should not be randomized prior to providing baseline data on the outcome variable. Also, if outcome data are available they should be included in the final analysis as well—even for participants who did not complete the protocol, comply with it, or actually receive the intervention. To facilitate this process, as part of the informed consent procedure, participants should be asked to supply outcome data at the proper point in time, even though they have already withdrawn from the experiment (although they are obviously under no obligation to do so), giving rise to our 15th principle:

PRINCIPLE #15: In the presence of any significant degree of experimental attrition (differential or otherwise), conduct post hoc intent-to-treat and data imputation analyses in order to ascertain the degree to which attrition (and/or noncompliance with the protocol) potentially affected the final study results.

While disciplines differ with respect to the acceptability of both data imputation and post hoc comparisons of dropouts vs. non-dropouts, investigators (or their statisticians) should conduct such analyses whether they are reported or not. If the investigators themselves have questions concerning the validity of their results they should either (a) not publish those results or (b) communicate their doubts clearly in their final reports. At the very least, any discrepancies between results obtained with and without data imputation should always be reported.

Methodological Note: Last Score Carried Forward (LSCF) and Other Data Imputation Strategies

With the increased use (and acceptance) of mixed linear models analyses, the imputation of missing data has lost some of its impetus, since list-wise deletion of missing cases (i.e., deleting all of a participant's data if one assessment is missing) is no longer necessary—especially for experiments employing two or more assessments following baseline. However, modeling missing EOT and follow-up outcome values is not widely acceptable. This is especially true of the LSCF procedure, which in a pretest-posttest design would entail substituting participants' baseline scores for their missing EOT scores.

Originally proposed as a conservative strategy to prevent attrition from producing false positive results, LSCF can have the opposite effect, as it completely ignores the possibility that such participants may have dropped out because their outcomes were deteriorating. LSCF is also not defensible from a technical perspective, since the presence of identical baseline and EOT scores artificially inflates the correlation coefficient, thereby potentially invalidating the final results. For this and other reasons, LSCF and outcome imputations should be employed and interpreted with extreme caution. (It should be mentioned, however, that this is a subjective opinion on the part of the present author and practices differ from discipline to discipline.)

TYPES OF CONTROL AND COMPARISON GROUPS

For our purposes three types of control groups and two types of comparison groups commonly used in experimental research involving human participants will be discussed:

1. No-treatment control groups
2. Placebo controls
3. Attention (placebo) controls

4.   Treatment-as-usual (aka standard-care) comparison groups
5.   Alternative-treatment comparison groups

Each will be discussed in turn and compared with respect to 10 of the 12 experimental artifacts introduced so far. (Instrumental changes and volunteerism have been deleted for this exercise because the former can only be prevented by procedural means, in which case it can be avoided in all types of designs, while volunteerism is unavoidable in all types of designs except the rather esoteric patient preference strategy, discussed in Chapter Six.)

The evaluative metric employed for this purpose will be:

√ [Effective]
≈ [Somewhat Effective]
× [Ineffective]

No-treatment control groups: This is the classic, "pure" control group in which "nothing" is done to participants except measure them on the outcome variable concurrently with those receiving the intervention. The quotation marks are necessary here because something is always "done" to control participants. They sign an informed consent agreement, know they are part of a scientific experiment, and are typically aware they have been selected not to receive the intervention in a study (at least when a no-treatment control group is employed). They also are either altruistic enough to volunteer their time for the betterment of science, do so because they need the money (if remuneration is offered), or have fewer outside commitments such as jobs or families. And sometimes they must undergo invasive or time-consuming testing, all of which suggests that they can hardly be considered representative of the population from which they are drawn (whether college students, healthy adults, or individuals diagnosed with a specific disease).

While a no-treatment control is often suitable for nonclinical experiments (a) of relatively brief durations conducted in laboratory (or laboratory-like) settings or (b) that employ unique interventions or outcome variables, it is not well suited for experiments using the following:

1.   Participants with serious medical diagnoses that require treatment of some sort. (Locating such individuals is becoming increasing difficult and often requires withdrawing them from treatment prior to baseline in order to employ a no-treatment control—which of course is sometimes impossible for ethical reasons.)
2.   Outcome variables susceptible to placebo effects (e.g., pain or depressive symptoms).
3.   Interventions already known to produce effects on a specific outcome. (An educational researcher, for example, would not use this type of control group to evaluate the effects of a new instructional intervention on learning, since any accruing results would be tautological.)
4.   Any health condition for which an effective alternative treatment exists.

A final consideration in the decision of whether or not to use a no-treatment control involves its potential effect on the participants assigned to receive it. In experiments involving interventions perceived to produce potential benefits, participants are typically disappointed when they are told they will not receive said intervention. As will be discussed in Chapter Six, this potentially results in either depressed or artificially inflated results when self-reported or observational outcomes are employed. (It can also result in differential attrition occurring in the control group for experiments spanning any significant length of time.)

All in all, however, no-treatment controls are quite successful in controlling for several of our inferential artifacts, as depicted in the chart below. Regression to the mean, for example, is perfectly controlled, because both the intervention and control group will exhibit equivalent amounts of the artifact if participants with extreme outcome scores are randomly assigned to it. Placebo effects, demand characteristics (e.g., the good-subject phenomenon), and reactivity effects (Hawthorne-like effects) are uncontrolled by the design itself, but are not necessarily problematic for certain types of experiments, outcome variables, and/or interventions. The strategy is awarded an "X" designation for attrition because the addition of a second randomized no-treatment group does nothing to reduce attrition in the intervention group. It also has the potential of introducing differential treatment under certain circumstances.

	No-Treatment Control
Selection	√
Natural History	√
Placebo Effect	X
Regression	√
Repeated Testing	√
Extraneous External Events	√
Demand Characteristics	X
Reactivity Effects	X
Attrition	X
Differential Attrition	X

A Few Disclaimers Regarding Design Ratings

Note that these comparisons are not absolute and all could be contested via the introduction of special circumstances. Placebo controls, for example, are given the only unqualified "√" for controlling the placebo effect, but that generalization is based on the assumption that the placebo procedure is properly constructed—which often isn't the case, even in drug trials. All randomized control groups are likewise given a "√" with respect to the control of extraneous external events, but unusual, unanticipated circumstances could arise for an individual experiment in which such an event occurred in one group and not another. Many of these possible exceptions can be anticipated or detected by carefully monitoring the conduct of a trial, but that is the subject matter of Chapter Ten.

Finally, and probably most irritating, some of the control/comparison group labels employed here are not mutually exclusive and are subject to subjective interpretations. Specifically, the same comparison group might be labeled as an attention control, alternative-treatment, or a standard-care group by different investigators or research consumers depending on their orientation, thus the ratings that follow must be interpreted cautiously. In fact, ultimately every experiment must be rated on its own merit in relation to how well it controls or avoids experimental artifacts and alternative explanations for its results. Thus disconnected from a specific experiment these ratings are of heuristic value only, but the charts that contain them are presented to encourage you, the reader, to "think" in terms of evaluating design decisions (yours and those of others) in terms of these inferential artifacts.

Placebo controls: True placebo controls are possible (and necessary) only for certain types of research. The rationale for their use is to prevent experimental participants (and preferably everyone else with whom they come in contact) from knowing whether they are receiving the actual intervention or a placebo (i.e., an inactive intervention theoretically indistinguishable from the "real" one). Placebos are most commonly used in drug research, where great care is often exerted in the manufacture of inactive pills to make them look and taste as similarly to their active counterparts as possible. Similar precautions are then taken to ensure that neither treatment nor study personnel are able to uncover the identity of participants' group (placebo or intervention) assignments (hence some of the more elaborate randomization strategies suggested earlier).

Placebo controls have been developed for a wide range of procedural interventions, such as surgery (Moseley, O'Malley, Petersen, et al., 2002) and acupuncture (Bausell, Lao, Bergman, et al., 2005), that partially hide group membership from participants but not from the treatment staff with whom they come in contact. Thus, like most strategies in both science and life, theory is more impressive than reality. Even in drug trials, where despite the necessity for placebo pills to look and taste as much like their active counterparts as possible, evidence exists that a high proportion of trials fail to take adequate steps to ensure blinding (Hill, Nunn, & Fox, 1976) or do not report doing so (Fergusson, Glass, Waring, & Shapiro, 2004). (A now rather famous experiment designed to assess the effectiveness of vitamin C [whose investigators claimed they did not have adequate time prior to the trial to secure a perfectly matched placebo] and conducted using medical-oriented participants found, via a questionnaire administered at the end of the trial, that a significant number of participants had broken the blind by tasting their medication [Karlowski, Chalmers, Frenkel, et al., 1975]. Vitamin C typically has a distinctive acidic taste.)

Definitional Interlude: Experimental Blinding

Blinding: This term is used in research to refer to the practice of designing a study in such a way that certain key actors are kept ignorant of participants' group membership. Trials in which only the participants do not know to which group they have been assigned are often described as *single-blind* trials. Those experiments in which group membership is also unknown to the staff interacting with participants (especially those who administer the experimental conditions and collect outcome data) are referred to as *double-blinded*. (Some methodologists even advocate blinding the statistician, but this suggestion has not received widespread implementation, since anyone with access to a data set can usually ascertain group membership with relative ease.)

Blinding of participants is always preferable when feasible, although it can be challenging outside of pharmaceutical trials. The primary purpose of blinding participants is to attempt to equalize the occurrence of a placebo effect among all experimental conditions (although it has a salutary effect on a number of other potential artifacts, such as demand characteristics and differential attrition). The primary purpose of blinding research and clinical staff is also to prevent (a) their elicitation of a placebo effect via purposeful or subliminal communication of expectations to participants (which has been empirically documented [Gracely, Dubner, Deeter, & Wolskee, 1985]) and (b) the administration of compensatory treatment based on group membership (e.g., empathetically administering the intervention to favored or especially needful participants).

Since placebo controls are seldom 100% effective, it is a good practice to evaluate them after implementation. When queried at the end of an experiment, for example, participants can often correctly guess their group assignment at a significantly greater rate than chance expectancies (e.g., Boasoglu, Marks, Livanou, et al., 1997; Fisher & Greenberg, 1993; Morin, Colecchi, Brink, et al., 1995). The etiology of this phenomenon undoubtedly varies from study to study and from discipline to discipline, but most likely includes the following:

1. Communication (subliminal or elicit) from therapists or research staff (for single-blind trials).
2. Comparing notes with other participants.
3. Side effects from certain interventions (e.g., potent drugs, effective or not, are often accompanied by potent side effects). Placebos themselves are capable of producing negative placebo effects that masquerade as side effects (Oddmund, Brox, & Flaten, 2003). Called "nocebos," these symptoms are rarer and less severe than those emanating from active treatments.
4. Inadequacies of the placebo employed.

Increasingly, investigators of placebo-controlled trials are querying their participants after the trial's completion about whether or not they had guessed their group assignment. (Present-day IRBs usually require participants to be told they will be assigned to receive either a specified intervention or a placebo group as part of the informed consent process, although some permit investigators to sugarcoat the latter by calling it something to the effect of "a treatment we believe will help you in this or that way.")

Often, post-experimental perceptions of group membership are stated quite simply, such as: Which treatment do you believe you received?

☐ Active Treatment (usually the actual drug or treatment is named)
☐ Placebo
☐ Not Sure

Alternately, sometimes multiple questions (occasionally administered at multiple times during the trial) are used regarding the self-reported degree of participant confidence in their guess (e.g., on a scale from 1 [Not at all Sure] to 10 [Absolutely Sure]).

While it has been known for some time that participants can correctly guess their group membership significantly above chance levels, the effects of this guessing have not been extensively investigated. The following single-blinded acupuncture trial provides a tantalizing hint in this regard, however.

EXAMPLE OF USE OF PLACEBO CONTROLS AND THE IMPORTANCE OF PARTICIPANT PERCEPTIONS IN RESEARCH

Is Acupuncture Analgesia an Expectancy Effect? Preliminary Evidence Based on Participants' Perceived Assignments in Two Placebo-Controlled Trials (2005)

R. Barker Bausell, Lixing Lao, Stewart Bergman, Wen-Lin Lee, and Brian Berman

This experiment contrasted traditional Chinese acupuncture with three types of placebo control groups in two separate trials using pain following dental surgery as the outcome variable. (*All* participants were initially provided the standard local anesthetic, with provisions for rescue medication if warranted, since it would have unethical not to have done so.)

The placebo procedures, which had been developed through preliminary work designed to ascertain if they could be differentiated from real acupuncture, involved combinations of (a) needle insertions at irrelevant points (as defined by traditional Chinese medical theory), (b) mock insertions at traditional points (involving an elaborate strategy using guide tubes for the needles following initially scratching the skin before being taped to it), and (c) shallow insertions at irrelevant points. (A screen was used for both the intervention and placebo control to prohibit participants' from seeing the actual procedures employed.)

Following the trial, participants were asked (using a single item such as the one just presented) if they knew to which group they had been assigned. Overall, they were slightly (but statistically significantly) more likely to correctly guess their group membership than would be expected by random guessing. (This wasn't surprising since the practitioners could not be blinded, which in turn meant that they could have inadvertently passed this knowledge on to the patients.)

What was most interesting from a design perspective, however, was that participant *beliefs* regarding which treatment they had received were significantly related to the pain they experienced, while their actual group membership had no effect at all. In other words, those individuals who *believed* they were receiving acupuncture experienced significantly less pain than those who *believed* they were receiving a placebo, while participants who actually received acupuncture did not experience significantly less pain than those who received a placebo (see Figure 5.1).

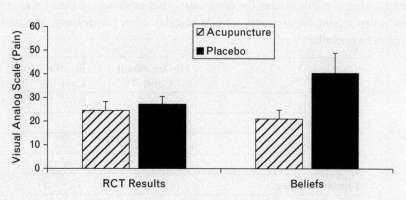

FIGURE 5.1: Differences Between Beliefs and Reality: Acupuncture vs. Placebo Effects on Pain.

At least two alternative explanations exist for these results. First, beliefs regarding group membership may have *caused* the differences in pain relief. While this is quite plausible, unfortunately, the experiments in question were designed to test cause and effect only for acupuncture effects, not beliefs. (To ascertain causation, it would be necessary to experimentally manipulate beliefs, as was done quite successfully in the Price et al. [1999] experiment described in Chapter One.)

Second, the differences in pain might have caused (or influenced) the differences in patients' guesses regarding which treatment they were receiving. In other words, patients who experienced the most pain may have simply guessed that they were not receiving a "real" treatment. From a design perspective, however, the true explanation for these results isn't particularly important because we know that the participants most likely did not make their guesses based on the effects of *acupuncture*, since there weren't any analgesic effects attributable to the actual acupuncture procedure (i.e., there were no statistically significant differences between the acupuncture and placebo conditions). Thus, one way or another the participants probably made their guesses on the basis of their personal beliefs and expectations, that very likely would have masqueraded as an intervention effect if a (a) no-treatment or (b) treatment-as-usual control had been employed instead of a placebo control group.

At the risk of overinterpretation, studies such as this illustrate another fact of experimental life. Regardless of the type of control employed (or the hypothesis being tested), participants who enroll in clinical experiments do so for multiple reasons, one of which is that they either *believe* or *hope* that the intervention described to them during the recruitment process will affect them in some particular manner. At the very least it is important for investigators to realize that their participants' agendas are different from their own and are capable of influencing the results of experiments that have not been properly designed to mitigate as many of these agendas and expectations as possible—both known and unknown. And one method of moving them from the unknown to the known side of the ledger is to routinely conduct a post-experimental interview with participants, as suggested in Principle #14.

The following chart illustrates the advantages that randomized placebo controls possess over their no-treatment counterparts when a placebo effect (or demand/reactivity effects) is considered to be operative:

	No-Treatment Control	Placebo Control
Selection	√	√
Natural History	√	√
Placebo Effect	X	√
Regression	√	√
Repeated Testing	√	√
Extraneous External Events	√	√
Demand Characteristics	X	√
Reactivity Effects	X	√
Attrition	X	X
Differential Attrition	X	√

Attention (placebo) controls: True placebo controls are difficult to implement properly and are not possible for many types of interventions. As discussed earlier, however, when the hypothesis calls for testing the efficacy of one of these interventions against no treatment at all, a worrisome experimental confound exists: One half of the experimental participants know they are receiving a potentially useful treatment (which also customarily involves social and professional contact with study personnel), while the other half are often painfully aware that they are receiving none of these benefits.

This realization may result in some "resentful demoralization" on the part of the controls, which in turn could be manifested by creating differential attrition if the experiment takes place over any length of time. (It also potentially affects recruitment if it is clear to potential participants that they have a 50% chance of receiving no treatment at all.) Of equal concern, intervention participants may consequently (a) behave differently (and respond differently to any self-reported outcomes), based on their appreciation and beliefs regarding the purposes of the experiment, as well as (b) be less likely to withdraw from the study.

Historically, behavioral investigators have attempted to address these potential artifacts by concocting placebo-like control groups to which something *known* not to strongly affect the outcome variable can be sold to participants as potentially useful. (While such controls are designed to mimic placebos, they usually do not result in actually blinding participants or staff, hence are not placebos in the true sense of the word.) The primary purpose of such a control group is to (a) prevent feelings of resentment among those receiving *nothing* in the form of a beneficial (or interesting) treatment for volunteering their time to participate in an experiment and (b) eliminate the potential confound of participants of only one experimental condition interacting with study or clinical personnel.

In nonpharmaceutical psychological and psychiatric therapeutic research, attention controls (sometimes called *active controls* when a minor effect is expected) may involve a relaxation-type condition or group education sessions designed to require approximately the same amount of time and contact with experimental personnel as the actual treatment. (Educational interventions of this sort have been repeatedly demonstrated to be ineffectual for a wide range of outcome variables—e.g. behavioral change, weight loss, compliance with medical regimens, pain relief.) Attention controls also provide a parallel control group that can be assessed on the outcome variable in the same manner and at the same time intervals as the intervention group—thereby controlling for such potential artifacts as repeated testing, regression to the mean, maturation, and natural history.

On the negative side of the ledger, however, while it may be possible to convince some individuals that they are receiving something of value, others often realize that they are not receiving the treatment of choice and therefore may be more likely to drop out of the study. Delivering an attention control can also be problematic if the individuals charged with administering the condition develop rapport with participants and are tempted to engage in "compensatory equalization of treatments" (which will be discussed in the next chapter) as the occasion arises. Whether it is better to have the same individual deliver both the intervention and the attention placebo when feasible is not known and is probably specific to the individual involved. In either case, the attention control condition should be monitored to ensure that it does not mutate into a potentially active intervention (or degenerate into an obviously bogus exercise).

Perfectly acceptable attention controls are possible, however, at least in some disciplines and under certain circumstances. In an educational experiment involving, say, the degree to which instruction in one topic *transfers* to (or is a prerequisite for) learning a related topic, it could be quite reasonable to use a control group receiving instruction in a completely different topic for the same amount of time required to teach the experimental unit. In general, the construction of attention controls requires a certain amount of creativity to ensure their (a) credibility and (b) theoretical unlikelihood of affecting the outcome variable.

To a certain extent, the success of this design resides in how well it is "sold" to participants; that is why placebo, demand characteristics, reactivity effects, and differential attrition are given an equivocal rating ("≈") rather than a "√".

	Attention Controls
Selection	√
Natural History	√
Placebo Effect	≈/X
Regression	√
Repeated Testing	√
Extraneous External Events	√
Demand Characteristics	≈
Reactivity Effects	≈
Attrition	X
Differential Attrition	√/≈

EXAMPLE OF AN EXEMPLARY ATTENTION CONTROL (OR ACTIVE CONTROL OR ALTERNATIVE INTERVENTION) GROUP

A Randomized Controlled Clinical Trial of Psychoanalytic Psychotherapy for Panic Disorder (2007)

Barbara Milrod, Andrew Leon, Fredric Busch, et al.

This trial illustrates the blurred and/or arbitrary distinction between alternative treatment and attention placebo control groups. The study itself was described by the investigators as the "first time a psychodynamic treatment has undergone formal efficacy testing for any *DSM-IV* anxiety disorder, despite common clinical use." Participants were randomly assigned to two conditions, described by the investigators as "panic-focused psychodynamic psychotherapy and applied relaxation training for subjects with primary *DSM-IV* panic disorder with and without agoraphobia." The latter group involved muscle relaxation and information about panic disorder and, according to the authors, had been used in five controlled trials involving cognitive-behavior therapy and demonstrated efficacy for panic disorder in one of them. The primary outcome was measured via the clinician-administered Panic Disorder Severity Scale, with a 40% reduction from baseline constituting the criterion for "response."

Thus, how relaxation therapy should be classified here is somewhat subjective, and perhaps the term *active control* might be a better descriptor. (The authors safely described it as the "comparator.") In any event, the psychodynamic intervention proved superior (as hypothesized) to the relaxation alternative intervention, active control, or however one prefers to categorize it. And the investigators accordingly concluded that the trial had "demonstrated preliminary efficacy of panic-focused psychodynamic psychotherapy." The present author might have added "in comparison to relaxation therapy," but he is somewhat of a stickler in these matters.

Treatment-as-usual (standard-care) comparison groups: There are occasions in which none of the three control group options just discussed is viable. In medicine, for example, if an effective treatment exists for a particular condition, which is the case for chronic conditions such as diabetes or acute conditions such as infections, then a pure control group is neither ethical nor scientifically meaningful. Similarly, in a discipline such as education, children are mandated to receive a certain number of hours of instruction, which even accompanied by poor instruction normally begets at least some learning (thus no-treatment controls are similarly neither possible nor of any scientific interest).

In situations such as these, a separate randomized group of participants is still needed for comparative purposes, the most common options being either a standard-treatment condition or the introduction of an alternative intervention. Naturally, the formulation of standard-care comparison groups are discipline, disease, and/or situation specific, but the precise and detailed specification of what standard care (or treatment as usual) entails should always be (a) operationally defined, (b) carefully monitored, (c) evidence or consensus based, and (d) formally documented.

When standard care is under the control of or implemented by the investigators, it should be designed to be as effective as possible while reflecting usual clinical practice in the relevant discipline—whether medical, psychological, or educational. Finally, as with no-treatment controls, investigators should recognize that participants may be unhappy with their group assignment and therefore more likely to drop out of the experiment or augment their treatment in some manner. Demand characteristics are probably adequately controlled via this type of control under optimal conditions, but reactivity effects are always possible (although perhaps not particularly likely). The placebo effect (when operative) is not well controlled, although standard care would be expected to elicit a small effect, just not as much as a promising intervention.

	Standard-Care Control
Selection	√
Natural History	√
Placebo Effect	X/≈
Regression	√
Repeated Testing	√
Extraneous External Events	√
Demand Characteristics	√/≈
Reactivity Effects	≈
Attrition	X
Differential Attrition	√/≈

Active treatment comparison: There are occasions in which an effective intervention exists and investigators wish to demonstrate that their intervention of choice is either superior or equivalent to it. (Examples might be two teaching methods or a head-to-head comparison of two behavioral therapies.) A number of complexities accompany experiments designed to demonstrate equivalence (or non-inferiority) and these will be discussed in Chapter Nine. For present purposes let's consider the case in which an intervention is contrasted with a specific active treatment (as opposed to the often more diffusely defined "standard-care" comparison group) solely to demonstrate the superiority of the former over the latter.

Suppose, for example, that a new intervention (I_{NEW}) is contrasted with a well-established alternative intervention (I_{ALT}) that has previously been shown to be more effective than, say, a no-treatment control group. If the results accrue as planned ($I_{NEW} > I_{ALT}$), then all is well as long as there is some assurance that I_{ALT} was properly formulated and the experiment was properly conducted. Irritating advocates of I_{ALT} may not be above arguing that their cherished treatment was somehow shortchanged in the experiment and would have been more effective if administered differently or by more competent hands, but generally speaking, investigators of such a study would be quite pleased with this particular outcome.

However, what if no difference is found between I_{NEW} and I_{ALT} (i.e., $I_{NEW} = I_{ALT}$)? On one level the results would be interpreted the same as if a no-treatment control group had been employed (i.e., there was simply no difference between the two groups). End of story.

Most investigators, however, while disappointed with the results overall, would probably prefer to interpret them in terms of their new and better alternative treatment being as effective as the established treatment. Unless I_{ALT} was *extremely* well established and its dosage easily standardized, however, a critic might claim that an alternative interpretation of the results was perhaps neither I_{NEW} nor I_{ALT} was efficacious (or that a sufficiently large sample size had not been employed). The same type of argument could also be leveled at a two-group study involving an intervention vs. a standard-treatment comparison group ($I_{NEW} = C_{STANDAD\ CARE}$). To prevent (or definitively counter) such arguments, a third experimental group is normally required, as discussed in the next section.

The methodological effectiveness of an active treatment comparison group is very difficult to compare to the other control/comparison groups just discussed because so much depends on the acceptability and attractiveness of the alternative intervention. If it is equal to the "new" intervention in these regards, it can be as effective as a placebo control in neutralizing the experimental artifacts introduced to this point. More realistically, however, it is probably more likely to reside somewhere between a true placebo and an attention control. The "$\sqrt{}/\approx$" ratings in the following chart reflect the difficulty (but certainly not impossibility) of making the alternative intervention as desirable as the new intervention.

Survey pilot work can be helpful in ascertaining any obvious equivalent vs. differential attractiveness. (The way in which the two conditions are initially described in the informed consent process to potential participants can also impact this factor.)

	Alternative-Intervention Comparison Group
Selection	$\sqrt{}$
Natural History	$\sqrt{}$
Placebo Effect	$\sqrt{}/\approx$
Regression	$\sqrt{}$
Repeated Testing	$\sqrt{}$
Extraneous External Events	$\sqrt{}$
Demand Characteristics	$\sqrt{}/\approx$
Reactivity Effects	$\sqrt{}$
Attrition	X
Differential Attrition	$\sqrt{}/\approx$

Combinations of control and comparison groups: It will be suggested later that occasions exist (e.g., when the sample size is limited) that it is preferable to employ only two experimental groups. As with all design decisions, however, scientific concerns take precedence (which is why so much of the advice offered in this book is accompanied by irritating disclaimers such as "whenever possible" or "when scientific considerations permit").

There are occasions, therefore, when investigators' aspirations for an experiment or scientific considerations require additional control or comparisons groups. As mentioned earlier, these studies frequently involve (but are not limited to) the possibility of no-difference findings emanating from two active treatments ($I_{NEW} = I_{ALT}$) or an active treatment vs. a treatment-as-usual comparison group ($I_{NEW} = C_{STANDAD CARE}$).

Whether a no-treatment, placebo, or attention placebo would be selected as the third condition for such trials would depend largely on the outcome variable's vulnerability to placebo effects and the clinical situation in general (e.g., when a no-treatment control is ethically or politically contraindicated). For the I_{NEW} vs. I_{ALT} scenario, let's assume that a no-treatment control (C) was so selected, in which case the "desired" (hence hypothesized) outcome would most likely involve both interventions being superior to the control, with the new intervention also proving superior to the alternative ($I_{NEW} > I_{ALT} > C$). For the I_{NEW} vs. $C_{STANDAD CARE}$ study, on the other hand, a placebo control might be in order, yielding the following hypothesis: $I_{NEW} > (C_{STANDAD CARE} = C_{PLACEBO})$.

Earlier it was suggested that all of the possible outcomes for an experiment be delineated at the design level with a probability of occurrence attached to each (Principle #7). This can become complicated in a three-group study. Thus, for the head-to-head comparison between two interventions (I_{NEW} vs. I_{ALT}) and a no-treatment control (C), in addition to the hypothesized outcome just delineated ($I_{NEW} > I_{ALT} > C$), there are myriad other possibilities (most of which would be highly improbable for any given experiment) including:

$$I_{NEW} = I_{ALT} = C$$
$$I_{NEW} < I_{ALT} < C$$
$$I_{NEW} < C < I_{ALT}$$
$$I_{NEW} > (I_{ALT} = C)$$
$$I_{NEW} < (I_{ALT} = C)$$
$$I_{ALT} > I_{NEW} > C$$
$$I_{ALT} < I_{NEW} < C$$
$$I_{ALT} < C < I_{NEW}$$
$$I_{ALT} > (I_{NEW} = C)$$
$$I_{ALT} < (I_{NEW} = C)$$
$$C > (I_{NEW} = I_{ALT})$$
$$C < (I_{NEW} = I_{ALT})$$

The a priori consideration of all of the possible outcomes for an experiment should facilitate both (a) an a priori evaluation of its meaningfulness and (b) an interpretation of the results that eventually accrue. (Many investigators appear to experience considerable difficulty in both regards, but unlike meaningfulness, interpretation of multigroup experimental results is not subjective.) Whether the failure to properly interpret such results is due to ignorance, bias, or paradigmatic induced blindness is unknown and ultimately irrelevant, since the outcome (an erroneous inference) remains as a blot on an investigator's experimental record, as illustrated by the next example.

EXAMPLE OF DUAL CONTROL/COMPARISON EXPERIMENT AND HOW NOT TO INTERPRET A $(I_{NEW} = C_{PLACEBO}) > C_{STANDARD\ CARE}$ RESULT

German Acupuncture Trials (GERAC) for Chronic Low Back Pain: Randomized, Multicenter, Blinded, Parallel Group Trial with 3 Groups (2007)

Michael Haake, Hans-Hedge Müller, Carmen Schade-Brittinger, et al.

Continuing with acupuncture experiments, one very large German trial (Haake et al., 2007) compared acupuncture (I_{NEW}) to a (a) placebo acupuncture group $(C_{PLACEBO})$ involving irrelevant placements of acupuncture needles and (b) a standard-care comparison group $C_{STANDARD\ CARE}$. This apparently well-designed and well-conducted trial provided a typical alternative medical finding: (a) no difference between the intervention and placebo control groups with (b) both being superior to treatment as usual $[(I_{NEW} = C_{PLACEBO}) > C_{STANDARD\ CARE}]$. When confronted with their results, however, the authors' conclusions completely ignored the logic of their design. In their published article they began referring to the placebo control as an acupuncture treatment in its own right. They also introduced a new artifact into the annals of experimental design: the "superplacebo effect." To quote:

> The superiority of both forms of acupuncture suggests a common underlying mechanism that may act on pain generation, transmission of pain signals, or processing of pain signals by the central nervous system and that is stronger than the action mechanism of conventional therapy. The underlying mechanism may be a kind of superplacebo effect produced by placebo and all nonspecific factors working together. (p. 1897)

As one published, rather boorish commentary on this article, entitled "Acupuncture Research: Placebos by Many Other Names" (Bausell & O'Connell, 2009), explained,

> the epistemological reason for using a placebo control in a clinical trial is to test the hypothesis that (1) any therapeutic benefit exhibited by the intervention (be it an alternative therapy or a drug) is due to some specific effect of that intervention rather than the nonspecific effects associated with placebos or (2) according to a recently proposed definition of a placebo agent, the observed effect is not due to the "simulation of a therapeutic intervention." Thus, if no difference is obtained between a "true" acupuncture group (or an experimental drug for that matter) vs. its placebo control, then the scientifically correct conclusion is that acupuncture (or the drug) is no more effective than the placebo. In the acupuncture trials in question, the hypothesis tested by the inclusion of a "usual care" control is primarily useful only in ascertaining whether the placebo effectively produced a placebo effect. (p. 1813)

It is worth noting, however, that the most direct method of illustrating the existence of a placebo effect is to compare a placebo to a no-treatment control. To make things a bit more complicated, Kaptchuk, Stason, and Davis (2006) (and Kaptchuk, Goldman, Stonea, & Stason, 2000) have noted that all placebos are not created equally, with procedural placebos (e.g., sham surgery or acupuncture) probably producing larger effects than pills and capsules. There is even some evidence that different-colored placebo capsules (blue is better than red), being prescribed a larger dose of placebo pills, or being more compliant with taking placebos produces differential placebo effects (Kienle & Kiene, 1997).

Internalizing the logic underling the use of control/comparison groups: There is no question that the use of control/comparison groups (especially when accompanied by their handmaiden, randomization) represents one of the most innovative developments in the history of science. Being able to select the proper category of this innovation is not sufficient, however. An *understanding* of exactly how a control/comparison group does what it does so miraculously must be acquired so that it and its components can be matched with both the intervention and its accompanying hypothesis.

The example just presented illustrates a properly selected (and apparently properly constructed) placebo control group accompanied by a standard-care comparison group—only to be confounded by an illogical interpretation. Let's next look at an example of an experiment involving the selection of an inappropriate control group accompanied by an inappropriate interpretation of the findings it produced. For ultimately, the selection, construction, and implementation of *both* the intervention and the control group determine an experiment's operational hypothesis tested (irrespective of the one the investigator composes) and the results produced.

ANOTHER EXAMPLE OF FAILURE TO RECOGNIZE IMPLICATIONS OF CHOICE OF A CONTROL GROUP

Pre-School Teachers Can Use a Media-Rich Curriculum to Prepare Low-Income Children for School Success: Results of a Randomized Controlled Trial (2009)

William Penuel, Helley Pasnik, Lauren Bates, et al.

This experiment involved 398 low-income children from 80 preschool classrooms. Their "teachers were randomly assigned to implement either a 10-week technology-supported literacy curriculum or a 10-week technology-supported science curriculum." Students were administered both a baseline and an EOT learning test specifically keyed to the literacy concepts taught in the intervention group. (Thus so far we have the makings of what seems to be an excellent educational experiment employing randomization to an instructional intervention vs. an attention control group, the latter being comprised of the same amount of instruction and monitoring as the former, but the instruction used was completely irrelevant to the outcome measure.)

No hypothesis or research question was presented per se, although the following sentence came closest to such a specification: "Described here is a study on the efficacy of a media-rich curriculum—based on the idea that children can learn best from *media synergy,* that is, when children have opportunities to learn a focused set of skills by engaging in repeated practice with them in many different formats and media." Ignoring the phrase "learn best" (which no experiment can demonstrate because this would entail comparing the intervention to all possible alternatives), the authors at least clearly identified their study as an "efficacy" trial designed to test the effects of a media-rich curriculum taught by providing practice using different types of media.

Relevant to the present topic is the reason why the investigators chose to employ an attention control group—especially since by doing so they had purposely designed a very obvious experimental confound into their expensive and otherwise elaborately planned study—namely the mismatch between the control group, the intervention, and the outcome variable.

The outcome variable (administered at baseline and EOT) consisted of items specifically keyed to the experimental curriculum (e.g., naming letters, knowing letter sounds, knowledge of story and print concepts). This outcome was entirely appropriate for the intervention group because it matched what was taught and was more sensitive to that than a commercial, standardized test (most items contained in such a test would assess content other than what could be taught in a 10-week instructional unit). Unfortunately for the authors' stated purpose, the outcome variable was completely irrelevant for the control group because its participants were not taught what was tested.

The data were apparently analyzed properly via a hierarchical linear model (since classrooms rather than individual students were randomly assigned) and the results came out as expected. The students taught the literacy curriculum registered significantly greater gains on the literacy test than the students who were taught the science curriculum. Of course, one would expect that if the science curriculum had been tested instead of the literacy curriculum the attention control would have then registered significantly greater gains than the literacy group.

So how were the results interpreted? Without any consideration at all regarding what was in effect a reasonable attention control group:

> These results show that a media-rich curriculum with integrated professional development for teachers can prepare low-income children for school success. The results also provide evidence of the success for the Corporation for Public Broadcasting in its *Ready to Learn Initiative*, which promotes literacy using multiple forms of media to deliver educational programming in a variety of settings, including preschools. (p. ii)

As was the case for the German acupuncture trial, a disconnection exists between the design employed and the investigators' conclusions (which appear to be influenced by their motives or aspirations for conducting the trials in the first place). Certainly both trials reflect a failure on the part of their investigators to understand (or acknowledge) both (a) the logic behind the use of a control group and

(b) the effect the choice thereof has on the permissible interpretation emanating from an experiment's final results.

It is worth repeating that the choice and construction of a control/comparison group is as crucial to an experiment as the intervention. The authors of the present study would appear to have understood the importance of *employing* an attention control group, since they carefully constructed one with the same amount of "attention," instruction, and instructional time as was present for the intervention. Given the fact that control students were not beneficiaries of the curriculum tested, however, what their study truly showed was that

> *If preschool children are taught literacy concepts appropriately for a sufficient period of time they will learn a statistically significant amount of what was taught.*

Or more generically:

> *If children are taught something, they generally learn something of what is taught.*

A conclusion which has no scientific significance whatsoever, since humans have known this since at least the dawn of civilization.

From a design perspective this trial illustrates (in addition to the importance of avoiding experimental confounds) the importance of choosing an appropriate control (which in this case did not match the investigators objectives: to "provide evidence of the success for the Corporation for Public Broadcasting in its *Ready to Learn Initiative*, which promotes literacy using multiple forms of media to deliver educational programming in a variety of settings, including preschools").

As mentioned earlier, while a statement of the study hypothesis was listed as the first of 10 steps in the design of an experiment, the design process is iterative. Thus the manner in which the intervention and control groups are defined in relation to one another ultimately defines the actual hypothesis being tested, the implications derivable from the study results (irrespective of whatever an investigator's motivations were for conducting the trial), and ultimately the meaningfulness of the experiment itself.

In the present case, the experiment was unfortunately not designed to "provide evidence of the success for the Corporation for Public Broadcasting in its *Ready to Learn Initiative*." This might have been the investigators' (or their clients') aspiration for the experiment, but the actual research hypothesis is dictated by what the experiment is *capable* of testing. And in this case that hypothesis is more accurately stated as follows:

> *Low-income preschool children whose classrooms have been randomly assigned to be taught a 10-week media-enriched literacy curriculum by teachers receiving specialist support will learn more literacy concepts than children whose classrooms are taught a science curriculum by teachers under otherwise similar conditions.*

Or, in other words:

Children taught a topic will learn more than children not taught the topic.

Or, to be fair, and ever so slightly alter their title:

"to demonstrate that pre-school teachers can use a media-rich curriculum to" teach literacy content when supplied with instructional support.

Of course the authors, and certainly their sponsor, would argue that few individuals would bother to read a research report whose design ensured positive results. But that is part of the point here, as well as the primary purpose of this book: to facilitate its readers' ultimate conduct of *meaningful* experiments (and to prevent them from conducting tautological experiments).

But perhaps these investigators deemed this effect worth demonstrating; in that case we'll settle for encapsulating this chapter's two unfortunate examples into yet another experimental principle.

PRINCIPLE #16: Choose the experiment's control or comparison group with exceeding care in order to match what the study actually assesses with its scientific objective or hypothesis.

On one level, this principle may appear painfully obvious. Putting it in the context of our earlier discussions involving *meaningfulness* and the importance of explicitly recognizing one's motivations for conducting an experiment, however, makes it one of the book's most important experimental principles, because it underlines the present author's belief that an explicitly stated hypothesis serves two crucial scientific functions that the substitution of research aims, purposes, or objectives fails to do.

First, regardless of the investigator's aspirations, an experiment always results in one or more explicit comparisons between groups of participants on one or more explicit outcomes. A clearly stated hypothesis that articulates what those groups are as well as the identity of the outcome variable(s) helps to explicate those comparisons. This in turn will hopefully prevent investigators from being disappointed if none of the possible outcomes from these comparisons match their aspirations for conducting the experiment (as was undoubtedly the case in the preschool education experiment just discussed). And perhaps, if the investigators and their sponsors had circulated a properly stated a priori hypothesis among themselves prior to the experiment, they would have designed their study differently. (Or, if the experiment was secondary to the development, implementation, and evaluation of the curriculum, perhaps their interpretation of the results would have been moderated accordingly.)

Second, while no amount of experimental principles can prevent anyone from purposeful biasing or spinning their experimental results, a formally stated hypothesis based on the comparison permitted by the proposed intervention and control group(s) could prevent anyone from doing so unconsciously. Thus, in the German acupuncture experiment described earlier, perhaps the very existence of a formal, a priori hypothesis might have resulted in a completely different, non-disingenuous conclusion to their published journal article (especially if it had appeared in the IRB application as well as the funding proposal), had it been signed off on by all the investigators, and had it been required by the journal editors who published the study results. Especially if that hypothesis had originally been as follows:

> *Participants with chronic low back pain randomly assigned to receive traditional Chinese acupuncture over a 5-week period will report less pain at 6 months than participants who receive either (a) multimodal medical treatment according to German standards or (b) shallow inserted needles administered at irrelevant nontraditional points.*

Now that we've discussed the role, logic, and types of control groups employed in research involving human participants, it is time to configure them with their intervention counterparts in actual experimental designs capable of (a) addressing more complex hypotheses and (b) controlling different combinations of experimental artifacts. That task begins with Chapter Six, in which eight different multigroup designs along with, alas, four additional experimental artifacts are introduced.

SUMMARY

Two of the most important innovations in human experimentation were discussed: the use of control/comparison groups and the randomization of participants to all experimental conditions. Random assignment was defined in terms of ensuring that each participant possesses an equal chance of being assigned to each experimental group compared to all other participants, to prevent our 11th experimental artifact:

> *Experimental Artifact #11*: **Selection**, or the possibility that the experimental groups initially contain participants with different propensities to change on the outcome (or to be differentially responsive to the intervention[s]).

The primary purpose of a control or comparison group was described in terms of preventing (or subtracting out) the effects of 9 of the 11 experimental artifacts presented to this point. (Instrumentation changes must be prevented procedurally and volunteerism is not completely preventable in prospective research, although it can be reduced via a seldom-used design introduced in the next chapter).

Five types of control/comparison groups were discussed: (1) no treatment, (2) placebo, (3) attention, (4) treatment as usual/standard care, and (5) alternative treatments. The importance of selecting and formulating an appropriate control/comparison group was stressed in terms of ensuring (a) its fit with a study hypothesis, (b) the ultimate meaningfulness of an experiment, and (c) the avoidance of our 12th experimental artifact:

> *Experimental Artifact #12:* **Differential attrition**, defined as occurring either when different proportions of participants withdraw from the study groups or when withdrawal potentially results in false positive or false negative results.

A judicious use of an appropriate, randomly assigned control was recommended for avoiding differential attrition, as indicated in the chart below. The use of five genres of randomly assigned control groups are compared to the single-group pretest-posttest design with respect to the control or prevention of 10 of the 12 experimental artifacts discussed to this point.

Artifact	(a) No-Treatment Control	(b) Placebo Control	(c) Attention Control	(d) Standard Care	(e) Alternative Treatment
Selection	√	√	√	√	√
Natural History	√	√	√	√	√
Placebo Effect	X	√	≈/X	X/≈	√/≈
Regression to the Mean	√	√	√	√	√
Repeated Testing	√	√	√	√	√
Extraneous Events	√	√	√	√	√
Demand Characteristics	X	√	≈	√/≈	√/≈
Reactivity Effects	X	√	≈	≈	√
Attrition	X	X	X	X	X
Differential Attrition	X	√	√/≈	√/≈	√/≈

Note that all five of the control/comparison groups are effective in preventing the occurrence of selection and controlling for regression to the mean, repeated testing, and extraneous concurrent events. Note further, however, that the latter—if sufficiently disruptive—is still capable of producing either a false positive or negative result.

Four additional experimental principles were presented relevant to the control of experimental artifacts and the importance of choosing the appropriate genre of control/comparison group:

Principle #13: When conducting an experiment, always use at least one control or comparison group and (for designs using different participants in the study groups) always randomly assign participants to all experimental conditions.

Principle #14: Whenever possible, conduct a post-experimental "exit" interview to ascertain information on undetected protocol violations, guesses regarding group assignment (when applicable), reactions to experimental procedures (e.g., noncompliance with them), and reasons for withdrawal.

Principle #15: In the presence of any significant degree of experimental attrition (differential or otherwise), conduct post hoc intent-to-treat and data imputation analyses in order to ascertain the degree to which attrition (and/or noncompliance with the protocol) potentially affected the final study results.

Principle #16: Choose the experiment's control or comparison group with exceeding care in order to match what the study actually assesses with its scientific objective or hypothesis.

Two seemingly well-conducted trials that violated Principle #16 were presented to underline the importance of understanding the logic underlying the use of the different genres of control/comparison groups available to investigators.

REFERENCES

Bausell, R.B,. Lao, L., Bergman, S., et al. (2005). Is acupuncture analgesia an expectancy effect? Preliminary evidence based on participants' perceived assignments in two placebo-controlled trials. *Evaluation & the Health Professions, 28,* 9–26.

Bausell, R.B., & O'Connell, N.E. (2009) Acupuncture research: Placebos by many other names. *Archives of Internal Medicine, 169,* 1812–3.

Boasoglu, M., Marks, I. Livanou, M., et al. (1997). Double-blindness procedures, rater blindness, and ratings of outcomes: Observations from a controlled trial. *Archives of General Psychiatry, 54,* 744–8.

Chow, S.C., & Chang M. (2006). *Adaptive design methods in clinical trials.* New York: Chapman and Hall/CRC Press, Taylor and Francis.

Chow, S.C., Chang, M., & Pong, A. (2005). Statistical consideration of adaptive methods in clinical development. *Journal of Biopharmaceutical Statistics, 15,* 575–91.

Fergusson, D., Glass, K.C., Waring, D., & Shapiro, S. (2004). Turning a blind eye: The success of blinding reported in a random sample of randomised, placebo controlled trials. *British Medical Journal, 328,* 432.

Fisher, S., & Greenberg, R.P. (1993) How sound is the double-blind design for evaluating psychotropic drugs? *Journal of Nervous and Mental Disease, 181,* 345–50.

Gracely, R.H., Dubner, R., Deeter, W.R., & Wolskee, P.J. (1985). Clinicians' expectations influence placebo analgesia. *Lancet 1*(8419), 43.

Haake, M., Müller, H.H., Schade-Brittinger, C., et al. (2007). German Acupuncture Trials (GERAC) for chronic low back pain: Randomized, multicenter, blinded, parallel group trail with 3 groups. *Archives of Internal Medicine, 167,* 1892–8.

Hill, L.E., Nunn, A.J., & Fox, W. (1976). Matching quality of agents employed in "double-blinded" controlled clinical trials. *Lancet, i,* 352–6.

Kaptchuk, T.J., Goldman, P., Stonea, D.A., & Stason, D.B. (2000). Do medical devices have enhanced placebo effects?' *Journal of Clinical Epidemiology, 53,* 1786–92.

Kaptchuk, T.J., Stason, W.B., & Davis, R.B. (2006). Sham device vs. inert pill: Randomized controlled trial of two placebo treatments. *British Medical Journal, 332,* 391–7.

Karlowski, T.R., Chalmers, T.C., Frenkel, L.D., et al. (1975). Ascorbic acid for the common cold. A prophylactic and therapeutic trial. *Journal of the American Medical Association, 231,* 1038–42.

Kienle, G.S., & Kiene, H. (1997). The powerful placebo effect: Fact or fiction?' *Journal of Clinical Epidemiology, 50,* 1311–8.

Lind, J. (1753). *A treatise of the scurvy. In three parts. Containing an inquiry into the nature, causes and cure, of that disease. Together with a critical and chronological view of what has been published on the subject.* Edinburgh: Printed by Sands, Murray, and Cochran for A. Kincaid and A. Donaldson. Retrieved from https://archive.org/details/treatiseonscurvy00lind

Milrod, M., Leon, A., Busch, F., et al. (2007). A randomized controlled clinical trial of psychoanalytic psychotherapy for panic disorder. *American Journal of Psychiatry, 164*(2), 265–72.

Morin, C.M., Colecchi, C., Brink, D., et al. (1995). How "blind" are double-blind placebo-controlled trials of benzodiazepine hypnotics? *Sleep, 18,* 240–5.

Moseley, J.B., O'Malley, K., Petersen, N.J., et al. (2002). A controlled trial of arthroscopic surgery for osteoarthritis of the knee. *New England Journal of Medicine, 347,* 82–9.

Oddmund, J., Brox, J., & Flaten, M.A. (2003). Placebo and nocebo responses, cortisol, and circulating beta-endorphin. *Psychosomatic Medicine, 65,* 786–90.

Penuel, W.R., Pasnik, S., Bates, L., et al. (2009). Pre-school teachers can use a media-rich curriculum to prepare low-income children for school success: Results of a randomized controlled trial. New York and Menlo Park, CA: Education Development Center, Inc., and SRI International.

Price, D.D., Kirsch, I., Duff, A., et al. (1999). An analysis of factors that contribute to the magnitude of placebo analgesia in an experimental paradigm, *Pain*, *83*, 147–56.

THE DESIGN OF SINGLE-FACTOR, BETWEEN-SUBJECTS EXPERIMENTS

Designs involving intervention and comparison groups to which different participants have been assigned constitute the backbone of experimental research. In research parlance they are considered *single*-factor designs if the groups are conceptually independent of one another (i.e., are arranged in such a way that they can share no additive, synergistic, or interactional effects). They are called "between-subjects designs" if different, unrelated subjects (i.e., participants) are assigned to groups.

Single-factor experiments are not limited to a single intervention and a single control/comparison group. They can involve multiple interventions and/or multiple control groups such as were used in the Lind scurvy or the Haake et al. (2007) acupuncture examples. For our purposes here, we will define a single-factor, between-subjects design as one in which unrelated individuals are assigned to experimental conditions that do not have the capacity to interact with one another. To avoid confusion, experiments in which two or more groups of participants are measured at multiple time points to assess the efficacy of an intervention (such as baseline and end of treatment [EOT]) will still be considered between-subjects designs as long as the same or matched participants were not assigned to the different experimental *groups*.

The key advantages of using more than one group of participants in an experiment (as compared to a single-group pretest-posttest design) were discussed previously. The primary advantage to contrasting multiple interventions (either to one another or to a comparison group) and/or multiple comparison groups in the same experiment involves (a) the additional information potentially generated and (b) the ability to test more than one hypothesis.

Unfortunately, as illustrated in Chapter Five via the introduction of selection and differential attrition, an additional genre of experimental artifacts has the potential to raise their ugly heads when two or more groups are contrasted. This chapter will introduce four additional such artifacts, two that require procedural control and avoidance and two that are rather specialized, less virulent, and less commonly occurring. The bulk of this chapter, however, is given over to an in-depth discussion of six different randomized designs and three nonrandomized (two quasi-experimental and one hybrid) compromises.

Definitional Interlude: Single- vs. Multiple-Factor Experiments

Although the distinction between single-factor and multiple-factor (factorial) designs will be discussed in detail in Chapter Eight, Dr. Lind's scurvy trial will be used here to illustrate the primary difference between the two approaches.

Lind used six different groups (some of which were presumably conceptualized as potential interventions, some as control groups) in his ground-breaking study designed to find a cure for scurvy. His design, therefore, is conceptualized as consisting of a single factor, because none of the experimental conditions (i.e., intervention or control groups) were "crossed" with one another (i.e., the six interventions did not have the capacity to interact, interfere, or moderate the effects of one another). Said another way, the investigator was not interested in ascertaining (a) if some *combinations* of interventions were superior to one or more of the other interventions or (b) if certain interventions were more effective for certain types of patients than others. Diagrammatically, the scurvy trial can be depicted one-dimensionally, as in Figure 6.1.

FIGURE 6.1: The Lind Scurvy Trial.

Cider	Sulfuric Acid Compound	Vinegar	Seawater	Barley Paste	Citric Fruit

And the same logic would have held had he included a no-treatment control group (i.e., the experiment would remain a single factor study) (see Figure 6.2).

FIGURE 6.2: The Lind Scurvy Trial with a Control Group.

Cider	Sulfuric Acid Compound	Vinegar	Seawater	Barley Paste	Citric Fruit	No Treatment

However, let's now pretend that our good doctor hypothesized that one or more of his six interventions might be effective only for relatively mild cases (i.e., early onset) of scurvy. To test this additional hypothesis he would have needed to recruit two types of patients (those with mild cases and those with advanced cases) and to have administered each experimental condition to each type of patient, producing the two-dimensional design presented in Figure 6.3

FIGURE 6.3: The Lind Scurvy Trial Redesigned as a Factorial Study.

Interventions	Disease Severity	
	Mild Scurvy B_1	Advanced Scurvy B_2
Cider A_1	A_1B_1	A_1B_2
Sulfuric Compound A_2	A_2B_1	A_2B_2
Vinegar A_3	A_3B_1	A_3B_2
Seawater A_4	A_4B_1	A_4B_2
Barley Paste A_5	A_5B_1	A_5B_2
Citric Fruit A_6	A_6B_1	A_6B_2

Now, the trial is comprised of two factors: the six experimental conditions (i.e., things he was able to manipulate) and the two levels of disease severity (which were preexisting conditions that could not be manipulated and in other disciplines are sometimes called attribute variables). Each level of one factor is said to be *crossed* with each level of the other, because individuals with each degree of disease severity receives each experimental condition and each experimental condition is administered to each level of severity. Thus Cell A_4B_2, for example, consists of patients with advanced cases of scurvy who were given seawater, while Cell A_4B_1 consists of patients with mild cases of scurvy who were given seawater. (More detail will be provided on factorial designs in later chapters, so for the time being it is enough to recognize the difference between [a] a multigroup study that is crossed and [b] one in which the experimental conditions and/or attributes are not.)

THE RANDOMIZED VS. NONRANDOMIZED PRETEST-POSTTEST CONTROL GROUP DESIGNS

In the previous chapter randomization was assumed in the discussions involving the logic of control/comparison groups, and the advantages of multigroup over single-group experiments were discussed. There are occasions, however, when a control/comparison group is used in the absence of randomization.

Let's begin, therefore, with a comparison between the (a) randomized pretest-posttest control group design and its (b) nonrandomized counterpart. For expository purposes two groups (one of which is a control) will be assumed, although the principles presented extend to multiple interventions and multiple comparison groups.

As depicted in Figures 6.4 and 6.5, the two designs are architecturally identical, with the exception of how participants are assigned to groups. Participants are administered the baseline assessment, assigned to groups (either randomly or purposefully according to some other criteria), administered the experimental conditions, and assessed at the end of treatment (EOT). (Both designs can use any of the five types of control/comparison groups discussed in Chapter Five.)

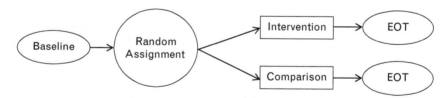

FIGURE 6.4: Randomized Pretest-Posttest Control Group Design.

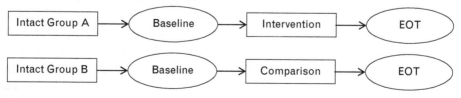

FIGURE 6.5: Nonrandomized Pretest-Posttest Control Group Design.

The randomized pretest-posttest control group design: Recall that the primary advantage of a control group is to (a) capture as many inferential artifact effects as possible, (b) quantify their cumulative effect, and (c) allow their statistical subtraction from the intervention effect (via the final intervention vs. control comparison). The accuracy of this function is made possible by the primary advantage of randomization, which is to help guard against initial nonequivalence between experimental groups prior to the intervention (i.e., our 11th experimental artifact—selection).

Selection was defined as *the possibility that two or more experimental groups initially contained participants with different propensities to change on the outcome variable (or to be differentially responsive to the intervention)*. This artifact (or experimental confound) is potentially more problematic than any other experimental inferential impediment because of its prevalence, size, and reputation. And because of its *potential* to completely invalidate an otherwise perfectly conceived experiment, its "guilt by suspicion" extends to all nonrandomized studies.

While this may not be "fair," it is understandable because of the potential harm this artifact is capable of inflicting. It is also important to note that randomizing participants to groups does not absolutely *guarantee* initial equivalence of groups—although its use greatly increases the probability thereof. Randomization also shifts the burden of proof from investigators to critics *if* the investigator (a) presents a between-group comparison on key pre-experimental variables (assuming that equivalence was demonstrated), (b) employs an appropriate randomization procedure, and (c) describes that procedure in the final research report.

While perhaps not necessary in laboratory research involving a homogeneous participant pool, such as undergraduate psychology majors, a test of the randomization process is otherwise mandated. Thus, while not deserving of the status of an experimental principle, the following procedure still constitutes good experimental practice:

> In between-subjects experimental designs, always test the pre-intervention equivalence of the different experimental groups with respect to potentially important participant characteristics (including pretest outcome values if collected) and describe how participants were randomized.

The description of the randomization process can involve only a phrase for the simplest procedures (e.g., "participants were randomized to experimental and control groups by the statistician using a computer program") or several sentences for some of the more complex procedures described. An example of an analysis designed to test the success of the randomization process can be presented quite simply in the final research report, as depicted in Table 6.1.

A reasonable question (seldom considered until the "unthinkable" occurs) is what happens when randomization "fails" as defined by a statistically significant result in an analysis such as that represented in Table 6.1? The answer may seem counterintuitive. However, just as the presentation of seemingly equivalent results represented in Table 6.1 does not guarantee initial equivalence on important unmeasured or unknown variables, neither would a statistically significant finding on a preexisting variable automatically invalidate the final experimental results.

As an example, if a statistically significant between-group gender distribution had occurred in Table 6.1, this finding would not necessarily invalidate a statistically significant EOT superiority for the intervention group over its control. Investigators finding themselves in this situation should conduct a post hoc subgroup analysis to ascertain if, for the specific outcome variable, there was any trend for males and females to differentially benefit from one condition

Table 6.1: Hypothetical Randomization Test.*

Participant Characteristics	Intervention ($N = 55$)	Control ($N = 55$)	p-value
Baseline pain	M = 4.81 (0.95)	M = 4.75 (0.89)	NS**
Years since initial diagnosis	M = 7.21 (1.1)	M = 7.10 (1.0)	NS
Knee replacement			NS
One	10 (18.2%)	8 (14.5%)	
Both	2 (3.6%)	2 (3.6%)	
None	43 (78.2%)	45 (81.1%)	
Gender			
Female	40 (72.7%)	42 (76.4%)	NS
Age (years)			NS
<50	20 (36.4%)	18 (32.7%)	
51–65	26 (47.3%)	25 (45.5%)	
>65	9 (16.4%)	12 (21.8%)	

* t-Tests were performed on continuous variables and chi-square analyses on categorical data. Standard deviations are in parentheses.

**NS = not statistically significant ($p > .05$).

over another. A significant positive finding here would certainly be extremely disappointing to an investigator, but neither a positive nor negative finding would be conclusive, since these contrasts were not causal in nature and were not originally hypothesized. (Another reason that negative findings from such analyses are not considered conclusive resides in the fact that most experiments do not have sufficiently large sample sizes for such analyses to have a high probability of achieving statistical significance.)

Since there is no completely satisfactory answer to the question of what effect a breakdown in the randomization process will have on the validity of the experimental outcome results, the best course of action for investigators who feel a need for additional insurance against this possibility is to employ either

1. A covariate known to be related to the outcome variable—the addition of such a variable will enable even minor initial between-group discrepancies to be statistically controlled—or
2. A blocking variable (as discussed in the Chapter Seven) which will procedurally facilitate the creation of equivalent groups.

Regardless of whether one of these strategies is employed or not, investigators should routinely

1. Ensure that the randomization process is performed properly and with compulsive care,
2. Ensure that factors known (or suspected) to be related to the outcome variable (or differentially responsiveness to the intervention) are assessed at baseline,

3. Conduct a test of the randomization process,

4. Report the results transparently (including the presence of a randomization "failure"), and

5. Dispassionately attempt to assess the likelihood that any initial nonequivalence was capable of invalidating the final experimental inference.

The nonrandomized (quasi-experimental) pretest-posttest control group design: Naturally, nonequivalence is considerably more likely to occur in the nonrandomized pretest-posttest control group design depicted in Figure 6.5 than its randomized counterpart. And while non-randomized designs with control groups are superior to more primitive single-group designs, the magnitude of this advantage depends to a large extent on the methods used to decide how participants are selected to represent the various groups being compared. While none of these methods are anywhere nearly as acceptable as randomization (which is why this design is classified as *quasi-experimental*), let's consider three possibilities.

Options #1: the concurrent use of intact groups. This is the option depicted in Figure 6.5 where two apparently equivalent and available groups of participants are located, such as classrooms, hospital units, schools, and so forth. Let's examine a hypothetical use of this strategy as a mechanism for illustrating some of the considerations arising in the design and conduct of a quasi-experimental study.

Suppose a psychology professor wishes to contrast the effects of two different textbooks on student learning. Fortuitously, several sections of the same introductory course are being taught in her department during the upcoming semester and our hypothetical investigator finds another instructor who is willing to cooperate with her on the project. The two agree to use the same final exam, which will be employed as both a pretest and a posttest for the experiment. It is also agreed that our professor will use the new textbook ("B") and her colleague will use the existing one ("A"). Each then teaches her class as usual and at the end of the semester students who used Textbook B learned significantly more than those who used Textbook A. Both investigators were quite proud of their study and resolved to henceforth use Textbook B in their courses. Fortunately, the two instructors didn't have to face Dr. Jones's uncivil biostatistician, but let's identify some of the potential confounds present in this study.

First and foremost, the possibility of selection can be conceptualized as a confounding variable in this experiment. Since randomization was not used, the possibility exists that the two intact groups of students may have had different abilities, aptitudes, motivations, or prior knowledge. (For example, perhaps scheduling conflicts resulted in more students majoring in the subject matter being taught gravitating toward one section than toward the other.)

Second, instructor differences (which might involve one being a better or more motivated teacher) are perfectly confounded with the experimental groups (i.e., textbooks). And to make matters worse, instructor differences could interact with selection if more serious students were more likely to opt for the instructor who was known to be a better or more conscientious teacher. (Or, just as likely, perhaps less motivated students purposefully enrolled in the section taught by the instructor with a reputation for being an easier grader.)

Myriad other potential confounds exist, such as the possibility that one instructor emphasized (purposefully or by happenstance) the test content more than the other. Or, if one section was taught in the morning and one in the evening, perhaps student fatigue would be a factor, making time of the day a confound. It is difficult, in fact, to design any non-laboratory experiment involving human participants in which confounds of *some* sort do not exist. One of the most important, if not the most important, purposes of the experimental design process is to set up an environment in which as many confounds as possible are automatically controlled (such as individual differences among participants, external events, natural history, and temporal differences).

Random assignment helps make the control of some confounds easier, but most must be anticipated and controlled by *procedural* means. Some may seem trivial, such as the fact that in the present example the classes were taught in different rooms (but even here the thermostat in one of the rooms might malfunction frequently, or the room itself might be located near a noisy construction site). However with care, serious forethought, and periodic monitoring of the ongoing experiment, many such confounds are avoidable or correctable—but only if they are recognized and enumerated at the design phase.

Without further ado, therefore, let's award this concept of confounding as our next experimental artifact, followed by its own experimental principle.

EXPERIMENTAL ARTIFACT #13:
OTHER EXPERIMENTAL CONFOUNDS

For present purposes, *experimental confounds* are defined *as any factor or condition (other than tested differences) unique to one experimental group but not the other(s).* The prefixed adjective "other" acknowledges that many of the previously designated experimental artifacts can also be conceptualized as confounds. When viewed in this context, the following principle is certainly one of the most important presented in this book:

> *PRINCIPLE #17*: **Prior to conducting an experiment, always (a) identify all potential confounds, (b) eliminate those which are plausibly related to the study outcome by standardizing and/or counterbalancing procedures across experimental conditions to the maximum extent possible, and (c) monitor the effects of those confounds that cannot be eliminated or counterbalanced.**

Counterbalancing simply means that a potential confound is controlled by ensuring that it occurs equally in all experimental groups. In our present textbook example, if the investigators were sufficiently worried about potential instructor differences, they could trade sections at mid-semester, although this would be a relatively obtrusive procedure and instructor effects would still be confounded with instructional content (i.e., the curriculum taught in the first half of the course vs. that taught during the second half).

The first step in preventing or controlling confounds (à la Principle #17) is their identification. These involve (a) selection, since the random assignment of students to conditions was not feasible, (b) the fact that only two instructors were available to teach one section each, and (c) the fact that two sections had to be offered at different times in different rooms. If our investigators were privy to Principle #17, however, they might have identified other correctable confounds as well—some of which would involve previously delineated artifacts.

Once identified, of course, a serious attempt should be made to ameliorate confounds to the maximum degree possible. For example, if counterbalancing was deemed too obtrusive, the potential instructor differences could be ameliorated by standardizing the instructional content of the two sections by delineating discrete instructional objectives for both instructors to cover. The outcome variable (the final examination also administered as a pretest) could then be based on these objectives, thus helping to at least ensure that the instructors taught the same content.

A misconception regarding random assignment in quasi-experimental designs: In this hypothetical study, the two instructors decided who would introduce Textbook A and who would continue to use Textbook B. At first glance it might appear that randomly assigning the two instructors to the two conditions would help result in partially controlling this particular confound, thereby bolstering the design. It would not, however. If the two professors had flipped a coin to see which instructor would assign which textbook, for example, the strategy would do nothing to control for either the selection artifact or any other experimental confound. If one classroom or one instructor, for example, turned out to be systematically different from the other in some manner sufficient to produce a false positive or false negative result, randomization of this sort simply ensures that said incorrect inference will have a 50% chance of favoring Textbook A or a 50% chance of favoring Textbook B.

Experimental confounds can often be avoided only procedurally. In the present study, for example, the same instructor could teach each section or the two instructors could team teach the two sections together. Probably the latter option would be preferable but regardless, the bottom line is that adherence to Principle #17 is a crucial aspect of designing any experiment. Fortunately, experimental confounds once identified can usually be avoided or at least weakened, but the first step is their identification.

Option #2: the use of intact groups with temporal or physical separation. When intact groups from different time periods are used in lieu of randomly assigned participants, the experimental conditions are confounded not only by time but also often by staff, geographic, and institutional structural differences that are considerably more likely to involve the potential for selection than our hypothetical textbook example. Participants tend to self-select themselves (or some other set of circumstances tends to influence their entry) into a particular facility, and this selection process always has the *potential* of being related to propensity to change on the outcome variable.

Or alternately, returning to our hypothetical example, the initiating investigator might have decided to avoid confounding instructors with conditions by opting to use Textbook A in one semester and Textbook B in the next. This strategy would avoid some of the instructor-related confounds present in the original design but would introduce others, such as (a) differences in the investigator's personal life over time, (b) a practice effect with respect to both teaching the keyed content and to implementing the experimental protocol in general, and/or (c) unconsciously biasing the results (since the investigator would undoubtedly personally or professionally prefer one text over another).

This strategy of using temporally separated intact groups would also not constitute a substantive improvement over the original study, since the students within these groups still cannot be assumed to be equivalent. Also, as a rule, it is always a good practice to (a) simultaneously run the intervention and the control group and (b) not permit the principal investigator to implement either an intervention or its control group.

Option #3: the use of matching to constitute more equivalent comparison groups. Occasionally it is possible to select participants at large to serve as controls for an intact intervention group.

Continuing with our textbook example, this might involve our professor deciding to introduce Textbook B in her assigned introductory psychology section during the upcoming semester and selecting control students from the remaining sections.

Let's assume, therefore, following considerable lobbying and the calling in of favors, that she was able to convince the other instructors to administer her pretest with only the experimentally relevant subset of items embedded in it being repeated on the final exam. So far, this design is quite similar to Option #1 and suffers from the same limitations, except perhaps the additional instructors might slightly reduce the instructor-instructional difference confound. A question remains, however, as to how she should select her control group from the much larger pool of possibilities.

One possibility would be to randomly select the same number of students from the seven other sections as was contained in her section. This would produce equal sample sizes in her two groups, but there would be no advantage to this strategy since the data were already available for a much larger number of students. (As will be discussed in Chapter Nine, although the advantage of unequal allocation of participants to conditions drops off dramatically as the sample size in two groups diverts, the more participants involved in a study, the more statistical power is available.)

A second possibility would be to select matching control participants based on one (or at most two) baseline variables known to be related to academic achievement (e.g., pretest scores, GPA, psychology majors vs. non-psychology majors, or some other academic measure). Matching intervention and control participants has a negative reputation among methodologists (and journal reviewers), but this option has a number of advantages to accompany its pitfalls, including a *reduction* in the threat of initial nonequivalence of the two experimental groups (i.e., selection). (Yet another possibility would be to use all the control students available as the primary contrast and present a matched control as a secondary analysis.)

Completely unacceptable options: While problematic, all of these alternatives are superior to the single-group pretest-posttest design. Quasi-experimental strategies exist, however, that are worse than no research at all, such as soliciting volunteers to receive an intervention and then contrasting their outcomes to non-volunteers—almost guaranteeing the two groups will differ on important outcome-related variables.

Other unacceptable solutions include knowingly selecting nonequivalent participants (from different facilities, classrooms, or other sources) to represent the intervention and control groups, based on the rationale that these preexisting differences can be statistically controlled. This isn't as common in prospective experimentation as in large-scale analyses of databases, such as those performed by economists, educators, or think tank denizens, but it is almost always ineffectual when it does occur. Two nonequivalent groups simply cannot be statistically manipulated into equivalency. Even when the correlation between the control variables and the outcome variable is high, it is always possible that this relationship is due to other unmeasured *causal* factors influencing either (or both) set(s) of variables.

The bottom line is always the same, à la Principle #13. The best design strategy for producing high-quality causal inferences in research involving human participants remains their random assignment to experimental conditions—which will also greatly facilitate publishing the resulting studies in a credible, peer-reviewed journal.

Strategies for "selling" the randomization process: One obstacle to randomly assigning participants to groups, especially in practice settings, resides in administrative and staff reluctance to deny a potentially effective treatment to clients. Added to this is a reluctance to disrupt everyday institutional practices or to increase the workload of already overextended treatment staff.

All of these issues are normally surmountable. Even the knowledge that an individual has a 50% chance of receiving a placebo is an acceptable risk for most people who volunteer for a randomized control trial. From an institutional perspective, it is incumbent upon the investigator to convey the importance of randomization and to design the study to be minimally disruptive to usual practice. Potentially helpful strategies in these regards include the following:

1. *Logic.* Explain that it isn't known whether the intervention is beneficial or not. (There may even be untoward effects.) If the intervention proves not to be effective, participants who do not receive it will miss nothing of value. If a randomly assigned comparison group is not used, however, the beneficial vs. non-beneficial nature of the intervention may never be determined.

2. *Giving everyone a chance to receive the intervention by delaying its implementation to the comparison group.* Both treatment personnel and their administrators' objections to denying half of their clients the possibility of receiving a potentially beneficial intervention can be mitigated by simply randomly assigning the order in which participants receive the intervention. This relatively common strategy, called a *delayed treatment design*, will be discussed in detail shortly. Its primary disadvantage resides in the additional effort required on the part of experimental staff, but it does effectively counter many of the objections to randomization and may improve recruitment and prevent attrition.

3. *Purposefully choosing too large a setting or participant pool.* If an intervention cannot be logistically administered to everyone available, random selection of intervention participants via a lottery-type strategy can suddenly become a more acceptable, democratic method of deciding who will and will not receive it. (An example of this option is presented in Chapter Twelve, involving a natural experiment regarding the effectiveness of New York charter schools.)

4. *Increasing the attractiveness of the comparison group.* One of the more pervasive objections to random assignment emanates from the use of a no-treatment control. Of the five genres of control/comparison discussed (no treatment, placebo, attention, treatment as usual, and alternative interventions), providing the comparison group with nothing of value is the option most objectionable to administrators, staff, and participants themselves. Thus, when scientific considerations permit, employing one of the other four genres can make random assignment more palatable. From an institutional perspective, an attention control or an alternative intervention may constitute the best choices to counter objections and improve recruitment.

5. *When all else fails, consider changing the study environment from the "real world" to a laboratory (or laboratory-like setting).* As experimental research becomes more and more common, randomization appears to be encountering less institutional resistance. When insurmountable resistance does occur (or when randomization is simply not feasible), investigators should consider the possibility of conducting an experiment in a different setting. Occasionally, this setting must be constructed, such as in a laboratory (see Chapter Eleven). Of course, this compromises generalizability, but promising results (even accompanied by a degree of artificiality) may open the way to the possibility of gaining future access to more veridical settings.

Before introducing a number of more preferable randomized designs, let's contrast the randomized pretest-posttest control group design with its nonrandomized counterpart on the artifacts discussed to this point via the chart presented in Figure 6.6. For simplicity's (and brevity's) sake we'll assume that both designs (a) use an effective placebo control group and (b) structure the instructions provided participants (on the informed consent statement and during the course of the experiment) to reveal as little about the design as ethically defensible.

FIGURE 6.6: Randomized vs. Nonrandomized Pretest-Posttest Control Group Report Card.

	Randomized Pretest-Posttest (Placebo) Control Group Design	Non-Randomized Pretest-Posttest (Placebo) Control Group Design
Selection	√	X
Natural History	√	≈
Placebo Effect	√	√
Regression to the Mean	√	≈
Repeated Testing	√	√
Extraneous External Events	√	≈
Demand Characteristics	√	√
Reactivity Effects	√	√
Attrition	x	x
Differential Attrition	√	√
Other Confounds	≈	X

Thus, while the prevention of selection is by far the greatest advantage of a randomized vs. nonrandomized design, it is not the only one. Since initial equivalence cannot be assumed, neither can regression to the mean be assumed to be equal, since this artifact is defined as being problematic (a) when participants are selected for an experiment *because* they exhibit more extreme scores (either high or low) on that outcome variable than the population from which they are drawn or (b) when participants' baseline scores happened to be more extreme than is typical for those particular individuals. In other words, the possibility of selection can go hand in hand with the possibility of differential regression to the mean, as participants selected for the experimental conditions may be drawn from different populations (e.g., which possess different propensities to exhibit the regression artifact), thus the "≈" rating. The same logic holds for natural history and extraneous external events in those instances in which the two groups of participants cannot be run in the same environment. (The randomized design was given an equivocal rating for the "other confounds" artifact because randomization only facilitates the avoidance of a limited number of confounds; specific procedural steps are normally required for the control of others.)

Now that the single-most common randomized and quasi-experimental designs have been contrasted with one another, let's consider three additional randomized designs. All are completely acceptable alternatives to the randomized pretest-posttest design, although the acceptability of the first (the randomized posttest-only control group design) may be counterintuitive to those readers who have not yet internalized the most impressive characteristic of the randomization process (the initial equating of experimental groups on preexisting attributes, thereby preventing the selection artifact).

THE RANDOMIZED POSTTEST-ONLY CONTROL GROUP DESIGN

This design is identical to its randomized pretest-posttest control group counterpart (see Figure 6.4) with the exception that no baseline or pretest assessment is performed (see Figure 6.7). A pretest or baseline assessment of the outcome variable is always preferable, but situations exist in which a pretest is either not available or contraindicated, such as the following:

1. The outcome variable is dichotomous and the inclusion criterion mandates that no one exhibiting the desired (or deleterious) behavior be permitted in the study. Thus if abstinence is the goal of a trial, only individuals who smoke or otherwise partake of a contraindicated substance would be recruited. Study investigators would be wise, however, to include a variable known to be related to abstinence as a covariate (such as risk-taking behavior, length of addiction, desire for achieving the stated outcome, and so forth).
2. The outcome variable is simply not available as a pretest. Examples might include length of stay in a treatment facility, recidivism, adverse events, or graduation from an educational institution. In such instances past performances predictive of these outcomes might be available from institutional records.
3. The outcome variable is considered too reactive to be used as pretest (e.g., our psychology professor's hypothetical textbook study is an example of such a scenario, since most college professors would be loath to share final examination questions with students at the beginning of their courses).

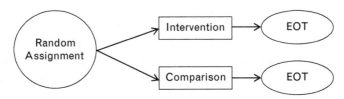

FIGURE 6.7: Randomized Posttest-Only Control Group Design.

At first glance, the lack of an initial assessment may appear problematic since there will be no pre-intervention outcome values upon which either to (a) establish pre-intervention equivalence or (b) compute between-group changes before and after the intervention. Randomization takes care of both problems, however, as it *permits* the assumption of initial equivalence of the experimental groups on all parameters—known or unknown, relevant or irrelevant. The success of the randomization process can, of course, be tested on variables other than the pretest.

To illustrate this point, let's return to Dr. Jones's hypothetical acupuncture experiment and explore what effect both (a) a randomized pretest-posttest (placebo) control group design (Figure 6.4) and (b) a randomized posttest-only (placebo) control group design (Figure 6.7) would have had on his original single-group pretest-posttest results. Most obviously, each design tests a slightly different hypothesis:

> *Dr. Jones's single-group pretest-posttest hypothesis*: Patients with osteoarthritis of the knee receiving six traditional Chinese acupuncture treatments over a 2-week period will report significantly less pain at the end of treatment than at baseline.
>
> *His pretest-posttest control group hypothesis*: Patients with osteoarthritis of the knee receiving six traditional Chinese acupuncture treatments over a 2-week period will report a significantly greater reduction in pain from baseline to end of treatment than randomly assigned osteoarthritis patients receiving six sham acupuncture treatments involving shallow needle placement at irrelevant points.
>
> *His posttest-only control group hypothesis*: Patients with osteoarthritis of the knee receiving six traditional Chinese acupuncture treatments over a 2-week period will report significantly less pain at the end of treatment than randomly assigned osteoarthritis patients receiving six sham acupuncture treatments involving shallow needle placement at irrelevant points.

Now, let's visualize Dr. Jones's hypothetical data resulting from each design. Revisiting the single-group study from Chapter Four which employed a baseline and EOT assessment, we already know the results (assuming only a placebo and regression to the mean artifact occurred) were as shown in Table 6.2.

Table 6.2: Dr. Jones's Original Single-Group Pretest-Posttest Results.

	Average Pain at Baseline	Average Pain at EOT	Difference
Intervention Group	5.000	4.270	−0.730

We also later estimated what the results of his randomized pretest-posttest control group study would have been following an inevitable regression to the mean and placebo effect (see Table 6.3).

Table 6.3: Dr. Jones's Estimated Results Had a Placebo Control Group Been Used.

	Average Pain at Baseline	Average Pain at EOT	Difference
Intervention Group ($N = 10$)	5.000	4.270	−0.730
Control Group ($N = 10$)	5.000	4.635	−0.365

Note that the operative numbers which would be used to test the first hypothesis change from $5.000 - 4.270 = -0.730$ to $[(5.000 - 4.270) - (5.000 - 4.635)] = (-0.730) - (-0.365) = -0.365$.

Now let's look at the same study results, had a randomized posttest-only (placebo) control group design been employed. If everything else had been equal (which in reality it seldom is), the results would have been as shown in Table 6.4.

Table 6.4: Dr. Jones's Randomized Posttest-Only
Design Results.

	Average Pain at EOT
Intervention Acupuncture Group	4.270
Placebo Group	4.635
Difference	−0.365

In other words, the contrast of interest, as specified in the third iteration of his research hypothesis, would be 4.270 − 4.635 = **−0.365** (which is the same as the contrast relevant to the second hypothesis (i.e., the randomized pretest-posttest design).

A natural question might then be: what is the best guess for what the pretest scores would have been had a pretest been employed? Unfortunately, that particular question cannot be answered on the basis of the data produced by a posttest-only design. And while it might be interesting to know how much less pain patients experienced from baseline to EOT in both groups, that bit of information is irrelevant as far as the hypothesis and the final inference are concerned.

It is also irrelevant clinically, because −0.365 represents an accurate estimate of the amount of pain relief resulting from the acupuncture treatment. Why? Because the random assignment of participants to the two groups allows us to assume that (a) the two groups were initially equivalent with respect to preexisting pain and (b) the resulting contrast subtracted out the same proportion of the effects due to the same experimental artifacts (assuming the repeated testing artifact was not operative).

Admittedly, the simulated data presented for the two-group pretest-posttest design (Table 6.3) are unrealistic, since even with randomization the intervention and the control group are quite unlikely to wind up with exactly the same outcome values at baseline. It should be remembered, however, that even if this did occur, the two groups' possession of the same pretest means would not imply that they were initially *exactly* equivalent on the outcome. All measurements contain a degree of error, and since this error is assumed to be random, the quantity of error present in one group would not be exactly the same as in the other even if the pre-intervention means had been identical. In addition, since familiarity with the pretest (which is more unlikely for pain than for outcome variables such learning) can influence scores on the posttest (i.e., the repeated testing artifact), another minor source of error is possibly added (minor because this artifact would manifest itself for both groups and thereby be controlled).

The bottom line here is that there is much less difference between the methodological rigor of a randomized pretest-posttest design and its posttest-only counterpart than appears on the surface. However, the use of a baseline (pretest) assessment is always recommended, except for those relatively uncommon instances in which (a) there is no premeasure available on the outcome variable (e.g., length of stay in treatment facility), (b) the outcome variable is used as an exclusion criterion (e.g., participants are selected because they have zero amounts of the outcome), (c) the outcome occurs only once (e.g., mortality), or (d) it is hypothesized to be overly reactive (as would be the case for using the entire final exam as a pretest in our hypothetical textbook study). The primary reasons for this recommendation are as follows:

1. *Affective.* Most research consumers and journal reviewers prefer a baseline value on the outcome.

2. *Increased precision.* As will be explained in Chapter Nine, a preexisting measure highly correlated with the EOT outcome increases the statistical power available for a hypothesis test. And almost without exception the highest correlation between any baseline variable and an EOT outcome is produced when the same measure is used for both.

Fortunately, a completely acceptable alternative exists for those scenarios in which baseline values on the outcome cannot be assessed that ameliorates both of these relatively minor disadvantages (i.e., affective and loss of precision).

THE RANDOMIZED COVARIATE-POSTTEST CONTROL GROUP DESIGN

While always preferable, there are occasions when a pretest is either not feasible or available as delineated for the posttest-only control group design (e.g., a pretest is considered too reactive). In these instances the randomized covariate-posttest design depicted in Figure 6.8 is employed which resides somewhere between a randomized pretest-posttest control group and a posttest-only control group design with respect to experimental precision. Its advantage over the previous posttest-only design is almost completely dependent on the strength of the correlation between this preexisting variable (called a covariate) and the EOT outcome variable.

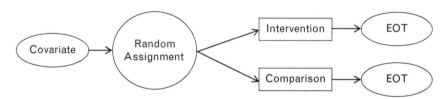

FIGURE 6.8: Randomized Covariate-Posttest Control Group Design.

The covariate in Figure 6.8 serves several important functions. First (and least important), it serves to help test the success of the randomization process by comparing the groups on the covariate (along with any other preexisting demographic or clinical information). Second, if minor initial differences do occur on the covariate (as slight variations almost always do on all pre-intervention variables despite the randomization process), the EOT outcome results will be adjusted on the basis of these differences by including the covariate in the analysis. Third, the existence of a covariate increases the statistical power available for the final hypothesis test (Chapter Nine), which in turn permits a reduction in the required sample size. And finally, in the design depicted in Figure 6.8, the covariate and the outcome variable need be administered only once, hence reactivity may be reduced and the repeated testing artifact is not operative.

The Weis and Cerankosky (2010) video-gaming study abstracted in Chapter Three is an example of an experiment that substituted multiple covariates for pretests and thereby approximates the design depicted in Figure 6.8. (The disclaimer "approximates" is used because this experiment also fits the delayed intervention design discussed later.) Although often repeated, this particular study illustrates the fact that components from different designs (and control groups) can be interchanged with one another. Thus, there is nothing to prohibit one or more covariates from being added to any other multigroup designs—including the pretest-posttest control group design just discussed. There is also nothing to permit the use of multiple covariates in the same study, other than the difficulty of identifying two or more viable candidates having *independent* relationships with the EOT outcome assessment. To be useful, however, the covariate should have a statistically significant correlation with the posttest which is independent of the correlation between the pretest and the posttest—a difficult criterion to meet in most experiments with limited sample sizes.

A numeric example of how a covariate serves to control for initial between-group differences in a randomized experiment. Although for simplicity's sake we have not conceptualized it in this manner with our hypothetical data, the baseline values in a randomized pretest-posttest design also serve to *adjust* the EOT results, based on any initial discrepancies. (In our previous examples we simply subtracted EOT from baseline values to represent the adjustment process.) To visualize how this adjustment process occurs in the presence of a covariate (or a pretest for that matter), let's return to Dr. Jones's hypothetical acupuncture study and change the results so that the same EOT mean pain value (4.27) was obtained for both groups (i.e., the same value emanating from his single-group design). However, let's assume that a covariate (positively related to pain) was substituted for the baseline pain assessment. The hypothetical effects of three different scenarios for the initial baseline covariate values are illustrated in Table 6.5: (a) identical covariate scores at baseline (Scenario A), (b) higher covariate scores obtained for the intervention group than the control (Scenario B), and (c) lower scores exhibited by the intervention group at baseline than for the control (Scenario C).

Table 6.5: Dr. Jones's Slightly Altered Two-Group Experimental Results Illustrating How a Covariate Helps to Statistically Control for Baseline Differences Between Groups.

	Average Baseline Covariate	Average EOT Pain	Adjusted EOT Pain Based on Covariate at Baseline
Scenario A (Equal Baseline Covariate Scores)			
Intervention Group	22.14	4.27	4.27
Control Group	22.14	4.27	4.27
			Δ0.00
Scenario B (Unequal Baseline Covariate Intervention Higher)			
Intervention Group	24.14	4.27	4.07
Control Group	20.14	4.27	4.47
			Δ-0.40
Scenario C (Unequal Baseline Covariate Control Higher)			
Intervention Group	20.14	4.27	4.47
Control Group	24.14	4.27	4.07
			Δ+0.40

In Scenario A, since there were no between-group discrepancies on the covariate, no adjustment would be made for EOT pain scores, regardless of how highly the baseline scores correlated with the EOT scores. Thus the zero intervention vs. control EOT difference stood up, and there was no treatment effect emanating from this study.

In Scenario B, however, the randomization process appeared to have suffered a rare breakdown, since participants with higher covariate scores were assigned to the intervention group. It would not be reasonable, therefore, to evaluate the between-group EOT pain without making some adjustment for this discrepancy, and indeed that did occur, with the unadjusted intervention EOT mean of 4.27 being "penalized" for its participants' greater covariate scores (remember, this would indicate greater pain, since the covariate was positively correlated with it) and the control EOT mean of 4.27 being "compensated," based on its participants' initial disadvantage. The result was a 0.20 adjustment downward for the intervention and a 0.20 adjustment upward for the control, yielding a positive intervention effect of 0.40 on the visual analog scale (VAS) (positive because less pain is "better" $4.07 - 4.47 = -0.40$). Finally, Scenario C represents the opposite baseline discrepancy from Scenario B, except this time the intervention group received lower scores on the covariate and the opposite adjustment occurred. Thus the adjusting process would also occur in the opposite direction.

These admittedly stylized and exaggerated scenarios were constructed to illustrate how a covariate basically operates. It is extremely rare that adjustments of the magnitude represented by Scenarios B and C would occur, because failures in randomization of this magnitude are likewise quite rare. In the presence of random assignment, the normal adjustment process is much closer to Scenario A and is usually trivial in nature, with the primary advantage being a boost in statistical power concomitant with the strength of the covariate–outcome variable correlation.

Suffice it to say that the use of covariates, either via a randomized covariate-EOT control group design or an add-on to another multigroup design, is a perfectly acceptable research strategy if and *only* if the covariate

1. Is at least moderately correlated with the EOT outcome,
2. Is roughly equally correlated with the EOT outcome for all the experimental groups,
3. Is selected a priori rather than after the EOT data have been collected (because the latter practice increases the probability of obtaining false positive results),
4. Represents a *preexisting* variable and is therefore not capable of being affected by the experimental conditions, and
5. Is not in some way conceptually or empirically related to the experimental purpose or conditions.

This fifth criterion probably deserves some additional explanation, because the covariate adjustment function must be considered carefully at the design stage to ensure that it does not somehow relate conceptually to one of the experimental conditions. If participants had been stratified into older vs. younger groups to ascertain if acupuncture is differentially effective for different age groups (thereby resulting in a two-factor experiment, as will be discussed in Chapter Seven), then age (or variables correlated with age, such as length of time since the participants were first diagnosed with arthritis) would certainly not be a reasonable choice for a covariate because any initial discrepancies between *all* of the study groups would be adjusted and two of the groups (i.e., older vs. younger patients) were chosen *because* they initially differed from one another. The resulting adjustment would therefore automatically invalidate any inferences involving acupuncture's age-related effects.

A PSYCHOLOGICAL EXAMPLE OF A COVARIATE USED FOR MEDIATING PURPOSES

The Value of Believing in Free Will: Encouraging a Belief in Determinism Increases Cheating (2008)

Kathleen Vohs and Jonathan Schooler

Although not common, covariates can be used in secondary analyses for mediating purposes, in which case the injunction against employing only preexisting variables no longer applies. Returning to the video-gaming study, since participants in both the intervention and control conditions played video games during the course of the experiment (the intervention group simply played more), the average duration of video-game play was used as a covariate to see if it would mediate the relationship between video-game ownership and test scores at follow-up (obviously and purposefully in violation of the fifth criterion presented earlier). When this was done the initial intervention vs. control effect disappeared, strengthening (in the investigators' opinion) the conclusion that it was video-game playing that affected academic performance.

Vohs and Schooler (2008) provide an example of a similar secondary analysis, in an experiment designed first to ascertain if being read an anti-free-will passage would decrease beliefs in the construct as compared to a control passage. It did. (The passage took the position that free will is an illusion or "a side effect of the architecture of the mind.")

In the second part of the experiment, both groups were given a computerized mental arithmetic task, during which the students were "told that the computer had a programming glitch and the correct answer would appear on the screen while they were attempting to solve each problem, but that they could stop the answer from being displayed by pressing the space bar after the problem appeared." Of course, the experimenters could tell when and how often cheating occurred.

Again, as predicted, the anti-free-will passage was associated with a statistically significant greater amount of cheating among participants than occurred with the control passage. So far this is a straightforward, well-designed psychological study to see if both beliefs in free will and cheating could be experimentally manipulated. Then, presumably to reinforce the causal conclusion that free will is causally associated with cheating, the free-will attitudinal measure administered after the free-will passage intervention was entered as a covariate. This time around there was no cheating effect attributable to the differences in passages after changes in free-will beliefs had been factored out (i.e., statistically controlled).

Whether this use of a covariate in a mediating analysis in an experiment is actually needed to elucidate the causal mechanism involved is a matter of opinion, but certainly no harm is done as long as it is clearly specified and interpreted as a secondary analysis, which both these and the video-gaming investigators clearly did. In any event, this example was included not because of its utility or supplementary value in experimental research but to illustrate the injunction that the use of a covariate deserves careful thought regarding *what is being controlled*. For a more thorough explication of mediation considerations, see MacKinnon and Fairchild (2009); for the distinction between mediating and moderating variables, see Baron and Kenny (1986).

The use of propensity scores as control variables: One method of ensuring a reasonable correlation between the outcome variable and the covariate (our first criterion for selecting a covariate) is to actually construct the latter via a linear combination of multiple preexisting variables known to be related to the outcome, based on the literature or a pilot study. Called *propensity scores*, these variables tend to function more effectively as covariates than any of the individual variables making them up (although the use of a pretest, where available, would probably still be superior). While most commonly employed in nonrandomized, quasi-experimental designs using intact groups (D'Agostino, 1998) or participant-matched designs (Austin, 2008; Rosenbaum & Rubin, 1983), propensity scores can also be employed profitably as the covariate component of a randomized covariate-posttest comparison group design when necessary.

From an experimental perspective the major limitations of the procedure involve

1. The amount of preliminary work required for their construction and, as with any non-randomized study, and
2. The fact that the most important factors differentiating the groups may not be known.

EXPERIMENTAL ARTIFACTS IMPERVIOUS TO RANDOM ASSIGNMENT

Before introducing the final two single-factor, randomized designs covered in this chapter, let's now consider some additional experimental artifacts that are, like selection, relevant only to multigroup designs. The first is the most problematic, while the final two (resentful demoralization and compensatory rivalry) are somewhat less so and certainly more easily prevented. None of them, however, imply that the single-group pretest-posttest design (or any nonrandomized strategy yet discussed) is a viable option to any of the randomized designs discussed to this point. Instead, if one or more these artifacts are considered problematic for the type of (a) setting, (b) outcome variable, or (c) intervention employed, two specialized randomized designs exist that between them potentially address all four artifacts. Before introducing these options, however, let's consider the final three miscreants, in order of virulence.

EXPERIMENTAL ARTIFACT #14: TREATMENT DIFFUSION

This potentially serious artifact is defined as the unplanned leakage of the intervention (or elements thereof) to other comparison groups, thereby eroding the designed procedural difference between conditions. It can occur when intervention and control participants (or the therapists who interact with them) are in close physical proximity or have the potential to routinely communicate with one another. At an absurd level, no investigator would knowingly assign dyads (e.g., husband–wife, significant others, siblings) to different experimental conditions. Only slightly less obvious, it would not be wise to assign members of captive institutional audiences (e.g., students within the same classroom or who share the same teacher; residents within an assisted living community) to different experimental conditions that encompassed more than a single session since either they, or treatment staff, could potentially share elements of an intervention with one another. (As an extreme example, there were anecdotal reports of some AIDS patients participating in early randomized placebo clinical trials pooling their theoretically indistinguishable capsules with one another to increase the probability of receiving at least some active ingredients.)

For educational and complex behavioral interventions, it is doubtful that most participants would be capable of communicating enough of the components to their control counterparts to affect the study outcome. Also, for interventions involving lifestyle changes (e.g., weight loss experiments), it is difficult enough to elicit compliance first hand, much less via secondary sources. However, such communication can alert participants to elements of the design that investigators would prefer to remain hidden, such as their assignment to attention control conditions, which may then encourage dissatisfaction and result in differential attrition. Thus, when intervention and comparison participants are in close proximity to one another, certain design alternations are necessary. It is also possible that treatment diffusion may be in the process of becoming increasingly problematic as social media continues to increase in all arenas of life.

Amelioration: Many types of interventions (and outcomes) are relatively immune from the effects of this artifact. The most obvious preventive strategy for those that are vulnerable involves not using participants with close social or institutional ties. Others include the following:

1. Changing the unit of assignment for captive audiences. Many modern educational studies, for example, now randomly assign classrooms (or even entire schools) to experimental conditions rather than individual students. (This strategy involves significant design and analytic adjustments, which will be discussed shortly when group [cluster] randomized designs are introduced.)
2. To avoid less obvious within-unit (e.g., classrooms, treatment facilities) dependencies, asking participants not to communicate with anyone else known to be involved or contemplating involvement in the experiment may be helpful. Altruism constitutes one of the most common motivations for experimental participation, hence at least some people will conscientiously comply with such requests.
3. When possible, avoiding communicating the experimental purposes to participants.
4. Keeping the experimental interval as brief as scientifically feasible.
5. Avoiding self-reported outcomes and overly reactive experimental conditions (Principle #11).

EXPERIMENTAL ARTIFACT #15: RESENTFUL DEMORALIZATION

This artifact is defined as *a depression in control/comparison respondents' outcome values due to their belief (or realization) that they are receiving a less desirable treatment than their intervention counterparts.* Resentful demoralization is more likely to occur for reactive outcome variables and interventions and can also result in differential attrition in the affected group(s).

Amelioration: While probably not as virulent or prevalent as selection and differential attrition in multigroup experiments, this artifact can be minimized by

1. Employing one of the alternatives to a no-treatment control group, discussed in Chapter Five, which offers more contact and benefits (or pretends to do so) to non-intervention participants. Placebo controls are especially helpful in this regard if they are carefully constructed. So are alternative-treatment comparison groups (if they are attractive to participants) and attention controls (which unfortunately are difficult to construct and thus are often more helpful in theory than in reality).
2. Reducing the duration of the experiment (single-session interventions, when scientifically defensible, almost completely preclude attrition).
3. Employing less reactive outcome variables and interventions.
4. Paying participants for their time.
5. Offering the intervention (or an abbreviated version) at a later time (see the Randomized Delayed Intervention Design, later in this chapter).

EXPERIMENTAL ARTIFACT #16: COMPENSATORY RIVALRY

This potential artifact is the other side of the resentful demoralization coin. Compensatory rivalry theoretically occurs when knowledge of group assignment encourages participants (or their service providers) to compensate or "try harder." Cook and Campbell (1979), who apparently first posited the existence of this and the previous artifact, nicknamed compensatory rivalry the "John Henry Effect," after the railroad steel driver who died from overexertion in a race against a machine. To the present author's knowledge, there are no controlled documentations of this effect actually occurring in experimental research, but the following ameliorative strategies constitute good experimental practice anyway.

Amelioration: Preventive strategies similar to those for resentful demoralization include reducing the experimental interval, using a different type of control group, and selecting nonreactive outcome variables. Others include the following:

1. Masking the experimental purpose and communicating *only* what participants need to know concerning the experimental procedures (such as what is required of them and any risks involved).
2. Monitoring both the implementation of the intervention and control conditions throughout the conduct of the trial.
3. Employing either of the two randomized designs which follow.

A Less Plausible Experimental Artifact: Compensatory Equalization of Treatments

Another variation of this theme was also originally posited by Cook and Campbell (1979) and named "compensatory equalization of treatments." In their words, "when the experimental treatment provides goods or services generally believed to be desirable, there may emerge administrative and constituency reluctance to tolerate the focused inequality that results" (p. 54). The authors use one of the most expensive, largest, and, unfortunately, poorest designed educational experiments (Follow Through, which was a "follow-through" of Head Start and part of the United States' ultimate defeat in its War on Poverty) to illustrate how supplying control sites with almost as many resources as their intervention counterparts doomed the effort to failure. There is no controlled demonstration, however, that this particular artifact was responsible for the accruing negative results for this "experiment" since it contained a plethora of additional design flaws; hence this construct (only barely distinguishable from "compensatory rivalry") is not listed as a separate experimental artifact here.

Let's now discuss the two randomized designs which, between them, help to prevent the occurrence of one or more of the previous three artifacts. It should be noted that these two designs can be employed with all of the randomized strategies presented to this point (i.e., designs employing pretests, covariates, or neither) as well as with the additional options presented in later chapters.

THE RANDOMIZED CLUSTER (GROUP) DESIGNS

This strategy, which involves the random assignment of clusters or groups of participants to conditions rather than the participants themselves, constitutes the most effective method known of preventing *treatment diffusion* in situations in which experimental participants routinely interact. To the extent that the randomized clusters are geographically separated, resentful demoralization and compensatory rivalry are also less likely to occur.

When participants are in close contact (especially within the same institution) or receive the same clinical care, the randomization of individual participants to experimental conditions can be contraindicated. Since randomization is always optimal, however, groups or clusters of individuals can be randomly assigned to receive or not receive the intervention without risking treatment diffusion. (Examples of such clusters include dyads [e.g., husbands and wives], physician practices [where clients can interact in the waiting room], clinics [in which considerable communication exists among participants], classrooms, schools, or even entire communities.) Behavioral, public health, and educational interventions in which blinding is not possible can be particularly vulnerable to treatment diffusion (as well as the somewhat less likely threats of compensatory equalization, compensatory rivalry, or resentful demoralization).

The success of this design in preventing the selection artifact (which is the primary advantage of randomization) depends to a large extent on the number of groups (or clusters) randomized. From that perspective the design itself resides on an acceptability continuum between a nonrandomized and a randomized experiment, depending on the number of clusters randomized. The number actually necessary to provide the randomization process a reasonable chance of ensuring pre-intervention equivalence depends on several variables which will be discussed in more detail in Chapter Nine. (As mentioned previously, and taken to an absurd level, if only two clusters [e.g., schools or treatment facilities] are employed, randomization is irrelevant because pre-intervention differences between groups will still be present and produce either false positive or false negative results.)

The primary disadvantage of randomized cluster designs, aside from the potential of initial nonequivalence of the clusters, resides in the possibility that the participants *within* those clusters are more homogeneous than participants *between* clusters (i.e., are more similar in their reactions to the experimental conditions or on the outcome variable within than between groups). The seriousness of this threat therefore depends on the *degree* of homogeneity and heterogeneity within and between clusters, as well as on which of three statistical procedures are used to analyze the individual participant outcome values.

As an example, suppose 40 clusters, each composed of 20 participants, were randomly assigned to receive either an intervention or a comparison—thereby resulting in two groups comprised of 20 clusters and 400 individuals each. (While it is advantageous to assign the same number of clusters to experimental conditions, it is not necessary to have the same number of participants present in each cluster.) Theoretically, three approaches exist for analyzing the resulting data.

> *Strategy #1: Individual outcomes are analyzed in the same manner as is done in a randomized pretest-posttest (or posttest-only) control group design.* In other words, the contrast of interest would consist of the 400 individual intervention outcome values vs. the 400 control group outcomes. This approach is inappropriate, however, because (a) the participants within groups are not independent and (b) it was clusters (not individuals) that were randomly assigned. Employing this strategy therefore results in an increase in the probability of finding spurious, false positive results and pretty much precludes the experiment from being published in a high-impact journal.
>
> *Strategy #2: Individual outcomes are not employed as the unit of analysis at all; instead, mean cluster outcome values constitute the unit of analysis.* Here the contrast of interest would be the 20 mean outcome values for intervention clusters vs. the corresponding 20 mean outcome values for the control clusters. Most methodologists would also eschew this strategy because it ignores individual participant differences (or similarities) within clusters. An argument could be made, however, that this analysis is not inappropriate per se because it employs the proper unit of analysis and in effect changes the experimental strategy from a cluster randomization design to a randomized pretest-posttest (or posttest-only) comparison group design. (This argument is difficult to refute if the clusters randomized were naturally occurring entities [e.g., classroom or treatment facilities] and the investigator was primarily interested in generalizing the intervention effect to such entities rather than individuals per se.) The primary disadvantages of this strategy are that (a) it generally results in slightly less power than the third, preferred strategy (hence increases the probability of false negative results) and (b) it will be frowned upon by most modern peer reviewers who favor a hierarchical approach which takes into consideration all of the sources of variation.
>
> *Strategy #3: Individual outcomes are analyzed but in a hierarchical data analytic approach in which all systematic sources of variation are taken into account, including individual*

participant outcome differences (both within and between) clusters. This is the preferred method of dealing with cluster randomization. Here the data are conceptualized as residing on different levels. On one level of the hierarchy are the intervention and control groups. Within each of these two groups reside the clusters, which in this case were randomly assigned but are *nested* within groups. (In other words, the intervention group has 20 completely unique clusters nested within it, as does the control group.) Next, within each cluster reside the 20 participants who are assumed to be more similar to one another than they are to participants within any other cluster. Whether or not this is actually the case is assessed by what is termed the intra-cluster correlation coefficient (or ICC). (The higher the ICC [and the fewer clusters randomized], the larger the sample size requirement [with the number of clusters employed assuming more importance than the number of participants within them, although both parameters are important].)

Besides the possibility of a high ICC (which appears to be relatively rare for many outcome variables and/or settings), a secondary disadvantage of cluster randomization involves the possibility of higher attrition for clustered studies, since participants can be lost both within clusters and, even worse, entire clusters can drop out of the study (e.g., should administrative personnel change or develop different priorities). A third disadvantage of the strategy involves the requisite statistical analysis of clustered data, which requires a certain degree of statistical sophistication (although this should not be a determining factor in the choice of an experimental strategy, as the necessary statistical expertise [or specialized software] is normally available in most universities and research institutions).

Advantages of the design, in addition to the fact that there are occasions when no viable option exists, include the possibility that the protocol may be easier to administer to groups of participants geographically clustered together than to individual participants. Otherwise the conduct of these experiments is similar to conventionally randomized trials, although their reporting should include additional details on the rationale for the design, the ICC, and its effect on the sample size employed and the analysis. An extension of the CONSORT (Consolidated Standards of Reporting Trials) statement (Schulz, Altman, Moher, for the CONSORT Group, 2010) to randomized cluster trials is now available for guidance in this respect (Campbell, Elbourne, Altman, for the CONSORT Group, 2004).

As with all the designs discussed here, adaptations and extensions on the basic cluster randomization architectural form exist. (For example, covariates, assessed at either the individual participant or clustered levels, increase both the power and the precision of the design via the statistical control of between cluster differences.) Another rather creative example of a large-scale experiment occurred in India, where practical and administrative constraints precluded the random assignment of individuals (Banerjee, Cole, Cuflo, & Linden., 2007). In this case, however, instead of randomly assigning schools to intervention vs. control groups, the investigators randomly assigned schools to one of two blocks. In Block 1 all the third-grade students would receive the intervention while the fourth-grade students would receive the control. The opposite, of course, would occur for the second block. This permitted the third graders in Block 2 to serve as the control for their third-grade intervention counterparts in Block 1 and the fourth graders in Block 1 to serve as the control for the fourth-grade intervention in Block 2. Although the experiment remained a randomized cluster design and sites were still confounded with conditions, the two grade-level comparisons additionally served as a quasi-replication of one another.

RANDOMIZED DELAYED-INTERVENTION DESIGNS

All of the randomized designs discussed to this point (including the randomization of clusters of participants) *potentially* suffer from resentful demoralization (Artifact #15) involving a group (or groups) perceived to be less attractive than others. Disappointment or demoralization is problematic, however, only if it (a) affects performance on the outcome variable (which is more likely for reactive or self-reported than more objective outcomes), (b) differentially increases attrition in the affected group(s), (c) decreases compliance with the protocol, and/or (d) makes recruitment more challenging.

A number of strategies have been offered for preventing this problem (e.g., increasing the attractiveness of all experimental conditions, paying participants, using placebo controls) and the artifact itself is often neither prevalent nor virulent. However, when (a) investigators consider participant disappointment to be potentially problematic in any given situation, (b) administrators consider it to be politically undesirable to deny some of their clients a potential treatment, and/or (c) denial of treatment is unethical, it is often possible to provide participants randomly assigned to the control group the opportunity to receive the intervention (or a truncated version thereof) after the experiment has been completed. (The individuals can even be informed that they may well receive an improved intervention based on the lessons learned the first time through the trial.)

Diagrammatically, this option added to the randomized pretest-posttest design might look like that depicted in Figure 6.9.

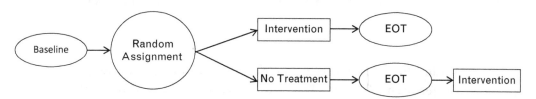

FIGURE 6.9: Randomized Delayed Intervention.

From the perspective of the group contrasts and the hypothesis test, this experiment effectively ends at the EOT assessment and is therefore architecturally identical to the original randomized pretest-posttest design. As mentioned previously, the video-gaming experiment presented earlier (Weis & Cerankosky, 2010) is one of many architectural variations of this design (in this case employing covariates rather than pretests for some of the outcomes).

A wrinkle sometimes added to the delayed intervention option presented in Figure 6.9 involves administering a second EOT assessment to the comparison participants who opt to receive the delayed intervention. In theory, this would constitute an additional single-group pretest-posttest replication of the original randomized design. In practice, however, this is seldom done, because (a) the single-group design is so much weaker methodologically that it adds little of scientific value, and (b) the results are further weakened by the number of comparison group participants who normally turn down the opportunity to continue past the original EOT assessment.

Either strategy has two major disadvantages, however, one obvious and one perhaps not so obvious.

First there is the increased time, effort, and expense involved in repeating the intervention for half of the participants. (Many, perhaps most members of the control/comparison group will not avail themselves of this opportunity, but it must be offered to anyone who desires it.) The investigator does have the option of offering a less intensive dose of the intervention following the EOT assessment. (This latter option was employed in the Haake et al. [2007] acupuncture example; only six sessions [down from the 10 administered to the intervention group] were offered to the control group.)

Second, there are settings and situations in which this approach is not possible. Many trials, for example, employ multiple follow-up sessions (sometimes extending to 6 months or longer following the EOT assessment) to judge the degree of decay that normally occurs following withdraw of the intervention. In a study such as this the control group can be offered the option of receiving the intervention only after the final follow-up session, which would reduce its value as an incentive. Similarly, some educational interventions are implemented for a full school year, hence making a delayed intervention impractical.

The following study illustrates the implementation of a psychological intervention using this design accompanied by a wait-list control. The online setting is especially well suited for this design as it avoids the inconvenience (for both participants and investigators) of scheduling the second implementation of the intervention.

A PSYCHOLOGICAL EXAMPLE OF A DELAYED INTERVENTION DESIGN ADMINISTERED ONLINE

Guided Internet-Delivered Cognitive Behavior Therapy for Generalized Anxiety Disorder: A Randomized Controlled Trial (2011)

Bjoörn Paxling, Jonas Almlöv, Mats Dahlin, et al.

This example illustrates the use of both a delayed intervention design and the increasing use of Internet-based experiments for which delayed interventions are especially appropriate, since investigators are not required to physically convene the second group. Eighty-nine participants were screened online, administered a structured psychiatric interview, and randomized to receive an 8-week program of text-based self-help relaxation steps (supplemented by the availability of a therapist to provide written feedback and to guide the participant through the program) or a wait-list control. (The wait-list control received the same intervention 8 weeks later.) The primary outcome variable was the Penn State Worry Questionnaire, accompanied by other anxiety, depression, and quality-of-life secondary indicators.

Statistically significant treatment effects were observed for all primary and secondary outcomes despite participants completing only 4.8 of the 8 sessions. One and three-year follow-up assessments were also performed, with the treatment gains apparently being maintained over time. Of course, no control comparisons for these follow-up assessments were available since the wait-list control had received the intervention prior to this. (As mentioned, the unavailability of a control group for follow-up comparisons is a drawback of the delayed intervention design.) The authors also considered the lack of an active control or placebo condition as a likely inflationary factor (arguing "it is known that wait-list controls tend to inflate effect sizes our results may be an overestimation.") The use of potentially reactive questionnaires, common in psychological research, is also problematic.

TWO ADDITIONAL QUASI-EXPERIMENTAL DESIGNS

So far in this chapter, five perfectly acceptable single-factor randomized designs have been presented, along with one contrasting quasi-experimental strategy (the nonrandomized pretest-posttest control group design). This latter design was deemed unacceptable primarily because of its failure to prevent the selection artifact.

In truth, we have barely scratched the surface of the experimental architectures that have been proposed and used over the past half-century. Many of these are quite creative (e.g., the regression discontinuity design discussed in Chapter Twelve), although most employ retrospective data which place them outside of our purview. For those interested in a more complete discussion of these nonrandomized approaches, Shadish, Cook, and Campbell's *Quasi-Experimentation: Design & Analysis Issues for Field Settings* (2002) is highly recommended.

This chapter will conclude with a brief discussion of two designs which, like the nonrandomized pretest-posttest control group design, serve to underline the epistemological basis of randomized experimentation in general. One of these models involves a comparison of both retrospective and prospective groups, while the other attempts to avoid one of the most troubling components of experiments involving human participants: the lack of choice regarding the intervention people receive. These approaches are sometimes categorized as "separate cohort" and "patient preference" designs, respectively.

The separate-cohort design: This strategy is feasible in situations (e.g., public schools, university courses, hospitals) in which similar treatments are delivered to cyclical cohorts of *presumably* equivalent groups for similar time intervals. The separate-cohort design often employs a prospective implementation of the intervention and compares those outcomes to a retrospective control—hence the hybrid designation.

The major disadvantage of the approach involves the necessity of assuming that the cohorts are equivalent (or nearly so) and that the institutional treatment of clients is static rather than dynamic. Since most institutions collect relatively extensive background data on their clients, however, the equivalence of cohorts can at least be grossly estimated and partially corrected via regression procedures. Unfortunately, the possibility that the cohorts receive different institutional treatments related to the outcome variable cannot be statistically controlled and hence any differences that do occur can only be described qualitatively. At the very least, however, the use of temporally separated cohorts is capable of providing reasonable preliminary data (or serving as a pilot study) for a randomized prospective experiment.

As a hypothetical example of such a study, our previously imagined psychology professor could have opted for this quasi-experimental option to evaluate the effectiveness of the new text-book under consideration in lieu of the intact-group design described (which, it will be recalled, involved a section concurrently taught by her colleague). To qualify as a separate-cohort design, she would have needed to extend the length of her study to two semesters, although a more common option would entail employing a previous section she had taught using the old textbook (i.e., a retrospective comparison group) and contrasted it with a prospective introduction of the intervention (i.e., the new textbook).

Of course, the same final examination (or at least a core of common items) would need to be used in the prospective class, as the previous ones and no pretest would be available for the retrospective option, but a common covariate could probably be identified (e.g., students' GPAs or SAT scores from the records office) to help control for initial cohort differences. This strategy, like all cohort designs, suffers from the possibility of selection (i.e., the cohorts could have differed in some unknown way). Even more problematic would be the possibility that our investigator-instructor (perhaps unconsciously) might "try harder" prospectively (than she did retrospectively) to gear her instruction to the content of the textbook or the final examination. And while this confound could be avoided by using a different instructor less emotionally attached to the study to teach the intervention (prospective) section, this option would have introduced yet another confound (i.e., instructor differences).

> *Bottom-line assessment:* This design has little to recommend it because of the possibility of selection and the fact that time is confounded with the experimental conditions. (Institutional policies could have changed or confounding extraneous events could have occurred during the different time intervals.)

Zelen's conditional consent (or patient preference) design involves a creative attempt to employ randomization while reserving the participants' right to choose their own group assignment. While the advantages of randomization are hopefully obvious by now, critics cite a number of disadvantages of the process, such as:

1. A reluctance of participants to volunteer for randomized trials because of the possibility of not being assigned to a preferred treatment,
2. Participants' increased propensity to drop out of the trial or to not comply with the study protocol because of resentment (or boredom or lack of novelty) resulting from not being assigned to a preferred treatment,
3. Ethical issues accompanying not providing participants with their preferred treatment, and
4. The tenuous nature of generalizing results produced under controlled (often artificial) conditions to veridical situations.

While there is little evidence supporting any of these objections (with the exception perhaps of attrition from an obvious no-treatment or attention control), lack of evidence does not constitute proof of a phenomenon's nonexistence. In any event, Marvin Zelen (1979, 1990), a statistician, originally proposed the following procedure for experiments contrasting a new intervention with the best standard treatment:

1. *Prior to informed consent*, participants are randomized via standard methods to receive either the intervention or the standard treatment. This, of course, is extremely unusual but is not unethical in the present author's opinion because when it occurs nothing has been done to participants, nor have they been contacted in any way. (Anyone aspiring to employ this design would be wise to describe its rationale carefully in their IRB proposal, however, since randomization prior to informed consent will raise multiple red flags among many reviewers.)

2. Participants assigned to the standard-treatment condition receive whatever treatment the institution normally provides and are not given the option of receiving the intervention, although they are not denied access to other options normally available to patients or clients. No informed consent is obtained from these participants, although if some additional data must be collected they would need to be consented. (Note that any design can be altered and mixed and matched with any other design at the discretion of the investigator [pending approval of the proposal of course], although the pros and cons of such alternations should be *very* carefully weighed.)

3. Participants who have been randomly assigned to the intervention group are contacted, asked for informed consent, and may receive the new intervention if they choose. If they decline, they are by default given the standard treatment.

The final contrast (the outcome usually being dichotomous but almost always available from institutional records—otherwise the design loses many of its advantages) then becomes between everyone assigned to the standard treatment control and *everyone* assigned to the new intervention whether they have opted to receive it or not. (This becomes, in a sense, a version of an intent-to-treat analysis).

Zelen (1979) concedes that this comparison results in a loss of statistical power (emanating from the decreased experimental effect size since a certain proportion of the intervention outcomes actually contain embedded standard treatment values). He suggests, however, that "any loss to statistical efficiency can be overcome by increased numbers."

This argument has a degree of validity, although the use of the design is accompanied by special disadvantages not present in conventional experiments (namely the participants who were randomly assigned to standard care during the first wave met the definition of random assignment; everyone else in effect chose their group assignment). The design, therefore, belongs to a hybrid category residing somewhere on the continuum between a true and a quasi-experimental designation.

Advantages of the strategy include the fact that some patients are free to choose their treatment and the experiment is not peopled with volunteers, since theoretically half of the sample do not know they are in a trial and nothing is required of the other half other than choosing their treatment. (Said another way, a randomly selected group of participants are given their choice of treatments, but no one formally volunteered to participate in a study such as this.) Of course, the fact that members of the intervention group are given a treatment option— while their control counterparts are not—potentially introduces an experimental confound of unknown magnitude. (Presumably, the outcomes of participants who chose standard treatment could be contrasted to those who were originally randomly assigned to receive it without their consent.) Also, many clinicians with ethical objections to traditional randomized clinical trials would undoubtedly prefer this design, since clients are not knowingly deprived of a preferred intervention. *Said another way, the very act of randomization may exert a causal effect in and of itself—thereby limiting the generalizability of all randomized trials.*

The design also has some major disadvantages, however, which undoubtedly explain its lack of acceptance. These include the following:

1. The purpose of a randomized trial is not simply to ascertain whether an intervention is significantly superior to its comparison group, but also to provide an estimate of the magnitude of this effect. Zelen's design will not provide an accurate estimate of the intervention's true effect because it is tainted with standard-care results. (Post hoc analyses can contrast intervention vs. standard-care subgroups within the second patient preference group, but there is no guarantee that the sample size will be sufficient to produce definitive results.) If the intervention is more efficacious than standard care, this design will underestimate the actual effect. If the intervention is actually harmful (i.e., produces more adverse events than standard care), these too will be underestimated (and perhaps masked).

2. While on one level Zelen's design initially fits the usual definition of random assignment (i.e., providing each individual with an equal chance of being assigned to treatment groups), group membership is no longer random once the intervention group is given the option to substitute standard care for their initial assignment, at least to the extent that participants exercise this option. Of course, following the initial random assignment, participants in *both* groups could be allowed to change treatments (sometimes referred to as a double-consent design), but if this occurs with any frequency, the purpose of random assignment is still subverted because initial equivalence between groups can no longer be assumed.

3. Participants in the intervention group, especially those who agree to receive the new treatment, are potentially exposed to more of a placebo effect that those not provided this opportunity. (The placebo effect is controlled if standard-care participants are also allowed to switch groups as well.)

4. Perhaps most critically of all, if participants are not consented, no additional information can be obtained on them that is not routinely collected as part of their clinical care. This is extremely unusual in experimentation and very few investigators would find this acceptable.

While in general the disadvantages of this particular design outweigh its advantages, there may be specialized applications for its use. Torgerson and Rolan (1998), for example, suggest that interventions such as those assessing the effectiveness of screening tests might employ the approach to avoid sensitizing unscreened individuals to seek available screening or preventive treatment, citing the first author's use of this approach in a randomized bone density screening trial (Torgerson, Thomas, Campbell, & Reid, 1997).

It should also be noted that there are other types of participant preference designs. Marcus, Stuart, Wang et al. (2012), for example, discuss the logic underlying what is referred to as a doubly randomized preference trial in which participants are first randomly assigned to either a randomized or a treatment preference arm. Then, those assigned to the randomized arm are randomized once again to experimental conditions. (Note that, like Zelen's design, the control here is usually standard care, since patient preference for no treatment makes little sense.) Those that have been assigned to the treatment preference arm are given a choice regarding which treatment they wish to receive, producing the configuration presented in Figure 6.10 (assuming two experimental conditions).

FIGURE 6.10: Doubly Randomized Preference Design.

	Intervention	Control/Alternative Intervention
Participants Randomized	a	b
Participants Given Treatment of Choice	c	d

The design depicted in Figure 6.10 is, like Zelen's version, a hybrid between a randomized and quasi-experimental design and has seldom been used prospectively. (An exception is an experiment conducted by Shadish, Clark, and Steiner [2008] involving student preferences for receiving either mathematics or vocabulary training.) The design would provide some evidence of generalizability regarding the intervention vs. control contrast. Specifically, it might answer the question of whether an intervention effect (positive or negative) emanating from a randomized trial would generalize to a more veridical practice setting where participants choose their own treatments (i.e., was $(a - b) \approx (c - d)$?). Since generalizability is determined by considerably more than whether or not participants were given their treatment of choice, this particular question would not seem to have a great deal of practical importance (i.e., if $(a - b)$ did differ from $(c - d)$, the extent of generalization to a nonexperimental setting still would not be known)—which, along with the obscurity of the design, most likely accounts for its lack of use.

With the introduction of these designs (especially the five randomized ones), we are now ready to consider a design genre capable of increasing both the amount of information and the explanatory power of an experiment. All of the single-factor designs introduced in this chapter are applicable to what are referred to as factorial designs, a cursory explanation of which has already been provided via our hypothetical of Dr. Lind's single-factor scurvy trial.

SUMMARY

Five randomized designs were introduced in this chapter. Four involve the conventional randomization of participants to conditions (the randomized pretest-posttest control group, randomized posttest-only control group, randomized covariate-posttest control group, and delayed treatment designs) and one involves the random assignment of clusters of individuals (the randomized cluster design). For expository purposes, two of the more commonly employed quasi-experimental designs (the nonrandomized pretest-posttest and the separate-cohort designs) were contrasted with their counterparts to illustrate the basic unacceptability of the latter. A hybrid, but seldom employed, experimental genre (patient preference designs) was also discussed briefly.

Although the appropriateness of a design is dependent on the specific intervention, outcome variable, sample size, control/comparison group characteristics, and research hypothesis employed, all the designs involving randomization of participants presented are effective in preventing selection (one of the most virulent of experimental artifacts), assuming sufficient numbers of participants and all facilitate the reduction of certain experimental confounds. The success of the randomized cluster design in preventing selection depends in large part on the number of clusters employed, with its primary utility residing in the avoidance of the treatment diffusion artifact. (Some nonrandom assignment strategies are superior to others, but basically none qualify as optimal research practice.)

In addition, the four additional experimental artifacts unique to multiple-group studies were introduced along with another experimental principle relevant to the first one:

Experimental Artifact #13: **Other experimental confounds**: *any factor or condition (other than planned differences) unique to one experimental group but not the other(s).* The prefixed adjective "other" acknowledges the fact that artifacts such as selection, natural history, the placebo effect, and so forth are also examples of experimental confounds. Some confounds are avoided in randomized designs, but most must be anticipated and controlled by procedural strategies such as counterbalancing—leading to our growing list of experimental principles:

Principle #17: Prior to conducting an experiment, always (a) identify all potential confounds, (b) eliminate those which are plausibly related to the study outcome by standardizing and/or counterbalancing procedures across experimental conditions to the maximum extent possible, and (c) monitor the effects of those confounds that cannot be eliminated or counterbalanced.

Experimental Artifact #14. **Treatment defusion**, defined as *the unplanned leakage of the intervention (or elements thereof) to other comparison groups, thereby eroding the designed procedural difference between conditions.* This artifact can be prevented by (a) randomly assigning clusters of participants (e.g., classrooms) in close proximity to one another, (b) appealing to participants not to discuss the experiment with others until its completion, (c) avoiding communicating the experimental purposes or hypotheses to participants, (d) keeping the experimental interval as brief as scientifically feasible, and (e) avoiding self-reported and overly reactive interventions.

Experimental Artifact #15. **Resentful demoralization**, defined as *a depression occurring in control/comparison respondents' outcome values due to their feeling that they are receiving a less desirable treatment than their intervention counterparts.* Its greatest threat resides in its potential for increased attrition among control participants (i.e., differential attrition), although resentment could conceivably negatively affect self-reported outcomes. It is perhaps best controlled by concealing experimental purposes and group assignment. It can possibly be mitigated by making the comparison group as attractive as possible. Of the randomized designs presented, the delayed intervention and (possibly) the randomized cluster designs provide the greatest protection against its effects, although some outcome variables are immune to this artifact. It is, however, not normally a particularly significant threat to the validity of most experimental inferences.

Experimental Artifact #16. **Compensatory rivalry**, defined as *an elevation in outcome scores caused by participants' knowledge that they have been assigned to receive a less desirable experimental condition, resulting in their (or their service providers') compensatory behaviors.* There is little, if any, controlled evidence that this artifact actually exists, although if it is considered to be a possible threat in certain specific clinical situations, it is good experimental practice to blind patients and service providers (depending on the presumed source of the effect) whenever feasible. It is, however, not a particularly credible artifact in most instances, and its likelihood can be further reduced by using a delayed intervention design.

REFERENCES

Austin, P.C. (2008). A critical appraisal of propensity score matching in the medical literature from 1996 to 2003. *Statistics in Medicine, 27*, 2037–49.

Baron, R.M., & Kenny, D.A. (1986). The moderator–mediator distinction in social psychological research: Conceptual, strategic, and statistical considerations. *Journal of Personality and Social Psychology, 51*, 1173–82.

Banerjee, A.V., Cole, S., Duflo, E., & Linden, L. (2007). Remedying education: Evidence from two randomized experiments in India. *Quarterly Journal of Economics, 122*, 1235–64.

Campbell, M.K., Elbourne, D.R., Altman, D.G., for CONSORT Group. (2004). CONSORT statement: Extension to cluster randomized trials. *British Medical Journal, 328*, 702–8.

Cook, T.D., & Campbell, M.K. (1979). *Quasi-experimentation: Design & analysis issues for field settings.* Boston: Houghton Mifflin.

D'Agostino, R.B., Jr. (1998), Propensity score methods for bias reduction in the comparison of a treatment to a non-randomized control group. *Statistics in Medicine, 17*, 2265–81.

Haake, M., Muller, H.H., Schade-Brittinger, C., et al. (2007). German Acupuncture Trials (GERAC) for chronic low back pain: Randomized, multicenter, blinded, parallel group trail with 3 groups. *Archives of Internal Medicine. 167*, 1892–8.

MacKinnon, D.P., & Fairchild, A.J. (2009). Current directions in mediation analysis. *Current Directions in Psychological Science, 18*, 16–20.

Marcus, S.M., Stuart, E.A., Wang, P., et al. (2012). Estimating the causal effect of randomized versus treatment preference in a doubly randomized preference trial. *Psychological Methods, 17*, 244–54.

Paxling, B., Almlöv, J., Dahlin, M., et al. (2011). Guided Internet-delivered cognitive behavior therapy for generalized anxiety disorder: A randomized controlled trial. *Cognitive Behaviour Therapy, 40*, 159–73.

Rosenbaum, P.R., & Rubin, D.B. (1983). The central role of the propensity score in observational studies for causal effects. *Biometrika, 70*, 41–55.

Schulz, K.F., Altman, D.G., Moher, D., for the CONSORT Group. (2010). CONSORT 2010 Statement: updated guidelines for reporting parallel group randomized trials. *British Medical Journal, 340*, c332.

Shadish, W.R., Cook, T.D., & Campbell, D.T. (2002). *Experimental and quasi-experimental designs for generalized causal inference.* Boston, MA: Houghton Mifflin.

Shadish, W.R., Clark, M.H., & Steiner, P.M. (2008). Can nonrandomized experiments yield accurate answers? A randomized experiment comparing random and nonrandom assignments. *Journal of the American Statistical Association, 103*, 1334–43.

Torgerson, D.J., & Roland, M. (1998). Understanding controlled trials: What is Zelen's design? *British Medical Journal, 316*, 606.

Torgerson, D.J., Thomas, R.E., Campbell, M.K., & Reid, D.M. (1997). Randomized trial of osteoporosis screening: HRT uptake and quality of life results. *Archives of Internal Medicine, 157*, 2121–5.

Vohs, K.D., & Schooler, J.W. (2008). The value of believing in free will: Encouraging a belief in determinism increases cheating. *Psychological Science, 19*, 49–54.

Weis, R., & Cerankosky, B.C. (2010). Effects of video-game ownership on young boys' academic and behavioral functioning: A randomized, controlled study. *Psychological Science, 21*, 463–70.

Zelen M. (1979). A new design for randomized clinical trials. *New England Journal of Medicine, 300*, 1242–5.

Zelen M. (1990). Randomized consent designs for clinical trials: An update. *Statistics in Medicine, 9*(6), 645–56.

FACTORIAL DESIGNS

T he distinction between a single-factor and two-factor design was touched on briefly in Chapter Six via a fanciful reconstruction of the 18th-century scurvy experiment. This chapter will expand on this important concept since the majority of experiments in most disciplines employ multifactorial designs of one sort or another.

2 × 2 FACTORIAL DESIGNS EMPLOYING TREATMENT AND ATTRIBUTE FACTORS

Let's begin by considering the simplest possible factorial design in which participants are randomly assigned to four groups representing two *factors*: (1) the experimental conditions possessing two levels (intervention vs. control groups) and (2) an attribute variable such as gender, which of course also has two levels (males and females). This particular experiment is labeled a between-subject design because different participants are represented in each of the four cells; it is labeled a 2 × 2 factorial design because it employs two independent variables or factors that may (a) independently influence the outcome variable or (b) interact with one another to differentially do so. To achieve this remarkable characteristic, participants are randomly assigned in such a design via a yoked procedure whereby each gender is randomly assigned separately to intervention and control groups, producing the perfectly *crossed* arrangement depicted in Figure 7.1. Of course, participants cannot be randomly assigned to male vs. female groups because gender is a human attribute, thus in this example there is only one manipulated factor (the intervention vs. the control conditions), and gender serves as a *blocking* variable within whose different levels (in this cases males vs. females) participants are randomly assigned.

For this reason, factorial designs employing one manipulated factor and one attribute-like factor are often called *randomized block designs*. These designs possess a subtle difference from factorial designs employing two (or more) *intervention* factors (i.e., factors or independent variables to which participants *can be* randomly assigned). These latter designs (which, among other things, can be used to ascertain if two intervention variables have an additive effect) will be discussed next, but for present purposes let's assume the presence of one manipulated factor and one attribute-like factor, as in Figure 7.1.

FIGURE 7.1: Example of a 2 × 2 Between-Subjects Randomized Block Design.

	Intervention	Control
Males	**Group 1:** males receiving intervention	**Group 2:** males receiving control
Females	**Group 3:** females receiving intervention	**Group 4:** females receiving control

Assigning participates: The design depicted in Figure 7.1 optimally requires a two-phase randomized assignment process in which participants of each gender would be randomly assigned separately to the intervention or the control conditions. To achieve maximum sensitivity, the same number of males and females should be recruited, but this is not an absolute requirement of a factorial design and might not be feasible if one of the levels of the attribute happened to be considerably rarer than the other (or harder to recruit).

If a large pool of eligible participants existed, the requisite number of each attribute level (which would be specified in the protocol) could be randomly selected, and then each gender could be randomly assigned separately to the two experimental conditions. If (as is often the case) subjects are run as they become available, the investigator could simply randomly assign participants of each gender to conditions separately as they present themselves.

For other attributes that are not evenly distributed, such as socioeconomic status, participants might need to be recruited from separate areas or institutions (e.g., schools) and randomly assigned separately. For an attribute variable such as a personality factor, participants would need to recruited, consented, and screened, with only qualifying (and consenting) individuals actually randomly assigned to the experimental groups.

Post hoc blocking, in which participants are recruited and randomly assigned to groups ignoring the attribute variable, is an option open to investigators when randomly assigning different levels of an attribute separately to conditions is not feasible. If the sample size is sufficiently large, random assignment will then usually result in *approximately* the same proportion of participants in each attribute level being assigned to each experimental condition. For an evenly distributed attribute such as gender, this would result in the four cells depicted in Figure 7.1 having similar numbers of participants in each cell. For a binary attribute with a 2:1 ratio in the participant population, however, approximately twice as many individuals of one type would wind up in one row of Figure 7.1 as the other, although the columns would have approximately equal *N*s. This would not be optimal statistically, but if the total sample size was sufficiently large it might be a reasonable option.

Another, probably more common, type of post hoc blocking occurs when the attribute is measured on a continuum and thus present to some degree in all participants. Investigators here often conduct the random assignment ignoring the attribute and then arbitrarily dichotomize (or otherwise divide) the participants' median value, resulting in "high" vs. "low" (or high, medium, and low) attribute groups, with almost identical *N*s in the factorial cells.

Post hoc blocking of either type most often occurs in secondary subgroup analyses, which should always be interpreted and reported as such (Principle #9). One of the two-phase a priori random assignment options discussed here is preferable for attributes considered important enough to be included in experiments' formal hypotheses for sensitivity purposes, but practical and scientific considerations may require a post hoc blocking procedure. The only incontrovertible rule here (as in most design decisions) is complete transparency with respect to *what was done and the reason it was done.*

Hypotheses emanating from a 2 (experimental conditions) × 2 (attribute) design: The data emanating from the study depicted in Figure 7.1 produce three hypothesis tests addressing the following three questions:

1. Ignoring any male and female differences on the outcome variable, did the intervention result in superior outcomes compared to the control?
2. Ignoring any intervention and control differences on the outcome variable, did one gender achieve superior outcomes as compared to the other?
3. Did one gender profit more from the intervention than the other?

In this study, the answer to question #2 would probably be of little scientific interest, the importance of question #3 might or might not be of interest, but certainly the answer to question #1 would be crucial.

Every two-factor, crossed experimental design produces some variant of these three questions, which are associated with three separate hypotheses, each of which is represented by its own p-value. All three questions are seldom of equal interest, and sometimes only one is of any substantive interest depending on the reasons for including the attribute variable. Such reasons are commonly one or more of the following:

1. Gender is known to be related to the outcome variable, in which case using it as a blocking variable and randomly assigning the intervention and the control groups to males and females separately will increase the precision and statistical power for the intervention vs. control contrast.
2. The intervention is expected to be differentially effective for one gender as compared to the other.
3. The investigator may not expect a differential intervention effect to occur, but theory may predict such an effect, or he or she may feel that the generality of the intervention effect might be enhanced by demonstrating the absence of such an aptitude × treatment interaction (assuming sufficient statistical power was available, as discussed in Chapter Nine).

So let's flesh out this study a bit by pretending that we had conducted an experiment designed to ascertain the effects of involving parents in ensuring their elementary school children's completion of homework assignments. We'll assume that the experiment lasted for 6 weeks, with the outcome variable consisting of the percentage of each day's assignment being completed (thus the final results would consist of the grand mean of assignments completed averaged over the 6-week period and consisting of a number between 0 and 100). Let's further pretend that we were interested both in (a) whether parents (regardless of the gender of their child) could have an effect on homework compliance and (b) whether their involvement would be more effective for one student gender than the other. Let's further assume that the reason we included the gender comparison was based on past research indicating that elementary school girls are usually more compliant with respect to homework completion than boys.

The intervention in this experiment operationally consisted of parents being (a) notified via e-mail each afternoon of the homework assigned that night, (b) asked to ensure that their children turned it in the next day, and (c) provided with online hints as to how to aid their children when needed. The control group consisted of students receiving the same homework assignments but involved no parental contact. The outcome variable was the percentage of homework completed by each student over the course of the experiment.

Let's further pretend that the results shown in Table 7.1 accrued.

Table 7.1: Hypothetical Results for the Parentally Supervised Homework Intervention.

	Intervention	Control	Total
Males	60%	40%	50% (60% + 40%)/2
Females	80%	60%	70% (80% + 60%)/2
Total	70% (80% + 60%)/2	50% (40% + 60%)/2	

Recalling the three research questions addressed by a factorial experiment such as this, the answer to the first two seems quite straightforward:

1. Overall, the intervention appeared to increase the amount of homework completed, irrespective of gender. This finding is represented by averaging the intervention results for males and females, doing the same thing for the control results, and comparing the percentages of assignments completed depicted at the bottom of each column (i.e., an overall 70% completion rate for the intervention as compared to only 50% for the control group).
2. Overall, female students were more likely to complete their homework than their male counterparts (also 70% vs. 50%, as depicted to the right of each row).

Note that the answer to both of these questions is ascertained by collapsing across groups. Gender is ignored for the first question, and the obviously crucial intervention vs. control contrast is ignored for the second. The third question, however, is of a completely different genre in the sense that it requires all of the available information in all four cells to answer the question (i.e., collapses nothing but analyzes the differences among four cells and is represented by what is termed an interactional effect).

In Table 7.1 this entails comparing the intervention's effect on males (60% − 40% = a 20% improvement in favor of the intervention) *versus* the intervention's effect for females (80% − 60%, also a 20% improvement). Thus, the answer to the third question is:

3. There was no difference between the intervention's effectiveness in increasing homework completion for males as compared to females.

Of course, we would need to examine the *p*-values associated with each question (or hypothesis) to ascertain whether or not these results were statistically significant, but hopefully this example illustrates the logic underlying a simple factorial experiment. The contrasts associated with the first two questions are often called *main effects*, because they are specific to only one of the independent variables (i.e., factors) while ignoring the other. The contrast associated with the third question is called an *interaction effect*, because it depends on the joint action of the factors (or independent variables).

Interactions are sometimes difficult for inexperienced investigators to interpret, although they can be scientifically more interesting than main effects. Even when the interactions' attendant hypotheses are not of primary interest, however, their interpretation precedes (and moderates) that of a hypothesized main effect. Said another way, the treatment (i.e., intervention vs. control) main effect in any factorial experiment is not interpretable without first examining any significant interaction effects between the treatment and any other factors.

To illustrate the explanatory potential of an interaction, let's look at the myriad possible results that can accrue from a two-factor statistical analysis. The results reflected in Table 7.1, in which both main effects were significantly significant but the interaction was not, is only one of the eight possible statistically significance/nonsignificance combinations emanating from a two-factor study:

	Possible Outcomes for p-values							
	(1)	(2)	(3)	(4)	(5)	(6)	(7)	(8)
Factor A: Intervention vs. Control	√	√	√	√	X	X	X	X
Factor B: Male vs. Female	√	√	X	X	X	X	√	√
AB: Interaction	√	X	√	X	X	√	X	√

√ = statistically significant; X = not significant.

The diversity of possible outcomes does not end here, however. While there are only two ways in which a *statistically significantly* two-group, two-level main effect can manifest itself (e.g., the intervention is superior or inferior to the control on the outcome), there are 10 ways that a significant 2×2 interaction effect can occur. In the homework trial, for example:

1. The control can be more effective than the intervention for males, but less effective than the intervention for females.
2. The intervention can be more effective than the control for males, but less effective than the control for females.
3. The intervention can be more effective than the control for both males and females, but proportionally more so for females.
4. The intervention can be more effective than the control for both males and females, but proportionally more so for males.
5. The control can be more effective than the intervention for both males and females, but proportionally more so for males.
6. The control can be more effective than the intervention for both males and females, but proportionally more so for females.
7. There is no difference between the intervention and the control for males, but the intervention is more effective than the control for females.
8. There is no difference between the intervention and the control for males, but the control is more effective than the intervention for females.
9. There is no difference between the intervention and the control for females, but the intervention is more effective than the control for males.
10. There is no difference between the intervention and the control for females, but the control is more effective than the intervention for males.

Given this diversity of possible statistically significant outcomes, 2 × 2 interactions are more difficult to interpret than main effects. One interpretative method was illustrated earlier (subtracting intervention vs. control effects for males and females separately and then comparing the two differences).

Alternately, graphing a statistically significant interaction can be more useful intuitively—both in interpreting the interaction and the two main effects that constitute it. To illustrate, let's begin with the hypothetical results presented in Table 7.1 (see Figure 7.2).

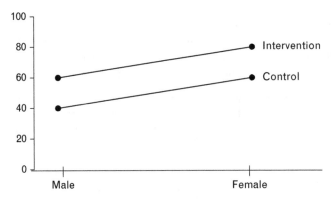

FIGURE 7.2: Both Main Effects Significant but No Interaction.

While the dichotomy on the horizontal axis can represent either factor, Figure 7.2 places the non-manipulated factor (gender) there and allows the lines to represent the manipulated intervention vs. control dichotomy. Here it is quite clear that the intervention group outperformed the control group overall for both genders (since the intervention line is consistently higher than the control's). The interaction effect, however, is represented by the relative *distance* between the intervention and control points for males and females. Since we already know from Table 7.1 that both of these distances are exactly the same (i.e., 20 percentage points), the two lines are perfectly parallel and there is no interaction between the two factors. This indicates, therefore, that the interpretation of neither main effect need be tempered (moderated), based on the presence of an interaction.

Since we're dealing with a hypothetical study here, let's illustrate how a simple line graph (a) can facilitate the visualization of a statistically significant interaction and (b) can force the investigator to reinterpret the existence *or* nonexistence of a statistically significant main effect. First, let's look at the seventh possibility for a statistically significant interaction listed earlier ("no difference between the intervention and the control for males, but the intervention is more effective than the control for females"). Numerically, one scenario for such results might be represented in Table 7.2, graphed in Figure 7.3.

Table 7.2: Hypothetical Example of Interaction Effect in the Absence of Main Effects.

	Intervention	Control	Total
Males	50%	50%	50% (50% + 50%)/2
Females	80%	50%	65% (80% + 50%)/2
Total	65% (50% + 80%)/2	50% (50% + 50%)/2	

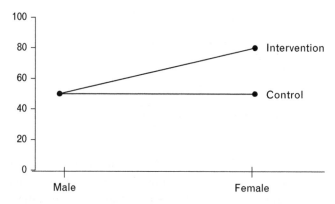

FIGURE 7.3: Significant Interaction (Intervention Effective for Females Only).

Here the two lines obviously are not parallel. Depending on the sample size used and the amount of within-group variability observed (neither of which can be ascertained via a line graph such as this), the two main effects might or might not be statistically significant. In either case, examination of the two lines in Figure 7.3 would indicate that this treatment × gender interaction is important here from a scientific perspective (assuming the p-value representing it was <.05). Specifically, the intervention was effective only for females, not males. (Presumably, since the investigator went to the trouble of randomly assigning males and females separately to the intervention and control groups, he or she would have hypothesized the direction of this effect a priori—which would make it more credible, especially if there was a theoretically plausible reason why the intervention *should* be more effective for female than males.)

Assuming that both the gender and treatment main effects were determined to be statistically significant, this graph illustrates the importance of using a statistically significant interaction to interpret such main effects. If the interaction had been ignored, we would have simply computed the intervention vs. control means collapsed across gender and declared victory. (An examination of Table 7.2 shows that the main effect means for the experimental conditions would be 65% for the intervention group [i.e., (50 + 80)/2] and 50% for the control.)

However, Figure 7.3 illustrates that the intervention was completely ineffective for males and quite effective for females. While space doesn't permit the graphing of examples for all 10 scenarios for a statistically significant 2 × 2 interaction, the most dramatic (and rarest) interactional effect (Scenarios 1 and 2) constitutes the clearest illustration of why the interpretation of interactions must precede and moderate the interpretation of the constituent main effects.

Table 7.3 presents one possibility for Scenario 1 in which neither the treatment nor the gender main effects would be statistically significant but the interaction is. (In other words, *overall* parental involvement was completely ineffectual in improving homework completion [the causal inference] and males did not differ from females on the outcome [the correlational or non-causal inference].)

Table 7.3: Hypothetical Example of Interaction Effect in the Absence of Main Effects.

	Intervention	Control	Total
Males	40%	80%	60% (40% + 80%)/2
Females	80%	40%	60% (80% + 40%)/2
Total	60% (40% + 80%)/2	60% (80% + 40%)/2	

A first glance at the row and column marginal (total) would lead to an understandable conclusion that neither treatment nor gender had any effect on homework completion. When the interaction is graphed (Figure 7.4), however, an entirely different conclusion becomes apparent (as would examination of the computer output, which would indicate a statistically significant p-value associated with the interaction). Now the two lines associated with the 2×2 interaction actually cross one another (hence are as far from being parallel as possible).

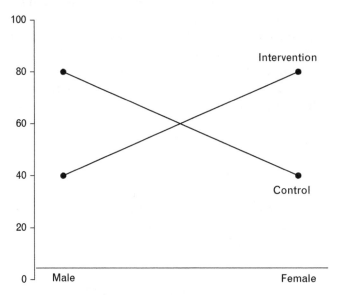

FIGURE 7.4: A Rare Orthogonal Aptitude × Treatment Interaction.

Correspondingly, the interpretation changes (pending inferential analysis) radically. It appears that the intervention was apparently effective for females and actually *harmful* for males:

Males Receiving Intervention minus Control Males = 40% − 80% = −40% Completion Rate

Females Receiving Intervention minus Control Females = 80% − 40% = +40% Completion Rate

Admittedly, results such as these almost never occur (certainly not in education), but hopefully these hypothetical data help to illustrate the logic behind interpreting interaction effects in simple factorial designs.

2 × 2 FACTORIAL DESIGNS EMPLOYING TWO SEPARATE INTERVENTIONS

Experiments often contrast more than one intervention. When each intervention is associated with different levels, doses, controls, or combinations with other interventions, a factorial design normally results. In this section, as with the combining of an attribute with a treatment factor, we will consider the simplest possible 2 × 2 factorial design in which two separate interventions are employed.

Let's simply call these Intervention A and Intervention B. One possibility would be to randomly assign participants to receive one of the two interventions and see which was more effective with respect to the outcome variable of interest. This would result in a single-factor design and would produce one of three somewhat equivocal results:

1. A > B, in which case we wouldn't know whether B was effective, ineffective, or harmful (in which case A might not be effective but simply not [or less] harmful),
2. B > A, in which case we wouldn't know whether A was effective, ineffective, or harmful (in which case B might not be effective but simply not [or less] harmful), or
3. A = B, in which case we wouldn't know whether either A *and* B were effective, ineffective, or harmful.

We could improve matters by adding a control group, thereby producing a three-group, single-factor design. This would produce all three of these outcomes and settle the issue of harm vs. no harm. However, while superior, this design leaves a potentially important question unanswered:

What would the effect on the outcome be if both A and B were administered together?

Adding a fourth group (A + B) nicely answers that question and clarifies all of the previously raised questions, producing the four-group design in Table 7.4 to which we'll hypothetically randomly assign 25 participants to each group.

Table 7.4 A Randomized Four-Group, Single-Factor Design

Intervention A Only ($N = 25$)	Intervention B Only ($N = 25$)	Both Treatment A + B ($N = 25$)	Neither A nor B (Control) ($N = 25$)

However, a single-factor experiment isn't the only or most efficient way to conceptualize this particular design. In comparison with the 2 × 2 randomized block design just discussed (which of course also has four groups), this one has an apparent disadvantage: It has no main effects that allow cells to be combined and thereby effectively double the sample size for these effects. To illustrate, let's review what our previous 2 (treatments) × 2 (gender) randomized block design would have looked like if we had randomly assigned 25 participants to each of its four groups (see Table 7.5).

Table 7.5: Effective Sample Size for a 2 (Gender) × 2 (Treatments) Randomized Block Design ($N = 100$).

		[B] Treatments		
		[B1] Intervention	[B2] Control	Main Effect (Males vs. Females)
Gender [A]	[A1] Males	[A1B1] $N = 25$	[A1B2] $N = 25$	$N = 50$
	[A2] Females	[A2B1] $N = 25$	[A2B2] $N = 25$	$N = 50$
	Main Effect (Intervention vs. Control)	$N = 50$	$N = 50$	

Assuming equal numbers of males and females were recruited (which would be optimal), Table 7.5 shows that each group has 25 participants, but the two main effects (one for the combined males vs. females contrast and one for the combined intervention vs. control contrast) *each have 50 participants per group*, thereby greatly increasing the statistical power for the intervention vs. control main effect collapsed across the male and female cells. (Note that the only difference between Tables 7.4 and 7.5 resides in how the four groups are conceptualized [and subsequently analyzed].)

However, our four separate group single-factor design suffers from another disadvantage as compared to a 2 × 2 design. The most common way to analyze the four separate groups represented in Table 7.4 is to contrast each group with the other group, thereby creating six pair-wise comparisons (A Only vs. B Only; A Only vs. A + B; A Only vs. Control; B Only vs. A + B; B Only vs. Control; and A + B vs. Control). Multiple contrasts such as this require a more stringent alpha level (via what statisticians call multiple comparison procedures) than is required by the orthogonal main effect and interactions resulting from a factorial model, thereby reducing the probability of obtaining statistical significance even more. (An orthogonal effect in this context simply indicates that the same cell mean is not employed separately in more than one contrast [e.g., A Only vs. B Only *and* A Only vs. A + B] per experimental analysis.)

Fortunately, two or more separate interventions and their combinations can be reconfigured into their own version of a crossed design. Many factorial variations exist on this theme, including factorial designs using (a) the same participants in some cells, as described in Chapter Eight, (b) the addition of one or more attribute factors, (c) covariates, (d) repeated assessments of the outcomes, and so forth. (Almost all designs can be mixed and matched to increase their sensitivity and experimental purposes.)

Table 7.6 represents the reconfiguration of the four-group experiment depicted in Table 7.4 (i.e., the two separate interventions, a combination of both, and a control/comparison group of some sort). This does seem to be the case for the four groups labeled in Table 7.5 (Intervention A only, Intervention B only, Both Intervention A & B, and Control), but in effect it is just a matter of labeling as shown in Table 7.6. If the two factors are conceptualized as Intervention A and Intervention B and labeled as "receives Intervention A (or Intervention B) in some version" vs. does "does not receive Intervention A (or Intervention B) in any version," then the two cells in each row and column contrast the presence of one intervention vs. the absence thereof.

Thus, for this design, as for the treatment × gender study, each main effect contrast (e.g., Intervention A vs. No Intervention A) has 50 observations available. It is only the Intervention

Table 7.6: A Two-Intervention 2 × 2 Factorial Design (Total N = 100).

	[B1] Receives Intervention B in Some Version (N = 50)	[B2] Does Not Receive Intervention B in Any Version (N = 50)	Intervention A Contrasts
[A1] Receives Intervention A in some version (N = 50)	[Cell A1B1] Both Intervention A and B (AB) (N = 25)	[Cell A1B2] Intervention A only (A) (N = 25)	Mean (A1B1 + A1B2) (AB + A)
[A2] Does not receive Intervention A in any version (N = 50)	[Cell A2B1] Intervention B only (B) (N = 25)	[Cell A2B2] Neither A nor B (Control) (N = 25)	Mean (A2B1 + A2B2) (B + Control)
Intervention B contrast (N = 50)	Mean (A1B1 + A2B1) (AB + B)	Mean (A1B2 + A2B2) (A + Control)	

The design can become somewhat complex for interventions that require carefully matched controls, such as placebo-controlled trials. Here, two different placebos might be indicated, with Cell A1B2 receiving placebo B, Cell A2B1 receiving placebo A, and Cell A2B2 possibly receiving both placebos.

A × Intervention B interaction that uses 25 participants per cell (since no cells are combined). As always, however, main effects cannot be interpreted independently of interaction effects. A nonsignificant interaction accompanying two effective interventions normally signals that the two interventions are additive when administered together. Conversely, a statistically significant interaction accompanying two effective interventions may signal that the interventions are either (a) less than or (b) more than additive (i.e., synergistic) in nature. Let's illustrate two of these scenarios with hypothetical data: Table 7.7 represents the additive scenario while Table 7.8 depicts a much rarer synergistic scenario. (Let's assume that a two-point difference between means corresponds to statistical significance in these two tables.)

Here both main effects are significant and have no hint of an interaction. Note that the difference between both interventions delivered together (i.e., A1B1) and the control (A2B2, in

Table 7.7: Both Interventions Are Effective and Together Their Effects Are Additive, Resulting in No Interaction.

	[B1] Receives Intervention B in Some Version	[B2] Does Not Receive Intervention B in Any Version	Intervention A Contrasts
[A1] Receives Intervention A in some version	8 [Cell A1B1] Both Intervention A and B	6 [Cell A1B2] Intervention A only	7 Mean (A1B1 + A1B2)
[A2] Does not receive Intervention A in any version	6 [Cell A2B1] Intervention B only	4 [Cell A2B2] Control: neither A nor B	5 Mean (A2B1 + A2B2)
Intervention B contrasts	7 Mean (A1B1 + A2B1)	5 Mean (A1B2 + A2B2)	

Table 7.8: Both Interventions Are Effective but Together Their Effects Are Synergistic, Thereby Resulting in an Interaction.*

	[B1] Receives Intervention B in Some Version	[B2] Does Not Receive Any Version of Intervention B	Intervention A Contrasts
[A1] Receives Intervention A in some version	10 [Cell A1B1] Both Intervention A and B	6 [Cell A1B2] Intervention A only	8 Mean (A1B1 + A1B2)
[A2] Does not receive any version of Intervention A	6 [Cell A2B1] Intervention B only	4 [Cell A2B2] Control: neither A nor B	5 Mean (A2B1 + A2B2)
Intervention B contrasts	8 Mean (A1B1 + A2B1)	5 Mean (A1B2 + A2B2)	

*The interaction is (Cell A1B1 – Cell A1B2) vs. (Cell A2B1 – Cell A2B2) = (10 – 6 = 4) vs. (6 – 4 = 2).

which neither intervention was delivered) is twice as great (8 – 4 = 4) as either intervention delivered alone [i.e., (A1B2 – A2B2) = (6 – 4 = 2) for Intervention A and (A2B1 – A2B2) = (6 – 4 = 2) for Intervention B)]. In other words, the intervention effects are additive and, in science and everyday life, 2 + 2 = 4. Note, too, that the two main effects, A1 vs. A2 and B1 vs. B2, also differ from one another by two outcome points (whatever that is).

Furthermore, since this is a factorial trial, the 2 × 2 interaction is assessed exactly the same way as was described previously: (Cell A1B1 – Cell A1B2) vs. (Cell A2B1 – Cell A2B2) = (8 – 6 = 2) vs. (6 – 4 = 2), hence no interaction. (As always, the column cells could be employed, yielding exactly the same results.)

Now let's illustrate two statistically significant main effects as well as a statistically significant interaction representing two synergistic interventions. (Note that both Tables 7.7 and 7.8 illustrate only a few of the possible permutations that can result from a 2 × 2 factorial design.)

When the two factors represent two interventions and the effects of the combination of the two interventions (Cell A1B1) is of equal or greater scientific interest to the effects of either intervention alone, the hypothesis should specify these specific contrasts a priori (i.e., Intervention A vs. control, Intervention B vs. control, and Interventions A + B vs. control), in which case the factorial design loses much of its inherent statistical advantage and the actual contrasts become three pairwise contrasts, which is much more similar to a single-factor design because it requires a p-value adjustment based on the number of pairwise contrasts employed. *In fact, it is a rare investigator who employs a factorial design involving two interventions who is not interested in the pairwise comparisons among all four cells, hence pretty much cancelling the statistical power advantage of employing a factorial design, since this will require the use of a more stringent alpha level.*

With this said, there are still advantages inherent to the use of a factorial design employing two interventions, although when (a) resources are scarce, (b) both interventions have been reliably established to be effective separately, *and* (c) their combined effects have not been tested, an option that might be considered is to conduct a "simple" two-group study (the combined interventions vs. a control). There are obvious advantages and disadvantages to both strategies which must be weighed against one another (an advantage being that a large effect for the combined intervention would have important clinical and meaningful implications). It is, after all, the bottom-line utility of the final results of a study that determines its ultimate meaningfulness, as illustrated by the following medical example in which clinical considerations determined the a priori hypotheses and the specific contrasts that would be tested.

EXAMPLE OF AN EXEMPLARY TWO-INTERVENTION FACTORIAL TRIAL

Comparison of Angioplasty with Stenting, with or without Abciximab in Acute Myocardial Infarction (2002)

Gregg Stone, Cindy Grines, David Cox, et al.

This example illustrates an unusual version of a crossed factorial trial that at first glance appears to not to qualify as a factorial trial at all. It seems to use no control group per se and what appear to be *three* active treatments, yet it manages to include all three treatments into a completely crossed 2 x 2 design in which 2,082 cardiovascular patients were randomly assigned to the four cells depicted in Figure 7.5. (The large number of randomized participants was a function of [a] the dichotomous endpoint [a dichotomous composite of deleterious outcomes of myocardial infarction, including death, a second myocardial infarction, disabling stroke] and the necessity of performing another reperfusion [return of blood supply to cardiovascular tissue] procedure, [b] the expected frequency of these outcomes' occurrence [most of which, fortunately, occur rarely], and [c] the study's two unusual primary hypotheses.)

At first blush the study appears to have three interventions (the drug abciximab and two procedures—stent and percutaneous transluminal coronary angioplasty [PTCA]), but the investigators clarify the issue by explaining that PTCA (a method designed to mechanically widen a blocked artery) and the insertion of stents (small tubes inserted in arteries to facilitate blood flow) are mutually exclusive procedures that are *not* performed in combination. Further, the drug (abciximab) is a supplementary intervention not used as a stand-alone treatment for acute myocardial infarctions.

The trial therefore qualifies as a two-intervention experiment (PTCA and abciximab), both of which were tested in combination (Cell **A1B1** in Figure 7.5) and both alone (Cells **A1B2** and **A2B1** respectively); Cell **A2B2** represents standard care and employs neither PTCA nor abciximab. (Patients with acute myocardial infarction obviously can't be assigned to receive no medical treatment.)

FIGURE 7.5: A 2 × 2 Factorial Trial Design (2 Treatments [PTCA vs. Stent and Drug vs. No Drug] with Stent Alone Serving as the Control/Comparison Group).

	[B1] Receives Abciximab in Some Version	[B2] Does Not Receive Any Version of Abciximab	PTCA Contrasts
Receives PTCA in some version [**A1**]	[**Cell A1B1**] (PTCA + abciximab)	[**Cell A1B2**] (PTCA alone)	**Mean** (Cell A1B1 + Cell A1B2)
Does not receive PTCA in any version [**A2**]	[**Cell A2B1**] (abciximab without PTCA but used with stenting)	[**Cell A2B2**] (neither abciximab nor PTCA but standard care (i.e., stenting)	**Mean** (Cell A2B1 + Cell A2B2)
Abciximab contrasts	**Mean** (Cell A1B1 + Cell A2B1)	**Mean** (Cell A1B2 + Cell A2B2)	

PTCA, percutaneous transluminal coronary angioplasty.

Classically, this design produces the following effects:

Main Effect A: Is there a difference in outcomes between the two reperfusion procedures (stents vs. PTCA) regardless of whether they are supplemented by abciximab [**Mean (Cell A1B1 + Cell A1B2) vs. Mean (Cell A2B1 + Cell A2B2)**]?

Main Effect B: Does abciximab supplementation improve outcomes for patients regardless of whether they receive stents or PTCA [**Mean (Cell A1B1 + Cell A2B1) vs. Mean (Cell A1B2 + Cell A2B2)**]?

AB Interaction: This can be stated numerous ways, but would normally be stated in terms of the combined interventions exerting an additive effect, such as:

Does the combination of PTCA plus abciximab over PTCA alone **(Cell A1B1 – Cell A1B2)** differ from abciximab without PTCA vs. stenting alone **(Cell A2B1 – Cell A2B2)**? Or the other side of the same coin, does the combination of PTCA plus abciximab compared to abciximab with stenting **(Cell A1B1 – Cell A2B1)** differ from PTCA alone vs. stenting alone **(Cell A1B2 – Cell A2B2)**?

However, as already noted, this is an unusual trial, so the authors stated their overall purpose as follows: "to determine the optimal reperfusion strategy in patients with evolving acute myocardial infarction." Then, interestingly, the study's two a priori hypotheses involved neither of the two main effects but a *specified directional interaction* that reduced to two pairwise comparisons—namely that (a) stenting without abciximab (i.e., standard care) is superior to PTCA without abciximab **(Cell A2B2 > Cell A1B2)** while (b) it is *not inferior to* the combination of PTCA and abciximab (i.e., **Cell A2B2 ≈ Cell A1B1**), hence obviously there would be no additive effect for this combination. (Note that this second hypothesis specifies no statistically significant difference between the two cells and, as will be explained in Chapter Nine, requires an adjustment to the usual *p*-level, since it is easier to *fail* to achieve statistical significance than to achieve it. The investigators chose to appropriately compensate for this fact in their initial power analysis by using a method described by Blackwelder [1982].)

Then, reflecting the trial's overall purpose ("to determine the optimal reperfusion strategy in patients with evolving acute myocardial infarction"), the investigators proceeded (as probably the vast majority of scientists in this situation would do) to test all six pairwise comparisons among their four groups. And, as all investigators employing this strategy *should* do, they adjusted their significance criterion downward to a more stringent level to help reduce the chances of a spurious finding. Their results? Cells **A2B1** (standard care with abciximab) and **A2B2** (standard care alone) were superior to the other cells, leading to the conclusion that "stent implantation (with or without abciximab therapy) should be considered the routine reperfusion strategy." (See McAlister, Straus, Sackett, and Altman [2003] for a systematic review of published examples of medical factorial designs as well as detailed recommendations for their reporting and analysis.)

EXPERIMENTS INVOLVING THREE OR MORE LEVELS PER FACTOR

There is no theoretical limit to the number of levels per factor that can be employed in an experiment (as long as there are sufficient observations to populate them). For ease of interpretation, two levels per factor are preferable and, as will be discussed in Chapter Nine, two levels are also optimal from a power-analytic perspective when the sample size is limited.

Scientific considerations take precedence over design issues, however, and there are many occasions when three experimental groups are necessary. Had the investigators in the acupuncture example presented in Chapter Five only employed an intervention and a placebo control rather than added a standard treatment comparison group, their results would have been quite different (i.e., no statistical significant results at all). Had they employed only an intervention and a standard-treatment comparison group, their results would have been unequivocally positive.

The logic of interpreting a two-factor interaction remains the same, however, regardless of the number of levels involved. For example, suppose our hypothetical homework experiment employed three levels of socioeconomic status (SES) instead of gender as the non-manipulated blocking variable and obtained a statistically significant interaction effect. A line graph (Figure 7.6) would remain a useful descriptive method for teasing out the "meaning" of a statistically significant interactional effect.

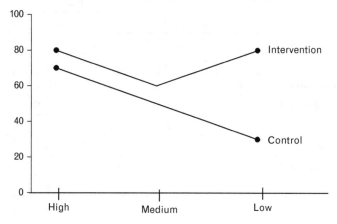

FIGURE 7.6: Hypothetical 2 × 3 Interaction.

Figure 7.6 illustrates one of many possible significant interactions emanating from a 2×3 interaction. Like all two-factor designs, this one would produce three p-values: two for the two main effects and one for the interaction between them. Assuming that all three p-values were <.05, the line graph in Figure 7.6 suggests that the intervention may really be effective only for children from lower SES families (perhaps because families from the higher SES levels may already be intervening to ensure homework completion). While graphs such as this are useful conceptually, all statistically significant interactions (especially those involving more than two levels per factor) should also be subjected to what are called special-effects tests, which allow their constitution parts to be subjected to inferential analysis. (This, as promised, is outside of our purview here, however.)

EXPERIMENTS INVOLVING THREE OR MORE FACTORS

Just as there is no limit on the number of levels that can be employed per factor, there is also no limit on the number of factors that can be employed in an experiment as long as each factor and each level within that factor contains a sufficient number of participants (two is the absolute numerical minimum). Our hypothetical homework experiment, for example, could have been designed as a two–experimental conditions (intervention vs. control) $\times$ 2 gender (males vs. females) $\times$ 3 SES (high, medium, and low) experiment.

This model results in 12 cells and produces seven p-values: (a) three for the three main effects/factors—treatments (intervention vs. control), gender (male vs. female), and SES (high, medium, and low); (b) three for the three two-way interactions between each pair of factors (treatments $\times$ gender ignoring SES, treatments $\times$ SES ignoring gender, and gender $\times$ SES ignoring treatments); and (c) one three-way interaction (treatments $\times$ gender $\times$ SES, which ignores nothing). To illustrate the latter, consider the hypothetical results presented in Table 7.9 for all 12 cells (which represent each level of each factor crossed with one another).

Table 7.9: Hypothetical Three-Factor Design of Parentally Supervised Homework Experiment.

		Intervention (C1)	Control (C2)	Total
High SES (A1)	**Males (B1)**	60% (a1b1c1)	40% (a1b1c2)	**50% (a1b1)**
	Females (B2)	80% (a1b2c1)	60% (a1b2c2)	**70% (a1b2)**
	Total	**70% (a1c1)**	**50% (A1C2)**	60% (A1)
Medium SES (A2)	**Males (B1)**	55% (a2b1c1)	30% (a2b1c2)	**42.5% (a2b1)**
	Females (B2)	75% (a2b2c1)	50% (a2b2c2)	**62.5% (a2b2)**
	Total	**65% (a2c1)**	**40% (a2c3)**	52.5% (A2)
Low SES (A3)	**Males (B1)**	30% (a3b1c1)	30% (a3b1c2)	**30% (a1c1)**
	Females (B2)	60% (a3b2c1)	30% (a3b2c2)	**45% (a1c1)**
	Total	**60% (C1)**	**40% (C2)**	37.5% (A3)

SES, socioeconomic status.

The overall main effect means here are as follows (and most likely all three would be statistically significant). Participants who received the intervention (C1) were more likely to complete their home assignments than (C2) control participants (ignoring gender and SES): 60% (i.e., 60% + 80% + 55% + 75% + 30% + 60%)/6 vs. 40%. Females (B1) were more likely to complete their homework than males (B2): 59.2% to 40.8%. SES was positively (and more or less linearly) related to homework completion: high SES (A1) = 60%; medium SES (A2) = 52.5%; low SES (A3) = 37.5.

The results for the three two-way interactions would be obtained by collapsing the 12 cells contained in Table 7.9 into one 2 × 2 table (for gender × treatment ignoring SES) and two 2 × 3 tables (treatment × SES and gender × SES, ignoring gender and treatment, respectively). Since we've already discussed two-factor interactions, let's only consider the three-way interaction.

Interpreting a three-way interaction: While this particular design has already produced a considerable amount of information, something is missing. Each of the six comparisons (the main effects and the three two-way interactions) ignored *something* (the main effects considered only one factor and ignored everything else; each of the two-way interactions ignore one main effect while comparing the joint action of the other two). None of the six comparisons, however, considered how all of the factors interacted *together*, and this is the function of a three-way interaction (or the highest level interaction available for any given factorial design): to ignore *nothing* but to consider all of the individual cells represented by the design. And, like the two-level interaction in a two-factor design, the highest level interaction—if statistically significant—must be taken into consideration and given preference—prior to interpreting both lower level interaction effects and main effects.

Although three-way interactions can be viewed from three different perspectives, they are all different looks at the same basic contrasts. For our purposes here, let's consider how treatment and SES interacted with one another for each gender separately. To examine this effect graphically, we would need to instruct the computer to construct two separate 2 (intervention vs. control) × 3 (high vs. medium vs. low) interactions: one for males alone and one for females alone (see Figure 7.7).

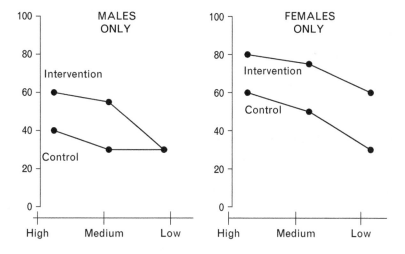

FIGURE 7.7: Three-Way Interaction: Males vs. Females.

To interpret this interaction, the entire "males only" line graph must be compared to its entire "females only" counterpart. If the two "males only" lines are more or less parallel (or isomorphic) to the two "females only" lines, then there is no interaction and the p-value will be greater than .05 (i.e., not statistically significant). Obviously, this isn't the case in Figure 7.7 since the difference between the pair of two-line graphs is quite striking. For both genders the intervention appears to be superior to its control for both high- and medium-SES families. However, the intervention appears to have no effect for males from low-SES families in comparison to control, while the intervention does appear to be superior for females from low-SES families.

Statistically significant three-way interactions can be difficult to interpret and rationalize unless their directions (i.e., meanings) are hypothesized a priori. (And since this is rarely done, the possibility of a higher level interaction should be considered at the design stage, along with the possible implications for the trial given its most likely manifestations.) Higher level (i.e., above two-way) interactions are also less likely to replicate because of chance occurrences unless their direction is hypothesized, which presumes a theoretical explanation for this effect. In general, this is true for all interactions and is important enough to warrant an experimental principle:

PRINCIPLE #18: All scientifically meaningful interaction effects expected to reach statistical significance should be hypothesized a priori along with their direction, based on the presence of a theoretical or clinical rationale.

A note on mixed (i.e., combinations of repeated measures and between-subjects) factorial designs: As with all experimental designs, it is possible to mix and match elements from seemingly diverse architectures. Mixed factorial designs combine one or more factors populated by completely different participants (as was the case with the previous example) with one or more factors made up of repeated observations on the same (or matched) individuals.

There are several reasons for using a mixed factorial design:

1. *Efficiency.* The number of participants required for higher level, between-subjects factorial designs can become burdensome with each additional factor. It will be remembered that our original 2 (treatments) × 2 (gender) iteration of the homework example employed four cells. Adding the third SES factor tripled that number. And while this may not have required tripling the overall required sample size, it would have required a considerably larger number of participants—especially to detect a statistically significant three-way interaction.

2. *The increased statistical power and precision available from repeated measures factors.* As will be explained in the next chapter, when there are no carryover effects and there is little danger of reactivity, the potential for error is much less (and sensitivity is considerably greater) when participants are compared to themselves as opposed to comparing them with completely different, randomly assigned individuals.

3. *In many experiments, more than two (i.e., baseline vs. EOT) assessments on the same participants are employed.* Technically, although it wasn't so classified here, the randomized pretest-posttest can be conceptualized as a mixed factorial design in which the between-subjects factor is the randomly assigned intervention vs. the comparison

group and the repeated measures factor is the baseline vs. EOT assessment. There are also occasions in which an interim assessment is added to ascertain when the intervention begins to exert its hypothesized effect. Or, more commonly, follow-up assessments (i.e., that occur after the EOT assessment) are employed to ascertain the permanence (or rate of decay) of an intervention effect. When these additional assessments are considered part of the overall analytic model (which investigators are not constrained to do if they specify a single post-intervention assessment as the primary endpoint), then the design contains a repeated measures factor (see Chapter Eight), which can be conceptualized as "time of assessment."

4. *Crossover designs technically constitute a mixed factorial design when participants are randomly assigned to order.* These designs, along with an important procedural strategy called counterbalancing, will be considered in more detail in Chapter Eight.

NESTED DESIGNS

The previously discussed randomized cluster design in which clusters (or groups) of participants rather than individuals are randomly assigned to experimental conditions is an example of a concept called *nesting.* Nested assignment is currently quite commonly used in educational experiments where students are contained in pre-assigned classroom units, making it impractical and disruptive, and risking the possibility of treatment diffusion to administer two experimental conditions within the same classroom. Instead, classrooms or schools (if there is a perceived danger of treatment diffusion) are randomly assigned to the experimental conditions, thereby producing a situation in which the assigned units are nested under the treatment variable (e.g., intervention vs. control groups).

Figure 7.8 depicts such a scenario, in which 12 classrooms consisting of 20 students each are randomly assigned to either the intervention or control groups. This strategy results in a *non-crossed* source of potential variation that must be accounted for—namely the teachers and their classroom nested within the two experimental conditions.

FIGURE 7.8: Teachers Nested Within Experimental Conditions.

			Pretest	Posttest
Intervention				
	Teacher/Classroom 1			
		Student 1		
		.....		
		Student 20		
	Teacher/Classroom 2			
		Student 21		
		....		
		Student 40		

FIGURE 7.8: (Continued)

	.....	.....		
	.....	.....		
	Teacher/Classroom 12			
		Student 221		
		.....		
		Student 240		
Control				
	Teacher/Classroom 13			
		Student 241		
		.....		
		Student 260		
	Teacher/Classroom 14			
		Student 261		
	.....	.....		
	.....	.....		
	Teacher/Classroom 24			
		Student 461		
		.....		
	.....	Student 480		

A nested variable typically reduces the statistical power (i.e., likelihood of obtaining statistical significance) of the variable within which it is nested (in this case the treatment [intervention vs. control] factor) as compared to that of a crossed design. While clusters are normally nested within experimental conditions, sometimes the strategy is used to account for a potential source of systematic variation within a non-manipulated factor.

Figure 7.9 illustrates a different scenario, in which students *within* classroom are randomly assigned to receive or not receive an intervention. (To avoid treatment diffusion, let's pretend that the intervention consisted of pulling out half of the classroom during the mathematics period to receive computerized instruction in a specified topic, while the other half remained in the classroom to receive routine instruction in the same topic from their regular teachers. Following testing, the same intervention was introduced to the other half of the class on a different topic via a delayed intervention control to allay student and parental concerns.)

On the surface we appear to have a routine, two-group experiment in which different participants are randomly assigned to experimental conditions. However, while teachers–classrooms were not nested within the experimental conditions, potential systematic effects still exist because of classrooms (e.g., students might be grouped according to ability level) or teachers (e.g., some might teach the experimental curriculum more conscientiously). Since the 12 classrooms were *crossed* with the treatment factor, however, this strategy results in a straightforward 2 (intervention vs. control) × 12 (classrooms/teachers) factorial design in which both factors contain independent observations. (Note that Principle #18 would most likely not apply here because there would be no theoretical reason to predict a statistically significant classroom × intervention interaction.)

FIGURE 7.9: Teachers–Classrooms Crossed with Experimental Conditions.

		Intervention	Control
Teacher/Classroom 1			
Teacher/Classroom 2			
Teacher/Classroom 3			
Teacher/Classroom 4			
Teacher/Classroom 5			
Teacher/Classroom 6			
.....			
Teacher/Classroom 11			
Teacher/Classroom 12			

Obviously, the crossed design (Figure 7.9) is the more precise design than its nested counterpart (Figure 7.8) since teacher/classroom differences are a non-issue when crossed with the experiment conditions because they are present to the same degree (i.e., each classroom and half of its students are represented in each experimental condition, as are all the teachers). Thus, if there are substantive differences among these classrooms and teachers, these differences can be accounted for (and "subtracted" out) of the study's unexplained variation (i.e., error)—thereby *increasing* the precision (statistical power) of the study over a conventional two-group randomized design (as long as the crossed teacher–classroom blocks are employed as a second factor in the statistical analysis).

The opposite is true for the nested design where teachers/classrooms were randomly assigned to receive either the intervention or routine instruction. Here, any differences in the classrooms/teachers assigned to the intervention group as compared to the control *decreases* the precision (statistical power) of the study over a conventional two-group randomized design if the nested teacher–classroom blocks are included in an appropriate hierarchical statistical procedure.

Hopefully, this example illustrates the primary difference between crossed and nested variables. It also provides the rationale for our 19th principle:

> **PRINCIPLE #19: Regardless of who analyzes the experiment's final data, ensure that all sources of systematic variation (e.g., covariates, factors, nested and blocking variables, counterbalanced procedural elements) are included (or at least modeled to ascertain if they should be included).**

LESS COMMONLY EMPLOYED PARTIALLY CONFOUNDED FACTORIAL DESIGNS

While factorial designs are unquestionably powerful strategies, they do have two distinct disadvantages:

1. It is a rare factorial experiment in which every main effect or interaction is of equal interest. While this isn't particularly problematic in two- or three-factor experiment, it

can become disadvantageous as the number of factors increase since each uninteresting term potentially increases the error term(s) used to test the study hypotheses. (For example, if a three-way interaction accounts for little or no variability in the outcome variable it still "consumes" what are called degrees of freedom, which has the same effect as slightly reducing the available sample size.)

2. As the number of factors (and number of levels contained in each factor) increases much past, say, a $2 \times 2 \times 2$ (2^3) factorial design, the cells proliferate and it becomes more difficult to recruit adequate numbers of participants for each cell (in which case the observations per cell tend to decrease). As an example, adding one level per factor to a 2×2 experiment produces a 3^2 (3×3) configuration and increases the number of cells from 4 to 9. Adding a third factor increases the number of cells to 8 and 27, respectively, which in turn means that the effective sample size for each individual cell is greatly reduced unless the overall number of participants is increased dramatically. When the overall sample size is limited, there will therefore typically be insufficient power to test the higher level interactions. (Note that this discussion does not apply to factors and interactions represented by repeated measures such as those employed in crossover designs or time of assessment factors [e.g., baseline vs. EOT vs. follow-up] and their interactions. No additional participants are needed to populate repeated measures cells.)

Generically, there are approaches to dealing with factorial experiments for which sufficient observations per cell are unavailable, the most obvious of which is being judicious regarding one's choice of factors and including only those for which there is good evidence for an interaction effect (and that effect is of scientific interest). Fishing expeditions are seldom successful in science but are even less successful in experimental work. Another is a design strategy known as fractional factorial designs. These designs are somewhat rare in experiments involving human participants, but they have applicability under certain circumstances.

Fractional factorial designs: While factorial designs are associated with certain disadvantages regarding the number of participants required to populate their sometimes daunting number of cells, they are also unquestionably powerful experimental strategies because of (a) the number of hypotheses they permit to be tested in a single experiment, (b) the definitiveness of their results due to fewer confounds resulting from the increased number of perfectly crossed variables, and (c) the unique hypotheses they permit.

There are occasions, however, when an investigator is faced with the need to perform preliminary work involving large numbers of potential interventions and attributes but does not have the resources (or feel justified in allocating them) to investigate the effects of these interventions via full factorial models. This is a scenario in which a fractional factorial design can constitute a viable approach since (as the name implies) only a *fraction* of the cells required for a full factorial model are populated.

Unfortunately, since nothing is without cost in either life or experimental design, the gain in efficiency provided by reducing the number of required cells is accompanied by a loss in specificity. Specifically, when all the cells required for a full factorial model are not employed, some of the experimental effects are confounded. Should a one-half fractional representation be employed (which means that the total number of cells to which participants are actually assigned are cut in half), for example, the highest level interaction is completely lost and some of the other levels are confounded with one another. The resulting confounds, or aliases, for one-half fractional factorial designs occur as follows:

1. For a three-factor study, the three-way interaction disappears and the main effects are confounded with the two-way interactions, which really makes no sense and is never used.

2. For four-factor studies, the four-way interaction is not computed and the main effects are aliased with the three-way interactions (which is not always disadvantageous, since three-way interactions are often not of major interest). More problematic, however, is the fact that the two-way factors are aliased with one another, which is usually not acceptable because some two-way interactions usually are of scientific interest.

3. For five-factor studies, all of the main effects and two-way interactions (of which there are many) are aliased with higher level interactions and therefore *interpretable* as long as it can be assumed that the three-way and four-way interactions are negligible and of no interest—which is why fractional factorial designs are most commonly used for factorial studies with five or more factors. For six-factor studies, even the three-way interactions are interpretable.

To illustrate the complexity of higher level factorial designs, let's begin with a review of a "simple" hypothetical study employing three interventions with two levels each. To flesh out the study, let's suppose that an educational software specialist was preparing an instructional module and needed to determine the best combination of characteristics to build into it—specifically, to ascertain whether it was more effective in eliciting learning when the written text had (a) a reading difficulty slightly below grade level or slightly above, (b) small vs. large fonts, and (c) animation (none vs. interspersed animated characters). A full factorial model would therefore employ the following eight cells comprised of all of the combinations of the three interventions and could be depicted as in Figure 7.10.

FIGURE 7.10: A 2^3 Factorial Design.

			ANIMATION (C1)	NO ANIMATION (C0)
Text written above grade level (a1)	Large font (b1)		a1b1c1	a1b1c0
Text written below grade level (a0)	Small font (b0)		a1b0c1	a1b0c0
Text written above grade level (a1)	Large font (b1)		a0b1c1	a0b1c0
Text written below grade level (a0)	Small font (b0)		a0b0c1	a0b0c0

And the eight cells would be defined as follows:

a0b0c0 (000) Text written below grade level with small font and no animation

a0b0c1 (001) Text written below grade level with small font using animation

a0b1c0 (010) Text written below grade level with large font and no animation

a0b1c1 (011) Text written below grade level with large font using animation

a1b0c0 (100) Text written above grade level with small font and no animation

a1b0c1 (101) Text written above grade level in small font using animation

a1b1c0 (110) Text written above grade level in large font and no animation

a1b1c1 (111) Text written above grade level in large font using animation

The seven p-values produced to test the full factorial model address the following seven questions (note that the questions associated with the interactions present directional examples that reflect only one of a multitude of actual possibilities):

Main Effect A: Does reading level of the text affect learning?

Main Effect B: Does the font size affect learning?

Main Effect C: Does the presence of animation affect learning?

Interaction AB: Is there an interaction between reading level and font size (e.g., does an easier reading level accompanied by a larger font size produce greater learning)?

Interaction AC: Is there an interaction between reading level and animation (e.g., irrespective of font size, does a lower reading level combined with animation produce more learning than a lower reading level without animation)?

Interaction BC: Is there an interaction between font size and animation (e.g., irrespective of reading level, does a smaller font size combined with animation produce more learning than a smaller font size without animation)?

Interaction ABC: Is there a three-way interaction between reading level, font size, and animation? (One of a multitude of ways in which such an effect could occur would be if animation seemed to only produce superior learning when accompanied by large font sizes and more difficult reading levels—which, like most directional three-way interactions, is somewhat of stretch.)

But what if our module developer had two more variables in which she was interested— say, whether or not the module was personalized to the individual student, which we'll designate "d": (0) not personalized vs. (1) personalized), and an attribute variable such as reading ability "e": (0) below grade level vs. (1) above reading above grade level?

At this point, the design (a 2^5 factorial) begins to become rather resource intensive (not to mention complicated). Instead of 8 cells the investigator must now populate 32, and instead of 7 hypotheses with associated p-values she has 30 to deal with (5 main effects: A, B, C, D, E; 10 two-way interactions: AB, AC, AD, AE, BC, BD, BE, CD, CE, DE; 9 three-way interactions: ABC, ABD, ABE, ACD, ACE, BCD, BCE, BDE, CDE; 5 four-way interactions: ABCD, ABCE, ABDE, ACDE, BCDE; and 1 five-way interaction).

Certainly our investigator would be interested in testing all five main effects and their interactions with one another, but in most cases the three-, four-, and five-way interactions may not be of primary interest, since

1. They are normally of negligible size and do not reach statistical significance,
2. They sometimes aren't interpretable scientifically or intuitively, in which case they aren't often hypothesized a priori (hence are less likely to replicate), and
3. They often have little scientific interest, partly because most behavioral and social science theories haven't reached the necessary degree of specificity.

Should any of these characteristics not apply, then a fractional factorial design should not be employed.

So let's assume that our hypothetical investigator opted to use a one-half replication for her five-factor experiment. This would mean that she would be required to populate only 16 of the 32 treatment combinations available in a 2^5 design. The 16 cells she would need to retain can be determined by summing the "1" (characteristic present) "0" (characteristic absent) nomenclature employed for each of the 32 cells and then applying modular arithmetic to the results as illustrated in Table 7.10, in which the "√'s" indicate the cells selected for use. (The odd sums have been chosen but comparable results would have been produced if the even sums had been chosen.)

Table 7.10: One-Half Fractional Representation of a 2^5 Design.

Cells	a	b	c	d	e	Sum	Interpretation
1	0	0	0	0	0	0	Text below grade level, small font, no animation, no personalization, low reading ability
2	0	1	0	0	0	√1	Text below grade level, large font, no animation, no personalization, low reading ability
3	0	0	1	0	0	√1	Text below grade level, small font, animation, no personalization, low reading ability
4	0	1	1	0	0	2	Text below grade level, large font, animation, no personalization, low reading ability
5	0	0	0	1	0	√1	Text below grade level, small font, no animation, personalization, low reading ability
6	0	1	0	1	0	2	Text below grade level, large font, no animation, personalization, low reading ability
7	0	0	1	1	0	2	Text below grade level, small font, animation, personalization, low reading ability
8	0	1	1	1	0	√3	Text below grade level, large font, animation, personalization, low reading ability
9	0	0	0	0	1	√1	Text below grade level, small font, no animation, no personalization, high reading ability
10	0	1	0	0	1	2	Text below grade level, large font, no animation, no personalization, high reading ability
11	0	0	1	0	1	2	Text below grade level, small font, animation, no personalization, high reading ability
12	0	1	1	0	1	√3	Text below grade level, large font, animation, no personalization, high reading ability
13	0	0	0	1	1	2	Text below grade level, small font, no animation, personalization, high reading ability
14	0	1	0	1	1	√3	Text below grade level, large font, no animation, personalization, high reading ability
15	0	0	1	1	1	√3	Text below grade level, small font, animation, personalization, high reading ability
16	0	1	1	1	1	4	Text below grade level, large font, animation, personalization, high reading ability
17	1	0	0	0	0	√1	Text above grade level, small font, no animation, no personalization, low reading ability
18	1	1	0	0	0	2	Text above grade level, large font, no animation, no personalization, low reading ability
19	1	0	1	0	0	2	Text above grade level, small font, animation, no personalization, low reading ability

Table 7.10 (Continued)

20	1	1	1	0	0	$\sqrt{3}$	Text above grade level, large font, animation, no personalization, low reading ability
21	1	0	0	1	0	2	Text above grade level, small font, no animation, personalization, low reading ability
22	1	1	0	1	0	$\sqrt{3}$	Text above grade level, large font, no animation, personalization, low reading ability
23	1	0	1	1	0	$\sqrt{3}$	Text above grade level, small font, animation, personalization, low reading ability
24	1	1	1	1	0	4	Text above grade level, large font, animation, personalization, low reading ability
25	1	0	0	0	1	2	Text above grade level, small font, no animation, no personalization, high reading ability
26	1	1	0	0	1	$\sqrt{3}$	Text above grade level, large font, no animation, no personalization, high reading ability
27	1	0	1	0	1	$\sqrt{3}$	Text above grade level, small font, animation, no personalization, high reading ability
28	1	1	1	0	1	4	Text above grade level, large font, animation, no personalization, high reading ability
29	1	0	0	1	1	$\sqrt{3}$	Text above grade level, small font, no animation, personalization, high reading ability
30	1	1	0	1	1	4	Text above grade level, large font, no animation, personalization, high reading ability
31	1	0	1	1	1	4	Text above grade level, small font, animation, personalization, high reading ability
32	1	1	1	1	1	$\sqrt{5}$	Text above grade level, large font, animation, personalization, high reading ability

The full range of fractional factorial designs cannot be given justice here, nor do they merit a great deal of attention in a book specializing in design issues involved in human experimentation. An absolutely bewildering array of fractional design options exist, involving one-quarter and one-third fractional factorials, the use of blocks of two or more different fractional factorials, and so forth. (Anyone desiring to set up higher level non-crossed factorial studies or more esoteric architectures should consider consulting one of the classic texts devoted to such designs, such as Box, Hunter, and Hunter [1978], Cochrane and Cox [1957], Cox and Reid [2000], Montgomery [2000], and Winer [1962]; employing generational software [e.g., SoftStat]; or accessing an online aid, such as http://www.itl.nist.gov/div898/handbook/pri/section3/pri3347.htm.)

For the purposes of this book, the primary application of fractional factorial designs probably involves pilot work and the provision of future investigative direction for new areas of research. They could also be useful in preliminary research to identify especially promising interventions and levels and doses thereof when insufficient information is available from the literature. This is especially true when the interventions are of brief duration (and can be simply implemented), such as different tasks or written scenarios in psychological research.

To summarize the advantages and disadvantages of the myriad types of fractional factorial designs, all share a common advantage: They produce a considerable amount of information while requiring fewer resources. They also share a common disadvantage that precludes their use for many scientific purposes: They all substitute confounded contrasts for certain hypothesis tests—which means that additional experimentation may be required to produce more scientifically precise results. This is the nature of preliminary work, hence fractional factorial replication designs should at least be considered as a method of complying with a later, extremely important experimental principle (*always conduct one or more pilot studies*).

Split-plot designs: While fractional factorial designs confound combinations of main effects and interactions, one class of experimental design confounds certain less interesting effects with what are termed "plots," after their agricultural roots, while preserving the integrity of other, more crucial ones. This approach is relatively rare in human experimentation (although perhaps more commonly used than fractional factorials). It should at least be considered in certain behavioral, educational, and social science applications, however.

A split-plot design thus might be used in an educational experiment where the different levels of one factor can be realistically introduced within, say, schools (i.e., plots) but the levels of a second factor cannot, yet it is important to at least estimate the interaction between the two independent variables.

As an example, let's pretend that an investigative team desired to assess whether two different mathematics textbooks (let's designate them A1 and A2) could be profitably supplemented by computerized review sessions (designated as computerized review [B1] and no such review [B2]).

Ideally, both interventions (textbooks and computerized review) would be introduced at all the schools involved in the experiment and students would be randomly assigned to conditions within each school (let's assume there are four), producing the perfectly crossed 2 (Textbook A vs. Textbook B) × 2 (computerized review vs. no review) × 4 (schools), depicted in Figure 7.11.

FIGURE 7.11: A Fully Crossed A (Textbooks) × B (Computerized Review) × C (Schools) Design.

		School 1 (C1)	School (C2)	School 3 (C3)	School 4 (C4)
A1 (Textbook A)	B1 (Computerized review)				
	B2 (No review)				
A2 (Textbook B)	B1 (Computerized review)				
	B2 (No review)				

But what if it was impossible to introduce both textbooks within each school because of practical constraints, hence necessitating schools being selected on the basis of the textbook already used? If the investigative team was not particularly interested in the textbook main effect (i.e., if one textbook was more effective than the other [A1 vs. A2]) but was quite interested in ascertaining (1) if computerized review was more effective than no such review (i.e., the main effect for B) and (2) if it was similarly effective for both textbooks (i.e., the absence of an AB interaction), then a split-plot design would appear to be a viable choice. The simplest possible such design is depicted in Figure 7.12, where type of textbook is confounded with the school effect (which the investigators also probably wouldn't be particularly interested in), but the computerized review main effect (B) is not confounded and the AB interaction is perhaps conceptually less so than the A main effect. (Naturally, the more schools per textbook used, the better the estimate of the AB interaction.)

FIGURE 7.12: A Split-Plot Design in Which One Factor (A) Is Confounded and the Other (B) Is Not.

SCHOOL 1 (PLOT C1)	SCHOOL 2 (PLOT C2)	SCHOOL 3 (PLOT C3)	SCHOOL 4 (PLOT C4)
Textbook A1	Textbook A2	Textbook A1	Textbook A2
Review (B1)	Review (B1)	Review (B1)	Review (B1)
No review (B2)	No review (B2)	No review (B2)	No review (B2)

Here, textbooks and schools are not crossed, hence any textbook main effect may be due to school differences (or the teachers/students associated with those schools). The investigator, therefore, will have a very imperfect, nonexperimental comparison of the learning differences between textbooks. Review and no review is crossed with schools and textbooks, however. Hence the design will provide a much cleaner test of the merits of computerized review (as opposed to none) and a reasonably interpretable test of whether or not this review is equally effective for the two textbooks—especially if an effective covariate (e.g., SES or previous test student standardized test scores) is employed to control potential initial differences in the "textbook" factor.

Other design genres and combinations of genres: There are many, many other factorial options available, some employing the arrangement of different design components in blocks while others use combinations of strategies, such as fractional factorial split-plot designs. The purpose of this chapter was to introduce only the most commonly used between-subjects factorial designs available to investigators, along with two factorial designs felt to have more potential than their frequency of use in experimentation with human participants suggests.

While this brief overview of factorial designs does not do justice to the field itself, hopefully it has provided a gestalt of the breadth of options available for increasing the amount of information available from experimentation involving multiple interventions and/or attribute variables. Chapter Eight greatly extends those options by introducing designs in which multiple experimental conditions are assigned to the *same* (or closely matched) individuals.

SUMMARY

Factorial designs were introduced as an efficient method of testing both the efficacy of multiple interventions as well as the existence of one or more moderating variables via the resulting interaction terms. The importance of these interactions, and the necessity of interpreting statistically significant ones prior to the interpretation of main effects, was stressed. The graphical interpretations of (a) two-level, two-factor, (b) multilevel, two-factor, and (c) three-factor interactions were illustrated.

Alternatives to classic factorial designs were also introduced, including nesting units within the levels of other factors. This strategy is especially useful in randomized cluster designs in which groups of participants (e.g., students within classrooms or clients within treatment facilities) are randomly assigned to avoid treatment diffusion, thereby resulting in a hierarchical design.

Finally, two more rarely used designs in experimentation involving human participants were introduced:

1. *Fractional factorials*, in which only a subset of the daunting number of cells produced by five or more factors need to be populated, which results in the confounding of higher level interactions—an acceptable tradeoff when the confounded effects are of little scientific interest, and
2. *Split-plot designs*, involving multiple factors, at least two of which are confounded with one another.

All the designs presented in this chapter, as well as their repeated measures counterparts discussed in the next chapter, informed two additional experimental principles:

Principle #18: All scientifically meaningful interaction effects expected to reach statistical significance should be hypothesized a priori along with their direction, based on the presence of a theoretical or clinical rationale.

Principle #19: Regardless of who analyzes the experiment's final data, ensure that all sources of systematic variation (e.g., covariates, factors, nested and blocking variables, counterbalanced procedural elements) are included (or at least modeled to ascertain if they should be included).

REFERENCES

Blackwelder, W.C. (1982)."Proving the null hypothesis" in clinical trials. *Controlled Clinical Trials, 3,* 345–53.

Box, G.E.P., Hunter, W.G., & Hunter, J.S. (1978). *Statistics for experimenters.* New York: Wiley.

Cochran, W.G., & Cox, G.M. (1957). *Experimental designs* (2nd ed.). New York: Wiley.

Cox, D.R., & Reid, N. (2000). *The theory of the design of experiments.* Boca Raton, FL: Chapman & Hall.

McAlister, F.A., Straus, S.E., Sackett, D.L., & Altman, D.G. (2003). Analysis and reporting of factorial trials: A systematic review. *Journal of the American Medical Association, 289,* 2545–53.

Montgomery, D.C. (2000). *Design and analysis of experiments* (5th ed.). New York: Wiley.

Stone, G.W., Grines, C.L., Cox, D.A., et al. (2002). Comparison of angioplasty with stenting, with or without abciximab, in acute myocardial infarction. *New England Journal Medicine, 346,* 957–66.

Winer, B.J. (1962). *Statistical principles in experimental research.* New York: McGraw Hill.

REPEATED MEASURES, WITHIN-SUBJECTS, AND LONGITUDINAL DESIGNS

W hile the randomized designs presented in the previous chapter are perfectly acceptable experimental strategies, they all have a common disadvantage. The intervention and comparison groups are populated by completely different individuals possessing different (a) genetic makeups, (b) motivations, (c) experiences, (d) agendas, (e) attributes, (f) personal characteristics, and (g) environmental conditions. And while the theory underlying randomization predicts that *most* of these initial differences can be equalized between groups prior to the beginning of an experiment, the statistical procedures used to compensate for these individual differences do so at a cost: the requirement of relatively large numbers of observations to achieve statistical significance for relatively modest between-group outcome differences.

Laboratory scientists using rodents as participants compensate for these problems by using genetically identical animals raised and kept in environmentally standardized cages—thereby permitting the use of considerably fewer animals in any given experiment than would be otherwise be possible. (Six per group appears to have been the magic number, since animal researchers have only recently been expected to conduct power analyses.) Investigators conducting research on human participants obviously do not have this luxury, although in certain specialized circumstances they are able to administer intervention and comparison conditions to the same (or closely matched) individuals. Such designs permit increased levels of precision accompanied by significantly reduced sample sizes. Since there are no free lunches in science, however, the advantages inherent in repeated measures and within-subjects designs come with their own price tag in the form of an accompanying set of sometimes untenable assumptions.

This chapter will consider when such research is appropriate via the presentation of three design genres using either the same individuals assigned to all experimental conditions or mimicking the approach via a matching strategy. All three optimally employ randomization, although in quite different ways from those previously discussed.

These three design genres are as follows:

1. Repeated measures (including crossover) experiments in which the same participants are administered multiple interventions and/or serve as their *own* controls.
2. Randomized matched block designs in which matched participants are randomly assigned to different conditions.
3. Time series designs in which participants in both intervention and comparison groups are measured repeatedly both before and after the intervention is implemented.

CROSSOVER (COUNTERBALANCED) DESIGNS

Several examples of experimental confounds have been presented earlier with strictures regarding their virulence and strategies for their avoidance. One of the most effective (and commonly used) methods for avoiding a common class of experimental *confounds* (notably time, order, and order-like effects) involves the concept of *counterbalancing*. This strategy is especially helpful when (a) the same participants are administered all of the experimental conditions and (b) the interventions are relatively brief in nature.

Single-group crossover designs: The simplest within-group architectural strategy using the same participants in both intervention and control/comparison groups involves the single-group crossover design, as depicted in Figure 8.1. (Note the distinction from the single-group pretest-posttest design, which doesn't involve an actual control/comparison group.)

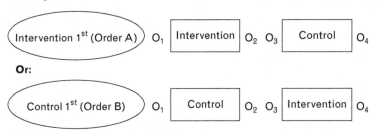

FIGURE 8.1: Two Options for a Single-Group Crossover Design.

Here the investigator is presented with two options: Either the intervention is presented first or the control/comparison group is presented first. (The O's represent assessments of the outcome variables; the numbers represent the order in which the assessments are performed.) In both, the contrast of interest resides in the $[O_2 - O_1]$ vs. $[O_4 - O_3]$ contrast (O_1 and O_3 serving as the baseline/pretest assessment with O_2 and O_4 serving as their EOT/posttest counterparts). But both options have an obvious confound: the order in which the conditions are administered. In Order A, the intervention experience could affect the comparison group (which could be a second intervention in some experiments) and the opposite effect would be possible in Order B.

More crucially, however, if there is an order effect for the two conditions (or the outcome variable does not return to baseline values (O_1) following the first experimental condition—i.e., $O_3 \neq O_1$) then the entire experiment is compromised. A key component of avoiding this $O_3 \neq O_1$ outcome (aside from selecting an appropriate outcome variable and intervention) is the correct specification of the time interval between O_2 and O_3, called the *washout* period, which requires a comprehensive knowledge of both the outcome variable's natural history and the persistence of the intervention's effects. (Such knowledge is obtained both through the research literature and pilot work undertaken as part of the design process for a crossover trial.)

This confound therefore relegates a single crossover design such as the two separate options depicted in Figure 8.1 to a similar status as its single-group pretest-posttest relative: an unacceptable experimental strategy potentially suffering from the same plethora of experimental artifacts as its predecessor (e.g., regression to the mean, natural history) plus some unique to repeated measures (e.g., practice effects, familiarity with the experimental setting and procedures).

Two-group simple crossover designs: The design of choice for a simple crossover comparison such as this is to (a) employ both possible orders and (b) randomly assign different participants to receive those two orders. Diagrammatically, the most stripped-down crossover model assumes the form presented in Figure 8.2.

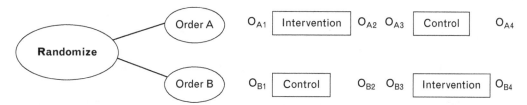

FIGURE 8.2: Two-Group Simple Crossover Design.

Alternately, when the nature of the outcome variable permits, it is more common for multiple baseline and follow-up assessments to be employed in each group (see Figure 8.3).

$$O_{A1}\ O_{A2}\ O_{A3}\ \boxed{\text{Intervention}}\ O_{A4}\ O_{A5}\ O_{A6}\ \boxed{\text{Control}}\ O_{A7}\ O_{A8}\ O_{A9}$$

FIGURE 8.3: Order A for a Two-Group Crossover Design with Multiple Observations.

For simplicity's sake, however, let's assume the presence of only one baseline and EOT assessment per condition per order, as depicted in Figure 8.2. These two-group configurations represent the simplest acceptable example of counterbalancing the order in which two experimental conditions are presented. (In this case the intervention and the control both precede and follow one another.) A randomized counterbalanced design has the obvious advantages of (a) identifying any potential confounding order effect and (b) controlling it (via the randomized counterbalanced order in which the experimental conditions are presented). And given that the same participants received both the intervention and the control conditions, it furthermore constitutes a very precise and powerful design if a number of relatively stringent assumptions can be made.

The first assumption is that the intervention effect is relatively transitory in nature (i.e., exerts no lasting effect on the outcome). If the intervention is a drug that has more than a very temporary outcome effect and can carry over from O_{A2} to O_{A3} in Figure 8.2 (Order A) or O_{A4} to O_{A6} in Figure 8.3, then obviously the intervention-induced changes (e.g., O_{A1} to O_{A2}) will not be comparable to the control changes (O_{A3} to O_{A4}) since the intervention carryover effects will be confounded with the control effects.

The second, related assumption is that the outcome itself must be transitory, thereby precluding most of those used in education and psychology since cognitive and affective outcomes typically do not recede quickly enough for crossover purposes. (This assumption can be circumvented under certain specialized conditions by additional factors, but a crossover design would not be the first choice for such a scenario.)

While violations of these assumptions (including the confounding effects of order) can be ascertained statistically, little can be done when they occur with any degree of magnitude. It therefore behooves investigators to employ interventions and outcome variables that have already been studied extensively (or of which sufficient clinical knowledge is available) *and* to conduct pilot work. Examples include (a) drugs in which the half-lives of specific outcomes (e.g., pain relief) are well known or (b) standardized behavioral tasks' effects on outcomes such as reaction time.

Interpretation of crossover designs: Conceptually, assuming the absence of carryover effects, the data accruing from Figure 8.2 can be conceptualized as a 2 (Order A vs. Order B) × 2 (intervention vs. control) factorial design possessing both a between-subjects and repeated measures factor. Order is represented as a between-subjects factor because *different* participants are assigned to receive each of the two orders (i.e., intervention first or control first). The primary factor of interest (the intervention vs. control comparison) is considered a repeated measure (or within-subjects) factor because the *same* individuals receive both conditions.

To represent these factors visually (and to analyze the resulting data), the two different orders can be reconfigured as illustrated in Figure 8.4, which simply combines the two intervention groups and their control counterparts. (Note that all that was done here was to switch cells C and D of the original design (for analytic purposes only) to permit the columns to represent the repeated measures intervention vs. control contrast and rows to represent the between-subjects order contrast.)

FIGURE 8.4: Reconfigured Contrasts of Interest in a Two-Group Crossover Design.

From:

	Intervention	Control
Order A	(**Cell A**) $\Delta(O_{A2} - O_{A1})$	(**Cell B**) $\Delta(O_{A4} - O_{A3})$
	Control	Intervention
Order B	(**Cell C**) $\Delta(O_{B2} - O_{B1})$	(**Cell D**) $\Delta(O_{B4} - O_{B3})$

To:

	Intervention	Control
Order A	(**Cell A**) $\Delta(O_{A2} - O_{A1})$	(**Cell B**) $\Delta(O_{A4} - O_{A3})$
Order B	(**Cell C**) $\Delta(O_{B4} - O_{B3})$	(**Cell D**) $\Delta(O_{B2} - O_{B1})$

While the analysis of a crossover design can be relatively intricate (as many of the individual assessment need to be analyzed separately to test the required assumptions), the primary contrasts of interest for our two-group, two-phase example are illustrated in Table 8.1 with the use of hypothetical data. An analysis of these contrasts would produce three *p*-values of varying interest.

The most interesting comparison (using the reconfigured cells) would be the *p*-value associated with two combined intervention groups vs. the two combined control groups, Mean [(**Cell A**: O_{A2} − O_{A1}) + (**Cell C**: O_{B4} − O_{B3})] vs. Mean [(**Cell B**: O_{A4} − O_{A3}) + (**Cell D**: O_{B2} − O_{B1})], which addresses the question of whether the intervention "groups" differ from the control "groups." Assuming that the outcome variable was pain as assessed via a 10-point visual analog scale (VAS; recalling that a lower value indicates less pain and is therefore desirable), Table 8.1 presents one of several possibilities for such an effect (i.e., −1.41 vs. −0.07).

Table 8.1: Hypothetical Positive Intervention Effect on Pain.

	Intervention	Control
Order A	(Cell A) −1.42	(Cell B) −0.12
Order B	(Cell C) −1.40	(Cell D) −0.02
Total (Mean)	−1.41	−0.07

The second contrast (and second main effect p-value) is not as interesting from a scientific perspective. It addresses the overall effect of the two orders by combining the intervention and control conditions within each order, Mean $[(\textbf{Cell A}: O_{A2} - O_{A1}) + (\textbf{Cell B}: O_{A4} - O_{A3})]$ vs. Mean $[(\textbf{Cell C}: O_{B4} - O_{B3}) + (\textbf{Cell D}: O_{B2} - O_{B1})]$. A p-value $< .05$ here would indicate either (a) that the randomization was not successful (e.g., one of the groups had a greater tendency for changing on the outcome variable than the other) or, more likely, (b) that the assumptions for the use of a crossover design were not met. An example of such a finding (accompanied by no suggestion of an intervention effect) is presented in Table 8.2.

Table 8.2: Hypothetical Overall Order Effect.

	Intervention	Control	Total (Mean)
Order A	(Cell A) −1.42	(Cell B) −1.40	−1.41
Order B	(Cell C) −0.12	(Cell D) −0.02	−0.05
Total (Mean)	−0.77	−0.71	

Another possibility, in which both an intervention and an overall order effect occur, is presented in Table 8.3.

Table 8.3: Hypothetical Overall Order Effect.

	Intervention	Control	Total (Mean)
Order A	(Cell A) −2.41	(Cell B) −0.12	−1.27
Order B	(Cell C) −1.42	(Cell D) +0.80	−0.31
Total (Mean)	−1.92	+0.34	

This latter result would be quite hard to explain (and fortunately, unlikely to occur) since participants were randomly assigned to orders. Such a finding would not necessarily be fatal, however, since the predicted intervention vs. control effect difference did not appear to be related to the order in which the intervention and control were presented (i.e., the predicted outcome occurred for both orders).

The third p-value produces a more refined test of the possible existence of a carryover effect by addressing the specific issue of whether the intervention was more effective than the control in one order than in the other *irrespective of any biased assignment of participants to order* (i.e., independent of any overall difference between Order A vs. Order B, such as depicted in Tables 8.2 and 8.3). As was discussed in Chapter Seven, this comparison involves an interaction (specifically a treatment × order interaction), but basically involves the following contrast (Figure 8.4): [Mean (**Cell A**: $O_{A2} - O_{A1}$) – Mean (**Cell B**: $O_{A4} - O_{A3}$)] vs. [Mean (**Cell C**: $O_{B4} - O_{B3}$) – Mean (**Cell D**: $O_{B2} - O_{B1}$)]. Conceptually, this contrast subtracts the effects of the intervention vs. control conditions in each order and then assesses whether this difference is statistically significant. It, like the combined intervention vs. control contrast, is also a repeated measure or within-subjects effect. A $p < .05$ result indicates a differential intervention effect for one order as opposed to another. Table 8.4 depicts one of many possible results that might occur (alternately, the interaction can be graphed as illustrated in the previous chapter [e.g., Figure 7.3]).

Table 8.4: Hypothetical Interaction Effect.

	Intervention	Control	Interaction Effect
Order A	(Cell A) **−1.42**	(Cell B) **+0.12**	(−1.42) − (+0.12) = **−1.54**
Order B	(Cell C) **−0.02**	(Cell D) **+0.02**	(−0.02) − (+0.02) = **−0.04**

Results such as this are every crossover investigator's worst nightmare. For some (possibly inexplicable) reason the intervention seemed to be quite effective for participants when it was administered first (Order A) but completely ineffective when it was administered after the control.

While the 2 × 2 crossover design just presented is conceptually quite simple, some behavioral crossover experiments can very quickly become rather complicated. To illustrate, consider the following example of an unpublished experiment designed to assess the effects of two types of stress-inducing interventions on three risk-taking (game-like) behavioral tasks.

Example of a More Complicated Crossover Design

This study departed from a typical crossover design in the sense that its dual interventions were not introduced to the same participants because of their likely reactivity effects on one another. Instead, each person was randomly assigned to receive either a performance-induced or stress-induced intervention, each of which was coupled with a common control condition (i.e., a guided imagery technique designed to be relaxing rather than stressful).

Healthy, paid participants were accordingly recruited to perform three risk-taking behavioral tasks (which we'll simply label as Tasks 1 through 3) under either performance or emotionally induced stress (i.e., Interventions A and B, respectively). All participants also performed the three tasks following the guided imagery control condition. The experiment itself was designed to select both (a) the type of stressful intervention that most strongly affected risk-taking behavior and (b) the type of risk-taking task most responsive to both interventions. It was, in effect, a pilot study for a larger experiment involving brain scans following intravenous injections of amphetamine as compared to placebo.

Procedurally, the experiment involved the following process:

1. Participants were randomly assigned to receive either performance-induced (A) or emotion-induced stress (B), which made type of stressor a between-subjects factor.

2. Each participant served as his or her own control (i.e., received the guided imagery condition), although each intervention and each control condition for each intervention was conducted on a separate day to avoid participant fatigue and hopefully to reduce any carryover effects. This meant that the (a) intervention vs. the control comparison, (b) Day 1 vs. Day 2 performance differences, and (c) the three performance tasks were represented as repeated measures factors (although the latter was not included in the overall model but instead each task was analyzed separately).

3. Then, to counterbalance the order in which the intervention and the control conditions were performed, participants who had been randomly assigned to receive Intervention A were randomly assigned once again to either receive either it on Day 1 or the guided imagery control on Day 1. (Naturally this meant that each individual so assigned would receive the opposite condition on Day 2.) The same procedure was then repeated for participants who had been randomly assigned to receive Intervention B. This resulted in a second between-subjects factor (the two randomly assigned orders).

To this point the design contained four factors. Two were between-subjects factors: the two types of interventions (to which participants were randomly assigned) and the two orders (intervention implemented on Day 1 vs. Day 2, also randomly assigned). The third and fourth factors were repeated measures factors comprised of the intervention (either A or B) vs. the guided imagery control and Day 1 vs. Day 2 overall performance (which was basically a nuisance factor that the investigators assumed and hoped would not prove to be statistically significant). Both variables were counterbalanced, resulting in four combinations:

1. Intervention A introduced on Day 1 (which meant that its guided imagery control would be run on Day 2),
2. Intervention A introduced on Day 2 (and its control on Day 1),
3. Intervention B introduced on Day 1 (with its control occurring on Day 2), and
4. Intervention B on Day 2 (with its control on Day 1).

As mentioned, there was an additional variable which did not necessarily require conceptualization as a fifth factor, but which did require counterbalancing: the three risk-taking behavioral tasks administered to each participant on each of the two days of the experiment. In other words, here, too, there existed the *possibility* that the order of presentation could influence the results via practice effects, learning, fatigue, or loss of interest.

When more than two levels or types of experimental conditions, procedures, and outcome variables require counterbalancing, the preferred strategy involves the use of a Latin square strategy, which will be described in more detail later in the chapter. This procedure is designed to ensure that each task will be performed an equal number of times in each possible order. For a 3 × 3 arrangement such as that used in this experiment, there are 12 different possibilities (these possibilities, as well as designs for additional numbers of entities in need of counterbalancing, can now be obtained from the Internet, as described later). For the present, let's assume the one randomly selected for this study took the form presented in Figure 8.5.

FIGURE 8.5: One of Twelve 3 × 3 Latin Square Designs.

	Performed First	Performed Second	Performed Third
Block 1/Task Order 1	Task 1	Task 2	Task 3
Block 2/Task Order 2	Task 2	Task 3	Task 1
Block 3/Task Order 3	Task 3	Task 1	Task 2

Participants were randomly assigned to one of the three blocks (or orders) indicated in Figure 8.5 separately for each intervention. Once assigned, this task order was kept constant for both days. From a procedural perspective, the challenge then became ensuring that each participant received the treatments and tasks in the prescribed orders to which they had been assigned, necessitating the creation of a log of assignments, such as that in Figure 8.6.

FIGURE 8.6: Log of Random Assignments for the Counterbalanced Example.

ID	Intervention	Day 1 vs. Day 2 Assignment	Task Order	First	Second	Third
#1	A (Performance)	Performance Day 1/Control Day 2	1	Task 1	Task 2	Task 3
#2	A (Performance)	Performance Day 1/Control Day 2	3	Task 3	Task 1	Task 2
#3	B (Emotional)	Control Day 1/Emotional Day 2	2	Task 2	Task 3	Task 1
#4	A (Performance)	Control Day 1/Performance Day 2	2	Task 2	Task 3	Task 1
#5	A (Performance)	Control Day 1/Performance Day 2	3	Task 3	Task 1	Task 2
#6	B (Emotional)	Emotional Day 1/Control Day 2	1	Task 1	Task 2	Task 3
#7	B (Emotional)	Control Day 1/Emotional Day2	1	Task 1	Task 2	Task 3
...	...	...	...	...	...	...

The contrast of primary interest here involved the relative effect of the performance stressor vs. its control *as compared to* the effect of its emotional counterpart vs. its control. Also of interest was the selection of the *single* task most contributive to that contrast (which could be ascertained separately or via a higher level interaction), which is why task order, once counterbalanced, was held constant across days and experimental conditions for the same individuals. The design itself, as procedurally conducted (and ignoring the three varying orders in which the tasks were performed) was as follows (where participants were first randomly assigned to performance vs. emotional interventions and then separately randomly assigned to order within interventions):

DAY 1		DAY 2	
Group A (Participants Assigned to the Performance Intervention)			
Order 1: Performance Intervention	Tasks 1–3	Guided Imagery Control	Tasks 1–3
Order 2: Guided Imagery Control	Tasks 1–3	Performance Intervention	Tasks 1–3
Group B (Participants Assigned to the Emotional Intervention)			
Order 1: Guided Imagery Control	Tasks 1–3	Emotional Intervention	Tasks 1–3
Order 2: Emotional Intervention	Tasks 1–3	Guided Imagery Control	Tasks 1–3

Theoretically, this design yields a staggering number of contrasts, many of which are of little interest (e.g., the Day 1 vs. Day 2 main effect collapsed across the other factors, or the overall Group A vs. Group B collapsed results). Some effects, while being of no scientific interest, were nevertheless essential to evaluate in order to ensure that (a) the final inferences regarding the overall effects of the two interventions (as compared to their controls) and (b) the differences between them were not in some way confounded with nuisance variables such as the order in which the conditions were introduced.

Investigators, of course, hope that no such nuisance (or moderating) effects occur, but to be safe they should all be investigated. Opinions differ among investigators (and some journals) regarding whether

1. To test order effects separately and then, assuming no statistically ones are found, conduct a final analysis using only the substantive contrasts of scientific interest, or
2. To test the entire factorial model.

In a study such as this one a sensible strategy might be to perform separate analyses involving the nuisance variables, employing perhaps three-factor models and then, assuming no nuisance effects surface, perform a final, more easily digested analysis for reporting purposes.

Thus, while the three tasks could be conceptualized as yet another factor in an already burgeoning factorial model, most investigators would analyze the interventions' effects separately for each task. However, since a Latin square design was employed to counterbalance order effects for these tasks, it would make sense to ascertain whether or not the order in which the tasks were introduced was related to performance, both in general and whether influenced by type of stressor.

Next, the treatment order effects can probably most easily be conceptualized via a separate analysis of the order effects for each intervention separately, as depicted in Figures 8.7 and 8.8.

FIGURE 8.7: Initial Reconfigured Data in a 2 × 2 Mixed Crossover Design for Intervention A.

	Intervention A	Control
Order 1	(Cell A) (Day 1)	(Cell B) (Day 2)
Order 2	(Cell C) (Day 2)	(Cell D) (Day 1)

FIGURE 8.8: Initial Reconfigured Data in a 2 × 2 Mixed Crossover Design For Intervention B.

	Intervention B	Control
Order 1	(Cell E) (Day 1)	(Cell F) (Day 2)
Order 2	(Cell G) (Day 2)	(Cell H) (Day 1)

Here the only real effect of interest (since the intervention vs. control comparisons will be analyzed next) is the interaction between the order factor and the intervention vs. control factor. These are interpretable, as described previously, via p-values and line graphs, with a lack of statistical significance for both analyses (assuming a reasonable sample size was used) indicating no intervention effect due to whether the intervention was introduced on the first day as opposed to the second.

Assuming no substantive moderating effect surfaced, the data can be subjected to a final reconfiguration of the key data, as depicted in Figure 8.9.

Of the three p-values produced by this analysis, only two are of *vital* inter-

FIGURE 8.9: Final (Conceptual) Reconfigured Data in a 2 × 2 Group Crossover Design.

	Intervention	Control
Group A (Performance Stressor)	(Cells A & C)	(Cells B & D)
Group B (Emotional Stressor)	(Cells E & G)	(Cells F & H)
Overall	(Cells A, C, E, & G)	(Cells B, D, F, & H)

est: (a) the main effect for the combined interventions vs. the control (which addresses the question, "Overall, did both interventions combined reduce performance in comparison to their controls?") and, perhaps more importantly, (b) the interaction between the intervention/control and the group factors ("Was the performance difference between Intervention A vs. its control different than that for Intervention B vs. its control?") The "group" factor, representing nothing more than the blocks to which participants were assigned (to permit the order effect to be tested), would be of little substantive scientific interest by itself. As always, however, the interpretation of a statistically significant intervention vs. control main effects must be moderated by order × treatment interaction (if one occurs).

While factorial designs such as this may appear unnecessarily complicated, a little complexity is a small price to pay for the amount (and the quality) of information they are capable of producing. Careful science absolutely requires the control of all potential confounds, and counterbalanced factorial designs provide a crucial mechanism for this task. And while experienced investigators may actually know which elements of a design are unlikely to confound the results of their experiments, their peer reviewers who judge the merits of their studies (at both the proposal and publishing stages) may not. Hence the need for another experimental principle:

PRINCIPLE #20: In addition to randomly assigning participants, counterbalance all procedural components employed in an experiment via the use of blocks and then randomly assign participants to those blocks to avoid confounding.

Advantages and disadvantages of crossover designs: This genre of design (and there are many variations) has both significant strengths and weaknesses. Let us summarize the more important of these. First, the strengths:

1. Crossover designs increase the statistical power of an experiment (hence the sensitivity of the hypothesis test) commiserate with the strength of the correlation between the same participants' outcomes across time [which in the case of the design represented in Figure 8.4 translates to the correlation between $\Delta O_{A2} - O_{A1}$ and $\Delta(O_{A4} - O_{A3})$ plus $\Delta(O_{B4} - O_{B3})$ and $\Delta(O_{B2} - O_{B1})$]. This in turn translates to permitting decreased sample sizes *or* the ability to detect smaller experimental effects.

2. The use of the same participants in the experimental conditions also provides a degree of procedural control. The same participants (when everything else is equal) always react more similarly to different situations than do different individuals reacting to different situations.

3. Since the participants in the groups or blocks used differ only with respect to the order in which they receive the experimental conditions, many of the potential participant/ institutional objections to random assignment are avoided. This potentially facilitates recruitment and decreases attrition.

The designs' drawbacks include the following:

1. Crossover designs are not applicable to the majority of experimental conditions because of their requirement of no lingering carryover effects for either the outcome or the intervention. Most interventions are designed to produce more than transitory effects, but there are many exceptions, such as brief-duration drugs or performance on certain tasks.

2. If a repeated testing effect (e.g., the simple act of responding to the outcome measure produces a practice effect) is suspected, these designs are contraindicated to the extent to which the expected size of the artifact is substantive or cumulative (i.e., continues to occur with each additional administration). While the repeated testing effect is controlled to a certain extent by counterbalancing (and the use of multiple assessments prior to the introduction of each experimental condition), the occurrence of the effect is potentially problematic.

3. While pilot work is recommended for all experiments, crossover and repeated measures studies normally require more such effort since incorrect timing of the washout period will most likely result in a ruined experiment.

4. Related to all three of the previous points, crossover studies seem to have a special capacity for producing equivocal results in which a hypothesized effect is produced along with an accompanying assumption violation (e.g., an unexpected and unexplainable carryover effect).

5. The methodology for testing order effects is imperfect because of the decreased statistical power available for testing order × treatment interactions. To avoid this weakness, experiments can be powered to test the interaction—which vitiates one of the primary advantages of the strategy (smaller required sample sizes)—or extensive pilot work can be conducted to ensure the absence of order effects.

6. The reactivity of crossover studies can be greater than a conventional experiment. Blinding is strongly recommended, as a no-treatment or treatment-as-usual control potentially introduces bias (e.g., good-subject or placebo effects). Placebo controls entail special challenges of their own in these designs, however, since individuals exposed to

both the intervention and its placebo are more likely to be able to differentiate between the two.

7. Attrition, when it occurs, is more costly, since data from participants withdrawing after receiving only one of the experimental conditions are lost because there is nothing with which to compare them. In a sense, one participant's withdrawal is equivalent to two withdrawals from a between-subjects design. However, to the extent that crossover studies are conducted in laboratory-like settings with brief experimental durations, missing data are usually not problematic.

8. While inexperienced investigators should not conduct experiments involving human participants without the tutelage of an experienced researcher, this adage is even more important for crossover studies, which generally require more specialized expertise than their between-subjects counterparts. It is therefore recommended that a concerted effort be made to obtain such help prior to the design of a crossover study.

These rather daunting disadvantages also change the advice of always conducting a pilot study to an absolute necessity for this design genre. Unless the experiment involves (a) interventions whose effects have a known duration (such as a drug with a carefully documented half-life), (b) an especially reactive outcome (such as blood pressure, which is known to fluctuate routinely), and (c) a good estimate of the duration of the effect of the intervention on the outcome (which is not available in many studies), conducting a full-blown crossover or repeated measures experiment without adequate pilot work borders on the irresponsible (if not the unethical). Even a small-sample, single-group crossover pilot designed to ascertain the probable existence and *duration* of a treatment effect on the selected outcome is better than none at all. (Of course, if two active treatments are involved, two groups are necessary. And if resources permit, using a control group is always preferable.) Finally, since determining the duration of an intervention effect (which is crucial for specifying the duration of the washout period) is as important as its strength, multiple observations following the intervention are required in crossover pilot work:

$$O_1 \text{ [Intervention] } O_2 \, O_3 \, O_4 \text{.... [Additional Observations As Needed]}$$

A marginally effective single-group alternative to the crossover design: Although not recommended, there are single-group repeated measures designs which constitute a significant improvement over the much-maligned single-group pretest posttest design discussed (or the primitive single-group crossover design depicted in Figure 8.1). One of these involves multiple implementations of all experimental conditions, as illustrated by the relatively simple version depicted in Figure 8.10.

$$O_1 \text{ [Intervention] } O_2 O_3 \text{ [Control] } O_4 O_5 \text{ [Intervention] } O_6 O_7 \text{ [Control] } O_8 O_9$$

FIGURE 8.10 The Single-Group Multiple-Intervention/Control Implementations Design

This design has both similar advantages and disadvantages to the randomized crossover design emanating from the same participants being exposed to all experimental conditions. It differs, however, in the sense that the multiple implementations of the intervention and the control conditions only *mimic* the counterbalanced procedural control of order effects without providing the capability of testing for them.

The design requires the same basic assumptions as its randomized counterpart but has the additional stipulation that none of the experimental conditions have an additive effect. In this latter regard, for example, if the second introduction of the intervention appears to produce a stronger effect than the first [i.e., $(O_6 - O_5)$ vs. $(O_8 - O_7) > (O_2 - O_1)$ vs. $(O_4 - O_3)$]—or the two control intervals do not produce comparable results [i.e., $(O_4 - O_3) \neq (O_8 - O_7)$]—then the results can be problematic to interpret.

Unfortunately, there are also other alternative explanations for false positive and false negative results in this design that could be avoided by randomization, such as the possibility that a significant effect for each intervention over its respective control could have simply been due to the same experimental artifact occurring twice. Given these weaknesses, therefore, this option normally cannot normally be recommended for anything other than a pilot study for a better designed subsequent experiment.

Latin square designs: When two conditions are contrasted in a repeated measures design, there are only two ways in which their order of presentation can be counterbalanced: Treatment A can be administered first, followed by Treatment B, and vice versa. When three or more conditions are employed, however, the counterbalancing possibilities begin to multiply exponentially.

For study experiments employing four conditions (let's simply call them A through D) there are 576 possibilities for how each condition is assured the opportunity of being administered first, second, third, and fourth (in case there is a practice or fatigue effect of some sort) *and* administered both prior to and following each other condition (in case receiving one condition affects the receipt of another). These 576 options are called Latin squares, and the design itself can be implemented as follows:

1. Access the Internet and have a 4 × 4 Latin square design randomly selected by one of the freely available Latin square generators. Let's assume that the following was selected (corresponding to the experimental conditions listed in Figure 8.11).

FIGURE 8.11: An Example of a Latin Square Design.

	1st	2nd	3rd	4th
Order 1	B	A	D	C
Order 2	A	B	C	D
Order 3	C	D	A	B
Order 4	D	C	B	A

2. The columns affixed to this square represent the order in which the conditions (designated A–D in the cells within each row) would be administered. The rows are simply blocks (or groups) to which participants will be randomly assigned and have no intrinsic meaning other than the assurance of a counterbalanced order since each person receives all four experimental conditions. Thus, one-fourth of the experimental participants will be assigned to the first block (row) and will receive Treatment B first, Treatment A second, Treatment D third, and Treatment C last. Another fourth of the sample will receive Treatment A first (row two) and Treatment D fourth, and so on.

3.   The effect of interest here is the difference in the outcome produced between the four experimental conditions. Of course, this design also allows the investigator to test the influence of order on the experimental conditions, although hopefully pilot work, experience, or theory would have suggested that this possibility was unlikely.

4.   The design perfectly controls for the order of administration, but not the number of times each condition *immediately* follows or precedes each other condition. Note that A and B immediately follow and precede one another twice, but A and C are never administered consecutively (although one is always administered prior to and following the other: For example, A is administered twice prior to C and twice followed it, but never adjacently. This failure of perfectly controlling all possible order effects is normally quite trivial, however, since it is unlikely, although not impossible, that unequal adjacent positioning would result in a substantive treatment effect.

Greco-Latin square designs: If our hypothetical investigator had decided it was necessary to counterbalance the order, another variable (such as the forearm positions in the Price placebo experiment or the behavioral tasks in the counterbalanced example), a Greco (or Graeco)-Latin square design, such as depicted in Figure 8.12, could have been employed, in which the capital letters A through D again represent our hypothetical experimental conditions as before and the subscripted numbers 1–4 represent the second repeated measures factor (e.g., site) to which these conditions would be applied.

This strategy enables two variables to be counterbalanced simultaneously. A Greco-Latin square is formed by the combination of two orthogonal Latin squares, as represented in Figure 8.12.

FIGURE 8.12: An Example of a Greco-Latin Square Design.

	1st	2nd	3rd	4th
Order 1	A_1	B_2	C_3	D_4
Order 2	B_4	A_3	D_2	C_1
Order 3	C_3	D_2	A_4	B_3
Order 4	D_3	C_4	B_1	A_2

Here participants are again randomly assigned to one of the four orders (blocks). Those assigned to Order 1 will be administered Intervention A at "site" 1 (the subscripts refer to sites) first. Those assigned to Order 4 will receive Intervention D applied to the third site first, and so forth.

Balanced incomplete-block designs: There are relatively rare occasions when a repeated measures design is appropriate but the large number of interventions (or other experimental conditions such as tasks in the counterbalanced example) necessitated preclude each participant from being given each intervention. An alternative design exists for such situations, referred to as *balanced incomplete-block designs*, in which participants are randomly assigned to complete a *manageable* number of interventions—but not the full number.

These hybrid designs employ *blocks* of interventions which are also "balanced" in the sense that each intervention is represented the same number of times in the blocks and each is presented in combination with every other intervention the same number of times. (This is yet another application of the blocking concept [as were the Latin square and Greco-Latin square designs, which also employed *blocks* of orders to which participants were randomly assigned], the identity or meaning of which has no scientific relevance other than permitting comparisons among interventions or other experimental conditions.)

Including blocks, there are five variables that determine the form that a balanced incomplete-block design takes: the number of (1) blocks [b], (2) treatments [t], (3) replications of each intervention across blocks (also called replicates) [r], (4) treatments per block [k] (i.e., the number of treatments to which any single participant will be exposed), and (5) times each pair of treatments appear within the blocks employed [Y]. Since all of these variables are interdependent, there is a finite (but large) number of combinations that can be used to ensure a balanced design (see Cochran and Cox's classic textbook [1957] for an extensive list of permissible t, k, r, b, Y combinations of blocks).

Borrowing an example from Winer (1962), suppose an experiment was comprised of five interventions [t] (designated A through E) but the investigator determined that it was feasible (e.g., because of time, fatigue, burden) for any one participant to complete only three of them [k]. One possibility would be to use 10 blocks [b], with each intervention being represented in 6 of them (called replications in this model [r]) and each pair of interventions appearing together in only three blocks [Y]. Participants could then be randomly assigned to the following 10 blocks and receive the interventions designated in Figure 8.13.

FIGURE 8.13: A Balanced-Incomplete Block Design (6 Interventions; 10 Blocks).

Block Number	Interventions Contained
#1	A, B, C
#2	A, B, D
#3	A, B, E
#4	A, C, D
#5	A, C, E
#6	A, D, E
#7	B, C, D
#8	B, C, E
#9	B, D, E
#10	C, D, E

This results in an "incomplete" repeated measures design in the sense that the same participants received only a subset of the study's interventions. Thus, if only one participant were assigned to one block, each intervention would be administered to six individuals and each pair of interventions would be administered to three different individuals.

In a complete design, of course, all participants would have received all five interventions, hence resulting in considerably more precision and power. The analysis of a balanced-incomplete block experiment takes these factors into consideration, however, and power can be compensated for by using as many participants per block as needed. (However, each block should contain the same number of participants to avoid confounding.)

A bewildering number of variations of incomplete, yet balanced designs exist. Here only the most basic strategies are discussed which (in the present author's opinion) are most applicable to experiments involving human participants. Even these are not commonly used in the behavioral, educational, and health disciplines, but they should be considered when completely balanced, repeated measures designs are not practical. (For investigators contemplating using one of these designs, it is recommended that a copy of Cochran and Cox [1957] be obtained through interlibrary loan or purchased for less than $10 via the Internet.) The design is, in a sense, a repeated measures single-factor analogy to the between-subjects, fractional factorial designs discussed earlier—having the same exploratory potential for identifying potentially effective interventions from a wide range of options.

Constructing balanced incomplete designs via the Youden square approach: A relatively simple method of constructing a balanced incomplete design can be employed via what is termed a cyclic square. This is a special case of the Latin square in which the dimension of square selected represents the number of interventions or tasks included in the design.

Thus, if eight treatments [t] are to be employed (which can be designated A–H), the cyclical Latin square in Figure 8.14 would be constructed, with the rows designating blocks to which participants will be randomly assigned and the columns (numbered 1–8) representing the number of treatments that would be presented to each participant in a full factorial design.

FIGURE 8.14: A Cyclical (Ascending Order Only) 8 × 8 Latin Square Design.

Columns							
1	2	3	4	5	6	7	8
A	B	C	D	E	F	G	H
B	C	D	E	F	G	H	A
C	D	E	F	G	H	A	B
D	E	F	G	H	A	B	C
E	F	G	H	A	B	C	D
F	G	H	A	B	C	D	E
G	H	A	B	C	D	E	F
H	A	B	C	D	E	F	G

Of course, employing the full 8 × 8 square would result in a completely balanced design in which each participant received all eight interventions. To reduce the number of treatments assigned (and to retain a balanced design), the investigator need only randomly select the number of columns representing the number of treatments each individual would receive.

Thus, if it were decided that each participant would receive four interventions, four columns could be randomly selected and individuals could then be assigned to the resulting eight blocks (which are represented by the eight rows in Figure 8.15). Assuming columns 1–4 were the ones selected (hence requiring deletion of columns 5–8), the following Youden square design would be generated (which is really a rectangle but called a square because it originated from one) with the following parameters: interventions [t] = 8, blocks [b] = 8, interventions per block [k] = 4, and replications [r] = 4.

Note that this design, in contrast to the first balanced incomplete block example, is constrained in the sense that the number of replications must be equal to the number of interventions per block and the number of blocks must be equal to the total number of interventions. Another difference is that the Youden square approach does not ensure the same number of times discrete pairs of interventions [λ] occur within blocks, but the most important factors are

FIGURE 8.15 Youden Square Balanced Incomplete Design (t = b = 8; k = r = 4).

Blocks	Order of Interventions Received			
	1st	2nd	3rd	4th
1	A	B	C	D
2	B	C	D	E
3	C	D	E	F
4	D	E	F	G
5	E	F	G	H
6	F	G	H	A
7	G	H	A	B
8	H	A	B	C

controlled by this strategy (i.e., the number of interventions received is the same for all participants, along with the assurance that each intervention is replicated an equal number of times across blocks). Also, since the number of blocks is restricted to the number of interventions, this design will almost surely require the random assignment of multiple participants to blocks. (The total N should again be equal for each block: $N = n \times b$.)

While other variations on this theme exist, such as *partially* balanced incomplete block *designs* (in which interventions of greater interest can be paired together more frequently in more blocks to produce more precision with scarce resources), these strategies are used more often in industrial than in human experimentation and thus will not be discussed here. For a more in-depth treatment of these additional options as well as further elaboration on fractional replications, see classic texts such as those by Cochrane and Cox (1957), Winer (1962), Winer, Brown, and Michels (1991), and Cox and Reid (2000).

THE RANDOMIZED MATCHED BLOCK DESIGN

The final design presented in this chapter employing the use of *blocks* involves an extremely powerful experimental approach called the randomized matched block design.

Definitional Interlude: Blocking

By now it should be clear that *blocking*, along with randomization, replication, and nesting, is a key design strategy involving the purposeful grouping of experimental units (e.g., treatments or participants) for the express purpose of eliminating (or controlling) extraneous sources of outcome variation. Usually these blocks have no intrinsic meaning in their own right (as illustrated via the Latin and Youden square designs) but serve only as a procedural strategy to isolate (or counterbalance) extraneous variation that can then be "subtracted" from the experimental error in subsequent statistical analyses.

The randomized matched block design typically involves (a) creating blocks of *closely matched* (on a variable related to the outcome) individuals (the number within each block being equal to the number of experimental conditions) and then (b) randomly assigning those individuals within each block to receive *one* (and only one) condition. Unlike the previous designs discussed in this chapter in which multiple experimental conditions are administered to the same individuals, the present design only *mimics* the control of individual differences afforded by a repeated measures design via the matching process. The randomized matched block design also has two very significant advantages: The assignment of each participant to only one experimental condition avoids (a) the possibility of a treatment carryover effect as well as (b) restrictions regarding the type of outcome variable that can be employed.

Because different participants are matched on a variable known to be correlated with the outcome variable, the randomized matched block design (like the crossover design) has considerably more precision than conventional between-subjects designs. This in turn allows investigators to use fewer participants than, say, a randomized pretest-posttest control group design. Unfortunately, the randomized matched block design has one requirement that precludes its use in many research scenarios: The identity of the entire participant pool must be known prior to the beginning of the experiment. (Many clinical studies involve administering the study protocol as participants are recruited and thereby become available.)

The primary procedural difference between the randomized matched block design and between-subjects (as well as repeated measures) designs resides in the randomization process. For the latter designs (as in a crossover design), participants may either be randomly assigned as they become available or a list of randomized group assignments can be made before the experiment begins, with individuals sequentially inheriting the assignment *following* informed consent and baseline assessment.

The randomized matched block design does not afford this degree of flexibility, however, since the entire matching and random assignment processes must be completed prior to the implementation of the experimental conditions. (The matching process itself requires two conditions: [a] all experimental patients must be available and consented prior to randomization and [b] a continuous baseline variable strongly related to the primary outcome variable must also be available at that time.)

To illustrate how this blocking variable is employed, let us assume an educational researcher designs a study to test two modes of presentation (Intervention A vs. Intervention B) with respect to their relative efficacy for facilitating learning mathematical content from a computerized instructional module. Having a limited number of students and computers available for the experiment, the investigator decides to randomly assign matched students to the two interventions. Nonrandomized matching has already been identified as an imperfect method of preventing the selection artifact, but coupling randomization with matching (a) prevents or controls such artifacts as selection and regression to the mean and (b) actually improves on the precision afforded by conventional random assignment.

Let's further assume that our hypothetical investigator decides to conduct her experiment using a single classroom of students whose educational records include a standardized mathematics achievement test. The two primary criteria for a randomized matched block design are therefore in place:

1. The existence of a continuous blocking variable (the standardized mathematics achievement test) that most likely correlates with the study's outcome variable (learning of the mathematics content taught via the computerized instructional module) and

2. The availability of the entire experimental sample prior to the initiation of the study protocol.

The first step in implementing the strategy entails the creation of blocks within which students can be randomly assigned to groups. Since this particular experiment involved the comparison of two interventions, the block sizes would be equal to two and the number of blocks would be equal to half of the number (N) of available students, or $N/2$. Block creation would be accomplished by (a) abstracting the previous year's test scores from the students' records, (b) entering each student's test scores into a spreadsheet such as Excel (or a statistical software data entry screen), next to his or her name or study I.D., and (c) instructing the program to rank order the scores. The resulting data would then look something like what is presented in Figure 8.16.

FIGURE 8.16: Rank-Ordered Student List.

Students	ID	Test Score Percentile	Student Rank
Mary Jones	#1	85.6	1
Robert Smith	#2	85.4	2
Beatrice McMillian	#3	79.0	3
Rebecca Weinstein	#4	79.0	4
		.	.
		.	.
		.	.
		.	.
Jonathan Brown	#29	42.1	27
James White	#30	41.2	28

Next, blocks of two students each would be formed, starting with Mary Jones and Robert Smith (who had the highest standardized test scores) and proceeding throughout the entire class enrollment to the two lowest scores, representing Jonathan Brown and James White. (If the class contained an odd number of students, the final student would not be used in the experiment, although she or he could receive one of the two interventions for the sake of convenience). Tie scores on the blocking variable are handled by randomly selecting which students would be assigned to an adjacent block. (A blocking variable that produces a large number of such ties is not a good choice for this design.)

The random assignment of students to groups would proceed as follows. Within each block, the first student would be randomly assigned to one intervention, and the second student, by default, would be assigned to the other. (While the actual random assignment would be done via the computer using a statistical package or online calculator, conceptually it would involve flipping a coin for the first of the two students in each block, letting, say, "heads" equal Intervention A and "tails" equal Intervention B.) If the experiment had involved three groups, blocks of three would have been formed, with the three students within each block being randomly assigned with the constraint that no two students could be assigned to the same condition. For the present example, the resulting group assignment might look as presented in Figure 8.17.

FIGURE 8.17: Rank-Ordered Student Assignment.

Block	Assignment	Students	Test Score Percentile	Student Rank
#1	Intervention A	Mary Jones	85.6	1
#1	Intervention B	Robert Smith	85.4	2
#2	Intervention B	Beatrice McMillian	79.0	3
#2	Intervention A	Rebecca Weinstein	79.0	4
.	.	.	.	.
.	.	.	.	.
.	.	.	.	.
.	.	.	.	.
#15	Intervention B	Jonathan Brown	42.1	27
#15	Intervention A	James White	41.2	28

The resulting groups would thus procedurally be forced to be almost perfectly equivalent on the matching variable. Assuming a reasonably strong correlation between the matching variable and the experimental changes in the outcome variable, the matching procedure also helps to assure the initial equivalence between groups with respect to those elusive, nonmeasurable variables affecting participants' propensities to change.

In addition to almost completely negating the possibility of a selection artifact by mimicking a repeated measures design, other advantages of the strategy include the following:

1. A significant increase in the amount of statistical power available for the study (and therefore a decrease in the necessary sample size) depending on the strength of the relationship between the blocking variable and outcome changes.
2. The fact that the assignment strategy still meets our definition of randomness, since at the beginning of the experiment each participant has an equal chance of being assigned to each experimental group as compared to all other participants.

Disadvantages include the following:

1. The necessity of having the entire sample available at baseline. Many experiments do not provide this luxury.
2. The occasional difficulty of coming up with a strongly correlated blocking variable.
3. The design is contraindicated for experiments expected to encounter significant attrition. (If one member of a block drops out of the study, this in effect precludes the use of the data from the remaining member[s] of the block.)

INTERRUPTED TIME SERIES DESIGNS

The final genre of repeated measures approach to be discussed in this chapter involves time series designs, which employ repeated assessments of the outcome variable as their primary control mechanism. There is no agreed-upon template for a time series design other than the use of at least three assessments before and after the introduction of the intervention(s) (Bero, Grilli, Grimshaw, et al., 2002), although considerably more assessments are usually used. (In a review involving the use of interrupted time series experiments in behavioral change experiments, the median number of observations was nine before the intervention and six afterward [Ramsay, Matowe, Grilli, et al., 2004].)

The length between assessments varies widely as well, although it is normally considerably longer than occurs in a crossover design. Optimally, these repeated assessments are of the same length and can be a day, a week, or even a year apart.

The most basic architecture for a single-group interrupted time series design (which is *not* recommended) looks like some variant of Figure 8.18.

$$O_1 O_2 O_3 O_4 O_5 O_6 O_7 \text{ [Intervention] } O_8 O_9 O_{10} O_{11} O_{12} O_{13} O_{14} O_{15}$$

FIGURE 8.18: A Sample Single-Group Interrupted Time Series Design.

Time series designs are often (a) retrospective in nature, employing (b) outcome assessments involving data that are routinely collected for other purposes, and (c) units of measurements other than individual participants. They are sometimes used to evaluate large-scale societal interventions and as such may involve a nonrandomly selected control group, such as another geographic region in which the intervention is not implemented. For present purposes, unless otherwise stated, we will assume that multiple measures on individual participants are used, although the architecture and logic of the designs themselves apply to groups of individuals as well.

Retrospective experiments are outside our stated purview, although time series designs are also used prospectively. The design represented in Figure 8.18 (or some variant thereof), for example, could be employed using an entire school as the designated group, with the number of tardiness episodes accruing weekly serving as the outcome variable. The intervention could be a new policy implemented after the seventh week involving the denial of recess privileges to students each day a student was late for school, regardless of the reason (except, perhaps, a school bus failure).

The comparison of interest would depend on the time interval required for the intervention effect to manifest itself and its duration. Figure 8.19 represents an outcome effect that occurs immediately but is transitory in nature.

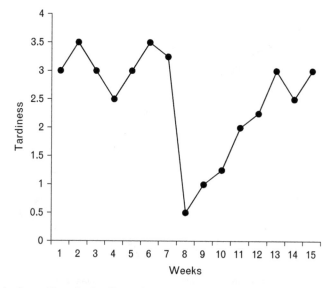

FIGURE 8.19: Single-Group Time Series (Immediate but Transitory Effect).

Alternately, our hypothetical tardiness intervention might last as long as the policy was in place (see Figure 8.20).

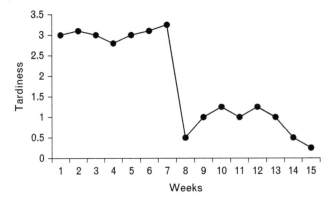

FIGURE 8.20: Single-Group Time Series (Delayed, Persistent Effect).

In either case, from an inferential perspective, single-group time series designs are superior to a single-group pretest-posttest design, since the multiple pre-intervention observations provide a degree of quasi-procedural control. In a single-group pretest-posttest design, on the other hand, a change in the outcome variable immediately following the intervention is much more likely to be attributable to (a) a chance finding, (b) an extraneous external event, or (c) regression to the mean than one occurring following the intervention than is the case of a change occurring exactly at Week 7 (Figures 8.19 and 8.20) in a time series design. Of course, sometimes the intervention effect does not occur immediately, but in that case its timing should be hypothesized on the basis of pilot work or a theory. (If the timing of the effect occurs at a nonhypothesized time point, the credibility of a change [even if it occurs in the hypothesized direction] is greatly reduced.)

The relatively flat, pre-intervention pattern depicted in Figure 8.20 is only one of a multitude of possibilities. Perhaps equally probable are gradually descending (see Figure 8.21) or ascending

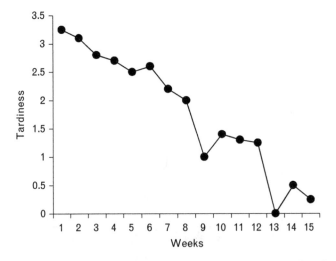

FIGURE 8.21: Single-Group Time Series (Delayed Intervention and Descending Baseline).

slopes which may themselves be a function of external factors other than the intervention and even statistically significant in their own right. (This might occur in our hypothetical tardiness study, by students being likely to be late toward the end of the school year rather than at the beginning of it.) Alternately, the repeated assessments may appear more "jagged" because of error-induced instability or seasonal effects. None of these pre- or post-intervention trends preclude the documentation of an intervention effect, but the statistical analysis employed must be capable of controlling for them.

Like its more primitive ancestor, the single-group pretest-posttest design, interrupted time series designs can be significantly buttressed by the addition of a comparison group. The random assignment of participants to such a group would be optimal, of course, but is often not feasible. However, just as a nonrandomized comparison group marginally buttresses the single-group pretest-posttest design, the same is true for a single-group interrupted time series design. In our tardiness experiment, for example, the selection of one or more "comparable" comparison schools in which the intervention is not scheduled to be implemented (but which collects the same data in the same manner) would help to control for seasonal or extraneous effects attributable to the local environment or changes in school district policies (see Figure 8.22).

Experimental Site: O_1 O_2 O_3 O_4 O_5 O_6 O_7 [Intervention] O_8 O_9 O_{10} O_{11} O_{12} O_{13} O_{14} O_{15}
Control Site: O_1 O_2 O_3 O_4 O_5 O_6 O_7 [No Intervention] O_8 O_9 O_{10} O_{11} O_{12} O_{13} O_{14} O_{15}

FIGURE 8.22: A Sample Multiple-Group Interrupted Time Series Design.

In such a scenario, results as dramatic as those depicted in Figure 8.23 would be difficult to discount.

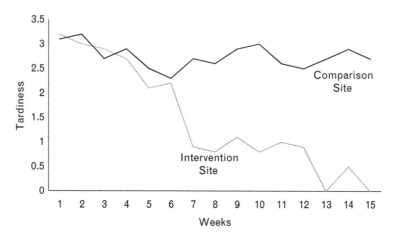

FIGURE 8.23: Two-Group Quasi-Experimental Time Series Data (Dramatic Intervention Effect at Week 8).

A multiple-group strategy such as this is obviously superior to its single-group counterpart and approaches inferential credibility if (a) properly implemented (e.g., the outcome variable is routinely collected and not reactive), (b) the comparison group can be demonstrated to be relatively comparable to the intervention group (historical outcome data, if available, could be used, such as previous-year tardiness data in our hypothetical example), and (c) the experiment is conducted prospectively rather than retrospectively. However, when randomization is absent, the attendant alternative explanations for the results remain problematic.

Many variations exist on both single- and multiple-group interrupted time series designs:

1. Multiple introductions of the intervention (which, like crossover designs, are only feasible when the intervention's duration is brief or well established).
2. The introduction of the same intervention at different sites at different time points. Figure 8.24 depicts a design described in Biglan, Ary, and Wagenaar's (2000) study, in which baseline assessments involved observations of young people attempting to buy tobacco products. In two of the communities the intervention was introduced following the fourth baseline assessment. After it became clear that the intervention had produced an effect, it was then introduced after the eighth assessment to the other two communities. The entire experiment was then replicated with four additional communities. (This example illustrates the flexibility creative investigators have in creating design alternations to fit their special needs and to increase the credibility of their findings.)

Site #1: $O_1O_2O_3O_4$ [Intervention] $O_5O_6O_7O_8O_9O_{10}O_{11}O_{12}O_{13}O_{14}O_{15}$
Site #2: $O_1O_2O_3O_4$ [Intervention] $O_5O_6O_7O_8O_9O_{10}O_{11}O_{12}O_{13}O_{14}O_{15}$
Site #3: $O_1O_2O_3O_4 O_5O_6O_7O_8$ [Intervention] $O_9O_{10}O_{11}O_{12}O_{13}O_{14}O_{15}$
Site #4: $O_1O_2O_3O_4 O_5O_6O_7O_8$ [Intervention] $O_9O_{10}O_{11}O_{12}O_{13}O_{14}O_{15}$

FIGURE 8.24: A Multiple-Site Interrupted Time Series Design (Phased Intervention).

Advantages and disadvantages of interrupted time series designs: For certain types of interventions that can only be implemented institution- or community-wide because of the probable occurrence of treatment diffusion (and/or political realities, such as the hypothetical tardiness and actual tobacco prevention experiments, respectively), interrupted time series designs constitute a less expensive alternative to randomly assigning entire facilities or communities to intervention and comparison groups. Their methodological utility is greatly enhanced through the additional procedural control available from the use of comparison groups or multiple sites (especially when the latter staggers implementation of the intervention, as illustrated by some version of the Biglan, Ary, and Wagenaar design).

However, interrupted time series designs require a very special genre of outcome variables that are often impractical to collect from individual participants. To the extent that data are collected from individuals specifically for research purposes, repeated testing or Hawthorn-like effects may also operate. When the data points involve institutional or community totals (as was the case in the tardiness example), it is possible that study results can be influenced by turnover, missing data, and/or instrumentation changes, especially in experiments taking place over relatively long periods of time. Treatment diffusion must also be guarded against in multigroup time series designs since between-site communication among administrators and staff is always possible. Finally, all of these designs involve a certain degree of analytic sophistication because of the possibility that the error components of the multiple assessments may be correlated, thereby violating the assumptions of conventional analytic approaches. (Auto-regressive integrated moving average [ARIMA] and latent growth models exist for this purpose but require specialized training and possibly statistical consultation for many investigators.)

This chapter ends our formal in-depth treatment of the most common designs employed in research involving human participants. (Chapter Twelve will present an overview of a number of more specialized designs unique to three less mainstream-paradigmatic approaches to conducting experiments involving human participants—i.e., single-case, program evaluation, quality improvement research.) The next section of the book, Part III, consists of two chapters dealing with issues that are absolutely essential for consummating the inferential potential of the powerful randomized experimental designs just presented. The first, Chapter Nine, involves maximizing the chances of avoiding something every investigator dreads (producing false negative results); the second, Chapter Ten, deals with implementing the design properly by ensuring that the experiment is conducted correctly and with exceeding care (which if not done reduces the most carefully and appropriated designed study to complete irrelevancy).

SUMMARY

Repeated measures (also called within-subjects) designs can be extremely powerful experimental options when it is feasible to introduce the experimental conditions to the same or matched participants. Two acceptable repeated measures/within-subjects designs were discussed along with a third marginally acceptable one:

1. Repeated measures designs in which all participants receive all the experimental conditions but are randomly assigned to receive them in a counterbalanced order. A variety of these crossover designs were illustrated. (A specialized alternative to these strategies, called *balanced incomplete block designs*, was described in which subsets of interventions, rather than the total number being evaluated, are administered to blocks of participants.)
2. Randomized matched block designs in which participants are matched and then randomly assigned to blocks. This is done in order to mimic the advantages of the same participants receiving all experimental conditions while avoiding many of the disadvantages of repeated measures designs.
3. Multiple-group quasi-experimental time series designs (the marginal option) in which multiple assessments of the outcome variable before and after implementation of the intervention provide a degree of procedural control when an a priori specification of the exact assessment at which the intervention effect will occur is hypothesized.

Two powerful experimental strategies (supplementary to randomization) and especially essential (but not limited) to repeated measures designs were introduced:

1. *Counterbalancing* (which controls for order effects and aids in the avoidance or facilitates the detection of carryover effects), and
2. *Blocking* (which involves the purposeful grouping of experimental units—such as treatments or participants)—for the express purpose of eliminating (or controlling) extraneous sources of outcome variation.

The utility of these two procedures consequently informed an additional experimental principle:

Principle #20: In addition to randomly assigning participants, counterbalance all procedural components employed in an experiment via the use of blocks and then randomly assign participants to those blocks to avoid confounding.

Alternative repeated measures designs discussed included the following:

1. The multiple-site/group interrupted time series design (preferably with a phased intro-duction of the intervention), which is capable of producing credible experimental inferences.
2. The single-group interrupted time series design, analogous to the multiple-group time series design, but without the additional control afforded by a comparable (preferably randomly assigned) comparison group.

REFERENCES

Bero L., Grilli R., Grimshaw, J.M., et al. (2002). *The Cochrane Effective Practice and Organisation of Care Group (EPOC) Module.* In: The Cochrane Library. Oxford: Update Software, Issue 1.

Biglan, A., Ary, D., & Wagenaar, A.C. (2000). The value of interrupted time-series experiments for com-munity intervention research. *Prevention Science, 1,* 31-49.

Cochran, W.G., & Cox, G.M. (1957). *Experimental designs* (2nd ed.). New York: Wiley.

Cox, D.R., & Reid, N. (2000). *The theory of the design of experiments.* Boca Raton, FL: Chapman & Hall.

Ramsay, C.R., Matowe, L., Grilli, R., et al. (2003). Interrupted time series designs in health technol-ogy assessment: Lessons from two systematic reviews of behavior change strategies. *International Journal of Technology Assessment in Health Care, 19,* 613–23.

Winer, B.J. (1962). *Statistical principles in experimental research.* New York: McGraw Hill.

Winer, B.J., Brown, D.R., & Michels, K.M. (1991) *Statistical principles in experimental design* (3rd ed.). New York: McGraw Hill.

PART III

MAXIMIZING AND IMPLEMENTING EXPERIMENTAL DESIGN

CHAPTER 9

ENSURING SUFFICIENT STATISTICAL POWER

S tatistical significance has already been described as both an a priori criterion for judging the acceptability of a research hypothesis and an a posteriori probability level generated as a byproduct of the statistical analytic process. For better or worse, the latter is often the arbiter of experimental success, as it determines whether or not the research hypothesis is accepted. And definitely for worse, it sometimes determines where and even *whether* an experiment is published.

Statistical significance is computed **after** a study is completed and its data are collected and analyzed. It is used to estimate how **probable** the study's **obtained** differences or relationships (both of which are called **effect sizes**) would be to occur by chance alone. Based in large part on Sir Ronald Fisher's (1935) recommendation, this probability level is commonly set at $p \leq .05$. If a probability level of .05 or below is obtained, the result is said to be "**statistically significant**" and the researcher has, by definition, supported his or her research hypothesis. If it is greater than .05, then statistical significance is not obtained and the research hypothesis is not supported.

Statistical power, by contrast, is computed **before** an experiment's final data are collected. It is sometimes incorrectly defined as the probability that an experiment will result in statistical significance. It is more commonly defined as the probability that a study will result in statistical significance if its research hypothesis is correct. However, both definitions are oversimplifications because the calculation of statistical power involves a two-step process involving (a) hypothesizing both the direction *and* the size of the effect most likely to occur as a result of the intervention and (b) estimating how **probable** the study's results are to result in statistical significance **if** both the direction and the size of the effect were correctly specified. But since both steps occur prior to the conduct of the experiment, the resulting probability is contingent on how appropriately that experiment is **conducted**—both with respect to its design and the implementation of its protocol.

Statistical power, therefore, is more accurately defined *as the probability that an experiment will result in statistical significance if that experiment is properly designed and properly conducted and its hypothesized effect size is correct*. Statistical significance is, in many ways, a conceptually easier concept than statistical power for most investigators to wrap their minds around since (a) the former's more common definitions are so much more succinct than the latter's and (b) there is something a bit counterintuitive about analyzing one's data before they are collected. There is also something very comforting to many scientists about the definitiveness of a decision making process in which "truth" is always obtained at the end of a study and questions can always be answered with a simple "yes" or "no" and not prefaced with such qualifiers as "perhaps" or "maybe."

The probability that an experimental inference finding would result by chance alone (i.e., the study's *obtained* statistical significance or *p*-value is ≤.05) must also be interpreted contingent on such issues as how it was designed and how that design was implemented.

So while the dichotomous nature of hypothesis testing is a comfort to many of us, it is profoundly discomforting that, following the conduct of an experiment, we are never 100% (or even 95%) certain whether our results were valid or invalid. We may know that the study was worthless because of a mistake (or some debacle that occurred during its conduct), but even then we could have achieved the correct results for the wrong reasons. And even if an experiment is competently designed and conducted, the final inference its results support may still be incorrect due to chance alone.

THE CONCEPTUAL BASIS OF STATISTICAL POWER

Therefore, since scientists never know with absolute certainty what truth is, the best they can do is design their experiments as thoughtfully as possible and conduct them as carefully as possible. And while, as scientists, we never know for sure whether our results were correct or not, fortunately, we do have a mechanism for determining how likely certain facets of our hypothesis tests are to be correct if we do our jobs properly. Diagrammatically, this process is depicted in Figure 9.1, where *it is assumed that the (a) experiment's significance (alpha) level was set at .05, (b) statistical power was set at .80, (c) the protocol was appropriate for the hypothesis, and (d) the study was conducted properly.*

FIGURE 9.1: Four Experimental Outcomes and Their Probabilities.

	What is Actually True	
	The Hypothesis Is Correct	The Hypothesis Is Incorrect
Possible Experimental Outcomes		
The Hypothesis Is Confirmed (*p* ≤ .05; power set at .80)	[a] Correct *[(p of occurrence) = statistical power = .80]*	[b] Incorrect [Type I Error] *[p of occurrence) = .05]*
The Hypothesis Is Not Confirmed (*p* > .05; power set at .80)	[c] Incorrect [Type II Error] *[p of occurrence]= 1 − statistical power = .20]*	[d] Correct *[p (of occurrence) = 1 − alpha = .95]*

In many ways, the chart is useful only from a conceptual or theoretical perspective, since we seldom if ever know whether the hypothesis was truly correct or incorrect. For while conventional wisdom teaches that we can assign probabilities to each of these cells as indicated in italics, these numbers are only a priori theoretical estimates based on perfectly run, and designed, experiments—conditions to which we can only aspire. Such probabilities are also based on the normal curve, which is a wonderful mathematical model but is nothing more than that—a model based on the assumption of an infinite number of data points used to make inferences regarding much smaller numbers.

But since this model *is* used to determine statistical significance (and will probably be used for the foreseeable future), it is necessary for investigators to understand the conceptual basis for these probability levels. Figure 9.1 is therefore interpreted as follows:

1. For any given hypothesis test, there are two theoretical possibilities (either the hypothesis was true or it was false—represented by the second and third columns in Figure 9.1).
2. Since there is no way that we can know which is true, we conduct an experiment as the best known way to choose the more likely possibility. (Remember, in research, we never deal with truth, only the probability of being correct in our quest for it.)
3. There are two, and only two, possibility outcomes for our experiment: either we will confirm the hypothesis or we will not (the table's two bottom rows).
4. While both the columns and rows in this table are somewhat problematic (especially the columns because we can never be absolutely sure about "what is actually true"), it is within the individual cells representing the combination of these rows and columns where things get interesting.

Cell a represents the probability that a **correctly** hypothesized effect will occur in an appropriated designed and conducted experiment. This, it will be remembered, reflects our definition of statistical power ("the probability that an experiment will result in statistical significance if that experiment is properly designed, properly conducted, and its hypothesized effect size is correct"). In other words, if the experiment is powered at .80 to achieve statistical significance equal to .05 and if (a) if the hypothesized ES was correct and (b) everything goes perfectly as planned, then (c) the probability that statistical significance will be obtained is .80.

> *Disclaimer*: The value .80, like .05, is an arbitrary statistical convention with no basis in "reality." In those cases when false positive results are considered especially serious, investigators may be wise to raise this value to .90 (or even .95 if resources are adequate and a compelling justification can be made).

Cell b represents the probability that an incorrect hypothesis will be experimentally confirmed (in other words, statistical significance will be obtained erroneously). This represents what is called a *Type I error* (or a false positive result) and is simply defined as the alpha level, which in turn is defined as the probability that any given experimentally generated effect size would occur by chance alone.

Cell c represents the probability of a completely different genre of error occurring, this time the probability that a correct hypothesis that should have been confirmed will not be confirmed. It is called a *Type II error* (or a false negative result) and constitutes a scientific nightmare for an experimental investigator: being right but not being able to demonstrate it. It is the complement of statistical power, which, it will be recalled, was defined as the probability that a correct hypothesis will be confirmed on the basis of an appropriately designed and conducted experiment. It is worth noting that the probability of this genre of error (.20) occurring is greater than the probability of occurrence of a Type I error (.05), based on the scientific value judgment that false negative results (as reflected in this cell) are more damaging to the fabric of science than false positive results. Whether or not this is a reasonable assumption is open to question, but there is no question that a false negative finding (a) can be extremely damaging to an investigator's career, by making the results more difficult to publish (as we will discuss in Chapter Thirteen, there is a bias against publishing studies that do not obtain statistical significance); (b) wastes resources; and (c) produces an incorrect inferential decision that the design process is supposed to avoid—all because the investigator did not employ a sufficiently large sample size (or failed to properly implement one of the other 11 power-enhancing strategies presented in this chapter). Ergo, the 17th experimental artifact that this entire chapter is designed to help prevent:

EXPERIMENTAL ARTIFACT #17: UNDERPOWERED EXPERIMENTS

These are defined as experiments whose design decisions unnecessarily increase the probability of producing false negative results.

Cell d represents the probability that the experiment will correctly fail to achieve statistical significance when the original hypothesis is incorrect. This is the complement of the alpha level $(1 - .05 = .95)$.

In a sense, the entire structure of inferential statistics and hypothesis testing rest on *statistical significance, statistical power,* and their relationship with one another, as laid out in Figure 9.1. This chapter is primarily devoted to discussing how the probabilities desired for Cells a and c can be estimated as accurately and cost-effectively as possible. (The book as a whole is devoted to the avoidance of all types of inferential errors, and to the goals that the hypothesized effect is *meaningful* and that it was tested by an appropriately designed and conducted experiment.)

If a power analysis is a quasi-statistical analysis performed on data before they are collected, something obviously must be used to represent these nonexistent data. And this "something" turns out to be proposed values for the following four parameters, any three of which can be employed to compute the fourth if *we can assume that the design, implementation of that design, and the statistical analysis were appropriate.*

(a)　*The significance criterion (or alpha level) that will be used to declare a given difference to be "real" or "statistically significant."* For the remainder of this chapter, we will follow Sir Ronald Fisher's suggested level of $p \leq .05$ and assume that this value is fixed at that level. (In an actual power analysis the desired significance level can be set at any value between zero and 1.00.)

Statistical Interlude: One- vs. Two-Tailed Tests

One- versus two-tailed tests: Throughout, when statistical significance (or the alpha level) is mentioned, the assumption is made that what is called a two-tailed or nondirectional statistical hypothesis test has been employed. This does not mean that the hypothesis itself is nondirectional, only that the statistical distribution used to test that hypothesis will be nondirectional, in the sense that the resulting analysis will include the possibility of declaring a "negative" finding as statistically significant (e.g., that the control group is significantly superior to the intervention group).

If a one-tailed statistical test is employed, an actually harmful intervention (no matter how dramatic the results) cannot be declared as statistically significant. There are occasions when it may be completely appropriate to discard the entire negative end of a statistical distribution, but scientific convention requires a persuasive a priori justification for doing so. (One reason for this requirement resides in the practice's potential for abuse, since a considerably smaller effect size is required to achieve statistical significance using a one-tailed test than that for its two-tailed counterpart. Thus, if an unethical [or inadequately trained] investigator's data analysis indicated that the final intervention vs. control contrast was associated with a $p = .10$, he or she could report that it was statistically significant at $p = .05$ using a one-tailed test.) Throughout the discussions that follow, therefore, a two-tailed significance level is assumed. This is not meant to deter investigators from hypothesizing directional, one-tailed effects. Such investigators are counseled, however, to provide a persuasive, scientifically based (but always a priori posited) rationale for this decision in their final research report.

(b)   *The desired power level.* This, by convention (and we can't blame it on Sir Ronald), is normally set at $p = 0.80$. This means, in turn, that the probability of being incorrect when (as always) everything else is done properly is 0.20 (i.e., a Type II error, or $1.00 - 0.80$).

(c)   *The number of subjects to be used in the experiment.* This is often the parameter that is estimated if the power is fixed.

(d)   *The size* of the intervention's hypothesized effect. Of the four parameters, the hypothesized effect size is by far the most problematic (Lipsey, 1990) because (a) if investigators *knew* what the experiment effect was before conducting the study there would be no need to conduct it in the first place and (b) the method by which the effect size is computed yields a completely ordinal estimate (as are all statistical concepts based on the normal curve). Like p-values, however, we're stuck with the concept, and its use—while imperfect—is a reality that at least appears to work serviceably well. (Although somewhat less common, the maximum detectable effect size can also be calculated when the sample size and desired power are fixed.)

The effect size (ES) concept: The final parameter (the hypothesized effect size) is considerably more difficult to specify than the others, so let's examine it in a bit more detail. ESs take numerous forms, based on (a) the characteristics of the outcome variable (e.g., whether it is continuous or categorical) and (b) the type of statistical procedure that will be used to analyze the data. For two-group studies, the most common formulation used is a descriptive statistic called Cohen's *d*, which is applicable to continuous variables analyzed via *t*-tests but can be converted to (or from) many other types of ESs (e.g., a dichotomous outcome variable analyzed by a chi-square, a relationship assessed by a correlation coefficient) via a variety of online calculators (e.g., http://

www.uccs.edu/~lbecker/ or http://www.campbellcollaboration.org/resources/effect_size_input.
php). The computation of a two-group ES involves the following very simple formula (with
apologies but sometimes formula can be conceptually simpler than prose):

Formula 9.1: Effect Size Formula for Two Independent Groups

$$ES = \frac{M_{INT} - M_{CON}}{S.D._{POOLED}}$$

Where M_{INT} stands for the mean of the intervention group; M_{CON} = the mean of the control group,
and S.D. usually stands for the pooled intervention and control standard deviation (Cohen's d, also
commonly used, involves the use of the control group's standard deviation in the denominator).

For those who prefer prose, all that is involved in this formula (to which other ESs can
be algebraically calibrated, including between-subjects, repeated measures, and mixed factorial
designs with and without covariates) is the estimation of (a) the most likely mean outcome difference to occur between the two group involved and (b) their pooled standard deviation. The
process of dividing this hypothesized difference by the pooled standard deviation results in a
generic ES independent of the outcome variable's scale of measurement. In other words, regardless of whether an outcome variable's values ranged from 0 to 10 (e.g., a visual analog scale) or
from 200 to 800 (e.g., graduate record exams), this formula reduces both disparate measures
to the same scale expressed in standard deviation units. Thus an ES of 1.0, regardless of the
measure itself, means that the difference between the intervention and the comparison group is
hypothesized to be one standard deviation on the outcome variable. An ES of 0.50 indicates a
hypothesized difference of one-half of one standard deviation.

For power analytic purposes, however, this ES formulation is helpful only as an initial point
in the power-analytic process. *Most of the design strategies mentioned so far (e.g., the use of a
pretest/baseline measure, the addition of covariates, factors, blocking variables, and repeated measures) possess the capacity of effectively increasing the experiment's ES, based on the relationship
between these added design features and the outcome variable.* This procedural ES increment
in turn reduces the required sample size for achieving a given level of power (or increases the
amount of power available for an experiment if the unadjusted sample size estimate is retained).
(The most notable exception to this generalization is the use of a nested factor as used in cluster
randomization, which tends to increase the required sample size, as will be illustrated shortly.)

While these statistical adjustment processes will not be discussed here, the first step in the
power/sample size analytic process remains a key part of the investigator's job description—
namely the task of hypothesizing the most likely between-group ES to accrue as represented in
Formula 9.1.

For power/sample size analyses this ES value can be obtained

1. Directly from a pilot study (which is preferable, because the relationship between other
   design components such as covariates or repeated measures can also be obtained),
2. Indirectly from a single-group pilot study followed by "guessing" what the mean of the
   control group (and any relevant correlations) would have been had they been employed,
   or
3. From a very similar study in the literature (or a meta-analysis based on similar studies).

The most common use of the ES, once hypothesized, is to estimate the number of participants required to achieve a desired level of power. However, in those cases in which the number of participants available is fixed (based on their availability or the amount of resources available to recruit and run them), statistical power can be estimated for the hypothesized ES. Alternately, given a fixed sample size, power can be set at 0.80 (or an alternative level if appropriately justified) and a maximum detectable ES can be calculated. In keeping with the pledge not to assault readers with statistical concerns, the actual calculation of statistical power (or an optimal sample size) will not be addressed here. Online calculators, free software available on the Internet (e.g., G*Power), commercial software, and numerous books (e.g., Bausell & Li, 2002) are available to facilitate that process. However, beginning investigators would be wise to have their results checked by more experienced hands.

Regardless of the analytic option chosen, however, a key component of the experimenter's job description is to maximize the sensitivity of his or her chosen design, which translates to ensuring that all investigations (except pilot studies) have sufficient statistical power to detect a defensible effect size without *wasting* resources. Toward that end, 12 strategies for increasing statistical power (thereby reducing the required sample size) will be briefly discussed.

Statistical Interlude: Studies Designed to Demonstrate "No Differences" or "Noninferiority"

The relationships presented in Table 9.1, as well as the power-analytic strategies that follow, assume an experimental framework in which two or more experimental conditions are compared to one another in order to ascertain if they differ from *zero* (and the relevant hypotheses are stated in terms of the expectation of obtaining *differences*). Occasionally, however, investigators begin the design process with a completely different agenda involving the expectation that two or more experimental conditions do *not* differ from one another (i.e., they are equivalent or one is not inferior to the other). The difficulty here is that *p*-values associated with our statistical distributions are based on comparing differences to *zero*, but zero is not the point of comparison when we wish to ascertain if two groups do *not* differ from one another.

Although not particularly common in the psychological, educational, social, behavioral, and health disciplines, *noninferiority and equivalence designs* are used in medical and drug research to deal with this issue. As their names imply, the noninferiority approach can be used to demonstrate that a new intervention (which is perhaps cheaper, less invasive, or more efficient [e.g., less time consuming] or has fewer effects than a specific standard intervention) is no *worse* than the standard, while an equivalence approach is used to demonstrate that the two are interchangeable. (The primary difference between the two is that a noninferiority analysis employs a directional, one-tailed test, while equivalence employs a two-tailed test.) Since noninferiority designs are probably more applicable to the disciplines addressed by this book, the following discussion will concentrate on them.

Both approaches, however, solve the problem associated with comparing two entities to a non-zero value by requiring the investigator to specify what constitutes a *trivial* or *clinically nonsignificant* difference. Called the *noninferiority point*, this specification is perhaps the Achilles heel of the entire noninferiority process, owing to the difficulties (and potential subjectivity) involved in defining what constitutes a "meaningless" or "trivial" difference between two groups. Occasionally, an element of objectivity exists for such definitions based on the research literature (e.g., a relevant meta-analysis), practice guidelines, consensus statements, or actual studies designed to establish benchmarks for certain outcomes (most notably pain [e.g., Cepeda, Africano, Polo, et al., 2003; Farrara, Young, LaMoreaux, et al., 2001]).

Once specified, however, the logic of statistically analyzing a noninferiority experiment is relatively straightforward, although beyond our promised scope here. Conceptually, the resulting hypothesis test is most clearly represented by constructing confidence intervals (which are computed by all commonly employed statistical packages and are interpreted as regions within which other values are *not* statistically significant, but outside of which they are). Five discrete outcomes that can accrue with respect to the point of noninferiority for a two-group experiment are illustrated by Figure 9.2 (adapted from Figure 17.8 in Friedman, Furberg, & DeMets, 2010) in which A is the intervention of interest and B is the standard intervention to which it is compared. (For convenience, the metric employed is the two-group effect size just discussed.)

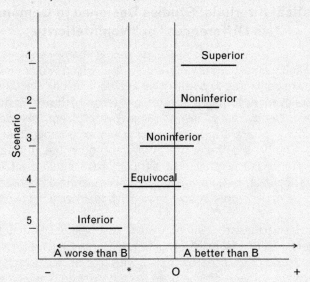

FIGURE 9.2: Illustration of Noninferiority Regions.

[*] Noninferiority point (anything between this point and zero [0]) was declared not clinically relevant, while anything to its left was considered (a priori) to be clinically relevant.

Scenario 1 represents a hypothetical study in which the 95% confidence interval representing the effect size for the difference between Interventions A and B is clearly in the positive direction and greater than zero. Here, A is superior to B (in conventional experimental terms), hence there is no question that A is not inferior to B. And, since this confidence interval does not include the noninferiority point [*], the results are declared *noninferior*. (Strictly speaking, however, A *cannot* be declared superior to B because a noninferiority analysis involves a one-tailed hypothesis test—which means that statistically significant results opposite to those hypothesized are not interpreted.)

Scenario 2 represents a slightly different situation. Here, A remains numerically superior to B (the midpoint of the confidence interval represents the mean), but the confidence interval representing this difference *includes* a zero difference. By itself, however, this fact is irrelevant in a noninferiority analytic framework, since a statistically significant *superiority* favoring A is not part of the hypothesis. *What is relevant is that the Scenario 2 confidence interval (like the one in Scenario 1) does not include the noninferiority point.* Thus, inferentially, A is again declared *not inferior* to B.

Scenario 3 represents a result in which Intervention A's mean is less than that of Intervention B, hence A is numerically inferior to B. However, since the effect's confidence interval does not include the noninferiority point, this too indicates that Intervention A is *not inferior* to Intervention B.

Scenario 4 represents a finding that most sources (e.g., D'Agostino, Massaro, & Sullivan, 2003; Friedman, Furberg, &DeMets, 2010; Piaggio, Elbourne, Pocock, et al., 2012) label as *equivocal*, but one which a noninferiority investigator would be quite disappointed to obtain (and many journal editors would consider to be a negative finding). Here the mean of A is numerically inferior to B but the confidence interval includes *both* zero and the noninferiority point.

Scenario 5 is quite definitive since A is significantly inferior both classically (the confidence interval does not include zero but favors B, which again is irrelevant) and from a noninferiority perspective (the confidence interval excludes the point of noninferiority in the negative direction).

Viewed from another perspective, the conventional Type I and Type II errors discussed in Figure 9.1 are completely reversed in a noninferiority design, which means that statistical power is reversed as well. In turn, this means that it easier to achieve noninferiority by choosing a liberal definition of what constitutes a trivial difference or (nonintuitively) by violating the design strategies presented next specifically to *increase* power—such as using a small sample size rather than one adequate for achieving conventional statistical significance!

An important (but often misunderstood) implication of this process is that if the investigator's intent is to demonstrate that two groups do not differ substantively, failing to achieve statistical significance via a conventional analysis does not "prove" that the intervention of interest is equivalent or not inferior to whatever it is being compared to. Instead, investigators must design and analyze their experiments in such a way that the .05 level of significance applies to the *intent* to demonstrate noninferiority (a major part of which is to choose a reasonable and defensible noninferiority point). And normally this will entail using a substantially larger sample size than is required for a conventional experiment.

12 STRATEGIES FOR INCREASING STATISTICAL POWER

Now, let's put the noninferiority/equivalence exception aside and concentrate on methods of enhancing statistical power in conventional, efficacy experiments. (Beginning investigators contemplating designing a noninferiority or no-difference study might be wise to seek specialized statistical consultation.) While our earlier delineation named three parameters that affect the statistical power available for a two-group, between-subjects experiment (the [1] sample size, [2] hypothesized effect size, and [3] significance level to be employed in the final hypothesis test), it will probably come as no surprise that there are other parameters involved when the design architecture becomes a bit more complex (e.g., when repeated measures, covariates, or additional factors and/or experimental groups are involved). Of course there is another consideration, perhaps best conceptualized as an *assumption*, which the discussion that follows will assume is met (i.e., the experimental protocol is properly implemented). Let's also assume, since we'll basically be discussing methods of increasing power or reducing sample size here, that the significance level is fixed at .05 (two-tailed) and that the outcome variable is continuous in nature. When downward adjustments to the alpha level are required (e.g., the use of noninferiority designs or the use of multiple comparison procedures), then these more stringent alpha levels will be used in lieu of .05. This typically decreases the amount of available power and forces the investigator to compensate through the use of one or more alternative strategies. Many of these strategies have been discussed in more detail in the second chapter of Bausell and Li (2002), and a number of the tables supporting them have been condensed here from that book.

The effect of each strategy will be illustrated by providing examples of how it affects the amount of power available for a study. (For simplicity's sake, two-group studies have been used in these examples whenever possible, but the relationships described generalize directly to three or more groups as well.) While some of the resulting increments may not appear especially dramatic, it should be recalled that statistical power represents a probability level (hence ranges between 0.00 and 1.00) that in turn is sometimes visualized (rightly or wrongly) by investigators as the probability that their experiments will be **"successful"** if their hypotheses are correct and their experiments are properly conducted. Thus, while a rise in power from, say, .50 to .60 may seem trivial from a purely numeric point of view, if visualized in terms of the corresponding boost in one's chance of obtaining statistical significance, perhaps the relevance of this particular topic will become more apparent.

THREE POWER-ENHANCING STRATEGIES INVOLVING SAMPLE SIZE ADJUSTMENTS

Strategy #1: *Increasing the sample size.* This is by far the most common, direct, and resource-*intensive* means of increasing statistical power available to an investigator. Without exception, regardless of design and statistical procedure employed, increasing the number of participants increases statistical power.

However, a disclaimer is probably in order here, since the emphasis in this chapter is overwhelmingly devoted to ensuring adequate statistical power. While it is crucially important to include a sufficient number of participants in an experiment, it is wasteful of participants' time, effort, and good will to employ a substantively larger sample size than is required to achieve a reasonable level of power or a practically significant effect size (Lenth, 2001).

The relationship between sample size and power can be succinctly illustrated for a two-group example in Table 9.1, where (a) the hypothesized ES is 0.50 (i.e., the difference between the intervention and comparison group outcome means is one-half of a standard deviation) and (b) the alpha level is .05. (An ES of 0.50 has been found to be the average value for educational and behavioral studies based on an analysis of thousands of experiments [Lipsey & Wilson, 1993], hence is used as a benchmark for this and several of the other strategies that follow.)

Table 9.1: Impact of Sample
Size on Power
(Two-Group Design).*

N/Group	Power
5	.09
10	.18
15	.26
20	.33
25	.41
30	.47
35	.54
45	.65
55	.74
65	.81
80	.88
100	.94
140	.99

*Two-tailed alpha = .05; ES = .50.

Note that the amount of power available for a two-group, between-subjects experiment becomes optimal only around a total sample size of 130 (actually, exactly 128, or an N/group of 64 for power = 0.80).

Strategy #2: *Assigning more participants to groups (often control/comparison groups) which are cheaper to run.* This strategy is really a corollary of the first suggestion, since it is simply a more cost-effective means of increasing a study's overall sample size. Equal numbers of participants per group are always optimal. However, if practical constraints limit the number who can be exposed to the intervention as compared to the control/comparison group, it would be unwise to artificially truncate the overall sample size by limiting the number of individuals assigned to the latter (if doing so results in an underpowered experiment).

Instead, if additional power is needed, the researcher should consider randomly assigning more participants to the cheaper condition in order to achieve the desired level of power. However, this strategy does reach a point of diminishing returns relatively quickly, as illustrated in Table 9.2.

Table 9.2: Effects of Different Ns/Group
Ratios.*

N_{INT}	N_{CON}	Ratio	Power
64	64	1:1	.80
43	85	1.2	.75
32	92	1:3	.67
26	102	1:4	.62

*ES = .50; two-tailed alpha = .05.

This table can be interpreted as follow. Beginning with our venerable 64 per group example in the first row (which we know will produce power of .80), if an investigator had allocated this sample size via a 1:2 ratio, the power for the experiment would have been reduced to .75 (row 2)—while the trend continues unabated for even more uneven allocation ratios. And, looking at the other side of the coin, if the sample is increased over 128 but the allocation is unequal, the resulting increase in power will be considerably less than would occur for the same increase evenly distributed among groups.

However, increasing the sample size and assigning more participants to a control or comparison group should be considered if the following conditions are met:

1.   More power is required,
2.   More participants are available, but
3.   Running additional experimental participants is too costly in terms of time or resources.

Strategy #3: *Using as few groups as possible.* As has been mentioned previously, most of the design advice and experimental principles tendered in this book must be tempered by scientific considerations. Thus the acupuncture example by Haake et al. (2007) would have been notably weakened by using one rather than two comparison groups and thus not clarifying the etiology of their effect.

However, from a purely statistical power perspective, when the available sample size is limited, multiple-group studies also have the potential of substantially reducing the probability of achieving statistical significance for the resulting pairwise comparisons. As an example, let's imagine a scenario in which an investigative team had obtained promising preliminary weight loss results from an uncontrolled pilot study testing an intervention involving multiple sessions of dietary instruction combined with supervised exercise. The investigators subsequently decided that the original results should be replicated via a larger, controlled experiment involving randomly assigning participants to an intervention vs. a no-treatment control group. Some members of the team, however, favored a more involved, multiple-group study designed to determine the original effect's etiology. The latter contingent, therefore, suggested the following five-group, single-factor study in which (a) the first two groups were designed to ascertain if the two constituent elements of the combined intervention's (presumed) effect were equally effective, (b) the third and fourth groups were designed to replicate the original effect (as well as to ascertain if the combined effect of dietary instruction and exercise was greater than that with either constituent alone), while (c) the fifth group was designed to ensure that the (again presumed) intervention effect was not simply a function of some sort of attention, placebo, or demand characteristic artifact:

(1)   E-1: Exercise only
(2)   E-2: Dietary information only
(3)   E-3: Exercise and dietary information
(4)   C-1: No-treatment control
(5)   C-2: Attention placebo control

Now, let's further suppose that the maximum number of participants available to the investigators was 120. Table 9.3 illustrates the relative **loss** in power associated with the pairwise comparisons as groups are added to the original two-group for a medium ES.

Table 9.3: Pairwise Power Loss for ES = 0.50 and Fixed Sample Size (N = 120) as Number of Experimental Groups Increase.*

	2 Groups N/Group = 60	3 Groups N/Group = 40	4 Groups N/Group = 30	5 Groups N/Group = 24
No Adjustment (*t*-test)	0.77	0.59	0.48	0.39
Adjustment (Tukey's HSD)	Not applicable†	0.45	0.25	0.15

*Pairwise power loss is with and without Tukey's HSD multiple comparison adjustment.

†Not applicable because multiple comparison procedures are not required for two-group studies.

Since the total sample size available to the investigators was fixed, each additional intervention and comparison group decreased the number of participants per group from (a) 60 for two groups to (b) 40 for three groups, (c) 30 for four groups, and (d) 24 for five groups. We already know, based on Strategy #1, that each reduction in the per group sample size will drastically reduce the power available for each of the pairwise comparisons as the number of groups are added to the experiment. If the team was not forced to adjust the alpha level for these multiple comparisons, the available power would reduce from an acceptable 0.77 for two groups to 0.39 for five groups (i.e., the "no adjustment" row in Table 9.3). If they applied a multiple comparison procedure such as Tukey's "honestly significant difference," the power decrement is even larger. (Multiple comparison procedures, of which there are a number of options, provide a mechanism for adjusting an experiment's alpha level, thereby allowing multiple comparisons among the various groups employed. They are not required for two-group studies.)

While the addition of experimental conditions has the potential for greatly increasing the explanatory value of a study, this advantage must be paid for by increasing the overall sample size and/or other power-enhancing strategies. With respect to the two-group vs. five-group dilemma facing our hypothetical investigators, if their sample size was restricted to 120 participants (and if they were reasonably confident in the hypothesized ES of 0.50 for the contrast[s] of interest), they would be better advised to first attempt to replicate their single-group pilot study via a randomized two-group experiment. (All too often, promising pilot results wilt in the presence of a control group.) Whether the no-treatment control group should be retained (or substituted for an attention control group) is less clear and depends on the literature and discipline-specific preferences.

FIVE POWER-ENHANCING STRATEGIES INVOLVING ES AND DESIGN ADJUSTMENTS

Strategy #4: *Increasing the size of the hypothesized ES.* It is much easier to achieve statistical significance when the intervention produces a powerful effect on the outcome variable. In experimental research, this translates to large differences between group means on the outcome (or large difference in proportions for dichotomous variables).

Table 9.4 illustrates the strong relationship between the hypothesized ES and power—more direct even than the relationship between sample size and power. Continuing with the two-group, single-assessment example, power increases (a) from .10 to .41 when the hypothesized ES rises from .20 to .50 (for a fixed 25 participants per group) and (b) from to .41 to .79 when the ES rises to .80.

Table 9.4 Impact of
Hypothesized Effect Size
on Power*

ES	Power
.20	.10
.30	.18
.40	.28
.50	.41
.60	.54
.70	.68
.80	.79
.90	.87
1.0	.95

*N/Group = 25 (two-group design; alpha
= .05).

Of course, increasing an experiment's ES is considerably more complicated (and fraught with more scientific tradeoffs) than increasing the sample size. Assuming that participants are to be randomly assigned to the two groups and that none of the other strategies discussed here are implemented, three avenues exist for increasing an ES: (a) strengthening the intervention, (b) weakening the comparison group, and (c) recruiting homogeneous participants (or participants who are most likely to be impacted by the intervention). Let's consider all three in turn:

Strengthening the intervention: The strength of an intervention is most directly affected by

(a)   Increasing the dose (e.g., literally, in the case of a drug trial or, in behavioral studies, offering more or longer training sessions) and
(b)   Adding additional components to the intervention.

Our hypothetical weight loss intervention was an example of a multiple components (i.e., both diet and exercise) treatment. If the investigators had felt the need to increase the ES further, they could have, among other strategies, made the exercise more strenuous and/or increased the length of sessions or the number thereof.

Naturally, the tradeoffs for both strategies would require serious consideration before altering the design. Adding multiple sessions or increasing their intensity, for example, might increase experimental attrition, reduce compliance, and make the intervention too costly or impractical to implement clinically. (And, as we've already discussed, adding multiple components to an intervention clouds the etiology of any effect produced, since the investigators have no way of determining whether the resulting superiority of the intervention over its control was *primarily* attributable to dietary instruction, exercise, or some combination or interaction between the two). Decisions such as these must simply be made on the basis of the investigators' ultimate scientific objectives of the study and balanced by power and sample size concerns.

Weakening the control (comparison) group: Since the ES formula presented earlier involves the mean difference between the experimental and control/comparison group in the numerator, weakening the latter is as effective as strengthening the former. One method of weakening the control group is to use (a) a no-treatment as opposed to a placebo (or an attention placebo) control or (b) any type of control group instead of an *effective* treatment-as-usual comparison group (or any other type of previously documented efficacious intervention).

As with altering the intervention, scientific and clinical considerations must always take precedence over purely statistical ones, *but unacceptably low power can (and should) prohibit an experiment from being conducted in the first place* (excluding pilot tests, of course).

The best existing evidence indicates that the choice of a control group is capable of increasing or decreasing the experimental ES by as much as 0.20 under certain conditions. Based on the results of their meta-analysis of educational and behavioral meta-analyses, for example, Lipsey and Wilson (1993) estimated that the use of a no-treatment control is likely to increase an ES by approximately .20 as opposed to use of an attention placebo group. This finding is consistent with other estimates, such as a meta-analysis directly comparing placebo with no-treatment controls in medical experiments involving pain reduction (Hrobjartsson & Gotzche, 2001).

Using participants who are most likely to change on the outcome variable: Obviously, only individuals in need of an intervention (or capable of responding to it) should be included in an experiment. In pain research, for example, it is not enough to recruit patients on the basis of a diagnosis such as arthritis, as some participants will not be experiencing pain at the time of the trial and thereby reduce the final ES even if the intervention was otherwise effective. Or, in our weight loss example, only obese or overweight participants should be recruited. Or in learning research, only participants (a) who have not mastered a substantive portion of the experimental curriculum or (b) who possess the necessary prerequisites for learning that curriculum should be used (thereby avoiding ceiling and basement effects, respectively).

Increasing participant homogeneity: Since the denominator of our ES formula was the pooled standard deviation of the experimental conditions, and since the standard deviation is an indicator of individual differences between individuals on the outcome variable, increasing the homogeneity of the experimental sample directly increases the ES. The previous strategy (using participants who are most likely to change on the outcome variable) not only increases the numerator of the ES formula but is also likely to increase the homogeneity of the sample and thereby reduce the denominator. So, too, does employing more stringent inclusion/exclusion criteria (e.g., restricting participation to certain specific age groups, diagnoses, or the absence of comorbidities) or limiting recruitment to participants with as many environmental or demographic factors in common as possible (e.g., college students or assisted living residents).

Strategy #5: *Employing covariates and/or blocking variable.* Most present-day investigators collect additional (often too much) baseline data that they suspect (or hope) may have a bearing on their experimental outcomes. This additional information has one of three potential uses: It can be used to (a) describe the sample to give the research consumer a feel for the types of participants used (and hence make an informed decision about how far the results may be generalized), (b) exert statistical control purposes to increase the experiment's statistical power (as a covariate or a blocking variable), and/or (c) test additional hypotheses regarding potential differential effects of the treatment (e.g., as the interaction between an attribute variable and the experimental intervention).

In truth, both covariates and interactions should be specified a priori as part of the study hypotheses, since fishing expeditions employing one candidate after another to locate those possessing sufficiently high correlations with the outcome have the potential of slightly increasing the probability of a Type I error. (Such exercises are also seldom effective, since it takes a thorough knowledge of the literature surrounding an outcome variable to identify its substantive correlates.) Successfully locating such a variable, however, can definitively increase a study's statistical power (and thereby reduce the required sample size), depending on the degree to which the additional covariate(s) or blocking variable(s) is (are) related to the study's outcome variable.

Table 9.5 illustrates the increment to power that accrues from using a covariate having a moderate relationship with the experimental outcome. As indicated in the table, little advantage is realized by a covariate until its relationship with the outcome reaches .40 or higher. However, assuming (a) an ES of .50 and (b) an N/group of 64, an r of .40 between the covariate and the outcome variable increases a study's power from .80 to .86. This reflects a potential decrease in the required sample size from 64/group in the absence of a covariate to 54/group with a covariate/outcome relationship of .40 (or a 16% reduction in sample size). This is hardly trivial, as it also reflects the need to recruit 20 fewer participants. For an r of .60, the corresponding values are (a) an increase in power of 18% and (b) a decrease in the required sample size, from 64/group to 42 per group (a 34% reduction from no covariate at all). Correlations within this range are possible, but rare. (Covariates should be hypothesized a priori on the basis of prior evidence emanating from the literature or pilot work.)

Table 9.5: Relationship Between Covariate–Outcome
Correlations and Power and Sample Size Requirements.*

r (Covariate-Outcome)	Power	N/Group = 64
.00	.80	64
.20	.82	62
.40	.86	54
.60	.94	42
.80	.99	24

*ES = .50.

Strategy #6: *Employing a repeated measures design.* In addition to procedural control, the primary advantage of crossover, repeated measures and randomized matched-block designs resides in the increased statistical power (hence sample size reductions) provided. The statistical origins of these repeated measures advantages are similar to those of covariates. However, the relevant correlations are between outcome variables for the same participants, hence both the correlations and their effect on power are considerably greater.

Thus reproducing Table 9.5 for a repeated measures design (or its randomized matched-block simulation) reveals a considerably more dramatic relationship between the size of the relevant correlation and power and required sample size (see Table 9.6).

Table 9.6: Relationship Between Outcome Correlations
of Same Participants across Time and/or Experimental
Conditions with Power and Sample Size Requirements.*

r (Repeated Measures Correlations)	Power	N/Group = 64†
.00	.80	64
.20	.88	51
.40	.95	39
.60	.99	27
.80	.99	14

*ES = .50.

†N/group necessary to achieve power of 0.80 for a within-subjects, two-group
ES of 0.50.

Table 9.6 illustrates the increased effect of the correlation resulting between individuals' performance when exposed to two or more experimental conditions (i.e., via a repeated measures, randomized matched-block, or crossover design). The effect is especially apparent in the "N/Group" column, which represents the required sample size for the various correlation coefficients listed in the first column where, for a correlation of .60, the required number of participants is reduced by (a) 58% (74 total participants) for a repeated measures design in comparison to, say, a randomized posttest-only design and (b) 36% (30 total participants) as compared to a comparable between-subjects covariate design (r = .60).

As explained in Chapter Eight, the circumstances permitting the same participants to receive all of the experimental conditions are limited. When procedurally feasible, however, it is an extremely powerful experimental procedure.

Strategy #7: *Hypothesizing between-subjects main effects rather than interactions.* The rational for this strategy is both statistical and conceptual. From a statistical perspective, more power is available for a main effect contrast than an interaction in between-subjects designs. And when all other things (e.g., sample size, hypothesized ES) are equal, two factor interactions possess more power than higher level ones (as do factors involving two levels vs. three or more, à la Strategy #3). As always, scientific considerations take precedence, but when the sample size is limited, investigators are better served to design their studies to detect main effects unless there is good empirical or theoretical evidence for a specific interaction.

Another consideration involves the fact that there are many more possible ways for an interaction to manifest itself than a main effect. The specific configuration of an interaction should be hypothesized, which adds a degree of difficulty in supporting such a hypothesis. Neither this difficulty, nor the extra power interactions required, however, should be a determining factor. Scientific concerns are always preeminent.

Strategy #8: *Randomizing individual participants rather than groups of participants.* This strategy, like all of the others (except #12) presented in this chapter, must be weighed against practical and scientific constraints. Randomized cluster designs, however, are often necessitated by the potential for treatment diffusion or political objections to randomizing individuals within the same administrative unit.

From a power analytic perspective, however, the use of this design almost always requires relatively large sample sizes—depending on the size of the intra-cluster correlation coefficient (ICC), which ranges from zero to 1 and is simply a statistical representation of how similar the participants within clusters are to one another at the end of the experiment on the final outcome variable. It is the extent of this intra-cluster dependency, in fact, that mandates the use of hierarchical data-analytic procedures (and therefore different power-analytic procedures) for evaluating a randomized-cluster research hypothesis. The preferred option, it will be recalled, involves a hierarchical analysis in which the clusters are nested under the treatment factor. And for a randomized cluster design there are three unique pieces of information that are required for performing a power analysis. These are:

1. The ICC (which can be determined by the literature, a pilot study, or the very general "yardstick" [which might be acceptable under certain circumstances], suggested by Murnane and Willett [2011]: .01 for small ICCs, .09 for medium, and .25 for large ones),
2. The number of clusters randomized, and
3. The number of participants per cluster.

Armed with these data (or estimates thereof), the total sample size computed for a conventional experiment can then be divided by a correction factor called the design effect (DE) to produce the adjusted total sample size for a randomized cluster design (Donner, 1998):

Formula 9.2: The Correction Factor for a Randomized Cluster Design
$$DE = 1 + ICC\,(\#\ clusters - 1).$$

What accrues from this process is a situation in which the number of clusters random- ized strongly influences the total necessitated sample size for a given level of power. Table 9.7

Table 9.7: Sample Size Costs of Randomizing Clusters vs. Participants.*

ICC	# Clusters	N/Cluster	Total N
0	NA	64/2 Groups	128
.20	30	24	720
.20	40	7	280
.20	50	4	200
.10	14	100	1400
.10	20	16	320
.10	30	7	210
.10	40	5	200
.10	50	3	150
.05	10	35	350
.05	20	9	180
.05	30	5	150
.02	20	7	140
.02	30	4–5	120–150
.02	40	3–4	120–160

*Power = 0.80; ES = 0.50.

illustrates this relationship rather dramatically, where the first bolded row indicates the number of participants required for the simplest possible two-group study (assuming a continuous outcome variable), which we already know will require 64 participants per group (for a total N of 128) to achieve a power of 0.80 to detect a hypothesized ES of 0.50.

Assuming the same conditions (i.e. power = 0.80 and two experimental conditions) for a randomized cluster design, this table is interpreted as follows:

1. When the ICC is unusually strong (0.20), adequate power cannot be achieved by randomizing many less than 30 clusters (15 per group). If 30 clusters with an N of 24 per group could be randomized, then the resulting total sample size of 720 (the Total N column) would produce power of approximately 0.80 as compared to the 128 participants required for a two-group study in which participants rather than clusters are randomly assigned. This, of course, is quite inefficient, but the use of more clusters reduces that inefficiency (for example, "only" 72 extra participants [200 – 128] would be required if 50 clusters with 4 participants each were randomized [i.e., 50 × 4 = 200 vs. the 128 required for a two-group experiment in which participants were randomized]). Fortunately, ICCs as high as 0.20 are rarely encountered.

2. This same pattern (use of more clusters with fewer participants being significantly more efficient than using fewer clusters with more participants) is apparent as the expected ICC becomes smaller. Thus, for ICCs of 0.10 (which still are relatively rare), randomizing 40 clusters of 5 participants each requires "only" 72 (56%) more participants than a non-cluster trial.

3. When an often not atypical ICC or .02 can be reasonably expected, the number of clusters can be reduced to 20 with only a modest increase of 12 participants.

With these relationships in mind, when a randomized cluster design is indicated for a particular study, the following design suggestions are tendered, if they are not contraindicated by scientific considerations:

1. The recruitment of numerous clusters (even relatively small ones) should be given preference over the recruitment of fewer large clusters.

2. If possible, enrollment should be limited to clusters that are as homogeneous as possible. This can be done relatively easily if a variable related to the outcome variable is already available for the targeted clusters (e.g., average standardized achievement test scores for a learning experiment in which classrooms will be assigned rather than students). This may impact the generalizability of the study, but reducing the ICC to .01 or below will greatly improve experimental precision.

3. Attempting to apply as many of the other strategies suggested in this chapter as possible, although some may require a bit of adaptation, as just illustrated. The fifth strategy (employing covariates), for example, can be quite effective in reducing the magnitude of the ICC if either strong cluster level *or* individual level covariates can be found. (Thus, if classrooms were randomly assigned in a learning experiment, either mean classroom [or individual] standardized test scores could be employed as the covariate. Individual-level covariates are usually preferable from a power perspective, when available.)

If none of these options apply and the ICC is relatively high, an investigator might be well advised to employ another design or another set of clusters.

FOUR STRATEGIES INVOLVING OUTCOME VARIABLES AND DATA ANALYSIS

Strategy #9: *Employing measures sensitive to change.* From an a priori, power-analytic perspective, an experimental ES is basically a descriptive statistics which indicates the improvement that an experimental group is expected to produce *over and above* that of a comparison group. The purpose of an experiment, therefore, is to produce *changes* in an outcome variable by introducing an intervention that is theoretically capable of *causing* such a change. If the outcome is extremely resistant to change (as many meaningful ones are), the experiment will require a strong intervention, a large sample size, or both.

As an example of what is meant by sensitivity to change, suppose a researcher hypothesized that using a focused health education intervention for individuals with high serum cholesterol levels would result in substantive learning gains as opposed to the type of hit-or-miss educational advice sometimes afforded to these patients by their primary care providers. Our hypothetical investigator would have several options for choosing an appropriate learning measure. He might, for example, opt to use a comprehensive test of dietary knowledge developed by a national association that had impressive psychometric characteristics and had been used extensively in both research and patient education. Ironically, such a measure might be considerably less likely to document an effect for the tested intervention than a briefer, less reliable (see Strategy #10) assessment tool constructed by the investigator to measure the specific content that would be taught during the course of the experiment.

A superior strategy, therefore, would entail constructing an instrument specifically tailored to the study whose items would be as representative as possible of the actual experimental instruction being offered. One method of doing so would be to (a) pretest a group of individuals (as comparable as possible to the projected experimental sample) on as many items as possible that were relevant to the experimental curriculum, (b) teach them the experimental curriculum, (c) retest the group, and (d) construct the final achievement measure based on those items on which performance changed most dramatically as a function of the instruction (although, of course, the repeated testing artifact would be operative here). Naturally, those items to which a high proportion of the sample answered correctly on the pretest would be deleted or changed, as would items that proved too difficult on both tests (unless the intervention itself was changed to emphasize the related content). This approach should, in effect, produce an outcome maximally sensitive to change and thereby increase (a) the experiment's ES and (b) the probability of obtaining positive learning results.

Of course, outside of educational research, investigators do not always have the luxury of creating their own outcome measures. In those cases, investigators should select those outcomes that are known to be maximally sensitive to change and, above all and always, to be maximally meaningful as defined earlier.

Strategy #10: *Employing reliable outcome variables.* Reliability is a psychometric term referring to the stability with which a construct, covariate, or experimental outcome is measured. Several different types of reliability exist, but the easiest one to visualize is aptly called *test-retest reliability*, in which an instrument is administered to the same group of participants twice within a specified time period in which no known outside influences occur to change the values on the measured variable. Reliability itself is, in this instance, measured by correlating the two values produced at the two different time intervals. The correlation coefficient (now known as a reliability coefficient) therefore constitutes the relationship of the measuring instrument with *itself* and ranges in value from zero to 1.0 (a negative correlation coefficient makes no conceptual sense). This coefficient has useful properties from a classic measurement perspective in the sense that it reflects the proportion of the resulting score that is systematic or stable. Thus, if an instrument's reliability is 0.50, 50% of any given person's score (on average) is "systematic" and 50% is "unsystematic," or *error*. (A reliability coefficient of 0.80, a more typical reliability estimate for educational, behavioral, and health outcomes, indicates that 20% of the score is erroneous, or noise.)

From a practicing perspective, the sensitivity (Strategy #9) of an outcome variable to change is more crucial experimentally than reliability, and sometimes the two concepts are mutually exclusive (i.e., some instruments and the constructs they measure [e.g., attitudes, personality] are so *stable* [hence psychometrically reliable] that they are not sensitive to change and thus are poor candidates for experimental research). With this exception aside, however, the more reliably an outcome variable can be measured, the greater the statistical power of an experiment employing it. (The relationship between sensitivity and reliability has not been explored extensively.)

Thus, the ES hypothesized as part of a power analysis is normally based on the assumption that the reliability of the outcome employed in the experiment will be identical to the reliability of the outcome on which the ES was based (e.g., a pilot test, a published experiment similar to the one being contemplated). So if the ES was estimated to be 0.50, based on a previous study, and the reliability of the outcome measures was found to be 0.70 in that study, it would be assumed that the reliability would remain the same for the hypothesized ES of 0.50 to be reasonable.

Normally, this is a relatively safe assumption, but what if the proposed sample was more homogeneous than the original sample and the reliability turned out to be lower? Or, conversely, the reliability turned out to be greater than expected? Or, alternately, what if the investigator, unimpressed by the reliability of the original outcome, decided to employ a more reliable indicator in his or her proposed study?

The answers to these questions (everything else, sensitivity included, being equal) are as follows:

1. If the reliability of an outcome variable is lower than expected, power will be reduced.
2. If the reliability of an outcome variable is higher than expected, power will be increased.

This relationship is illustrated in Table 9.8, where the investigator's hypothesized ES of 0.50 was based on the assumption that his or her outcome variable would possess a reliability of 0.70 (hence 30% of the resulting "score" would be error).

Table 9.8 is interpreted as follows. Assuming that the hypothesized ES of 0.50 is appropriate and the reliability of the final outcome variable turns out to be similar to the value that was observed in the pilot study (i.e., 0.70), then the power of the final experiment will be 0.70 for an *N*/group of 50. However, if the actual reliability turns out to be greater than expected, the power will also be greater (0.76 if the reliability is 0.80 and 0.89 when it is 0.90). Unfortunately, the opposite occurs when the obtained reliability turns out to be lower than expected (0.62 for a reliability of 0.60 and 0.55 for a reliability of 0.50).

Table 9.8: Changes in Power as a Function of Reliability
of Outcome Variable.*

Reliability Hypothesized	Reliability Obtained	Power
0.70	0.70	0.70
	Reliability greater than expected	
	0.80	0.76
	0.90	0.89
	Reliability less than expected	
0.70	0.60	0.62
	0.50	0.55

*ES = 0.50, N/Group = 50.

The bottom-line message from this discussion is that investigators should choose both reliable and sensitive measures of their outcomes, when possible. In the relatively rare instances in which the two appear to be mutually exclusive, it may be possible to increase the reliability of an unusually sensitive (and unstable) outcome. As one example, blood pressure is an unstable—hence not particularly reliable—indicator. Its reliability, however, can be increased by measuring it multiple times under carefully controlled circumstances and employing the mean of these multiple administrations as the outcome variable. (Or, if learning is the outcome and the specific test planned for its assessment is found to be unreliable based on pilot work, the number of items employed can be increased—which in turn will increase the test's reliability—although care should be taken that the additional items match the intervention.)

Strategy #11: *Using direct rather than indirect (or using Lipsey's [1990] terminology: proximal as opposed to distal) outcome variables.* In both behavioral and health experiments, power considerations sometimes preclude employing what investigators consider to be the most clinically important indicators as a study's primary outcome variable. This is one of the few times that statistical considerations take precedence over scientific ones, since there are occasions in which practical constraints (including sample size and time requirements) preclude employing the most meaningful experimental outcomes.

Some instances of this are obvious, such as the length of time it takes for certain outcomes to manifest themselves (or their relative rarity). For example, among the most meaningful health outcomes are variables such as length of life or the avoidance of chronic diseases. In education these variables might be professional success; in addiction it might be long-term abstinence. Unfortunately, such variables are typically beyond the scope of most experiments (and the resources of most investigators).

Other instances of this dictum perhaps aren't so obvious. In an experiment designed to evaluate the effects of a dietary education intervention for individuals with high serum cholesterol levels, the "ultimate" (or most important) purpose of such an intervention is to avoid adverse health consequences, such as the incidence of a myocardial infarction. Ignoring the obvious procedural difficulties of waiting the requisite time for such an outcome to manifest itself, a study designed to affect this outcome would require a huge sample size to detect an effect for knowledge gains on heart attacks, given the location (or link) the former occupies on the causal chain representing the etiology of a heart attack—assuming that knowledge is even causally related to that outcome (to which there is some question).

Perhaps the most appropriate way of estimating how many steps (or links) are involved in such a chain is to construct a theoretical model of the study itself. One possible model for this experiment is depicted in Figure 9.3, where the development of a heart attack is five outcome variables removed from learning, the most proximal outcome for the dietary education.

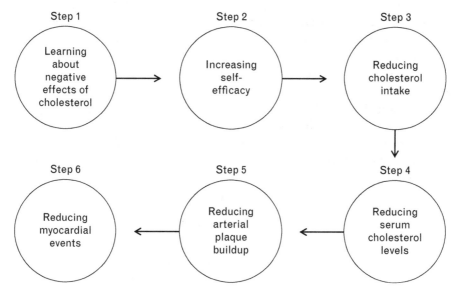

FIGURE 9.3: Theoretical Model of an Outcome Variable's Casual Chain.

Examination of this model indicates that, *everything* being equal, the education intervention's most direct (and hence the greatest accruing ES) outcome would occur for *learning* of the content of the experimental curriculum, which is Step 1 in the causal chain. (If the participants don't learn or retain anything from the instruction, this particular intervention is unlikely to affect outcomes further down the causal chain.) Unfortunately, Figure 9.3 illustrates something else: The length of this chain suggests learning to be a rather tenuous causal factor in reducing myocardial events (the preferred outcome), because even if individuals learn (and retain) the contents of the experimental curriculum they may do nothing *with* this knowledge. An equally uninteresting outcome would involve changes in self-efficacy (Step 2: a component of the behavioral theory [Bandura, 1986] guiding this hypothetical experiment) that are posited to result in behavioral change (Step 3) but might not occur for many individuals. Behavioral change itself, on the other hand, while designed to reduce serum cholesterol levels (Step 4), might constitute a dead end, as there is not a perfect linear relationship between cholesterol intake and cholesterol in the blood. And so on it goes, because, for reasons not completely clear, some individuals have high cholesterol levels without experiencing disruption in their cardiovascular blood flow (Step 5), and a few even have severely blocked arteries but do not experience heart failure (Step 6).

From a statistical perspective, where the selected outcome variable falls along this causal chain or continuum is quite important, because an intervention's ES is *reduced* at each link in the chain to the extent that the relationships between these successive outcomes are not perfect.

(And the relationships between disparate variables such as this are *never* anywhere close to perfect.)

To illustrate the impact on an experiment's ES when two variables are separated from one another along a causal chain, such as the one illustrated in Figure 9.3, consider the scenario in which the estimated ES between the intervention (instruction) and the first step in the causal chain (learning) is hypothesized to be 0.50. (We already know that we would need 64 participants per group to achieve power of .80 for this ES, assuming that we planned to conduct a simple *t*-test to evaluate the experiment.) But suppose further that an average correlation of .80 existed between each successive step leading to the final outcome of interest. (In reality, correlations this high are almost nonexistent in many areas of research involving human participants.)

Table 9.9 illustrates the degradation of statistical power and the associated increase in required sample size as a function of causal distance. Thus, while 64 participants provided power of .80 between the intervention and the actual learning outcome used in the study, had self-efficacy been employed in the same study along with learning, the hypothesized effect size for self-efficacy would be .40 (down from .50) and the power for achieving a statistically significant effect on this variable would have been .61 instead of .80. (The required sample size would be increased from 64 per group to 100 per group.) And the outlook for this particular study becomes bleaker at each successive step until it hopefully becomes obvious that this particular experiment shouldn't even be conducted by an investigator interested in preventing myocardial infarction, arterial plaque, or high levels of serum cholesterol who did not have access to an extremely large sample (and an extremely well validated theory).

Now obviously Table 9.9 represents an extremely stylized (and hypothetical) illustration of the relationship between causal distance and sample size requirements. The correlations between successive steps in a chain are seldom known and would almost surely be less than .80. (Sometimes even the identities of the steps themselves aren't known.) Or, even more problematic, the theory could be *incorrect*, thereby resulting in a break in a chain's causal effects and rendering all research conducted prior to that point irrelevant. The bottom-line message here, therefore, is that the power calculated for any given experiment (or the determination of an experiment's required sample size) is relevant only for the outcome on which the hypothesized ES is based and is completely irrelevant for outcomes more distally related to the intervention. And since these latter outcomes are usually of considerably greater scientific or societal import,

Table 9.9: Relationship Between Power/Sample Size and Causal Distance Between Outcomes.

Causal Steps from Intervention	ES Based on # Causal Steps	Effective Power with N/Group = 64	Required N/Group for Power = .80
Proximal	.50	.80	64
1 step removed	.40	.61	100
2 steps removed	.32	.41	165
3 steps removed	.26	.29	253
4 steps removed	.20	.20	394
5 steps removed	.16	.15	615

a careful consideration of the *theory* associated with the etiology of such outcomes is an important determinant of the ultimate experimental meaningfulness. *An experiment that has little probability (as defined by its available statistical power) of affecting a meaningful outcome has an equally small probability of being meaningful itself.*

Strategy #12: *Using appropriate data analysis procedures.* Since this book doesn't cover the statistical analysis of experiments, only their design, it won't be possible to go into much detail regarding what does and does not constitute an appropriate data analysis procedure. Failure to analyze data correctly, however, can result in either false positive or false negative results (more likely the latter) and is referred to by some methodologists (e.g., Cook & Campbell, 1979) as a lack of *statistical conclusion validity.* And even if someone else analyzes the data, a key component of the principal investigator's job description involves ensuring that (a) appropriate statistical procedures are employed and (b) the data meet the prerequisite assumptions of those procedures. To accomplish this it is necessary to be familiar with the statistical procedures employed in a discipline, gleaned perhaps by a careful examination of similar experiments found in the published literature.

Thus, if a second party does analyze an experiment's data, it remains the investigator's responsibility to have that individual explain his or her choice of analyses—especially if it differs from these published examples. Other minimal facets of an analysis which should be checked include whether

1. All systematic sources of variation were accounted for (Principle #19).
2. Variable distributions were checked, transformations of the outcome variable were employed, and the proper model specification was employed, if indicated.
3. Repeated measures were analyzed as such (and if covariates were employed they were included in the analysis).

The development of the expertise (including the management procedures) needed to meet this responsibility will be discussed in Chapter Ten, accompanied by its own experimental principle, but for the time being the following principles are tendered, based on the contents of this chapter. First:

> **PRINCIPLE #21: Always conduct a power/sample size analysis as part of the design process and ensure that the experiment has sufficient power to detect the hypothesized effect size.**

At present, the minimum acceptable power criterion for a study is usually considered to be 0.80. To conduct a study with a greater probability of a Type II error than 0.20 (i.e., 1.00 − 0.80) is risky and potentially wasteful of scarce resources. And while there is something to be said for adhering to current styles, there are also advantages (especially for high-stakes studies) to setting one's power at 0.90 (which has the effect of cutting the probability of a Type II error in half).

Second, as a corollary of our very first principle (functioning absolutely uncompromisingly and unfashionably honestly in all matters scientific):

> **PRINCIPLE #22: Do not subvert the power/sample size analytic process by making it a process for justifying a convenient, feasible, or easily available sample size.**

There may well be occasions in one's scientific career when sufficient resources are simply not available to, say, compete for funding to conduct an experiment and have sufficient power to conduct the study based on a sensibly hypothesized effect size. (It is always possible to project any level of power desired using any sample size if the hypothesized ES is set high enough.) In the absence of a truly defensible sample size, the best approach is to (a) shave as much excess from the budget as possible to produce as large a sample size as feasible, (b) explain the situation in the sample size section of the proposal, and (c) report the ES that will be detectable with a power of 0.80 expressed both as a statistical ES and in terms of the unique *scale* on which the outcome variable employs. (Alternately, a case for a lower power level can be made, if appropriate.) Transparency of this sort may occasionally put investigators at a competitive disadvantage, but it is also the type of behavior that builds positive reputations and in the long run will better serve both one's career and his or her science.

SUMMARY

Statistical power was defined as *the probability that an experiment will result in statistical significance if that experiment is properly designed and properly conducted and its hypothesized effect size is correct.* The theory behind statistical significance and statistical power was discussed in terms of two types of error: (a) the probability that a statistically significant finding is (or will be) due to chance (called *Type I error*) and (b) the probability that a statistically nonsignificant finding is (or will be) due to a lack of sufficient statistical power (*Type II error*). A relatively rarely employed genre of design was briefly discussed, in which the experimental purpose is to demonstrate noninferiority and equivalence between experimental conditions.

Twelve strategies were presented that possess the capability of increasing statistical power, which in turn is designed to avoid an especially pernicious experimental artifact:

> *Experimental Artifact #17*: **Underpowered experiments:** defined as experiments that have been improperly designed to avoid producing a false negative result.

The first 11 strategies also involve tradeoffs of one sort or another which must be evaluated on the basis of scientific considerations. (The 12th *is* an unequivocal scientific necessity.) Each of these strategies, however, should be considered at the design stage of any experiment because they all have the potential of increasing the sensitivity and validity of the hypothesis test itself. As a group they might be categorized as involving (a) sample size enhancements, (b) ES/design alterations, and (c) desirable characteristics of outcome variables. The final strategy involves a more general principle involving the analysis of experimental data. The 12 strategies were as follows:

> **Strategy #1**: *Increasing the sample size.*
> **Strategy #2**: *Assigning more participants to groups (often control groups) which are less resource intensive to run.*
> **Strategy #3**: *Using as few groups as possible.*
> **Strategy #4**: *Increasing the size of the hypothesized ES.*
> **Strategy #5**: *Employing covariates and/or blocking variable.*

Strategy #6: *Employing crossover or repeated measures designs.*
Strategy #7: *Hypothesizing between-subjects main effects rather than interactions.*
Strategy #8: *Randomizing individual participants rather than groups of participants.*
Strategy #9: *Employing measures sensitive to change.*
Strategy #10: *Employing reliable outcome variables.*
Strategy #11: *Using proximal as opposed to distal outcome variables.*
Strategy #12: *Using appropriate data analysis procedures.*

Finally, two addition experimental principles were tendered:

> **Principle #21:** Always conduct a power/sample size analysis as part of the design process and ensure that the experiment has sufficient power to detect the hypothesized effect size.
> **Principle #22:** Do not subvert the power/sample size analytic process by making it a process for justifying a convenient, feasible, or easily available sample size.

This chapter concludes our discussion of experimental design as it relates to

1. *Internal validity* (i.e., ensuring that the causal inference stated in the study hypothesis has a reasonable chance of being correct if the design is properly implemented) and
2. *Statistical conclusion validity*, as it relates to ensuring that sufficient statistical power is available for the data-analytic stage at the end of the experimental process along with a nod or two to the appropriate analysis of said data. (Statistical analysis, of course, is not covered here because it requires an even longer book than this one and is increasingly "outsourced" to a specially trained co-investigator.)

A third genre of experimental validity, not nearly as well defined and specific as the issues covered in the previous nine chapters, will be discussed in Chapter Eleven. Before considering that topic, however, we must explore one that impacts everything discussed to this point: the *implementation* of the experimental design—namely the conduct of the experiment itself. For no matter how beautifully an architect designs a building, if that building is constructed shabbily with little attention to detail, the resulting structure will be a disaster.

REFERENCES

Bandura A. (1986). *Social foundations of thought and action: A social cognitive theory.* Englewood Cliffs, NJ: Prentice-Hall.

Bausell, R.B., & Li, Y.F. (2002). *Power analysis for experimental research: A practical guide for the biological, medical, and social sciences.* Cambridge, UK: Cambridge University Press.

Cepeda, M.S., Africano, J.M., Polo, R., et al. (2003). What decline in pain intensity is meaningful to patients with acute pain? *Pain, 105,* 151–7.

Cook, T.D., & Campbell, D.T. (1979). *Quasi-experimentation: Design and analysis issues for field settings.* Chicago: Rand McNally College Publishing.

D'Agostino, R.B. Sr., Massaro, J.M., & Sullivan, L.M. (2003). Noninferiority trials: Design concepts and issues—the encounters of academic consultants in statistics. *Statistics in Medicine, 22,* 169–86.

Donner A. (1998). Some aspects of the design and analysis of cluster randomization trials. *Applied Statistics, 47*, 95–113.

Farrara, J.T., Young, J.P., LaMoreaux, L., et al. (2001). Clinical importance of changes in chronic pain intensity measured on an 11-point numerical pain rating scale. *Emergency Medical Journal, 18*, 205–7.

Fisher, R.A. (1935). *The design of experiments*. London, Hafner.

Friedman, L.M., Furberg, C.D., & DeMets, D.L. (2010). *Fundaments of clinical trials* (4th ed.). New York: Springer.

Haake, M., Muller, H.H., Schade-Brittinger, C., et al. (2007). German Acupuncture Trials (GERAC) for chronic low back pain: Randomized, multicenter, blinded, parallel group trail with 3 groups. *Archives of Internal Medicine. 167*, 1892–8.

Hrobjartsson, A., & Gotzche, P.C. (2001). Is the placebo powerless? An analysis of clinical trials comparing placebos with no treatment. *New England Journal of Medicine, 344*, 1594–602.

Lenth, R.V. (2001). Some practical guidelines for effective sample size determination. *American Statistician, 55*, 187–93.

Lipsey, M.W. (1990). *Design sensitivity: Statistical power for experimental research*. Thousand Oaks, CA: Sage Publications.

Lipsey, M.W., & Wilson, D.B. (1993). Educational and behavioral treatment: Confirmation from meta-analysis. *American Psychologist, 48*, 1181–209.

Murnane, R.J., & Willett, J.B. (2011). *Methods matter: Improving causal inference in educational and social science research*. New York: Oxford University Press.

Piaggio, G,. Elbourne, D.R. & Pocock, S.J., et al. (2012). Reporting of noninferiority and equivalence randomized trials. Extension of the CONSORT 2010 statement. *Journal of the American Medical Association, 308*, 2594–604.

CHAPTER 10

CONDUCTING AN EXPERIMENT

The most elegantly designed, but sloppily conducted, experiment is worthless. Our final (and completely avoidable) experimental artifact, therefore, is:

EXPERIMENTAL ARTIFACT #18: SLOPPILY CONDUCTED EXPERIMENTS

This artifact requires no definition. It is seldom listed as a threat to the validity of experimental inferences but is perhaps the most virulent and common of its 17 predecessors. The conduct of an experiment is an endeavor fraught with difficulties and must be planned and executed with great care, generic steps for which include the following:

1. Converting the experimental protocol to a comprehensive, detail-oriented manual of operation (MOP) containing the behaviors and materials required for implementation.
2. Wherever feasible, constructing checklists to match these behaviors and the temporal order in which they are performed.
3. Training staff in the use of these materials. (If the experimental staff involves only the investigator, this step can be performed by thorough review and memorization where indicated.)
4. Conducting a dry run of the procedures via one or more pilot studies.
5. Carefully supervising the implementation of the protocol.
6. Obsessively documenting compliance with it, as well as any changes to the MOP (or practical decisions required for the implementation of the protocol).
7. Reporting any protocol violations or substantive changes in the experimental procedures to the IRB (and study sponsor, if relevant).
8. Planning and implementing a secured data entry protocol.

CONSTRUCTING THE MANUAL OF OPERATING PROCEDURES

As discussed in Chapter Three, the design of any experiment involving human participants involves 10 key procedural decisions that constitute the methodological backbone (or protocol) that must be submitted to an IRB and/or funding agency. Seven of these decisions should be expanded on operationally in a formal, detailed, step-by-step experimental protocol to be shared with the experimental staff in order to help ensure the fidelity with which the design is implemented. The three decisions that do not apply are as follows:

#1: The research hypotheses (or study aims, purposes), which the investigator may or may not want to share with all study personnel, depending on whether they are considered capable of biasing the conduct of the study. (While there may be motivational advantages to sharing these with staff, there is something to be said for a "need to know" approach to communicating with both study personnel and participants.)

#6: The final comparison of interest (e.g., the intervention vs. control group or the post-test with the pretest), which is procedurally irrelevant to the individuals actually implementing the intervention and/or comparison groups.

#9: The statistical analysis plan (which is normally relevant only after the study is completed).

Of course, this information will be contained in the IRB and funding (if applicable) proposals but is not necessarily shared with study staff.

The procedural decisions that must be translated to detailed behavioral steps include recruitment, the implementation of the experimental conditions, the collection and storage of research data, and the training of staff for both the final experiment and any pilot studies that precede it.

RECRUITMENT

Recruitment of participants in some experiments may involve nothing more than in-class announcements by professors of the opportunity for undergraduates to participate in an experiment. Others may require print or online advertisement. Some may also have no inclusion or exclusion criteria other than the necessity of being a college student or an adult over the age of 18 who speaks English. Others may require the presence of a specific diagnosis with numerous comorbidity exclusions.

Regardless, all IRBs require the detailed specification of the types of participants to be recruited, how they will be contacted, and how informed consent will be assured. These details must then be operationalized in the MOP with respect to the methods by which participants are approached (or dealt with when they present themselves, either in person or via online or telephone contacts). Scripts should be written out for these purposes along with all other anticipated communication (such as how much to tell participants about the design and purpose of the study).

From the onset of the recruitment process, information (and descriptive statistics) on all contacts with participants should be kept, including those who

1. Inquire about the announced experiment,
2. Volunteer,
3. Do not volunteer (and the reasons given for not doing so),
4. Fail to meet the inclusion criteria (including statistics on each failed criterion),
5. Agree to participate but are not randomized for some reason (including what that reason was), and/or
6. Were randomized but lost to follow-up (including, when possible, the reasons given for dropping out of the experiment).

Some journals require a comprehensive flowchart containing this detailed information, such as the one depicted in Figure 10.1, recommended by the CONSORT Statement (Schulz, Altman, & Moher, for the CONSORT Group, 2010), which may be duplicated in part or its entirety by simple attribution of the original source.

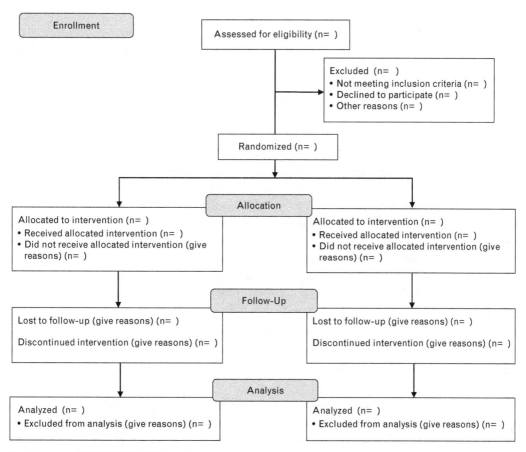

FIGURE 10.1: CONSORT 2010 Flow Diagram.

The number of participants recruited is, of course, specified in advance as part of the design and approved by the IRB. The recruitment process itself must be carefully monitored to ensure compliance with this number, since (a) exceeding it would constitute a protocol violation and (b) failing to meet the target might increase the probability of a Type II error. As a general rule, investigators are almost always overly optimistic about the availability of eligible and willing participants, so it is a good idea to have backup plans in place in the event that shortfalls occur. It is almost a logistic given (or an experimental law) that recruitment will wind up being more difficult (and take more time) than anticipated.

IMPLEMENTATION OF THE EXPERIMENTAL CONDITIONS

Arguably the most important step in the conduct of an experiment is the correct and complete implementation of the intervention(s) and comparison group(s). And the longer the duration of those conditions, the more crucial it becomes to ensure both participant and staff compliance with them. As with all of the procedural elements, detailed step-by-step behaviors and processes should be (a) written out and (b) converted to checklists whose completion are routinely monitored. Methods for dealing with participant noncompliance should be anticipated (such as the provision of makeup sessions for absences in multiple-session interventions), and IRB-approved strategies for maintaining contact with participants should always be part of the protocol.

Blinding: Procedures for blinding participants and experimental staff, when relevant, should be specified in detail. Individuals who collect data from participants should always be blinded with respect to group membership to avoid conscious and unconscious bias.

Placebo or placebo-mimicking groups are often quite difficult to implement cleanly, hence special care should be exercised in studies involving their use. In general, whether placebo controls or other comparison groups are used, participants should know as little as possible about the constitution of the experimental conditions, although they should know exactly what is required of them and what the risks (if any) are. As mentioned, a "need to know" philosophy is often a reasonable approach for running an experiment—both from the participants' and from the staff's perspectives.

Allocation of participants to conditions: Random assignment procedures (as discussed in Chapter Five) should likewise be specified in detail, and one experienced, trained individual (preferably a research methodologist or statistician) should be assigned the task of implementing them.

DATA COLLECTION

Even if the experimental conditions are properly implemented, complete and accurate outcome data are necessary to evaluate them. The MOP should contain standardized instructions for the collection of all study data along with written scripts and checklists for that purpose. If the data involve questionnaires, someone (e.g., research assistants) should check all instruments to avoid the presence of missing data at the time data are collected and ask participants to correct the omissions. If online data collection is employed, automated cues should be provided to participants concerning missing data. When data are abstracted from records, appropriate methods (e.g., the documentation of inter-rater reliability and extensive training) should be employed to ensure accurate transcription.

Ranges for acceptable time intervals before and after the completion of experimental conditions should be specified (and adhered to), as well as acceptable changes in data collection for participants who miss a scheduled assessment (e.g., if data collection normally involves a personal appearance by participants, a telephone interview might be appropriate if an in-person assessment cannot be scheduled, although this has the disadvantages associated with instrumentation changes). When research instruments need to be scored, obviously the key should be part of the MOP, and whoever is assigned to this task should be blinded with respect to group membership of the data.

Finally, complete copies of all study instruments in the order in which they are to be administered should be appended to the MOP, and appropriate personnel should have easy access to these. A record of permissions obtained (and fees paid) for copyrighted instruments should be kept along with other financial expenditures (the latter not being part of the MOP).

TRAINING

Training of research staff is almost always required for even the procedurally simplest of experiments. A pilot study constitutes one effective training mechanism for running the final study. If this is not feasible (e.g., when the pilot was conducted before the entire experimental staff was constituted), then all relevant staff should be conscientiously trained in as many aspects of the protocol as possible. If multiple individuals are involved, cross-training should also be employed in anticipation of illnesses or staff turnover. (A dress rehearsal employing role-playing and checklists is also a reasonable training aid.)

Checklists: In addition to their use as a training tool, the most simple and reliable way to ensure that each of the behaviors involved in the implementation of the protocol is performed in the correct order is via checklists in which the experimental staff simply mark whether or not the behavior was performed (or explains why it was not performed). Checklists have been advocated to increase both clinical (Gawande, 2009) and research (Stufflebeam, 2001) performance, primarily because of their ease of use and mnemonic facilitation. For a study of any complexity, therefore, checklists should be constructed (and continually monitored) for the experiment as a whole and each procedural category.

THE PILOT STUDY

At least one pilot study should always be employed, preferably a dry run of the entire protocol, but definitely involving such key components as (a) implementing the intervention, (b) gauging compliance with it, and (c) collecting the study data, including the primary outcome variable. The sample size can be quite small (perhaps five participants or so) for this purpose, although a larger sample will be required for estimating a credible effect size (ES) (or to serve as preliminary data for a funded proposal).

Pilot work is an absolute necessity for all experiments, including dissertation research. An investigator should be prepared for the fact that it may be necessary to change the protocol based on unanticipated difficulties encountered in this process. In the event such changes are required, a second pilot study may well be necessary. Thus, there are few dicta more important than our 23rd experimental principle:

> **PRINCIPLE #23: Always conduct at least one pilot study prior to initiating the final experiment.**

DOCUMENTATION

From the onset of recruitment, everything that occurs in the experiment should be compulsively documented. At the very least, the final protocol should be used to generate a study log in which each deviation from it (however minor) can be recorded. This is done for three reasons: (1) substantive protocol violations must be reported to the IRB, and in the final research report, (2) the resulting documentation serves as a mnemonic backup (since no one's memory is perfect) and (3) the document will serve to improve subsequent studies conducted by the investigator.

GENERAL GUIDELINES FOR CONDUCTING AN EXPERIMENT

Other than the absolutely essential steps just outlined, it is difficult to provide specific advice for running all types of experiments given the differences in complexity, procedures, types of participants, and settings. Individual studies also tend to differ dramatically with respect to regulatory requirements based on (a) their investigators' parent institutions, (b) the institutions from which participants are recruited (if relevant or different from one's affiliate), and (c) the degree of risk or obtrusiveness involved.

There are, however, some generic guidelines that apply to all investigations involving human participants. A universal one is the necessity for investigators to familiarize themselves with their IRB's requirements and to constantly query their staffs regarding any issues on which the latter may be unclear. Even small unfunded studies now require a considerable number of IRB forms, correspondences, and informed consent documents that should be locked, carefully organized, and stored in a central location.

These regulations are normally available online, and all research institutions require some sort of training in regulatory matters. Most IRBs also conduct audits, and compliance with these matters which, while sometimes constituting a minor irritant, is simply a cost of conducting research.

There are a few additional issues and considerations that often arise in the conduct of an experiment of which seasoned investigators are quite aware but which beginning ones should *anticipate*. Some of the more common of these follow:

1. Even when the experimental procedures have been piloted, it is sometimes necessary to fine-tune the protocol during the course of a trial. When this occurs, it is necessary

to obtain permission from the IRB (and the funding agency when relevant), document the change, and mention it in the final report (if the change is sufficiently substantive to conceivably affect the bottom-line experimental inference).

2. Everyone involved with any given experiment will not be equally competent, experienced, or conscientious. This truism is one of the primary reasons that, to the maximum extent possible, every procedural aspect of the design should be standardized to the maximum degree possible to avoid the necessity of staff needing to problem solve in real-time situations. Scripts should be written for recruitment, administration of the experimental conditions, and data collection when relevant. The necessity of adhering to the exact wording of these scripts over the course of the study (again, to the maximum extent possible) should be stressed and enforced. In addition, an attempt should be made to anticipate questions participants may have about the study, and a priori decisions should be made regarding what is appropriate and inappropriate to communicate to them.

3. To the extent that there is *any* subjectivity in the data collection process (e.g., if behavioral observations are employed as the outcome variable), the individuals charged with this task should be trained rigorously prior to beginning the study until an acceptable level of inter-rater reliability is obtained (preferably, using the kappa coefficient). Following that, unannounced spot checks should be conducted throughout the course of the study to ensure that slippage does not occur. (Unanticipated scenarios are the rule rather than the exception here, thus a codebook should be kept documenting ongoing decisions and shared with the data collectors as required.)

4. The implementation of the experimental conditions should always be monitored with extreme care to ensure their uniformity throughout the study. If the intervention has been piloted, the investigator knows that it *can* be implemented. What may not be as clear, however, is how conscientiously participants will comply with that implementation, thus it is important to record the dose (e.g., number of sessions attended) each recipient receives. This is referred to as *treatment fidelity* (Bellg, Borrelli, Resnick, et al., 2004) in some circles and should be quantified and recorded for each individual when relevant. (Intent-to-treat analysis precludes dropping noncompliant participants out of the final statistical analyses, but this information is important to report.)

5. Regardless of their core personalities, it is necessary for investigators to be assertive during the conduct of their experiments to ensure that no preventable extraneous events interfere with the implementation of the experimental protocol. The more individuals involved in the conduct of a study, and the closer the experimental environment is to everyday clinical practice (i.e., away from a controlled, laboratory setting), the more important it becomes for investigators to supervise the entire enterprise carefully and continuously. (A non-debilitating diagnosis of obsessive-compulsive disorder is also not a bad attribute for someone who runs experiments.) Murphy's Law (and especially Finagle's corollary) is also applicable to the conduct of research (i.e., anything that can go wrong, will—at the worst possible moment).

6. Running an experiment requires both a great deal of skill and a great deal of commitment. Often the only way to ensure that both of these attributes are present is for the investigator to be involved in as many of the activities as feasible and to delegate as little as possible. When circumstances prevent this, obtaining the services of an experienced, hands-on project director is absolutely essential. (All prospective investigators should

strive to obtain as much experience as possible actually conducting experiments as part of their education—preferably prior to their dissertation research.)

7. Even when investigators have the luxury of employing a project director, they should supervise that person and as much of the experimental process as possible. (It is unwise to simply assume that everything ran smoothly, based on their project directors' reports or lack of documentation of problems.)

8. Related to this point, while few scientists enjoy meetings, they are absolutely necessary when multiple individuals are involved in an experiment. These meetings should be regularly scheduled and everyone involved in the study should be required to discuss potential problems, issues, or even the lack thereof. These meetings do not have to be of any fixed duration, but they should be regular (and relatively frequent). This point, in fact, is important enough to deserve its own principle:

PRINCIPLE #24: When conducting (or planning) an experiment, schedule regular meetings with all staff and collaborators to discuss problems, solutions to those problems, and suggestions for improvement of the experimental process.

DATA ENTRY AND PROTECTION

While statistical concerns are generally outside of our purview here, both data entry and data monitoring are integral components of conducting an experiment. This is especially true of data entry since even if an investigator has access to a statistician, the statistician will usually expect to receive the data in an analysis-ready form, such as via an Excel spreadsheet, or directly entered into a preferred statistical package, such as SPSS or SAS. (Direct entry into the statistical package is preferable in many ways, as many of these offer more convenient options for documentation.)

Obviously, *accurate* data entry is a prerequisite for successfully conducting an experiment because the final inference will be based on these numbers. Entering data properly can be relatively labor intensive as well, often more so than anticipated because of the amount of subsidiary (often unnecessary) information collected. Six keys to ensuring that data are entered accurately involve the following:

1. Constructing a comprehensive code book, using study instruments when possible (multiple-item questionnaires must be entered item by item), and including acceptable values and codes. (IRBs require some form of participant identifiers in lieu of actual names. The links are normally stored under lock and key or password-protected electronic files available only to specified study personnel.)

2. Taking the time to fully document the data entered with transparent variable names, missing value codes, value labels when appropriate, and so forth. These labels should also be used in the code book and will prove valuable when the data are accessed in subsequent years for additional analytic purposes.

3. Using double data entry, preferably employing different entry personnel. If the latter is not practical, have the same individual enter the data twice, with a reasonable time intervening. User-friendly software exists for this purpose.

4. Periodically checking the data by running descriptive statistics on each variable (e.g., the mean, frequency distributions, and high vs. low values) to ensure that an incorrect value has not been entered by mistake. Alternately, software exists (e.g., Access) that prohibits data entry personnel from entering out-of-range values; running descriptive statistics that include high and low values for each variable or item provides an additional safeguard.

5. Protecting the integrity of one's data compulsively, assertively, and aggressively. It is absurd to take the time to conduct a clean, well-designed experiment (not to mention consuming scarce resources, including one's own time and that of participants) and then wind up with an incorrect inference because of inaccurate data entry. Large individual differences exist in data entry aptitude, thus this position should be filled carefully (and supervised).

6. Electronically saving one's data (and documentation) in multiple secure locations. Guidelines exist for the length of time investigators are required to keep their data, but there is really no excuse for ever destroying experimental results in this digital age (personal identifiable information being an exception).

DATA ANALYSIS

While the actual analysis of data is not discussed in any detail here, investigators should not absolve themselves of all responsibilities in the statistical analysis of their experiments. It is true that data analysis is becoming ever more specialized, with increasing emphasis placed on statistical assumptions and relatively esoteric procedures, but in many ways experiments are easier to analyze than observational studies.

And while investigators may be wise to involve a statistician in the final analysis that will appear in the refereed journal submission, 95% of the time a simple t-test, chi-square, or ANOVA will provide a comparable inferential conclusion to one produced by a more defensible and complex mixed linear, generalized estimating equations, or hierarchical modeling procedure. In fact, given the existence of point-and-click statistical packages such as SPSS, there is little excuse for investigators not to perform their own preliminary and cursory hypothesis tests involving one of the simple statistical procedure taught in every undergraduate introductory statistics course. The data are the primary product resulting from an experiment, and they are both the investigator's property and responsibility. It is therefore incumbent upon investigators to at least understand the data-analytic procedures employed, and it is exceedingly unwise to rely solely on someone else's interpretation thereof.

There are instances, of course, where a simplistic analysis produces dissimilar results from a more complicated one. (An example is analyzing the results of a randomized cluster design while ignoring the nested effect.) At the very least, however, a "quick and dirty" analysis provides an idea of whether one's hypothesis has been supported or not. And certainly, if a major discrepancy (positive or negative) exists between a simplistic and a more sophisticated analysis, the author of the latter should be asked for a simple, understandable explanation of the discrepancies. If none is forthcoming, the investigator should seek another opinion.

When investigators do employ a second party to analyze their data there should be an a priori agreement in place regarding the analyst's duties, including the following:

1. Providing the investigator with a Word document containing the final output plus descriptive statistics. The latter can be checked against the investigator's more simplistic analyses since unadjusted means and standard deviations should agree regardless of the technique employed.
2. Providing a prose synopsis, preferably journal ready, of the bottom-line results as they relate to the study hypotheses.
3. Providing a face-to-face meeting (after the output and written synopsis have been delivered) to explain each component of the output provided and answer questions.

The investigator, in turn, should prepare for the meeting by formulating questions (such as how is this or that source of variation accounted for) and by marking each part of the output he or she does not understand. During the meeting, copious (and legible) notes should be written on the output—both to (a) record the analyst's explanations for future reference and (b) possibly facilitate obtaining a second opinion if there is some question about the results that are not explained understandably. (A competent data analyst should be able to justify any decisions made and explain in simple terms any procedure employed. If not, this should be interpreted as a red flag signifying that the analyst may not understand the analysis.)

Working with a statistician can be a trying experience, however, one which our 25th and final principle should facilitate (and perhaps even avoid):

PRINCIPLE #25: Develop sufficient data-analytic expertise to either analyze your own data or to evaluate what has been analyzed for you by someone else.

This dictum may appear daunting to some, but user-friendly statistical packages exist, and it simply isn't that difficult to develop the expertise to perform serviceable, preliminary analyses of experimental data. And in those instances in which more sophisticated analytic strategies *are* required (such as when preparing the final report for publication or for accounting for all sources of systematic variation), it remains the principal investigator's responsibility to ensure that the analysis has been performed properly.

As a final suggestion, while it is important that data be entered as they are collected (as well as checked for accuracy throughout the study), it is often wise for the final statistical analysis of one's data to be delayed until the end of the study. This helps resist the temptation to take premature actions (such as terminating the trial, changing the protocol in some way, or "running just a few more subjects to get statistical significance") based on emerging trends in the data, which in turn can increase the probability of a Type I error. Obvious exceptions include studies involving a planned interim analysis or that involve a data safety and monitoring board (which are independent committees required for some funded studies) that requests interim looks at the data.

This concludes the third of the book's four parts. Our final task is to consider a few issues that are less cut-and-dried (and a bit more controversial) than those discussed to this point. These include (a) issues related to the *external validity* (or generalizability) of experimental research (which are not particularly amenable to specific experimental principles but which can be extremely relevant to experimental *meaningfulness*), (b) three unique paradigmatic approaches to conducting experiments involving humans, each possessing some designs relatively specific to it (some of which are more open to criticism than those covered to this point but have their own unique advantages under certain specialized circumstances), and (c) the uncomfortable topic of scientific bias, which manages to rear its ugly head in just about every experimental arena.

SUMMARY

Based on the reality that the design process is worthless if the experiment is *sloppily conducted* (our 18th and final experimental artifact), generic guidelines were provided for preserving the integrity of the final hypothesis test. These include the following behaviors:

1. Constructing a detailed manual of operations (MOP) mirroring but greatly expanding on (and operationally defining) the protocol.
2. Training and supervising staff, because like it or not, part of the job description of most scientists involves becoming an effective (if specialized) administrator.
3. Planning and conducting one or more pilot studies.
4. Implementing the protocol with careful attention to detail.
5. Documenting *everything*, including compliance with and deviations from the protocol with extreme obsessiveness, keeping careful records, based on the assumption of an eminent IRB or sponsor (if applicable) audit.
6. Planning and supervising a secured data entry protocol and developing as much statistical literacy as feasible.

Three experimental principles were tendered based on this crucial aspect of the experimental process:

Principle #23: Always conduct at least one pilot study prior to initiating the final experiment.
Principle #24: When conducting (or planning) an experiment, schedule regular meetings with all staff and collaborators to discuss problems, solutions to those problems, and suggestions for improvement of the experimental process.
Principle #25: Develop sufficient data-analytic expertise to either analyze your own data or to evaluate what has been analyzed for you by someone else.

REFERENCES

Bellg, A.J., Borrelli, B., Resnick, B., et al. (2004). Enhancing treatment fidelity in health behavior change research: Best practices and recommendations from the NIH Behavior Change Consortium. *Health Psychology, 23*, 443–51.

Gawande, A. (2009). *The checklist manifesto*. New York: Metropolitan Books.

Schulz, K.F., Altman, D.G., & Moher, D., for the CONSORT Group. (2010). CONSORT 2010 Statement: Updated guidelines for reporting parallel group randomized trials. *British Medical Journal, 340*, c332.

Stufflebeam, D.L. (2001). Evaluation checklists: Practical tools for guiding and judging evaluations. *American Journal of Evaluation, 22*, 71–9.

PART IV

OTHER EXPERIMENTAL
ISSUES, DESIGNS,
AND PARADIGMS

CHAPTER 11

EXTERNAL VALIDITY (GENERALIZABILITY)

To a certain extent, a dichotomy exists in human experimentation involving the sometimes conflicting goals of achieving high internal vs. high external validity. So far we have discussed internal (or inferential) validity in considerable detail while somewhat neglecting its complement—external validity, which was originally defined by Campbell and Stanley (1966) in terms of the following question:

> To what populations, settings, treatment variables, and measurement variables can this effect be generalized? (p. 5)

Unfortunately, over half a century later we have found few ways to answer this multifaceted question satisfactorily other than to repeat an experiment under another discrete set of conditions to see if the results replicate. Campbell and Stanley's question, as they fully realized, is basically not answerable via an efficacy experiment designed to provide a satisfactory answer to a discrete (usually dichotomous) question of the form:

> Under these specific conditions *does this intervention produce higher or lower "scores" than this comparison group with respect to this specific outcome?*

To this point, no known scientific methodology is capable of addressing questions such as:

> Given that, under these conditions, this intervention produces higher or lower "scores" than this comparison group with respect to this specific outcome, under what other conditions (i.e., populations, settings, treatment variables, and measurement variables) *will the same effect occur?*

Thus, while it is hardly a simple matter to assure adequate internal validity (i.e., for ensuring that the resulting inference, operationalized by the experimental hypothesis, is correct), ensuring external validity is far more difficult (other than to repeat the experiment under different sets of conditions). Historically, investigators have largely tended to ignore external validity and concentrate on internal validity, except to occasionally speculate on the former in their discussion sections. The reasons for this preference are relatively straightforward.

First, the assurance of internal validity is a logical prerequisite (i.e., necessary but not sufficient) for external validity. If an experiment produces false positive or false negative results, obviously the generalization of these results to other "populations, settings, treatment variables, and measurement variables" is irrelevant. Scientists are therefore understandably more interested in the accuracy (or validity) of an experiment's results than they are the question of how far these results can be extended. (And while this latter issue is of scientific importance, and of even greater societal interest, a prevalent—though largely unfounded—belief is that if the study is important enough, further research will automatically be conducted to determine what relevant conditions, if any, preclude an experimental finding from replicating.)

Second, the threats to internal validity (i.e., the validity of the inference generated by the experiment) are well documented, understood, and (largely) avoidable. Hopefully, this has been sufficiently illustrated by our discussion of natural history or maturation, the placebo effect, regression to the mean, the repeated testing artifact, instrumental changes to the outcome variable, extraneous external events, demand characteristics, Hawthorne-type effects, experimental attrition, and sloppily conducted research in general. While the Hawthorne effect is arguably more relevant to external than internal validity, the only completely unavoidable threat to the generalizability of experimental research is the inconvenience that >99.9% of all experimental research must rely on volunteers (the hand-washing experiment briefly described in Chapter Four [Munger & Harris, 1989] being an extremely rare counter example). For this and other reasons (e.g., the fact that experimental conditions are often purposefully *changed* from naturally occurring conditions in order to allow the intervention effects to be observed under controlled, uncluttered conditions), experimental research in general is usually accused of having lower external validity than the results accruing from other investigative genres (e.g., observational and correlational research).

Finally, examination of the brief but expansive definition of external validity just presented (which includes generalizability to different participants, settings, interventions, and techniques of measuring outcomes) raises some obvious questions: How could any experiment involving human participants with all of their vagaries be expected to address all of these issues? Or how could a consumer of any experiment (or another investigator for that matter) assess the degree to which a single experiment possesses acceptable external validity? Or even, what constitutes an acceptable degree of external validity?

The answer to the first questions is obvious: No one can categorically know how generalizable an effect is to a different environment in which it was conducted until the experiment is repeated in that environment. The reason is that, unlike other design elements, generalizability is not reducible to a discrete number of evidence- (or consensus-) based steps (e.g., random assignment, the use of an appropriate sample size, and so forth). There are several reasons for this, the most important of which are that (a) external validity is situational specific and (b) we simply do not know all of the reasons why some experimental results generalize while others do not.

Fortunately, individual scholars have been active in attempting to both (a) heighten awareness regarding the importance of external validity in the experimental design process and (b) provide guidelines for helping experimental consumers judge the degree of generalizability of experiments. Without question the most comprehensive and ambitious effort in this regard involved a taxonomy compiled by Lawrence Green and Russell Glasgow (2006) designed to

1. Provide standards similar to the CONSORT Statement to ensure adequate reporting of design elements impacting an experiment's external validity,
2. Provide criteria and standards for prospectively increasing external validity of experiments at the design stage, and
3. Ultimately develop a rating scheme by which the degree of external validity of an experiment can be quantified.

A list of these standards and their accompanying questions is presented in the next insert. (The original article provides a more thorough explanation and rationale for each standard.) Note that these questions do not ask whether the experiment was generalizable with respect to each issue (surely no studies are), but instead asked whether the investigators did or did not address each of the 16 issues in their final report. (At the very least, it is recommended here that investigators consider all 16 issues underlying these questions during the design of their experiments.)

QUESTIONS RELEVANT TO THE DETERMINATION OF EXTERNAL VALIDITY

Evaluating the Relevance, Generalization, and Applicability of Research: Issues in External Validation and Translation Methodology (2006)

Lawrence W. Green and Russell E. Glasgow

The following outline presents the questions these authors consider to be important in determining the external validity of experiments designed to impact public health practices.

I. REACH AND REPRESENTATIVENESS

A. Participation: "Are there analyses of the participation rate among potential (a) settings, (b) delivery staff, and (c) patients (consumers)?"
B. Target audience: "Is the intended target audience stated for adoption (at the intended settings such as worksites, medical offices, etc.) and application (at the individual level)?"
C. Representativeness—Settings: "Are comparisons made of the similarity of settings in the study to the intended target audience of program settings—or to those settings that decline to participate?"

D. Representativeness—Individuals: "Are analyses conducted of the similarity and differences between patients, consumers, or other subjects who participate vs. either those who decline, or the intended target audience?"

II. PROGRAM OR POLICY IMPLEMENTATION AND ADAPTATION

A. Consistent implementation: "Are data presented on the level and quality of implementation of different program components?"
B. Staff expertise: "Are data presented on the level of training or experience required to deliver the program or quality of implementation by different types of staff?"
C. Program adaptation: "Is information reported on the extent to which different settings modified or adapted the program to fit their setting?"
D. Mechanisms: "Are data reported on the processes or mediating variables through which the program or policy achieved its effects?"

III. OUTCOMES FOR DECISION-MAKING

A. Significance: "Are outcomes reported in a way that can be compared to either clinical guidelines or public health goals?"
B. Adverse consequences: "Do the outcomes reported include quality of life or potential negative outcomes?"
C. Moderators: "Are there any analyses of moderator effects—including different subgroups of participants and types of intervention staff—to assess robustness vs. specificity of effects?"
D. Sensitivity: "Are there any sensitivity analyses to assess dose–response effects, threshold level, or point of diminishing returns on the resources expended?"
E. Costs: "Are data on intervention costs presented? If so, are standard economic or accounting methods used to fully account for costs?"

IV. MAINTENANCE AND INSTITUTIONALIZATION

A. Long-term effects: "Are data reported on longer term effects, at least 12 months following treatment?"
B. Institutionalization: "Are data reported on the sustainability (or reinvention or evolution) of program implementation at least 12 months after the formal evaluation?"
C. Attrition: "Are data on attrition by condition reported, and are analyses conducted of the representativeness of those who drop out?"

EXPERIMENTAL CLASSIFICATION SYSTEMS AND EXTERNAL VALIDITY

So far we haven't mentioned the experimental classification systems used in the various disciplines involving human participants, for two reasons: They tend not to be mutually exclusive and many are largely discipline specific. In almost all of these systems, however, at least one experimental category is given over to testing some aspect of external validity (usually involving the applicability of an effect to clinical practice).

Drug experiments, for example, are normally categorized by the U.S. Food and Drug Administration (FDA) and National Institutes of Health (NIH) in terms of four phases. Phase I involves extremely small-scale, usually uncontrolled studies (i.e., no control group is deemed necessary) to assess the maximum safe dose (or potential toxicity) of a new drug. (This is accomplished through the use of stepped-up dosages, using as few as three healthy volunteers per dose.) Phase II, also normally uncontrolled, involves a few more participants (usually less than 15) to ascertain if there is any biological activity or disease-related effect from the drug. Phase III studies involve the types of controlled experiments in which we have been primarily interested and are designed to test the efficacy of an intervention on a meaningful outcome under carefully controlled conditions. Phase IV experiments are typically larger trials, often encompassing longer follow-up intervals and much larger sample sizes to better assess long-term outcomes (including side effects) under veridical clinical conditions. These trials may be controlled or relatively uncontrolled but are always more relevant to the assessment of external validity than Phase III experiments.

The educational analog to these four phases are represented by the Institute of Educational Sciences' funding structure, which are delineated in terms of "goals." Goal 1 studies are secondary analyses of data sets (or small descriptive studies) designed to "identify existing programs and practices that may be associated with better academic outcomes and examine factors and conditions that may mediate or moderate the effects of these programs and practices."

A Goal 2 study is designed to develop new educational interventions by getting them to the point at which they can be evaluated. Goal 3 experiments are analogous to controlled Phase III medical trials in the sense that they are designed to assess efficacy. Goal 4 provides evidence of effectiveness (and costs) of programs, practices, and policies "implemented at scale" and (although often bedeviled by a number of problems as described in the next example) are directly relevant to external validity. (Goal 5 doesn't really involve experimentation but is given over to the "development of data and measurement systems," which theoretically should at least help ensure the proper implementation and continued efficacy of an intervention.)

No classification system is perfect (or especially useful), however, and individual experiments often combine elements of more than one phase or goal. "Duration," one of Green and Glasgow's main criteria, for example, is addressed by many NIH-funded studies via the inclusion of relatively long follow-up intervals after the intervention's efficacy has been assessed. Other efficacy trials sometimes employ a declining "booster" level of the treatment to ascertain if a total cessation of benefit can be prevented once the intervention is completely withdrawn.

In recent years, efforts have also been instituted by the U.S. federal government to attempt to increase the payoff of society's huge investment in biomedical, health, and educational research. A number of funding agencies (e.g., the NIH, Department of Education, Centers for Disease Control and Prevention [CDC], Agency for Healthcare Research and Quality) have created initiatives for what is sometime called translational research involving funding for

1. Investigations designed to find practical or clinical applications for basic (sometimes even laboratory) research originally conducted solely for the sake of adding to knowledge or advancing theory,
2. Research into the translation process itself, and

3. What are variously termed practical, pragmatic, large simple, or "scaled-up" trials that are specifically designed to ensure their generalizability to clinical practice.

PRAGMATIC, PRACTICAL, LARGE SIMPLE, AND "SCALED-UP" EXPERIMENTAL DESIGNS

Pragmatic experiments (or large simple trials [Yusuf, Collins, & Peto, 1984]) are designed to straddle the boundary between internal and external validity. They are also designed to cross the boundary between efficacy (Type III trials) and effectiveness (Type IV trials). And like randomized cluster and noninferiority trials, they have a CONSORT extension of their own (Zwarenstein, Treweek, Gagnier, et al., 2009). Unlike the latter designs, however, they are associated with few specialized procedural or analytic components. Instead, they differ from efficacy trials primarily in their existential purpose, which is to ascertain an intervention's practicality or likelihood of effectiveness in the real world of professional practice (and service delivery).

In a table adapted from a presentation by Marion K. Campbell, the CONSORT pragmatic extension document (Zwarenstein, Treweek, Gagnier, et al., 2008) lists four primary differences between pragmatic and efficacy trials:

(1) *Experimental purpose*: For an efficacy trial the purpose is to ascertain, "Can the intervention work?" For its pragmatic counterpart the purpose is to ascertain, "Does the intervention work when used in normal practice?" It should be noted that these two questions do not translate to different hypotheses but to the investigators' purpose for conducting the experiment in the first place—a purpose the present author considers existential but may be better described as an "attitude" (Schwartz & Lellouch, 1967).

(2) *Experimental setting*: For an efficacy trial, a "well-resourced, 'ideal' setting is employed as opposed to 'normal practice.'" The former is chosen to maximize experimental control; the latter (which is difficult to define operationally) to maximize external validity. The opposite is the case for a practical or pragmatic trial.

(3) *Implementation of the intervention*: In an efficacy trial every effort is made to ensure both participant and practitioner compliance with the protocol and intervention implementation. In a pragmatic trial no more effort is expended in this regard than would be done in "normal practice." (In some disciplines this failure to ensure the implementation of the intervention is almost surely a recipe for negative findings, as witnessed by the majority of the Department of Education's "scaled-up" experimental efforts.)

(4) *Relevance to practice*: One "attitude" that some efficacy investigators have been accused of is that "applicability to practice is not our job." In a pragmatic trial the relevance to practice is of paramount concern.

While perhaps justifiable in certain disciplines, it is not clear that huge, expensive randomized trials are necessary to evaluate (a) effectiveness, (b) professional compliance, or (c) willingness to adopt a research finding. As illustrated by the example which follows, if an intervention is not implementable under current practice conditions, then perhaps resources can be better spent by documenting this fact via lower cost methodologies such as focus groups or surveys.

AN EDUCATIONAL EXAMPLE OF A PRAGMATIC, PRACTICAL, GOAL 4, OR SCALED-UP TRIAL

Effectiveness of Reading and Mathematics Software Products: Findings From Two Student Cohorts (2009)

L. Campuzano, M. Dynarski, R. Agodini, and K. Rall

The purpose of this large "scaled-up" experiment was to compare 16 reading and mathematics software instructional systems to "conventional" classroom instruction using standardized achievement tests as the outcome variable. Classrooms were randomly assigned (from 132 schools involving 439 teachers) to employ one of the software systems or none at all (in which case the classroom teacher taught the regular curriculum by "conventional" means).

While the experiment qualified as a randomized control trial (employing a randomized cluster design), it is also an example of both a translational research project (translational because the software systems were already developed but not as widely implemented as hoped) and a practical trial (because little or no apparent effort was made to persuade the experimental teachers to actually use the software). At experiment's end (data were collected over a 2-year interval), no statistically significant differences surfaced between the combined software intervention and conventional classroom instruction (a not particularly surprising finding, since the intervention group teachers opted to employ the software for an average of 5 minutes of each 50-minute class period).

The cost of the study was in excess of $14,000,000, but when the lead investigator was confronted with criticisms of the fact that all the study demonstrated was a lack of implementation, he defended the trial as follows: "We felt pretty confident that 10% of use reflects the sound judgment of the teacher about how often and for what kinds of instructional modules they wanted to use technology" (*Education Week*, April 11, 2007, p. 18).

As inane as such a statement sounds (since 10% of a 50-minute class period translates to 5 minutes of instructional use), what this individual seemed to be saying was that the purpose of this trial was to ascertain the effect of these software systems on learning under veridical educational conditions in which teachers controlled the instructional method used in their classrooms. In the present author's admittedly biased opinion, one would have hoped that the funding agency (U.S. Department of Education) would have required sufficient pilot work to avoid wasting millions of taxpayers' money on an experiment doomed from the onset to produce negative findings. But unfortunately, also from the present author's opinion and experience, such are the vagaries and inanities of our funding systems.

OTHER APPROACHES TO INCREASING
AND EVALUATING EXTERNAL VALIDITY

Meta-analysis: Another initiative designed to improve the generality of experimental results involves the ascendance of meta-analysis, a term coined by (Glass, 1976) and followed up by two seminal examples, one involving class size in education (Glass & Smith, 1979) and one assessing the effectiveness of psychotherapy (Smith, Glass, & Miller, 1980). The technique itself constituted an impressive effort (a) to make sense of the welter of often conflicting experimental results, (b) to arrive at a bottom-line conclusion regarding whether or not a particular intervention "worked" and, if it did, (c) to determine why certain experiments investigating the same hypothesis produced conflicting results. (The meta-analytic process involves retrieving experiments assessing the same or similar interventions, computing an effect size [ES] for each study, and statistically analyzing these individual study results much as the individual participant outcomes are analyzed in a single experiment.)

Figure 11.1 depicts a typical meta-analytic forest plot in which the ESs of each retrieved experiment is presented along with the *p*-value and confidence interval associated with the average ES (weighted on the basis of the sample size associated with each individual ES; see the diamond at the bottom of the plot). Each individual experiment's ES can also be assessed to determine if one or more is significantly heterogeneous, at which point the offending parties can be examined to see if they possess characteristics (e.g., lower methodological quality) different from those of their homogeneous counterparts.

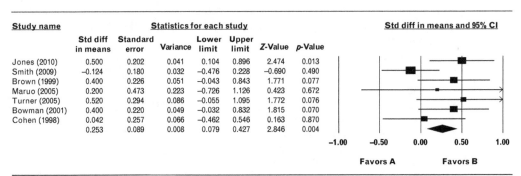

Study name	Statistics for each study							Std diff in means and 95% CI
	Std diff in means	Standard error	Variance	Lower limit	Upper limit	Z-Value	*p*-Value	
Jones (2010)	0.500	0.202	0.041	0.104	0.896	2.474	0.013	
Smith (2009)	−0.124	0.180	0.032	−0.476	0.228	−0.690	0.490	
Brown (1999)	0.400	0.226	0.051	−0.043	0.843	1.771	0.077	
Maruo (2005)	0.200	0.473	0.223	−0.726	1.126	0.423	0.672	
Turner (2005)	0.520	0.294	0.086	−0.055	1.095	1.772	0.076	
Bowman (2001)	0.400	0.220	0.049	−0.032	0.832	1.815	0.070	
Cohen (1998)	0.042	0.257	0.066	−0.462	0.546	0.163	0.870	
	0.253	0.089	0.008	0.079	0.427	2.846	0.004	

Meta analysis

FIGURE 11.1: Meta-analysis Output.

The numbers of meta-analytic studies have proliferated to an astonishing degree since the introduction of the technique four decades or so ago. As one example, John Hattie (2009) synthesized over 800 meta-analyses involving student achievement alone (although these included correlational as well as experimental studies). The technique has spawned one extremely impressive institution (the Cochrane Collaboration), which has conducted over 5,000 systematic reviews of medical and healthcare experiments, and its younger, more nascent sister institution (the Campbell Collaboration) has conducted reviews for social and behavioral research. Both groups attempt, with some success, to arrive at bottom line conclusions regarding the effectiveness of interventions conducted by different investigators at different sites and often employing relatively disparate patient/participant populations.

Multicenter trials represent another experimental approach to increasing external validity. Often necessitated by the difficulty of recruiting patients with rare conditions in medicine, these trials involve simultaneously conducting the same experiment at different sites. One of the sites functions as a coordinating center for the entire effort, but participants are randomly assigned within each site, with the results being pooled at the end of the experiment. Optimally, these sites are treated as a blocking variable and the experimental effects are compared across and within sites. If no interaction exists between sites and intervention effects, then some evidence of the generalizability of the overall results is provided—assuming, of course, that there are sufficient participants within each site to provide sufficient statistical power to detect such an interaction. Should some sites produce divergent results, the generality of the pooled results are questionable, although site-by-treatment interactional results are often not reported, thereby obviating one of the major advantages of the technique. (Graphical techniques such as that depicted in Figure 11.1 should probably be a required component of any multicenter trial.)

Replication: an experiment cannot possess external validity if its results cannot be replicated. (A multisite trial is a form of *non*-independent replication in the sense that the site investigators are part of the same team and the statistical analysis is normally supervised by the principal investigator.) When a replication is performed (whether performed by independent or non-independent investigators), the production of the same inference is a necessary but not sufficient condition for external validity (since the same conditions and procedures were employed in both studies).

Unfortunately, independent replication is relatively rare in many of the human sciences, partly because the stakes are seldom considered to be sufficiently high, partly because pure replications (i.e., experiments using exactly the same protocol) are considered less interesting by both investigators and peer reviewers. (A finding in physics such as the cold fusion fiasco in Utah [Wikipedia, 2014], however, can be subjected to replication with surprising rapidity.)

BOTTOM-LINE THOUGHTS ON THE EXTERNAL VALIDITY OF EXPERIMENTS

Many, many years ago (1961) when classic measurement theory's reputation was at its peak, an iconoclastic psychometrician (Robert Ebel) conducted an extensive analysis of the testing literature to ascertain the extent to which test validity (i.e., "whether a test measures what it purports to measure") was actually demonstrated for published psychological and educational assessment instruments. What he found was somewhat surprising, since the American Psychological Association and other groups considered the psychometric documentation of validity essential for any measurement instrument used for either clinical or research purposes. In the vast majority of cases, Ebel found little or no validity evidence for the assessment tools he investigated—leading the good professor to conclude:

> Validity has long been one of the major deities in the pantheon of the psychometrician. It is universally praised, but the good works done in its name are remarkably few.

In hindsight, this finding should have shocked no one since there are over a half-dozen distinct types of psychometric validity (e.g., construct, content, criterion, factorial, concurrent, predictive, face). Of course, Ebel's finding was largely ignored and until this day investigators in certain disciplines continue to blithely describe any measure they employ in their research as having been shown to be "valid and reliable"—providing an unnecessary illustration of the enduring "validity" of "The Emperor's New Clothes" parable. And while this is only the present author's opinion, the concept of external *validity* may be tailored from this same cloth.

In all, five approaches to increasing or assessing the external validity of experiments have been briefly discussed: standards for its documentation, pragmatic (or large practical) trials, meta-analysis, multicenter trials, and replications. All are useful, all have drawbacks, and all in combination do not solve the underlying question of how an experiment can be designed (or be evaluated) to ensure its external validity (or generalizability). From a "glass half-empty" perspective, let's consider their drawbacks in turn:

1. Standards are useful in many arenas, especially when they are reduced to a checklist, which Green and Glasgow (2006) envisioned doing with their list of external validity facets. The problem with standards is the difficulty of promulgation, ensuring acceptance, and mandating compliance. However, a significant benefit to consumers and investigators would accrue if the Green and Glasgow criteria were addressed in a separate document by each experiment's authors and made available either through the publishing journal's website or e-mail from the principal investigator.

2. Large practical trials suffer from their high costs, difficulty of mounting, and the potential number of them (one per promising intervention) that would need to be conducted.

3. Multicenter trials can be even more expensive than large practical trials and therefore suffer from the same disadvantage. They also seldom contain sufficient participants per site to allow for definitive inferential comparisons of between-site results.

4. Meta-analysis, while a brilliant concept, also has demonstrated a disconcerting propensity for producing positive results due to publication bias. The often mentioned meta-analysis of meta-analyses conducted by Lipsey and Wilson (1993), for example, found that of the 302 analyzed, only 6 reported numerically negative ESs and three of those were investigating the same topic. (Ninety percent of the 302 studies found ESs of .10 and over and 50% reported ESs of .50 or greater.) Even more disconcerting, meta-analyses conducted on the same basic intervention often produce disparate results—even when conducted by the same investigator (e.g., Ernst, 2002; Linde, Clausius, Ramirez, et al., 1997; Linde & Melchart, 1999).

This admittedly subjective presentation of the difficulties inherent in ensuring and/or evaluating external validity is not meant to disparage the concept and certainly not to discourage anyone's attempt to make their research efforts as generalizable as possible. Instead, the preceding discussion is offered as a single perspective for those experimental investigators who, at some point in their career, may be faced with a decision regarding how much emphasis to place on external validity in the design process.

Criticisms of randomized experiments: Also deserving of mention are criticisms of the randomized experimental designs in general, which argue that the very act of randomization may change affected individuals' responses to an intervention (e.g., Marcus, Stuart, Wang, et al. [2012] suggest that compliance, engagement, and motivation may be better with a preferred treatment than one assigned randomly, and Kaptchuk [2001] posits the existence of some potential biasing effects actually produced by blinding and randomization).

Even Sir Ronald Fisher, as fervent and effective an advocate for randomized experiments as any on record, recognized the possibility that experimental results may not generalize perfectly. While all of these conjectures undoubtedly have a degree of validity in certain situations, nothing has yet been demonstrated to be superior to the randomization of participants to different conditions for producing valid causal inferences. We simply have to exercise restraint in *what* we infer.

Also deserving of mention is the fact that while experiments involving human participants may employ random assignment to experimental conditions, they almost never randomly select their samples from *any* target population. Therefore, strictly speaking, they cannot be considered representative of any given population, much less of other populations. It should be noted, however, that the external validity of experiment involves generalizing a causal inference—hence the experimental sample is not required to be representative of its own (or any other) population with respect to demographics or other attributes not integrally related to susceptibility to the intervention's effects or lack thereof. This latter point is more eloquently made by Lucas (2003) and Zelditch (2007) with respect to theory testing in the next section.

EXTERNAL VALIDITY IN EXPERIMENTS EXCLUSIVELY DESIGNED TO TEST THEORIES

Much of the preceding discussion on external validity has centered on experiments in which the clinical efficacy of an intervention or treatment is of primary concern. This is also true of the examples presented to this point, with the exception of the Price et al. (1999) placebo study abstracted in Chapter One. However, when, the primary focus of an experiment is to test theory (as was the case in the placebo example), an argument can be made that external validity takes on a somewhat different meaning.

This is perhaps best illustrated by Lucas (2003), who states the case as follows:

> When testing theories... external validity can be assessed through determining (1) the extent to which empirical measures accurately reflect theoretical constructs, (2) whether the research setting conforms to the scope of the theory under test, (3) our confidence that findings will repeat under identical conditions, (4) whether findings support the theory being tested, and (5) the confirmatory status [i.e., the degree of previous empirical support] of the theory under test. (p. 236)

Lucas goes on to argue that in such experiments, external validity is not so much a matter of the methodology employed as it is the experiment's fidelity to the theory:

> If an experiment does manipulate every theoretically relevant variable and finds an effect, then to say that the effect will not generalize to *naturally occurring situations* is not a criticism of the experiment as having low external validity; rather, it is a critique of the theory for not taking every factor influencing the phenomenon of interest into account. (p. 238)

The phrase "naturally occurring situations" was italicized here because in a typical efficacy trial the research consumer is quite interested in this facet of generalization. Educational and medical experiments, for example, are often criticized by clinicians on the basis of their perceived lack of applicability to actual school instruction or healthcare practice.

However, Zelditch (2007), who basically adopts the same position as Lucas, makes an important point regarding the reason experiments are conducted in the first place rather than simply relying on careful observation: "The purpose of an experiment is to control the extraneities that muddle observation of a process in its nonexperimental settings" (p. 108).

Thus, regardless of the extent to which a result generalizes to *other* populations, settings, treatment variables, and/or measurement variables, which Zelditch also seems to consider a nearly impossible task, his conclusion (which very closely matches that of Lucas) regarding external validity as it relates to theory tests can be summed up as follows:

> An experiment is externally valid if the theory it supports predicts and explains the behavior of the process it describes in any situation to which the theory is applicable—that is, any situation that satisfies its instantiation [i.e., how its variables are operationalized from abstraction to concreteness] and the scope of the theory [i.e., what it explains and does not explain]. (p. 108)

And since theories very seldom specify the precise populations, conditions, and settings to which they are applicable (or are limited to), another option is to ignore the concept of external validity altogether and conduct one's experiments under the optimal conditions permitted by a laboratory—in which case the experimental focus changes from discovering "what is to what could be."

IN PRAISE OF WELL-CONDUCTED (LABORATORY-TYPE) EXPERIMENTS

And that's what one young investigator did long, long ago when he found himself faced with a rather troubling dilemma. When he conducted his educational experiments under existing classroom conditions presided over by public school teachers, even the most promising interventions tuned out not to be efficacious in comparison to instruction-as-usual control groups. (The same was largely true for the field itself and it largely remains true today, as witnessed by the Institute of Educational Sciences' plethora of negative scaled-up projects, à la the instructional software example provided earlier.)

However, when the young man in question introduced his interventions under controlled conditions using (a) carefully structured procedures, (b) brief instructional intervals, and (c) motivated undergraduates as the teachers, his experiments tended to result in significantly *increased* learning (even though they, too, were conducted in the public schools).

Not surprisingly, criticisms of using such a modified, laboratory model of school learning took the form of the dreaded "so what?" question. What applicability could such research possibly have for the existing high-noise, pandemonium-laced classroom model? All of which could be reframed as a rather *extreme* instance of the internal vs. external validity dichotomy.

For better or worse, he chose procedural control over generalizability, based on the following rationale (some might say rationalization):

> Was it the experimenter's fault that so many public school classroom environments bore more resemblance to a rave than his learning laboratories? Why not instead embrace a science of what

"could be" rather than "what is"? Why not find out what interventions were *capable* of influencing public school students' learning and then change the setting rather than conduct experiments destined to produce negative results?

Now, of course decisions such as this are individual and discipline specific and do not necessarily need to be resolved at the dichotomy's poles as this young investigator chose to do. He went on to conduct a successful program of experiments, such as comparison of tutoring vs. classroom instruction, the effect of manipulating teacher experience and teacher knowledge, and so forth, which to this day remain his favorite work.

Now certainly it is a matter of professional opinion whether large "scaled-up" or "practical" trials are worth the societal resources they consume. It is the present author's hope, however, that anyone who has read this far will prefer conducting a clean, small (but appropriately powered), definitive trial to conducting a large, sloppy one when given the choice.

In the final analysis, it is questionable whether any single educational, behavioral, or non-medical or drug-related health experiment, or program of experiments, is capable of changing professional practice or impacting public policy anyway. Perhaps the best we as scientists can do is to perform the best and the most meaningful work we can and hope that it will eventually be used to advance the public's good.

Our next chapter represents somewhat of a departure from the randomized designs and the generalization of findings discussed to this point. These designs are probably considered less epistemologically sound by the majority of mainstream investigators (including the present author), although this is by no means always the case. Regardless, beginning investigators would be wise to be conversant with all three (single-case research, program evaluation, and quality improvement research) of their philosophical orientations and relatively unique approaches to empirical inquiry.

SUMMARY

Perhaps the most comprehensive (and certainly the most venerable) definition of external validity is addressed by the question: "To what populations, settings, treatment variables, and measurement variables can this effect be generalized?" The construct itself is too diffuse, comprehensive, and ambitious to be definitively answered on the basis of any single experiment and no single experiment can address all of these issues.

The most specific and comprehensive sets of reporting standards for its documentation, proposed by Green and Glasgow (2006), were translated into 16 questions that the authors suggested be addressed by efficacy experiments—especially those designed to be implemented in public health practice. Four additional methods of assessing (or enhancing) generalizability include the following:

1. Pragmatic (or large practical) trials, which are designed to ascertain if an effect initially demonstrated under controlled conditions can or will be implemented in clinical practice (an educational example of which was discussed),
2. Meta-analysis, which is a method by which individual experiments addressing the same (or very similar) intervention (but usually using different populations, conditions, and

methodologies) can be analyzed both as a single group as well as compared to one another with respect to whether or not they produced similar or dissimilar results or inferences,

3. Multicenter experiments, in which the same experimental procedures are implemented at different sites (whose results can then be compared to ensure replication and generalizability to different, albeit similar, clinical settings), and

4. Replications of experiments by independent investigators, since an experimental effect that cannot be replicated cannot be externally valid.

Experiments designed specifically to test theory may constitute a special case with respect to external validity, since theories seldom specify the types of populations and settings to which their predictions apply or to treatment operationalization. A case is also made to give preferential attention to the assurance of internal validity over its external counterpart (as occurs in laboratory-type experiments), since internal validity is a necessary (but not sufficient) condition of external validity.

REFERENCES

Campbell, D.T., & Stanley, J.C. (1966). *Experimental and quasi-experimental designs for research.* Chicago: Rand McNally.

Campuzano, L., Dynarski, M., Agodini, R., & Rall, K. (2009). Effectiveness of reading and mathematics software products: Findings from two student cohorts (NCEE 2009-4041). Washington, DC: National Center for Education Evaluation and Regional Assistance, Institute of Education Sciences, U.S. Department of Education.

Ebel, R.L. (1961). Must all tests be valid? *American Psychologist, 16,* 640–7.

Ernst, E. (2002). A systematic review of systematic reviews of homeopathy. *British Journal of Clinical Pharmacology, 54,* 577–82.

Glass, G.V. (1976). Primary, secondary, and meta-analysis of research. *Educational Researcher, 5,* 3–8.

Glass, G.V., & Smith, M.L. (1979). Meta-analysis of research on class size and achievement. *Educational Evaluation and Policy Analysis, 1,* 2–16.

Green, L.W., & Glasgow, R.E. (2006). Evaluating the relevance, generalization, and applicability of research: Issues in external validation and translation methodology. *Evaluation & the Health Professions, 29,* 126–52.

Hattie, J. (2009). *Visible learning: A synthesis of over 800 meta-analyses relating to achievement.* London: Routledge.

Kaptchuk, T.J. (2001). The double-blind, randomized, placebo-controlled trial: Gold standard or golden calf? *Journal of Clinical Epidemiology, 54,* 541–9.

Linde, K., Clausius, N., Ramirez, G., et al. (1997). Are the clinical effects of homeopathy placebo effects: A meta-analysis of placebo-controlled trials. *Lancet, 350,* 834–43.

Linde, K., & Melchart, D. (1999). Randomized controlled trials of individualized homeopathy: A state-of-the-art review. *Journal of Alternative and Complementary Medicine, 4,* 371–88.

Lipsey, M.W., & Wilson, D.B. (1993). Educational and behavioral treatment: Confirmation from meta-analysis. *American Psychologist, 48,* 1181–209.

Lucas, J.W. (2003). Theory-testing, generalization, and the problem of external validity. *Sociological Theory, 21,* 236–53.

Marcus, S.M., Stuart, E.A., Wang, P., et al. (2012). Estimating the causal effect of randomized versus treatment preference in a doubly randomized preference trial. *Psychological Methods, 17,* 244–54.

Munger, K., & Harris, S.J. (1989). Effects of an observer on hand washing in public restroom. *Perceptual and Motor Skills, 69,* 733–5.

Price, D.D., Kirsch, I., Duff, A., et al. (1999). An analysis of factors that contribute to the magnitude of placebo analgesia in an experimental paradigm, *Pain, 83,* 147–56.

Schwartz, D., & Lellouch, J. (1967). Explanatory and pragmatic attitudes in 6 therapeutical trials. *Journal of Chronic Diseases, 20,* 637–48.

Smith, M.L., Glass, G.V., & Miller, T.I. (1980). *The benefits of psychotherapy.* Baltimore: Johns Hopkins University Press.

Wikipedia. (2014). Cold fusion. Retrieved from http://en.wikipedia.org/wiki/Cold_fusion#CITEREFBroad1989a

Yusuf, S., Collins, R., & Peto, R. (1984). Why do we need some large simple randomized trials? *Statistics in Medicine, 3,* 409–22.

Zelditch, M. (2007). The external validity of experiments that test theories. In M. Webster & S. Jane (Eds.) *Laboratory experiments in the social sciences.* Burlington, MA: Academic Press.

Zwarenstein, M., Treweek, S., Gagnier, J.J., et al. (2008). Improving the reporting of pragmatic trials: An extension of the CONSORT statement. *British Medical Journal, 337,* a2390

THREE ADDITIONAL EXPERIMENTAL PARADIGMS

Single-Case, Program Evaluation (Including Natural Experiments), and Quality Improvement Research

n this chapter we will discuss three approaches to experimentation that are accompanied by such unique attitudes or orientations that they are considered by some to have evolved into entirely different research paradigms. As a group they appear to value both (a) strategies other than the recommended randomized designs discussed to this point and (b) questions geared more to improving institutional (and professional) performance over uncovering the universal "truths" to which most scientific disciplines ostensibly aspire.

Each of the three genres also employs certain relatively unique designs with which, in the present author's opinion, investigators in all disciplines involving human experimentation should at least be conversant. But while philosophical and empirical differences exist, all three orientations share a common objective with all investigators involved with human experimentation: the production of valid causal inferences regarding the effects of specific interventions on meaningful outcomes. In order of appearance, these approaches are (a) single-case experiments, (b) program evaluations, and (c) quality improvement studies.

SINGLE-CASE EXPERIMENTS

As its name implies, this empirical genre does not randomly *assign* multiple participants to receive its interventions. Instead, most of its designs attempt to achieve experimental control by employing repeated assessments and/or repeated introductions of an intervention to a single individual. Originally developed in the laboratory (think Watsonian and Skinnerian behaviorism), single-case designs are still most commonly used in behavioral analysis, often involving attempts to decrease or extinguish aberrant behaviors in children or adults with psychiatric diagnoses. As would be expected, given the use of single participants (or sometimes single sites conceptualized as a single case), inferential statistical procedures are nowhere nearly as well developed, sophisticated, or satisfying as those employed to analyze the results of multiple-participant experiments.

With that said, a plethora of different designs exist for single-case experiments. Such a rich diversity of options exist, in fact, that only the more commonly employed will be discussed here which single-case investigators feel perfectly free to adapt as the situation requires. Conceptually, most single-case experimental designs are quite similar to the single-group crossover design discussed earlier. (Of course, single-case designs are additionally burdened by their inferential reliance on changes exhibited by a single participant who most commonly serves as his or her own control "group.")

A caveat: A common misperception regarding single-case experiments is that they are (a) performed on only one participant and (b) do not assign different participants to groups. In truth the majority of published single-case studies appear to use at least three participants (often more, but seldom more than five) as quasi-replications of one another. And sometimes three or more participants are even randomly assigned to intervention vs. control/comparison groups. What tends to distinguish them from conventional experiments is the practice of presenting the results graphically and interpreting them for each individual (usually referred to either via a first name or a letter) rather than as a group.

ABAB & ABABC designs: The most common architectural configuration of a single-case design employs a baseline period (A), followed by the intervention (B), and then followed by a complete repetition—thereby resulting in an ABAB designation. One example of such a design using only a single participant is depicted in Figure 12.1.

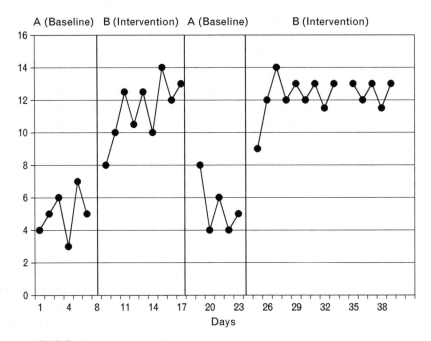

FIGURE 12.1: ABAB Design.

This basic ABAB architecture is normally accompanied by the following design characteristics:

1. Multiple assessments during both baseline and intervention phases. Thus, unlike multiple participant crossover designs that typically administer the outcome variable once or twice per phase, an ABAB single-subject design administers the outcome variable multiple times (e.g., for multiple days and often multiple times per day) during the two baseline and two intervention phases. (This is feasible because the outcome is normally behavioral and observational in nature, therefore requiring little or no participant burden, occurs frequently under normal circumstances, and is not reactive in nature.)

2. Single-case studies rely less heavily on inferential statistics and p-values than conventional experiments. While inferential techniques exist (see Kazdin [2011], p. 410, for a relatively complete list of techniques with references), visual inspection of graphical presentations of results is the most highly valued approach. This philosophy is often evidenced by an attitude that "if the results aren't obvious, they aren't important." This, in turn, implies the expectation of considerable greater effect sizes than in multiple-case trials.

Figure 12.1 illustrated a best-case scenario for the results of a participant's response to an ABAB design. The inferential logic here is that (1) since a dramatic change occurred after Day 7 coinciding with the introduction of the intervention (i.e., from A to B), (2) then reverted back to baseline (or at least changed dramatically toward the first baseline values) during the second baseline (A), and (3) once again changed substantively in the predicted direction when the intervention was introduced a second time (B), then strong experimental evidence exists for the efficacy of the intervention.

Conceptually, the investigator producing such results might reasonably argue that changes such as these are highly unlikely to have been mere coincidences. What else could they be, but an intervention effect?

Of course, curmudgeons such as the present author, while acknowledging that such results are undoubtedly not coincidental (i.e., most likely not due to chance alone and probably possessive of a p-value $< .05$), they could result from (a) investigator-to-subject cueing of some sort or (b) even from chance alone if this experiment were repeated multiple times with either the same or multiple participants until the desired results were produced. However, if none of these artifacts occurred and the experiment was conducted cleanly, results such as exemplified in Figure 12.1 are rather persuasive. And while a bewildering number of scenarios exist for the possible results of an ABAB design besides the one depicted, to be considered positive all the changes must occur in the predicted order, time, and direction.

Both ABAB design and all other single-case designs have a number of limitations that must be considered. First and foremost is their inapplicability to the vast majority of outcome measures (e.g., physiologic, learning, or anything else that does not fluctuate frequently or is not prone to return quickly to baseline). Others include the following:

1. The need to achieve relatively large effects relatively quickly (although latent effects can be acceptable if hypothesized a priori).
2. The possibility that the single participants chosen for study (or their current situation) may be somehow unique (and not generalizable to other participants).

3. The potential for increased reactivity (e.g., a Hawthorn-like effect or an increased tendency to attempt to please the experimenter) resulting from the tendency of single-case studies to involve more contact with experimental staff.

4. The very real possibility that the experiment will produce equivocal results, such as when the first introduction of the intervention results in a dramatic improvement, but the behavior does not return to baseline and the second introduction of the intervention does not seem to have any effect. (This could mean that the intervention result was permanent, longer lasting than hypothesized, or a product of an artifact such as a co-occurring extraneous event.)

5. Clinicians (or IRB reviewers) may be understandably hesitant to truncate a seemingly positive intervention (and hence reinstate deleterious symptoms, when applicable, as represented by the second baseline in the ABAB design) simply to verify efficacy. Unless the outcome variable is plausibly harmful, this argument can be countered by appealing to the rationale for conducting the experiment in the first place (i.e., to definitively determine whether the intervention truly is effective). However, in the rare instances in which the outcome behaviors are dangerous (or life enhancing), another design is called for since researchers should always ascribe to the Hippocratic injunction of "Above all, do not harm."

A number of variations exist for this relatively simple design, such as adding a reinforcement (or longer term follow-up) phase (C) to attempt to ensure permanence of the effect (ABABC). In addition, a rich variety of alternative single-case designs exist, only a sampling of which can be mentioned here.

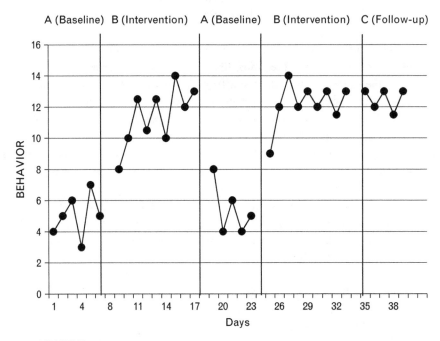

FIGURE 12.2: ABABC Design.

Staggered intervention designs: An alternative class of single-case designs involves staggered introductions of the intervention (also sometimes referred to as *multiple-baseline designs*). The primary advantage of these designs is their avoidance of some of the assumptions and weaknesses inherent in the ABAB and ABABC designs, the most important probably being not requiring the outcome variable to revert back to baseline. (This is made possible by substituting one or more additional sets of comparisons consisting of some variation on the original intervention.) In a sense, the staggered intervention design involves a series of introductions of similar interventions to the same individuals or within the same setting. As a hypothetical example of the latter, suppose a teacher with an especially problematic group of students decided to try out a class-wide intervention to ascertain the effectiveness of emailed messages sent to parents soliciting their help in increasing learning facilitative behaviors. Suppose further that a decision to employ three emailed messages targeting three different behaviors was made. The first (Behavior #1) involved sending parents e-mails requesting them to ensure that their children complete their homework assignments. Behavior #2 involved parental discussions at the dinner table about the importance of not disrupting class, while Behavior #3 involved requesting parents to take steps to avoid tardiness in arriving at school.

Three separate sets of baselines behaviors would be collected daily by the teacher as depicted in Figure 12.3: number of homework assignments not completed, number of classroom disruptions, and number of children late for school. As depicted in Figure 12.3, the interventions would be staggered with enough time in between for the previously introduced intervention to establish a stable pattern. Since the interventions were introduced during different periods, the baselines for each intervention were also collected at different times, which is why this genre of study is also called multiple-baseline designs. (Note that what makes this a single-case design is that behaviors are not linked to individual students but aggregated for the classroom as a whole, which makes it almost indistinguishable from some types of quality improvement studies.)

In this best-case scenario, depicted in Figure 12.3, all three behaviors would improve following the interventions. A less favorable outcome would be a scenario in which perhaps the third intervention failed to affect its outcome (Figure 12.4), which could be interpreted in a number of ways:

1. The third intervention was not effective and the first two improvements were due to extraneous factors or simple chance.
2. The third behavior (tardiness) was more difficult to correct or the intervention might not be appropriate for it.
3. Because order was not counterbalanced, the novelty of the experiment had been exhausted by the first two interventions.
4. And, of course, the first two interventions were effective but parents couldn't or wouldn't do anything about their children's tardiness. Our teacher investigator would then have several options. One might be simply to continue to maintain the first two behaviors while trying out a new intervention to affect tardiness.

As mentioned, and more realistically, this same genre of design can be applied to different settings in lieu of different behaviors. Using our hypothetical schooling study, this might involve

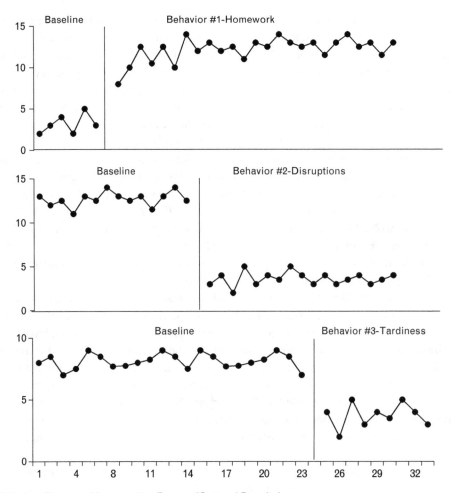

FIGURE 12.3: Staggered Intervention Design (Optimal Results).

a single behavior (say completing homework assignments) with the same intervention (e-mail reminders) introduced in a staggered manner to multiple classrooms or perhaps to three different participants rather than intact groups.

Changing criterion designs: This design is often employed in behavioral studies in which performance is immediately rewarded in some manner (e.g., via the use of tokens that can be later exchanged for inexpensive objects or desirable activities). Typically, the reward is first keyed to a small improvement (criterion) in performance, but when that level is achieved, the reward is only supplied when a slightly higher level of performance attained, and so on until relatively significant performance changes have been effected. The approach has the advantage that the intervention (unlike the ABAB design) need never be withdrawn.

Results are considered positive if they closely mirror the changing criteria as depicted in Figure 12.5 (or conform closely to their investigators' otherwise specified hypotheses). If there is no obvious match between the criterion changes and the results, then the results are negative or inconclusive.

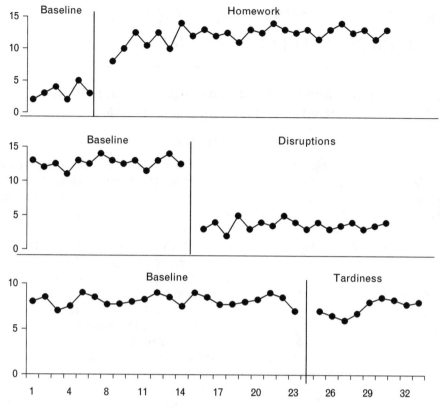

FIGURE 12.4: Staggered Intervention Design (Less than Optimal Results).

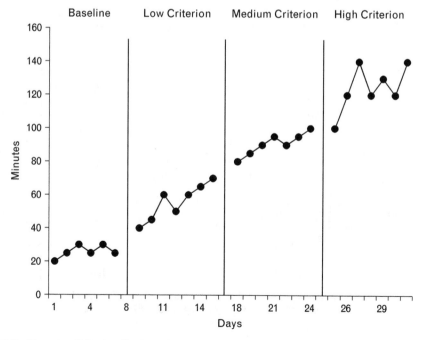

FIGURE 12.5: Changing Criterion Design.

EXAMPLE OF A COMPLEX SINGLE-CASE, HEALTH PROMOTION EXPERIMENT

Pedometers and Brief E-Counseling: Increasing Physical Activity for Overweight Adults (2004)

Jeffrey J. VanWormer

This exemplary single-case experiment used three (a typical number for single-case studies) overweight adults (designated as Jennifer, Brad, and Heather) to ascertain if the use of a pedometer, self-monitoring, and a 10-minute e-mail conversation per week could increase activity and result in weight loss. A family member provided interobserver agreement data for both outcomes.

Baseline consisted of a week in which the three participants wore their pedometers but were blinded to the results via a sticker covering the screen until the week's end when they recorded the results. Thereafter they recorded their results each evening on a spreadsheet and weighed themselves once per week. The intervention duration was 10 weeks and consisted of the following phases: baseline, self-monitoring, another baseline, another self-monitoring episode, self-monitoring plus e-counseling, self-monitoring alone, self-monitoring plus e-counseling, and follow-up. (Follow-up consisted of one day of blinded assessment conducted 6 months later after the study's first self-monitoring phase was begun.)

The results were presented graphically without statistical analysis as is typical of single-case experiments and reported as follows: "All participants increased their steps during treatment phases, with Jennifer and Brad roughly doubling their step counts by study end. Jennifer and Heather were able to maintain high levels of activity at follow-up, whereas Brad regressed toward baseline.... Jennifer and Brad also saw the most improvement in regard to weight loss"

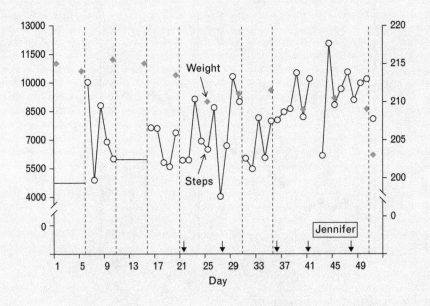

(6 lbs. for Jennifer [at 10 weeks], 5 lbs. for Brad, 3 lbs. for Heather by follow-up—her weight "was relatively stable" during the experiment). (The investigator [Dr. Van Wormer] kindly provided one of the graphs he prepared for this study ["Jennifer's" results].)

The author concluded that the results were promising and that "the intervention worked best for those who were the least active.... Considering the affordability of pedometers... and the high prevalence of computers in U.S. households, such interventions could feasibly be conducted across large segments of the sedentary population and be sustained over longer periods." Limitations of the study were also discussed, such as the use of noncalibrated scales, lack of control over variables such as illness and injury, and the use of family members as observers rather than using investigators.

SOME FINAL THOUGHTS ON SINGLE-CASE EXPERIMENTS

Single-case studies constitute several steps up from case studies (the most commonly used methodology in published medical articles) in producing credible causal inferences. They are also normally several steps down from-well designed randomized control trials (RCTs), however, both in applicability and the quality of the inferences produced. (Kratochwill and Levin [2010] proposed a number of situations—primarily in terms of phases and procedural elements—in which randomization can be applied to enhance the inferential validity emanating from single-case designs.) Also, while statistical procedures have been developed for single cases, they are neither as satisfactory nor as widely accepted as those developed for data emanating from multiple participants. And, of course, power is problematic (if even applicable at all) for detecting anything but large effects.

Strengths of the approach include (a) the *relative* ease with which they can be mounted (if there is such a thing as an "easy" experiment to conduct), (b) the relative rapidity with which they can be completed, and (c) their low expense (most can be conducted without external research funds if the necessary facilities exist—although ultimately all research must be supported somehow). The specialized nature of the methodologies involved can be problematic because of the need for (a) extensive training or (b) access to a hands-on help from an experienced single-case investigator (but then adequate training and expert guidance is a requirement for conducting all experiments).

This degree of flexibility and the timeliness with which single-case studies can be conducted also provide a major temptation, which (in Alan Kazdin's words) encourages investigators to "tinker" with the intervention and the design until the expected (or desired) results are obtained. And while single-case aficionados would (with some justification) most likely list this as an advantage of the approach (i.e., getting the intervention "right"), the practice has the potential of making it easier to discard negative and ambiguous experiments until an optimal outcome is achieved. To the extent that this occurs, and to be fair, there is no evidence that it does, it would have the effect of increasing the already inflated number of positive results gracing the published experimental record.

An impediment to the wider use of single-case designs includes the facts that they are nei-ther taught nor highly valued in many disciplines outside of applied behavior analysis. It is probable, therefore, that investigators in other fields might experience difficulties in publishing single-case results in their mainstream journals. There is evidence, however, that the use of these designs has recently increased relatively dramatically in psychology (Smith, 2012), and outlets such as the *Journal of Applied Behavior Analysis* and *Behavioral Interventions* routinely publish single-case studies.

However, the most serious disadvantage of single-case research involves the specialized nature of the interventions and outcome variables to which they are applicable. And even for those interventions that can be appropriately tested via these designs, few are capable of produc-ing effect sizes of the magnitude required for credibility. Such interventions exist (e.g., penicillin for bacterial infections, insulin for diabetics, or increased instructional time for learning), but most of these require no further documentation. A challenge for studies that do produce large effects, therefore, resides in avoiding trivial research questions.

Single-case designs can offer viable alternatives for pilot studies, however, when the intervention and outcome variables meet their assumption or can be adapted to do so. (The pedometer experiment above is an excellent example.) It should also be noted that there are always exceptions to generalizations such as those proffered here, especially in the presence of creativity or ground-breaking work. (For a far more positive assessment and in-depth dis-cussion of these and other single-case design issues, both Kazdin [2011] and Smith [2012] are recommended.)

TWO FINAL EXPERIMENTAL GENRES

The final two approaches to experimentation to be discussed here are, as were single-case designs, primarily included to widen investigators' options for generating researchable ideas and broadening their professional repertoires. Both constitute unique empirical paradigms that often value practicality over theory, local effects over universal generalizability, and (sometimes unfortunately) alternative designs to the classic random assignment of partici-pants to groups.

Both research genres have self-consciously developed their own specialized terminolo-gies, journals, and libraries of books. Program evaluation (the first of these alternative para-digms) is most similar to the types of experimentation we've discussed in this book because of both terminology similarities and the designs employed. The data points for the second approach do not normally use individual participant outcomes and hence bear certain simi-larities to those single-case experiments involving the introduction of interventions to entire workplace units or sites. Generically labeled as quality improvement research, these experi-ments involve monitoring events occurring within an organization, with the goal of improv-ing outcomes such as productivity, behaviors, performance, or the avoidance of adverse events. As such, quality improvement experiments bear more similarities to program evalu-ation than they do to conventional experimentation, but the catalog of tools developed espe-cially for their commission may have wider applicability to other types of experimentation than commonly realized.

PROGRAM EVALUATION (AND NATURAL EXPERIMENTS)

Program evaluation received its primary impetus with the U.S. government's funding of several large educational initiatives as a part of Lyndon Johnson's "War on Poverty"—many of which were accompanied by requests for proposals to evaluate their impact. Evaluation research typically approaches the design of experiments from a slightly different perspective than conventional educational or psychological research, often due to practical constraints imposed by (a) their large scope of effort, (b) administrative realities/preferences of often diverse intervention sites, (c) the limited amount of lead time between funding and implementation, and/or (d) difficulties in constructing appropriate comparison groups.

While as a discipline evaluation research's ultimate goal is, like efficacy experiments, to produce valid causal inferences regarding the effect of an intervention upon an outcome, the questions it addresses are usually generated differently and its practitioners almost always labor under more difficult circumstances than traditional scientific investigators. Evaluators also often approach their tasks with an "attitude" or "existential" purpose characterized by the objective of determining the overall *value* of a service, program, or intervention.

Without question the early "spiritual" and methodological leader of this "attitude" was Donald T. Campbell, whose essays and books constituted a clarion call for educational, social, and behavioral scientists to play a formative role in creating a different, evidence-based approach to improving quality of life. The titles of his essays themselves reflected the potential (and perhaps unrealistically optimistic) role of the discipline in achieving this agenda—titles such as "Methods for the Experimenting Society" (later reprinted in the *American Journal of Evaluation* [1991]), "Reforms as Experiments" (1969), and the "The Social Scientist as Methodological Servant of the Experimenting Society" (1973).

Campbell's and others' vision of a society that dispassionately evaluated its social programs was never fully realized, of course, and it seems somewhat antiquated given current political realities. Still, an entire discipline was launched and seemingly endless texts and articles on evaluation proliferated.

In public health and health education, evaluation came into its own as an identifiable *field* of endeavor at almost the same time as its social and behavioral counterparts—its development likewise facilitated by the availability of funding to assess the impact of large governmental and philanthropic initiatives.

In many ways the distinction between research and program evaluation was always a bit gray, as witnessed by a widely accepted definition by Michael Scriven (1991):

> Evaluation is the process of determining the merit, worth and value of things, and evaluations are the products of that process. (Note the embedded noun in "e*valua*te".)

Thus, at the risk of oversimplification, evaluation is not conducted for the primary purpose of generating knowledge for knowledge's sake or to test theory. Instead, it is conducted to provide useful, real-time, real-world guidance for assessing and improving a "program" or "service" in the "here and now"—not at some time in the future pending "further research." Its audience is variously conceived as including politicians, the public, policymakers, program administrators, staff, and/or clients (all of whom are often referred to as evaluation "stakeholders").

There are also many types of evaluation, including *nonexperimental* activities involving the assessment of worth, such as planning, evidence-based practice, rankings of institutions (e.g., hospitals, universities), product evaluations, accreditation, credentialing, quality assurance, and a plethora of other worthwhile endeavors. However, the only facet to be discussed here involves the *experimental* evaluation of "merit, worth, and value." And from this experimental perspective, the only defensible difference between the types of experiments and the experimental procedures discussed so far involve the fact that the investigator (now evaluator) does *not* define (or create) the intervention. The intervention already exists, and it is the task of a program evaluator to construct an experimental framework to permit the conduct of a controlled assessment of the effectiveness of that intervention (i.e., *program*).

A program can involve a major societal initiative (e.g., Head Start, Welfare Reform, or Medicare Prescription Reimbursement) down to a change in the way in which an individual facility delivers one of its services (such as an elementary school that institutes a computer lab to supplement mathematics instruction, or a hospital deciding to hire nurse anesthetists for the first time).

Evaluations can be either retrospective (when the intervention was instituted with little thought of later assessing its effectiveness) or prospectively (baseline data were purposefully collected on an outcome variable and a control group was constituted). Sometimes (although too rarely) clients are even randomly assigned to intervention vs. comparison groups, in which case the already tenuous distinction between evaluation and prospective experimentation becomes further blurred.

While evaluators do not commonly construct their own programs, in the best of possible worlds they are called in to design (or write proposals for the design of) the evaluation prior to the implementation of a program. Alternately, they may be asked to evaluate programs already implemented, but in either case the primary outcome variable (like the intervention) is usually specified (or obvious). Needless to say, such post hoc circumstances produce a challenging environment for the production of defensible causal inferences regarding the extent to which the intervention affected the outcome variable. Still, beginning researchers should not eschew these challenges for they offer empirical learning opportunities and when done properly (within the limitations of their settings) can constitute a meaningful contribution to society.

Another distinction between the design of a program evaluation and an experimental assessment of the efficacy of an intervention is the tendency for investigators involved in the latter genre to narrow the focus of their work as much as possible. Scientifically oriented investigators do this to isolate the causal effects of a single intervention on a single outcome variable for a homogeneous, clearly defined target population in order for the experimental setting to be as carefully controlled as possible. Evaluators, on the other hand, while interested in causation, have little interest in this degree of specificity. Instead, they are normally interested in the broad combined effects of a program's multiple components on anyone who might profit therefrom. Certainly the primary causal mechanism for any observed effect could theoretically be teased out by controlled *research* conducted one component at a time, but such an effort would be of little interest to an evaluator (or the stakeholders of the evaluation) because the program itself would be expected to evolve over time (as well as a result of being implemented in other settings under different conditions).

A final distinguishing characteristic of many program evaluations is their conceptualization as more comprehensive undertakings than a single experiment. Most experimental investigators would be reluctant to announce that they were investigating the "value" of *anything*, realizing that there are simply too many facets and connotations of the concept (e.g., economic, affective, existential, societal) for it to have much scientific meaning. From this perspective, while controlled trials usually employ multiple outcome variables, a primary endpoint is normally specified and the treatment of subsidiary outcomes is somewhat more guarded than in program evaluations. (For example, in efficacy experiments claims of causal results of the intervention on other outcomes are looked on with skepticism unless accompanied by sufficient disclaimers befitting a secondary analysis.) In evaluation, on the other hand, multiple outcomes are considered more integral to the overall enterprise.

In the end, most disciplinary distinctions have a degree of arbitrariness, and the evaluation/research dichotomy is no exception. This embracement of comprehensiveness does perhaps best differentiate the evaluative from the classic experimental process, however, as illustrated in Michael Scriven's (1991) exhaustive (although seldom if ever realized) 14-point "key evaluation checklist" detailing the type of information that could be included in a truly comprehensive program evaluation report:

1. A detailed description of what is to be evaluated, its component parts, their relationship with one another, the physical environment in which they are located, how the program is delivered, and so forth.
2. The background and context of the evaluation, including potential problems with clients and stakeholders, the type of evaluation proposed, and expected results.
3. Intended, actual, and potential consumers.
4. Resources available for use by the program being evaluated.
5. Values, including political and ethical, of the program, its objectives (e.g., choice of outcomes and needs), and the evaluator's discipline.
6. The process by which the intervention is delivered, the extent of delivery, and any factors that potentially affect the delivery and its effect on the outcome.
7. Outcomes produced (i.e., caused) by the program including long term, short term, and unintended.
8. Costs of the program.
9. Comparisons with other programs offering similar services.
10. External validity, including difficulties in exporting and delivering the services in other settings.
11. The overall importance of the program, its effects, and the evaluation itself.
12. Recommendations for improvement, taking into consideration practicality and resources required.
13. The report of the evaluation process (basically everything included up to this point). Also, in Scriven's words: "The report has to carry a scientific and commonsensical message, but it is also a case where data visualization and its aesthetic dimension is deeply involved" (p. 210).
14. Meta-evaluation, which is conceived of as a second level of evaluation of the evaluation process itself encompassing all of the above.

Other writers and organizations provide helpful (less extensive) lists for both elucidating the steps in (a) conducting a program evaluation and (b) reporting the results. The Centers for Disease Control, for example, suggests the following phases in a public health program evaluation (the first and last of which are not normally considered part of research practice):

1. Engage stakeholders (i.e., anyone with a special interest in the program itself, such as individuals within the organization offering the program, funders, consumers) in the evaluation,
2. Describe the program in detail,
3. Design and focus the evaluation,
4. Gather "credible" evidence,
5. Justify conclusions, and
6. Take steps to ensure use of the evaluation.

To the extent that an evaluation is experimental (and prospective) in nature, all of the experimental principles listed to this point apply (many evaluations are not experimental, such as those using qualitative approaches, historical control groups, or analyses of existing databases). The design should employ random assignment (Principle #13) whenever feasible; when truly not feasible a credible comparison group of some sort should always be used in preference to a single-group design. And, given the pressure that can be exerted by the funder or special interest groups, adherence to our first principle ("be absolutely, uncompromisingly, unfashionably honest") can represent a very real challenge in this experimental genre.

NONRANDOMIZED DESIGNS IN EVALUATION

A discussion of the full spectrum of quasi-experimental designs has largely been avoided to this point except for illustrative purposes. There is a school of thought, however, that some empirical *evaluation* of societal programs is better than none at all, and this is a difficult argument to counter. The present author does not happen to ascribe to this particular school of thought with reference to extremely weak designs such as the single-group pretest-posttest design, but he would be extremely hesitant to suggest that other quasi-experimental designs should not be undertaken to evaluate societal interventions. The following evaluation of a legislative intervention is an example of such a design that, while not employing randomization, probably resulted in a credible (and if so, an important) experimental inference. Judgments such as this, however, are in the eye of the beholder, but this experiment does represent a rather typical example of a large-scale program evaluation effort.

EXAMPLE OF A LARGE-SCALE PROGRAM
EVALUATION USING A QUASI-EXPERIMENTAL DESIGN

The Short-Term Impact of National (Finland) Smoke-Free Workplace Legislation on Passive Smoking and Tobacco Use (2001)

Antero Heloma, Maritta S. Jaakkola, Erkki Kähkönen, and Kari Reijula

The purpose of this evaluation study was to prospectively assess the impact of a Finnish Tobacco Control Act on workers' environmental tobacco smoke (ETS) exposure. Since the "intervention" (i.e., the legislation passed by the Finnish parliament) was national in scope, the random assignment of a control group was impossible. Instead, the investigators selected "12 medium-sized and large workplaces" (of which 3 were lost to follow-up) to participate—which consisted of (a) measuring employee nicotine levels using a gas chromatograph, (b) self-reported number of cigarettes smoked daily, and (c) self-reported daily hours exposed to tobacco the year before the legislation went into effect as compared to the year following its implementation.

As such, the design resembled a cross between (a) a single-group pretest-posttest strategy (although no effort was made to match the same participants across time given the anonymous nature of the data collection as well as employee turnover) and (b) an institutional cohort design (although completely different employees were not used). All three outcomes reduced significantly between the two years, leading the investigators to conclude that the legislation "worked."

Now obviously this study employed a weak quasi-experimental design that permitted numerous alternative explanations for its results. Its primary inference could perhaps have been strengthened had national data been presented on smoking rates for several years prior to the study itself to dismiss the possibility that the observed results were simply part of a national trend. (Alternately, perhaps existing data on tobacco use in a neighboring country during the two years of interest might have been available.) However, the use of a physiological indicator (nicotine levels), multiple workplace sites, and a plausible cause for the observed changes probably makes the study better than no evaluation at all. The study is also typical of a prospective evaluation experiment in general in the sense that the investigators did not create or introduce the intervention, nor were they able to use a credible control group.

A plethora of nonrandomized and single-group designs exist that can be used either prospectively or retrospectively in evaluation research and are discussed in detail by Cook and Campbell (1979). Interested readers are encouraged to access that resource (entitled *Quasi-Experimentation: Design and Analysis Issues for Field Settings*) or its updated version (Shadish, Cook, & Campbell, 2002). These designs will not be discussed here, however, since the majority are (a) rarely used, (b) often more appropriate for retrospective evaluations or scenarios in which a credible comparison group cannot be formulated, and (c) provide very little protection from the experimental artifacts discussed earlier. There may be one exception to this stricture, however, which is the regression discontinuity design.

The regression discontinuity design: This strategy provides a creative approach designed specifically for the unusual scenario in which the comparison group is *known* to initially differ systematically from the intervention group. As an example, suppose that an intensive intervention is prescribed to raise struggling students' SAT scores in a high school in order to provide them with a better chance of being accepted for college. Suppose further that the administration and teaching staff of that school were unwilling to deny half of the qualifying students (i.e., those at risk for receiving a substandard SAT score) with the opportunity to participate in the program in order to conduct a randomized evaluation thereof.

The intervention in question could still be evaluated via a regression discontinuity design in which *all* students at the appropriate grade level in the high school were administered a practice

SAT exam known to be highly correlated with actual SAT performance. All students scoring below a certain cut point (e.g., 480 on the practice exam) could then be provided the intervention while students scoring 480 or above would not (since they were in less need thereof). At the appropriate time, all students (those who received the intervention and those who did not) could then be readministered the practice SAT.

At first glance, evaluating the effects of this intervention would be quite challenging with anything other than a single-group pretest-posttest in which the intervention students' first scores were compared to their post-intervention scores. A control group from another high school could perhaps be constituted but might also be logistically difficult to constitute. Certainly the school's nonstruggling students (who did not receive the intervention because they did not need it) would not appear to constitute a sensible comparison group since by definition the two groups of students would be decidedly nonequivalent. (There would also be no way to control for regression to the mean since the upper group's scores would be expected to regress downward on the second test administration while the intervention group's scores would move upward—irrespective of the intervention.)

The regression continuity design, however, would be quite appropriate for such a scenario and would constitute perhaps the only viable option for comparing the performance of those who were administered the intervention and those who were not under these circumstances. Certainly statistical control employing (a) the practice test as a covariate or (b) propensity scores based on multiple correlates would not be appropriate nor could either option overcome the initial discrepancy between the two groups. (See Pion and Cordray [2008] for a sophisticated analysis and discussion illustrating both approaches in a failed attempt at evaluating the effects of a merit based award.)

The logic behind the regression discontinuity methodology, however, is creative, simple, relies on none of these strategies, and can be applied to the present case as follows:

1. Without an intervention it would be assumed that the relationship (i.e., correlation) between the practice exam pretest and posttest scores would be linear (visualized as a positively oriented scatter plot with a nicely appointed straight line of best fit approximating a 45-degree right-to-left angle).

2. However, if the intervention administered to the bottom portion of this distribution was effective, then this scatter plot would be different for the two groups and the line of best fit would be disrupted at or around the exact cut point at which the intervention stopped. This scenario is illustrated in Figure 12.6, where the disruption at the exact

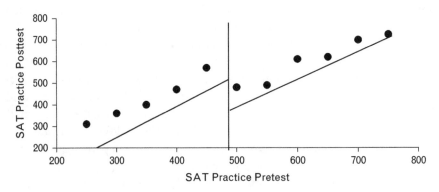

FIGURE 12.6: Hypothetical Regression Discontinuity Results.

point of the intervention (recalling that the points below the 480 score cut point represent the intervention and the scores above it represent no intervention) is suggestive of an intervention effect.

While not as methodologically clean as a two-group design that randomly assigned half of the students below the cut point to receive the intervention and half to not receive it, the regression discontinuity design controls for many of the artifacts a single-group design does not. It is not particularly plausible, for example, that an extraneous external event could have accounted for the change in the relationship that occurred at the a priori selected cut point since both groups of students were exposed to similar external and internal environments. The effect could not be attributed to regression to the mean since the group above the cut point would be expected to regress downward to the same degree the group below the cut point would be expected to regress upward. The effect also could not be a placebo effect (since placebos do not affect knowledge or learning), nor could it be due to the repeated testing artifact, because both groups were administered the test twice.

Of course, an actual statistical analysis would be required to determine if the two lines in Figure 12.6 were significantly discontinuous. And, given a choice, a randomized design employing an actual randomly assigned control would be preferable because it would provide (a) a better estimate of the magnitude of the effect) and (b) a more sensitive hypothesis test with greater statistical power. All in all, however, the regression discontinuity design is one of the stronger quasi-experimental options available to evaluators and constitutes a viable strategy for conventional investigators faced with one of those rare occasions when a credible control cannot be constituted. (For a considerably more detailed discussion of regression discontinuity designs, see Trochim, 1984; for accessible introductions and additional examples of their use, see Shadish, Cook, & Campbell [2002] or Linden, Adams, & Roberts [2006].)

NATURAL EXPERIMENTS

If prospective program evaluations can be basically indistinguishable from other experimental research (with the exception that the investigator does not construct the intervention in an evaluation), this is even more the case with natural experiments vs. program evaluations. Natural experiments tend to be retrospective rather than prospective and they overwhelmingly involve quasi-experimental designs, but both characteristics also apply to program evaluations.

In reality, definitional distinctions such as this make little sense anyway, but for pedagogical purposes let's attempt to classify natural experiments as a subset of program evaluation by using Wikipedia's definition of the former:

> A natural experiment is an empirical study in which individuals (or clusters of individuals) exposed to the experimental and control conditions are determined by nature or other actors outside the control of the investigators. (http://en.wikipedia.org/wiki/Natural_experiment)

(Part of this definition was omitted [i.e., "yet the process governing the exposures arguably resembles random assignment"] because obviously your author doesn't consider anything "resembling" random assignment as remotely *equivalent* to random assignment.)

The Wikipedia article goes on to briefly describe several examples of natural experiments (e.g., the Vietnam War draft on lifetime earnings, and a sort of crossover 6-month smoking ban that occurred in Montana in 2002). Remler and Van Ryzin (2010) also provide an extensive chapter on the concept, accompanied by many examples (which can, at least as of this writing, be found at http://www.sagepub.com/upm-data/33935_Chapter13.pdf).

Currently, in the present author's opinion, the most impressive natural experiments are being conducted by quantitatively oriented economists who identify promising social interventions and apply sophisticated statistical procedures to evaluate them. An exemplary example of such an evaluation that included a societally mandated randomized "design" and a strong theory suggesting why the social intervention should result in salutary outcomes will close out this section. It also supplements the randomized experimental design with observational evidence, both of which point to the same irrevocable conclusion. And while this particular evaluation is not prospective (the investigators did not implement the intervention or randomize the participants), hopefully, it reflects the *potential* of how natural experiments may be evaluated in the future.

A RARE EXAMPLE OF A RANDOMIZED NATURAL EXPERIMENT

Are High-Quality Schools Enough to Close the Achievement Gap? Evidence from a Social Experiment in Harlem (2009)

Will Dobbie and Roland G. Fryer, Jr.

The authors explain that the "Harlem Children's Zone is a 97-block area in central Harlem, New York, that combines reform-minded charter schools with a web of community services designed to ensure the social environment outside of school is positive and supportive for children from birth to college graduation." These schools (the Harlem Children's Zone [HCZ] Promise Academies) offer "an extended school day and year, with coordinated afterschool tutoring and additional classes on Saturdays for children who need remediation in mathematics and English Language Arts skills. Our rough estimate is that HCZ Promise Academy students that are behind grade level are in school for twice as many hours as a traditional public school student in New York City. Students who are at or above grade level still attend the equivalent of about fifty percent more school in a calendar year."

Armed with a strong theory predicting why these schools *should* produce increased student learning (a massive dose of extra instructional time), the investigators set out to evaluate whether this naturally well-designed experiment resulted in increased student achievement. They were aided in this task by the fact that New York law requires that oversubscribed charter schools allocate enrollment randomly via a lottery system, which provided a relatively unique experimental opportunity to study the effects of these charter schools on student achievement for students who won the lottery and attended the charter schools vs. those for students who had applied but were randomly denied entrance. The authors supplemented these analyses with observational (i.e., nonrandomized comparisons) comparisons comprised of (a) students from adjacent geographic areas (800, 1,600, and 2,400 meters outside the HCZ), (b) siblings of selected students, and (c) national norms. (In addition, supplementary intent-to-treat analyses were conducted, which contrasted [a] all students who were *offered* a spot in the charter schools, whether they attended or not, with [b] students who entered the lottery but *were not offered a spot*.) Available covariates were employed in the analyses, including gender, race, whether the student qualified for supplementary lunch aid, and prior achievement, when available.

Basically all the comparisons employed (i.e., the randomized, quasi-experimental, and intent-to-treat components) resulted in the same finding: "Harlem Children's Zone is effective at increasing the achievement of the poorest minority children. Students enrolled in the sixth grade gained more than four fifths of a standard deviation in math and between one-quarter and one-third of a standard deviation in English Language Arts (ELA) by eighth grade. Taken at face value, these effects are enough to close the black-white achievement gap in mathematics and reduce it by about half in ELA. Students in the HCZ elementary school gain approximately four fifths to one and a half a standard deviation in both math and ELA by third grade, closing the racial achievement gap in both subjects. HCZ students are also less likely to be absent. These results are robust across identification strategies, model specifications, and subsamples of the data." (The same basic benefits accrued for all subgroups in the analysis.)

SOME THOUGHTS ON THE BOTTOM-LINE APPLICABILITY OF PROGRAM EVALUATION

Since prospective program evaluations can be basically indistinguishable from other experimental research (with the exception that the investigator does not construct the intervention in an evaluation), little difference need exist in their design processes as well. It is therefore unfortunate that these evaluation studies often use weaker designs than other types of experiments, which might well be corrected if more experimentally sophisticated investigators became interested in program evaluation as a supplementary empirical activity. Retrospective evaluations and natural experiments represent another situation in which epistemologically weaker designs are often inevitable, but young investigators would be wise to keep abreast of opportunities to participate in these as well. It is almost always possible to bring additional methodological rigor to even retrospective experiments by an investigator who has a thorough understanding of experimental design and its attendant artifacts.

QUALITY IMPROVEMENT EXPERIMENTS

Quality improvement research can be visualized as a subset of evaluation and in at least one instance is indistinguishable from a single-case experiments design in which the "case" is a setting rather than an individual. Quality improvement experiments differ from conventional efficacy trials in the sense that they can be conducted using a unit within a larger institution (or the institution itself) and the outcomes (often consisting of behavioral or event counts) are not typically disaggregated to individual participants.

The primary focus of a quality improvement experiment is on determining the local effects of an intervention on an outcome variable with little or no concern for generalizability or such quintessential scientific concerns as (a) testing a theory, (b) elucidating the cause of a phenomenon, or (c) discovering a previously unknown relationship or phenomenon. Rather, the focus is on improving outcomes in a specific service delivery site, be it on an assembly line (e.g., reducing the number of times production must be shut down for maintenance or the number of widgets produced per hour), a pharmacy (e.g., reducing the number of medication errors), or a hospital unit (increasing staff hand-washing behaviors).

The design of a quality improvement study can take any of the forms discussed to this point, although randomization is infrequently employed. More commonly, designs are some variation of the single-group pretest-posttest or use nonrandomly assigned comparison groups, in which case everything said to this point applies to both the execution and interpretation of such studies.

The quality improvement process itself involves

1. Identifying opportunities for improving the quality (and efficiency) of different clinical processes, interventions, or methods of delivering a service by using a team effort involving representatives of all the components of the processes in question,
2. Systematically monitoring quality indicators (i.e., outcomes), and
3. Continuously attempting to improve the processes through a number of prescribed methods.

One "philosophical" or paradigmatic approach to this quality improvement process (total quality management, or TCM) deserves some mention here since it is associated with a number of unique experimental designs. It also assumes a distinct "attitude" quite divergent from the stereotypic lone researcher pursuing his or her career one study at a time. Instead, this approach to experimentation (especially to the development of interventions) becomes a continuous, cooperative endeavor involving service providers, management, and often feedback from clients. Its goal, rather than narrowing the area under study, is expandable to include anything and everything (thus the descriptor *total*) that might be capable of affecting the "outcome" of interest.

A movement such as TCM, which like evaluation research has waxed and waned in popularity over the years, may seem somewhat irrelevant to science. Originally it was largely confined to industry, where it was designed to help ensure the quality, efficiency, and consistency of whatever was being produced. Over the years, however, the approach has been applied to myriad settings, and some aspects of it have found their way into the delivery of healthcare and education.

For example, the Joint Commission (the primary accreditation institution of hospitals and other healthcare organizations) and the Centers for Medicare and Medicaid Services (CMS) have increasingly become advocates for quality improvement projects in general. During the 1990s, CMS changed its entire evaluation focus away from quality assurance (which is primarily designed to detect errors and practice aberrations) to quality improvement and recommissioned its quality assurance centers into "quality improvement organizations" that incorporate at least certain aspects of TCM. The following quality improvement study is an example of one of the projects supported by CMS which incorporates this philosophy.

EXAMPLE OF AN UNCONTROLLED
QUALITY IMPROVEMENT EXPERIMENT

Improving the Appropriateness of Blood Transfusions in Orthopedic Surgical Patients (1998)

Anne-Marie Audet, Chester Andrezejewski, and Mark Popovsky

Perhaps typical of the type of quality improvement studies resulting from the previously mentioned CMS quality improvement initiative (called the Health Care Financing Administration when this study was funded), these investigators identified an area of practice with "opportunities for improvement" in the form of unnecessary blood transfusions among elderly patients undergoing orthopedic surgery. Five hospitals volunteered to participate in the project and baseline data on indicators (i.e., avoidable transfusion events, single vs. multiple blood transfusions, whether the transfusion was performed as indicated by a recommended hematocrit level, and allogeneic blood exposure) were abstracted from the Medicare Claims Database for a 2-year period from 1992 to 1993 and for a 9-month period following the interventions' implementation.

Team members in each hospital were identified who would help create that hospital's individualized interventions, and baseline data were presented to them at a special meeting in which "transfusion practices were described at the level of each individual hospital, and comparative data from each of the hospitals and the overall group [were] also provided. This allowed the group to identify the hospitals that were the best performers on each of the indicators [see the discussion on benchmarking that follows].... The group identified opportunities for improvement and brainstormed various possible approaches to improve practice." (This, of course, is a classic TCM strategy). Each hospital was then charged with modifying its own transfusion processes via multiple

1. Clinician–patient level educational interventions (e.g., grand rounds, disseminating comparative data from the other participating hospitals) and
2. System-level interventions (e.g., establishment of project-specific quality improvement teams, policy revisions).

Statistically significant baseline to EOT results occurred for three of the four indicators:

1. Avoidable transfusion events decreased by 55.6%,

2. Appropriate hematocrit procedures by 7.6%, and
3. Single- vs. multiple-unit transfusion increased by 7.4%.

While acknowledging the methodological shortcomings of the uncontrolled design, the investigators themselves appeared to consider that they had accomplished their original purpose in conducting the study, which was not to discover impeccable causal conclusions but rather to improve the quality of care in the affected clinical facilities. They also presented evidence from a later, larger study suggesting that their improvements were not simply due to temporal trends. Of course, their study could have been strengthened by the formation of a control group from the same Medicare Claims Database, but for better or worse this is not commonly done in this genre of research.

Quality improvement as a discipline tends to employ a number of relatively unique experimental strategies focusing on (a) the use of desirable standards with which to compare experimental results rather than convening separate comparison groups and (b) ongoing monitoring of experimental results (as opposed to waiting until the intervention has been completely implemented), as illustrated by the following approaches.

Benchmarking: This process identifies clearly superior institutions (or service delivery practices) in order to use their results as a targeted improvement level for the planned quality improvement intervention(s). Conceptually the approach bears certain similarities to the use of a nonrandomly assigned control group except that in the present usage the "comparison (benchmark) group" is (a) initially chosen *because* it possesses outcomes that are patently nonequivalent to the group in need of improvement and (b) no inferential comparisons are made between it and the "intervention" institution at study's end.

However, not only are the benchmarking institutions used for comparative purposes, their production or service delivery processes are also examined and—when relevant—instituted as part of the quality improvement process. As a research strategy, this genre of quality improvement strategy is as vulnerable to experimental artifacts as the single-group pretest-posttest model but "true" quality improvement investigators are concerned much less with *why* they may have achieved positive results than the fact that they have achieved them. Said another way, the investigators initially set out to change a process (the intervention) in order to improve the quality of a service or product (the outcome). If they do so, they have achieved their purpose and have no need to suffer the slings and arrows of peer reviewers. Said yet another way, if a quality improvement researcher has achieved the desired results for the wrong reason, who cares? The next task is to improve it even more, or ensure that said improvement is maintained.

Control charts: This strategy encompasses an ingenious method for continuously monitoring outcome variables, whether processes, behaviors, or adverse events. The outcomes themselves are normally available from records, relatively easily collected, or nonreactive and/or involve no burden on individual participants.

The design of the originating quality improvement (or quality assurance) experiment is quite similar to that of a single-group interrupted time series experiment since it also relies on repeated measurements to substitute for procedural control (i.e., separate comparison groups). The control chart itself (and there are a plethora of different types) consists of a central line representing the outcome mean computed over a baseline period accompanied by three standard deviations computed from the same data.

Once the process starts both this mean and its standard deviations can gradually change as additional data become available. In industry, the chart is most commonly used to monitor some production process with the goal of keeping each observation close to the mean, with the expectation that the data points will adhere ever closer to said mean and certainly never stray outside three standard deviations thereof. (Of course, with constant improvement the standard deviations will gradually decrease as well.) This process is depicted in Figure 12.7, with the jagged line around the mean representing the individual data points collected during the study.

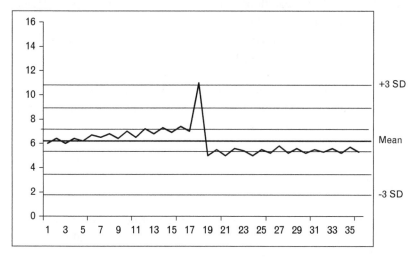

FIGURE 12.7: Hypothetical Six Sigma Control Chart.

The interpretation of the data emanating from a control chart is quite unique, however, and is based on the standard deviation (which is an algebraic representation of the mainstay statistical concept of variance). A "statistically significant" event, for example, is usually defined as (a) a single point falling above or below the three standard deviation boundary (thus the moniker "six sigma," since the Greek symbol σ designates the standard deviation), as illustrated at data (or time) point 17 in Figure 12.7, (b) two out of three consecutive points falling outside the two standard deviation line (in the same direction), (c) 10 out of 11 successive points on the same side of the middle (mean) line (which also occurs in Figure 12.7), and so forth. (These definitions are not arbitrary but provide reasonable protection against excessive Type I errors more or less comparably to conventional statistical tests in which an excessive number of inferential "looks" are not performed.)

While charts such as this are most commonly used to monitor production in order to avoid statistically significant untoward events from occurring as part of the quality improvement process, they can also be used to test the salutary effect of an intervention introduced at a specific point in time (which in the Figure 12.7 would hopefully have occurred at or around the 17th data point). Control charts such as this are rarely used in human experimentation and deserve mention here only as an heuristic addition to future investigators' "toolkits" (not to mention the somewhat unique and appealing philosophy behind the quality improvement concept that might be applicable to an investigator's ultimate research objective).

SOME THOUGHTS ON THE BOTTOM-LINE APPLICABILITY OF QUALITY IMPROVEMENT DESIGNS

In many ways the primary objective of quality improvement research (i.e., to improve outcomes and service delivery in an institution by whatever ethical means possible) is very close to the meaningfulness approach to experimentation advocated by this book. Furthermore, selected components of TCM can be a useful approach to monitoring, conducting, and reducing protocol violations in any type of experiment involving multiple staff members (e.g., frequent, regularly scheduled meetings to solicit suggestions from research staff regarding possible improvements in protocol implementation as advocated in Chapter Ten).

However, since quality improvement designs and empirical strategies are seldom included in the curricula of the disciplines targeted by this book, investigators interested in applying them to their own work should seek out continuing education or online courses dedicated to their use. (The description presented in this chapter is far too cursory and general to be of much help in their actual commission.) A good starting point for such an endeavor might be a textbook such as Nancy Tague's (2005) excellent *The Quality Toolbox*.

SUMMARY

Three unique experimental paradigms, none of which routinely employ randomized designs, and all of which are characterized by somewhat different philosophical objectives than typical efficacy trials, were introduced. Single-case experiments rely on analyzing a small number of individual results sequentially rather than collapsing them via descriptive statistics such as means and standard deviations. They employ designs often involving multiple administrations of intervention and control conditions to generate their inferences and employ repeated measurements to replace the control afforded by randomizing multiple participants to multiple conditions. Several different strategies for achieving this control were also discussed, including the ABAB, ABABAC, staggered intervention (multiple-baseline), and changing criterion designs.

The second paradigm, program evaluation (of which natural experiments are a subset), is designed to ascertain the "value" of a predeveloped intervention designed for a prespecified population (or institutional setting). Often the constitution of an appropriate control group is problematic for such situations, hence the use of quasi-experimental designs is more common than is the case for conventional efficacy experiments. An example of such a strategy was discussed, called the regression discontinuity design, which permits an obviously nonequivalent group of participants to serve as a comparison for the intervention group. Evaluation researchers tend to have less interest than conventional investigators in testing theories or generalizing their results to other settings or samples.

The final paradigm, quality improvement experimentation, also tends to neither emphasize generalizability nor randomize participants to groups. Instead, such efforts (including those supported by total quality management) focus on the continual improvement of products, services, and production efficiency—viewing individual experiments more as an ongoing process than a discrete stand-alone endeavor in their own right. Two experimental strategies used in this genre of research, benchmarking and control charting, were briefly discussed.

REFERENCES

Audet, A-M., Andrezejewski, C., & Popovsky, M. (1998). Improving the appropriateness of red blood cell transfusions in patients undergoing orthopedic surgery. *Evaluation & the Health Professions, 21*, 487–501.

Campbell, D.T. (1969). Reforms as experiments. *American Psychologist, 24*, 409–29.

Campbell, D.T. (1973). The social scientist as methodological servant of the experimenting society. *Policy Studies Journal, 2*, 72–5.

Campbell, D.T. (1991). Methods for the experimenting society. *American Journal of Evaluation, 12*, 223–60.

Cook, T.D., & Campbell, D.T. (1979). *Quasi-experimentation: Design and analysis issues for field settings.* Chicago: Rand McNally College Publishing.

Dobbie, W., & Fryer, R.G., Jr. (2009). *Are high quality schools enough to close the achievement gap? Evidence from a social experiment in Harlem.* Research Working Paper, No. 15473. Cambridge, MA: National Bureau of Economic Research.

Heloma, A., Jaakkola, M.S., Kähkönen, E., & Reijula, K. (2001). The short-term impact of national smoke-free workplace legislation on passive smoking and tobacco use. *American Journal of Public Health, 91*, 1416–8.

Kazdin, A.E. (2011). *Single-case research designs: Methods for clinical and applied settings* (2nd ed.). New York: Oxford University Press.

Kratochwill, T.R., & Levin, J.R. (2010). Enhancing the scientific credibility of single-case intervention research: Randomization to the rescue. *Psychological Methods, 15*, 124–44.

Linden, A., Adams, J., & Roberts, N. (2006). Evaluating disease management program effectiveness: An introduction to the regression-discontinuity design. *Journal of Evaluation in Clinical Practice, 12*, 124–31.

Pion, G.M., & Cordray, D.C. (2008). The Burroughs Wellcome Career Award in the biomedical sciences: Challenges to and prospects for estimating the causal effects of career development programs. *Evaluation & the Health Profession, 31*, 335–69.

Remler, D.K., & Van Ryzin, G.G. (2010). *Research methods in practice: Strategies for description and causation.* Thousand Oaks, CA: Sage Publications.

Scriven, M. (1991). *Evaluation thesaurus* (4th ed.). Newbury Park, CA: Sage Publications.

Shadish, W.R., Cook, T.D., & Campbell, D.T. (2002). *Experimental and quasi-experimental designs for generalized causal inference.* Belmont, CA: Wadsworth.

Smith, J.D. (2012). Single-case experimental designs: A systematic review of published research and current standards. *Psychological Methods, 17*, 510–50.

Tague, N. (2005). *The quality toolkit* (2nd ed.). Milwaukee, WI: Quality Press.

Trochim, W.M.K. (1984). *Research design for program evaluation: The regression-discontinuity approach.* Beverly Hills, CA: Sage.

VanWormer, J.J. (2004). Pedometers and brief e-counseling: Increasing physical activity for overweight adults. *Journal of Applied Behavior Analysis, 37*, 421–5.

CHAPTER 13

EXPERIMENTAL BIAS

While the subject matter of this entire book has been largely devoted to the avoidance of unintentional, procedurally induced bias, the time has come to discuss everyone's least favorite scientific topic: bias due to institutional incentives and individual failings. These two genres, which are sometimes difficult to distinguish from one another, fall under the broad categories of publication bias and investigator bias.

At first glance, the relevance of this topic may not be obvious, but it is crucial that investigators be able to base their experimental work on past work that is trustworthy (i.e., unbiased). To facilitate this process, it would be optimal if we could separate valid experimental results from invalid ones—but since this is an extremely difficult task, it is at least important to be aware of the presence of experimental bias in the research literature along with *some* of its indicators. In fact, when summing up the lessons based on this chapter, the present author will reluctantly advise his readers to evaluate all published experiments with jaundiced, critical mindsets.

PUBLICATION BIAS

As a graduate student the present author was once counseled by a well-published educational psychologist to always include a subsidiary contrast of some sort in his experiments that would be guaranteed to produce a significant p-value, even if it was irrelevant to the primary hypothesis. Thus, as an example, if the outcome variable was an especially developed measure of mathematical learning and the investigator was insecure about whether or not the intervention would significantly impact that outcome, this advice translated to hedging one's bets by, say, including a blocking variable known to always be related to learning. A safe bet might be a standardized cognitive (IQ or mathematical aptitude) test, dichotomized at the median to produce high and low groups crossed with the intervention of interest, as illustrated through the hypothetical results presented in Table 13.1.

Table 13.1: Ensuring at Least One Significant Effect for a Learning Outcome.

	Intervention	Control	Total
High math aptitude	24.0	24.2	24.1
Low math aptitude	14.4	14.0	14.2
Total	19.2	19.1	

Table 13.1, therefore, reflects a scenario in which there is obviously no intervention effect (19.2 vs. 19.1), nor any aptitude × treatment intervention, but at least the investigator would have a highly significant p-value to report for the mathematics aptitude main effect (24.1 vs. 14.2).

The reason for this rather silly advice was that in the late 1960s and the early 1970s, the premiere psychological and educational publishing outlets for learning research were loath to publish results that did not result in statistical significance. Today, peer-reviewed publications such as the *Journal of Educational Psychology* and other high-impact journals in the field retain this bias toward publishing nonstatistically significant results—although hopefully their reviewers are a bit too sophisticated to be fooled by the simplistic strategy just represented.

On one level, a preference for positive results on the part of editors, reviewers, sponsors, practitioners, and researchers themselves is understandable, since it is considerably more exciting to say that a new intervention "works" than that it does not. The scientific implications of this preference, however, are quite insidious, because their end result is a published literature with a decided overall trend toward Type I errors (ineffective interventions masquerading as effective ones) and/or trivial studies.

Called *publication bias*, the phenomenon has been documented in numerous ways. The most creative (and amusing) are experiments in which methodologically oriented investigators, with the blessings of the journals involved, send out two versions of the same bogus article to journal reviewers. (The two manuscripts tend to be identical in every way, except one reports a statistically significant result while other reports no statistical significance.) Not surprisingly, the positive version is considerably more likely to be accepted for publication (e.g., Atkinson, Furlong, & Wampold, 1982). Other investigators have demonstrated that psychological (Cooper, DeNeve, & Charlton, 1997) and medical (e.g., Easterbrook, Gopalan, Berlin, & Matthews, 1991) studies with statistically significant results are more likely to be published in the first place, to be published in prestigious journals, or published more quickly (Stern & Simes, 1997).

Over time, this bias toward positive results can feed on itself and possibly create a strong disincentive for investigators to even try to publish their "failed" experiments, leading to a methodological term called the "file drawer" tendency. (A survey of psychological investigators conducted several decades ago indicated that a decided minority would consider submitting a research study that failed to reject the null hypothesis [Greenwald, 1975].) And one of the most dramatic, although circumstantial, illustrations of the prevalence of publication bias has already been discussed via the Lipsey and Wilson (1993) meta-analysis of all the psychological, educational, and behavioral meta-analyses conducted at the time of publication. Half of these meta-analyses reported ESs ≥ .50, 85% had at least small intervention effects (ESs ≥ .20), and less than 2% reported results numerically favoring the comparison group. More recently, in an even larger study, Hattie (2009) analyzed the results of over 816 meta-analyses related to learning and found an average effect size of 0.40—all of which leads to a natural question: "If everything works so well in education, why are so many of our public schools in such abysmal condition?" (In fairness, it should be noted that none of these review authors attribute their meta-analytic results, which encompass tens of thousands of individual studies, to the omnipresence of publication bias.)

Publication bias (on the part of reviewers) and the "file drawer" problem (on the part of investigators), while serious, is only one consequence of our infatuation with the obtainment of statistical significance. Far more troubling are the career and financial incentives for producing positive results, for while none of us likes to admit it, science is a business, and many scientists' livelihoods are dependent on their publication records. This is true even of college professors, who increasingly find it difficult to obtain full-time positions (much less tenured ones) without (a) consistently garnering multiple peer-reviewed publications per year and (b) achieving significant grant support (few grants are awarded on preliminary evidence that an intervention isn't likely to prove beneficial).

In any event, the truly deleterious result of this practice—if left unchecked—is the existence of a major incentive for investigators (a) to *produce* positive effects or (b) to avoid work that *might* produce negative results. (There is even an adage among medical investigators that the NIH is loath to fund research whose outcomes aren't already known.) And if the fields of economics and criminal justice have taught us anything, it is that when an incentive exists to engage in an activity, many people will—especially when the disincentives (e.g., punishments) are not particularly severe.

From this perspective, then, publication bias and investigator bias are extremely difficult to differentiate, and basically reduce to the interplay between incentives, disincentives, and acculturation. Both types of bias are also capable of producing the same result: a flawed scientific literature that must be consumed with a large helping of salt. Entire books have been written on this topic (e.g., Bausell, 2007; Broad & Wade, 1982; Goldacre, 2008; Park, 2001), with the problem being more acute in certain areas of endeavor (and in certain areas of the world) than others.

As an illustration of the latter, consider a systematic review conducted by Andrew Vickers et al. (1998), entitled "Do Certain Countries Produce Only Positive Results? A Systematic Review of Controlled Trials." Vickers's group set out to ascertain if the nationality of the principal authors is related to the results of the trials they report. In the first of a two-part analysis, 252 published accounts of acupuncture trials were reviewed; the results of their survey appear in Table 13.2. (These findings are especially dramatic given that the best evidence suggests that high-quality alternative medical trials [including acupuncture] tend to produce no positive results over and above that attributable to the placebo effect [Bausell, 2007].)

More importantly, these results illustrate a strong (and suspicious) relationship between the principal investigators' countries of origin and their conclusions. China, for example, simply did not produce *anything* but positive acupuncture trials, while the rest of Asia and Russia weren't far behind. Next, to determine if these findings were an artifact of the admittedly specialized intervention, Vickers' group repeated the analyses with a larger sample of trials involving interventions other than acupuncture (most of which involved conventional medical treatments).

In this second analysis, a search was performed for all non-acupuncture randomized controlled trials (RCTs) published between the years 1991 and 1995 (1991 was chosen because changes in key words prohibited a comprehensive computerized search for RCTs prior to that date.) This time the search was restricted to the four largest countries that had been found to publish almost all positive trials in the first study (China, Russia, Taiwan, and Japan) plus the United Kingdom, which had "only" registered a 60% positive rate.

Table 13.2: Positive Acupuncture Results by Country or Region of Origin.

Country of Origin	# Acupuncture Trials	% Positive Results
(Non-US/UK English-Speaking) Canada, Australia, New Zealand	20	30%
United States	47	53%
Scandinavia (Sweden, Denmark, Finland)	47	55%
United Kingdom	20	60%
Other European Countries (e.g., France, Germany)	52	73%
Russia	11	92%
Asia other than China (Hong Kong*, Taiwan, Japan, Sri Lanka*, Vietnam)	16	94%
China	36	100%
Other Countries (Brazil, Israel, Nigeria)	3	100%

*Hong Kong was not part of China at that time. Sri Lanka produced the only nonpositive Asian CAM trial.

This search netted 1,100 qualifying abstracts (UK RCTs, because of their large numbers, were randomly sampled), producing the equally disturbing results presented in Table 13.3.

Table 13.3: Positive Randomized Control Trials by Country of Origin.

Country of Origin	# Trials	% Positive Results
United Kingdom	107	75%
Japan	120	89%
Taiwan	40	95%
Russia	29	97%
China	109	99%

While the same trend surfaced as in the previous analysis, the results for Russia and China were even *worse* than they appeared. Each was represented by only one negative study: (a) the single Russian "negative" drug efficacy trial involved a comparison between two antihypertension drugs (sans placebo), with the conclusion that they were equally effective, and (b) the single Chinese trial reported no statistically significant difference between two antibiotics (also sans placebo), with both being designated as "effective in more than 96% of cases." And what did our investigators conclude?

> Some countries publish unusually high proportions of positive results. Publication bias is a possible explanation. Researchers undertaking systematic reviews should consider carefully how to manage data from these countries. (Vickers et al., 1998, p. 66)

Certainly publication bias is a possible explanation here and a more politically correct one than the present author would have supplied. He might have even suggested that "researchers undertaking systematic reviews should consider ignoring studies conducted in these countries." And maybe even that an investigator contemplating basing his or her experiment primarily on work conducted in one of these countries might proceed with caution.

INVESTIGATOR BIAS

As far as can be ascertained, the Vickers et al. study has not been updated, so we can all hope that time, the flattening of the earth, and the hopefully cumulating effects of educational interventions such as the original CONSORT statement (Begg, Cho, Eastwood, et al., 1996) have reduced practices such as this. Unfortunately, we can't conclude that these regional effects are no longer with us, since one Chinese journal recently reported that 31% of the articles submitted to it were plagiarized (Zhang, 2010). Pharmaceutically sponsored trials also remain exceedingly problematic (Angell, 2004), producing (a) outcomes favoring the sponsor more often than drug studies funded by other sources (Lexchin, Bero, Djulbegovic, & Clark (2003) and (b) what appears to be a blatant example of scientific misconduct, uncovered by an analysis of drug efficacy trials, by Erick Turner and colleagues, in 2008.

Selective Publication of Antidepressant Trials and Its Influence on Apparent Efficacy (2008)

Erick Turner, Annette Matthews, Eftihia Linardatos, et al.

This study took advantage of a unique database to evaluate the possibility of bias in pharmaceutically funded research. The source of the data was FDA reviews of all randomized, placebo-controlled evaluations for 12 antidepressant agents approved by the FDA between 1987 and 2004. This agency must provide their approval prior to the marketing of drugs, and approval is normally based on efficacy demonstrated via randomized placebo trials. Part of this review process involves FDA judgments regarding whether a submitted trial is positive or negative with respect to the primary outcome (and normally this agency permits only one such measure to be so specified—if additional outcomes are approved, an adjustment of the alpha level downward is required).

Of the 74 FDA-registered studies, 38 were judged by the FDA as being positive and 37 (97%) of these were published. Of the 36 trials that were judged by the FDA to be negative ($n = 24$) or questionable ($n = 12$), only 14 (39%) wound up being published. (So far, only unneeded evidence of publication bias: positive results were almost two and a half times more likely to be published than negative studies.) The next finding, however, is unique in the scientific study of bias.

Of the FDA-judged positive studies published, all (100%) were presented as positive in the final report. (No surprise here.) However, of the 12 questionable studies, the 6 that were published all appeared in the experimental record as positive (i.e., a miraculous 100% improvement in efficacy between the time the FDA reviewed the trials and the time they appeared in print). Of the eight negative trials that were published, five (or 64%) of the drugs somehow changed from ineffective to effective during the publication process.

Other equally disturbing findings reported by the authors were (in their words):

The methods reported in 11 journal articles appeared to depart from the pre-specified methods reflected in the FDA reviews.... Although for each of these studies the finding with respect to the protocol-specified primary outcome was nonsignificant, each publication highlighted a positive result as if it were the primary outcome. The nonsignificant results of the pre-specified primary outcomes were either subordinated to non-primary positive results (in two reports) or omitted (in nine). (p. 255)

(Ergo, Principle #9: Always explicitly designate nonhypothesized subgroup analyses as such when reporting the results of an experiment. When reading someone else's results, put little or no credence in a nonreplicated subgroup analysis.)

The authors, whether by choice, fear of being sued, or as required by the editors of the *New England Journal of Medicine*, offered the following politically correct, mild conclusion:

By altering the apparent risk–benefit ratio of drugs, selective publication can lead doctors to make inappropriate prescribing decisions that may not be in the best interest of their patients and, thus, the public health. (p. 259)

Do you think? What the present author thinks is that we owe this (Turner et al., 2008) and the previous set of investigators (i.e., Vickers et al., 1998), along with many other methodologically oriented scientists, a debt of gratitude for the thankless task of studying the prevalence of different types of bias in the scientific literature (for more on drug trial abuses, see Angell, 2004). Both studies also illustrate the difficulties of attempting to separate publication bias from investigator bias—which perhaps is of little consequence, since the end result of both is the same: *experimental results that simply cannot be taken at face value.*

Investigator bias specific to the design, analysis, reporting, and interpretation of experiments: Experimental bias encompasses many forms, ranging from prosecutable fraud (such as the fabrication of data) to censurable misconduct (such as misrepresenting procedural components of a study) to noncensurable sins such as the following:

1. Reporting unjustified conclusions, as illustrated by some of our previous examples,
2. Selective reporting of statistically significant findings and not reporting negative ones,
3. Failing to mention procedural glitches occurring during the course of an experiment,
4. Changing the original hypothesis in the final report, including the identity of the a priori specified primary outcome or endpoint,
5. Hyping the abstract with positive reports and questionable conclusions,
6. Reporting subgroup or secondary analyses without identifying them as such, and
7. Selectively reporting supportive past research at the expense of nonsupportive findings.

Excluded from this admittedly rather narrow focus (i.e., bias specific to experimental design, conduct, reporting, and interpretation of experimental results) are such practices as (a) unethical practices involving research participants (such as not providing them with full disclosure of risks), (b) publishing issues (such as the insistence on unjustified authorships, gaming the peer review process by suggesting supportive reviewers to journal editors, or the failure to properly cite previous work), (c) outright plagiarism (which is included in the Office of Science and Technology Policy [OSTP]'s FFP [fabrication, fraud, and plagiarism] definition (Office of Science and Technology Policy, 2005) of scientific misconduct), as well as numerous other practices including investigator-initiated publication bias (e.g., not submitting the results of statistically nonsignificant experiments for publication because they might reduce the chances of future funding).

No one actually knows the extent of bias or scientific misconduct in general. And while reports of high-profile and flagrant cases often receive professional or media attention, such as (a) Cyril Burt's career-long fabrication of fraternal vs. identical twin IQs (Wade, 1976), (b) William T. Summerlin's painted mice (Hixson, 1976; Weissmann, 2006), (c) the Korean stem cell episode (Associated Press, 2006), or (d) the cold fusion "discovery" several years ago (Wikipedia, 2014), many less high-profile studies go unnoticed. However, a restricted amount of survey research has been conducted in an attempt to ascertain the overall extent of the problem. Two relatively small surveys reported that over 50% of respondents had firsthand knowledge of fraudulent scientific conduct (Greggie, 2001; Ranstam, Buyse, George, et al., 2001). The most extensive survey of misconduct to date was published in *Nature* and presented data on 3,247 NIH-funded investigators' reported misbehavior over the previous 3 years (Martinson, Anderson, & de Vries, 2005). While these investigators cast a considerably wider net than is being discussing here, the percentages of investigators admitting infractions impacting the validity of the experimental record are presented in Table 13.4. The good news here is that two of these behaviors (see asterisks) were committed less frequently by early-career than mid-career NIH grantees. The bad news is that the latter had more opportunities to commit these offenses, as they received their first R01 funding from 1999 to 2001 (in NIH parlance, an R01 is seldom awarded to a beginning researcher just out of a doctoral program), while the latter received their "starter" grant (either individual or institutional, but designed to provide new investigators with the wherewithal to successfully apply for an R01) from 2001 to 2002.

Table 13.4: Selected Misconduct Behaviors Committed by NIH-Funded Investigators Impacting the Integrity of Research Results.

Biased Behaviors	% Engaged in Practice
Falsifying or "cooking" research data	0.3
Failing to present data that contract one's own previous research	6.0
Withholding details of methodology or results in papers or proposals	10.8
Dropping observations or data points because of a gut feeling they were inaccurate	15.3
Changing the design, methodology or results of a study in response to pressure from a funding source	15.5%

Other ethical infractions surveyed in the Martinson, Anderson, and De Vries survey included human subject violations, plagiarism, inappropriate publishing practices, conflicts of interest, and several miscellaneous issues, such as inadequate records (which was hopefully sufficiently addressed in Chapter Ten, by calling for compulsive documenting of everything that occurs during the conduct of an experiment).

One item that does deserve some comment is the fifth most frequently questionable behavior in the 16-item survey: "Overlooking others' use of flawed data or questionable interpretation of data." The fact that 12.5% of respondents reported observing this type of behavior over the past 3 years is disheartening, to say the least. The seriousness of *overlooking* such behavior, however, is a rather gray area. The present author would advise beginning researchers who observe what they consider unethical behaviors such as this to seek advice from experienced, trusted colleagues or mentors before *reporting* them, for two reasons: first, to garner another, more experienced opinion regarding the egregiousness of the offense, and second, because "whistle-blowers" are sometimes inappropriately and unfairly punished for what they consider to be an altruistic, professional duty on their parts. Alternately, discussing the offense with someone more senior may in itself absolve you from the "overlooking" part of this item. So may voicing your disagreement with the practice to the perpetrator, perhaps by simply "innocently" asking him or her if this is an appropriate scientific action and thereby potentially decreasing the likelihood of the individual committing the offense again. Ultimately, of course, if you find yourself in the unfortunate situation of observing this type of behavior, you must decide on the appropriate course of action for yourself. Hopefully, you won't be in the unlucky 12.5% who does.

Surveys such as the three cited here undoubtedly produce underestimates of the problem, given the (a) relatively low response rates (typically below 50%) and (b) reluctance to self-report egregious misconduct. The real issue, however, is not the accuracy of the prevalence of such practices but the unfortunate fact that they occur at all. Whether such practices are increasing is not known, although Steen (2010) reports that published retractions for fraud and other reasons have increased sharply since the year 2000. (Steen admits that this trend could [a] "reflect either a real increase in the incidence of fraud or a greater effort on the part of journals to police the literature" and [b] that most retractions are for reasons other than misconduct.)

Even if the prevalence is low, the end result of this type of behavior is (a) diminished public confidence in the scientific process by a society (and species) in desperate need of scientific help (and which generously supports the conduct of science), (b) wasted expenditures of increasingly rare resources, and (c) precious time wasted by other scientists attempting to replicate and build on bogus experimental results. Another end product to which bias is a major contributor resides in the fact that practically anyone advocating practically any position on any topic addressed by experimental research can find support for that position somewhere within the scientific record. This occurs partially because too many experiments are

1. Performed by investigators with inadequate training, who are simply incompetent, or not sufficiently conscientious.
2. Not honestly reported because their investigators are unethical or (consciously or unconsciously) permit personal bias to influence their results.

And then there is the bizarre and reprehensible practice of using research as a purely marketing strategy.

Seeding trials: The present author's first experience with this genre of pseudo-research occurred when the television show *20/20* asked him to comment on camera concerning the claims made by a diet product in which "noncaloric tastant crystals" are sprinkled over food. The product purportedly then decreases the amount of the treated food eaten and thereby results in significant weight loss. As part of the product's promotional information, the owner of the company cited research he had previously conducted, including the following huge nonrandomized experiment, information for which was available on the company website as well as that of an affiliated company called the Smell & Taste Treatment and Research Foundation.

Use of Gustatory Stimuli To Facilitate Weight Loss

A.R. Hirsch

While the full report of this study on which this synopsis is based appears to be no longer available on the company-sponsored website (perhaps as part of a 26.5 million dollar settlement with the Federal Trade Commission, which accused the marketers of the miracles drug and Hirsch of false and deceptive advertising practices [Deardorff, & King, 2014]). As of this writing, however, an abstract is available at: http://www.trysensa.com/media/pdf/Abstract_Poster_Use_of_Stimuli_for_Weight_Loss.pdf. (Another version was delivered at the 90th Annual Endocrinology Society Conference [2008] in San Francisco.)

Methods: "Two thousand four hundred thirty-seven overweight or obese subjects, over a six-month period, sprinkled a variety of savory or sweet tastant crystals onto their food prior to mandiculation. Pre and post study weights were obtained and compared to one hundred non-treated controls."

Results: "1437 (59%) of the participants completed the trial. The average weight loss was 30.5 pounds, 5.0 BMI, versus control of 2 pounds, 0.3 BMI ($p < 0.05$)."

Conclusion: "Use of tastants to enhance or generalize sensory specific satiety demonstrated efficacy in the promotion of weight loss. Further investigation into this approach on the secondary effects of obesity (i.e., hyperlipidemia, cardiovascular disease, hypertension) is warranted."

Of course, this was a nonrandomized trial with no information provided on how the 100 control participants were chosen. The weight loss was also based solely on self-reports. It is not the design of this study that is of primary interest to us here, however, but the fact that the participants appeared to be recruited for the trial as a marketing ploy to sell the product and they were required to pay for it *themselves*. (No data are provided on the 1,001 participants who opted to exit the trial, perhaps because they were not getting the results they had hoped for or felt that the money they were spending for the product was not worth the results *they* were obtaining.)

The study was never published in a peer-reviewed journal, but its results have been repeatedly used to market the product. And to the present author's knowledge, no other trial this size (certainly no peer reviewed double-blinded randomized trial of any sort) has ever reported an *average* weight loss of 30+ pounds. However, an even larger uncontrolled trial ($N = 3{,}193$) by the author and a colleague (Hirsch & Gomez, 1995) was published that found surprisingly similar results. Here an inhaler (consisting of food aromas) was used three times per day (or whenever participants felt hungry) and those who used "their inhalers frequently, ate 2 to 4 means a day, felt bad about overeating, but did not feel bad about themselves lost nearly 5 pounds, or 2% of body weight per month" (p. 28). No mention is made of how many of the original 3,193 volunteers met these criteria appeared in the article, but given that this finding involved quadruple exclusion criteria, the size of this particular subgroup may have been very small indeed.

Surprisingly, despite *20/20*'s best efforts (not to mention the present author's cogent methodological critique and charismatic on camera presence), the product is apparently even more profitable a decade after the exposé aired and presumably remains the world's best first-line defense against the obesity epidemic.

By definition, "seeding trials" involve the selling of a product and a built-in conflict of interest. And unfortunately, few are as transparent as this example, which in practice often involves a pharmaceutical company's desire to familiarize physicians with a drug in the hope they will become prescribers in their own practices (Kessler, Rose, Temple, et al., 1994). (Obviously, neither volunteering participants nor IRBs are informed of the true purpose of such trials, otherwise the former would not volunteer for them, nor, hopefully, would the latter approve them.)

Krumholz, Egilman, Ross, et al. (2011) provide a rare beam of light into this practice through a narrative review of hundreds of documents obtained from a court order in a trial involving Pfizer and Franklin, the manufacturer of an antiseizure drug whose side effects were the subject of the litigation. (For another example, see Hill, Ross, Egilman, & Krumholz, 2008). The experiment in the litigated case was described as "a phase 4 uncontrolled, unblinded trial" in which 772 physicians were recruited to enroll 2,759 participants. Despite the study's size, the number of participants was limited since internal company documents suggested that the true purpose of the "study" was to recruit physicians (who were rewarded for meeting their recruitment targets), not their patients. In all, 11 of these patients died, and 73 others suffered serious adverse incidents. Strangely, Krumholz and colleagues report that the two published journal articles based on the trial results "were generally supportive, describing the drug as effective, safe, and tolerable" (p. 1101). (Many seeding trials are never published because they are conducted for an entirely different purpose—not to mention that most are so poorly designed, such as the Hirsch trial discussed in the insert, that they would have difficulty getting accepted in a reputable peer-reviewed journal.)

The bioethicist and philosopher, Carl Elliot (2011), sums up this particular practice as follows:

> Many patients volunteer for research in the hope that the knowledge generated will benefit others. When a company deceives them into volunteering for a useless study, it cynically exploits their good will, undermining the cause of legitimate research everywhere. (p. A27)

Like other forms of experimental bias, no one knows with any precision how prevalent this practice is, but there is no question that a significant amount of research is conducted for purely marketing purposes. While the practice may not be sufficiently prevalent to deserve a separate principle, a corollary to Principle #1 (to choose another field "if you are not prepared to be absolutely, uncompromisingly, unfashionably honest") will be provided instead:

Corollary #1 to Principle #1: Do not design and conduct experiments as a marketing ploy for yourself or anyone else. The practice will not only destroy your credibility but it will also contribute to weakening the credibility of science and exploiting people's altruism (not to mention making them less likely to volunteer for future scientific experiments.)

STRATEGIES DESIGNED TO DETECT BIAS

It would obviously be a major boon if publication and/or investigator bias could be identified on the basis of the research report itself. In Cyril Burt's case, this actually occurred when someone finally noticed, after his death, that the "father of educational psychology" hadn't bothered to change his published correlation coefficients of monozygotic and dizygotic twins' IQ scores after supposedly having twice added to his original sample. Since we can't count on everyone who fabricates data being this lazy (or arrogant), the question becomes: Is there any generalized, reliable method of detecting experimental bias and/or fraud? The short answer is "Not yet, but some of us keep trying." Two examples follow.

Meta-analytic procedures: The prevalence of publication bias constitutes a serious threat, not only to individual investigators exploring the likelihood of an intervention's effectiveness but also to the meta-analytic enterprise in general. Meta-analytic methodologists have developed a number of methods by which the presence of publication bias can be supposedly documented (or dismissed) for a group of experiments. The most common approach probably involves the use of a funnel plot (Light, Singer, & Willett, 1994) that checks for both (a) the underrepresentation of smaller studies (an hypothesized effect of publication bias) and (b) the potential differences in variability among ESs for smaller vs. larger sample experiments (one would expect the variability to be greater for small studies than for large ones). (Lipsey and Wilson [2001] and Hayashino, Noguchi, and Fukui [2005] have written quite readable critiques of these methods.) Ironically, however, Ferguson and Brannick (2012) report evidence that meta-analyses that included unpublished literature searches were more likely to evince publication bias than those which did not, hence suggesting that we have a long way to go in identifying and compensating for the phenomenon. The bottom line is that if publication bias is as rampant as the evidence suggests, no statistical procedure is going to be capable of *correcting* the situation.

Design quality as an indicator of bias: Unfortunately, none of the methods developed to detect the influence of publication bias are applicable to the detection of investigator bias or bias simply due to flawed experimental designs. However, a relatively large body of evidence has accumulated over time from a specialized genre of research that uses discrepancies in published experimental findings to identify those design characteristics that seem most likely to bias study results. The first study of this kind to have provided hard (albeit observational) evidence suggesting a link between study design and possibly biased results was conducted over 45 years ago (Chalmers, Matta, Smith, & Kunzler, 1977). In comparing treatment effects found in 32 trials of anticoagulation therapy for acute myocardial infraction, these investigators found that nonrandomized trials (including historical controls) reported substantially larger ESs than their randomized counterparts. (The assumption was that the larger ESs were indicative of bias *due* to use of weaker designs.)

The finding that poor methodological practices are associated with larger (presumably inflated) ESs was supported to one degree or another by several subsequent studies (Chalmers, Celano, Sacks, & Smith, 1983; Concato, Shah, & Horwitz, 2000; Emerson, Burdick, Hoaglin, et al., 1990; Miller, Colditz, & Mosteller, 1989; Sacks, Chalmers, & Smith, 1982; Smith, Oldman, McQuay, & Moore, 2000). Based on these promising results, rating scales of design and research quality began to proliferate, with one group of investigators (Moher, Jadad, Nichol, et al., 1995) identifying 25 different scales from a variety of disciplines designed to assess practically every component of the research process.

The most often used scale (especially in meta-analytic studies, which commonly rate their constituent RCTs with respect to methodological quality) came to be called the Jadad scale (Jadad, Moore, Carroll, et al., 1996; see Table 13.5). This five-item scale derived its popularity from (a) the ease with which it was administered, (b) its high inter-rater reliability (only the second and fourth items required any substantive degree of judgment on the part of raters), and (c) the fact that it was often correlated negatively with experimental ESs (i.e., the higher the Jadad score, the lower the individual ESs tended to be within relatively homogeneous groups of experiments).

Table 13.5: The Jadad Scale.

1. Was the study described as randomized?
2. Was the randomization scheme described and appropriate?
3. Was the study described as double blind?
4. Was the method of double-blinding appropriate?
5. Was there a description (reasons and numbers) of dropouts and withdrawals?

As provocative (and promising) as the results produced by this genre of research were, their interpretation suffered from a number of weaknesses. Perhaps the most serious challenge emanated from a study conducted by Juni, Witschi, Bloch, and Egger (1999) that employed *all* 25 of the quality rating scales identified by Moher, Jadad, Nichol, et al. (1995) in the assessment of a set of 17 unusually homogeneous randomized clinical trials (all 17 compared low-molecular-weight heparin [heparin is an anticoagulant] with standard heparin with respect to their efficacy in preventing postoperative thrombosis [blood clots]). This extremely well-conceived study found that some of the scales supported previous analyses (i.e., produced a statistically significant negative correlation with ESs), some demonstrating a significant positive relationship, but most found no relationship at all. This led Juni and his colleagues to the conclusion that their "data indicate that the use of summary scores to identify trials of high quality is problematic" (p. 1054).

Another disadvantage of quality/bias indicators unearthed by this line of research involved their probable discipline-specific nature. In much psychological, behavioral, and educational experimental work, for example, placebo control groups and double blinding are often not possible or relevant (there is no placebo effect in learning, for example). Perhaps because of this, there is less evidence that methodological quality is associated with ESs in these disciplines. Thus, while Lipsey and Wilson (1993) quite effectively documented the presence of publication bias in these fields (e.g., published studies were found to have larger ESs than unpublished dissertations), no discernible relationship was found between the ESs of high- vs. low-quality studies. In another analysis, Lipsey and Wilson also failed to find a difference in the ESs of randomized vs. nonrandomized trials, although single-group pretest-posttest designs were found to produce significantly larger ESs than experiments using control groups.

The final, and perhaps most important disadvantage of employing quality rating scales to assess their correlation with experimental ESs involves the fact that the true ESs for the experiments involved are *unknown*. We *assume* that smaller effect sizes are more likely to be valid indicators than larger ones, but this is after all only an assumption. If, on the other hand, we had access to a set of experiments involving a single discipline for which we had a priori information on what their results *should be*, then theoretically we could ascertain the most important design factors within that discipline.

Fortunately, such a research area exists: complementary and alternative medical efficacy trials. Given their common lack of plausible physiological mechanisms of action, statistically significant positive experimental effects in this area might reasonably be assumed to be due to chance findings (i.e. Type I error), investigator or publication bias, and/or design artifacts (e.g., placebo effects, sample size, experimental attrition). The following analysis suggested the latter as at least one of the contributing etiologies.

Are Positive Alternative Medical Therapy Trials Credible? Evidence from Four High-Impact Medical Journals (2009)

R. Barker Bausell

The purpose of this study was to ascertain the extent to which the proportion of positive complementary and alternative medical (CAM) trials would be reduced within high-impact general (i.e., not disease of body system specific) U.S. medical journals if certain negative methodological indicators were taken into account. These publishing outlets are reputed to provide more stringent credibility screening due to their (a) more rigorous peer review system (Laine, Goodman, Griswold, & Sox, 2007), (b) reputation for publishing higher quality trials in general (Reed, Cook, Beckman, et al., 2007), and (c) commitment to requiring well-established procedural controls (as witnessed by their endorsement of the original CONSORT Statement [Begg, Cho, Eastwood., et al.,1996]). The journals selected (in order of their impact level) were (1) *The New England Journal of Medicine,* (2) *The Journal of the American Medical Association,* (3) *The Annals of Internal Medicine,* and (4) *The Archives of Internal Medicine.*

Each trial was examined to determine the presence or absence of the following three design characteristics:

1. A randomly assigned placebo control group: The presence of a placebo control was deemed to be a biological *and* methodological necessity given the placebo effect's well-documented mechanism of action (i.e., endogenous opioid release [Amanzio, Pollo, Maggi, & Benedetti, 2001; Zubieta, Bueller, Jackson, et al., 2005]) on pain, the most commonly used outcome variable in CAM trials in general.
2. Fifty participants per group (which is the sample size required to achieve statistical power of 0.80 given a hypothesized medium effect size [0.50] for a two-arm trial assuming a correlation of 0.60 between the baseline and end-of-treatment assessments [Bausell & Li, 2002]).
3. Experimental attrition less than 25% (given the likelihood that any higher loss of participants could potentially significantly bias study results).

Randomized trials that met all three criteria were designated as having "high internal validity," and those failing to meet one or more criteria were designated as "low internal validity" trials.

All issues of the four journals between January 1, 2000, and August 1, 2009, were manually reviewed, and all original contributions constituting randomized, prospective experimental assessments of the efficacy of a CAM therapy were evaluated. CAM therapies were defined as those therapies included in the 2002 National Health Survey CAM Supplement (Barnes, Powell-Griner, McFann, & Nahin, 2004). In all, 26 randomized trials met all three of the quality criteria while 19 trials failed to meet one or more. As indicated in Table 13.6, reasons for failure involved the absence of (a) a placebo control ($N = 5$, 26%), (b) N/group < 50 ($N = 7$, 37%), and (c) attrition greater than 25% ($N = 3$, 16%). Four (21%) trials failed multiple criteria, three of which also involved the lack of a placebo control.

Table 13.6: Reasons for Low-Validity Judgments.

Failed Validity Criteria	Positive Results	Negative Results	Total
No placebo-control group	4 (80.0%)	1 (20.0%)	5 (26%)
N/Group < 50	1 (14.3%)	6 (85.7%)	7 (37%)
Attrition > 25%	2 (66.6%)	1 (33.3%)	3 (16%)
No placebo and N < 50	2 (100%)	0 (0%)	2 (11%)
No placebo and attrition > 25%	1 (100%)	0 (0%)	1 (5%)
N/Group < 50 and attrition > 25%	1 (100%)	0 (0%)	1 (5%)
Total	11 (57.9%)	8 (42.1%)	19 (100%)

Initially, the original trial authors' qualitative assessment regarding whether the therapy was superior to the control group was designated as the criterion for whether the study results would be judged as positive or negative. It soon became clear, however, that in trials in which there were two control groups (i.e., a placebo and either a no-treatment or "usual treatment" control), a number of investigators were reluctant to consider the placebo group as an actual control group and instead upgraded it to treatment status, as was done in the acupuncture example described in Chapter Five. Consequently, the actual p-value between placebo and treatment controls was used to determine whether a trial was positive or negative with alpha set at ≤.05.

Of the 26 trials employing a placebo control, N/Group ≥ 50, and attrition < 25%, only 2 (7.7%) were found to be more effective than its placebo control (see Table 13.7). In contrast, 11 (57.9%) of the 19 trials failing to meet one or more of the validity criteria were reported to have produced positive therapeutic effects. (One trial that achieved statistical significance at .05 was judged as negative because its authors hypothesized an a priori effect size that was not reached and they concluded that the therapy was not efficacious.)

Although the sample size was limited, these results were interpreted as suggesting a relatively strong relationship between design validity and efficacy trial

Table 13.7 Relationship between Design Validity and Complementary and Alternative Medicine Results

	Positive Results	Negative Results	Total
High-validity trials	2 (7.7%)	24 (93.1%)	26
Low-validity trials	11 (57.9%)	8 (42.1%)	19
Total	13	32	45

results for CAM therapies. A 2 (positive vs. negative results) × 2 (study met all four criterion vs. did not) chi-square was highly significant ($\chi^2 = 13.5$, $p < .001$), and the low proportion of positive trials (i.e., .077) using a credible placebo control, a modest sample size, and relatively low attrition approaches the 0.05 significance level itself (i.e., 5% of these trials would be expected to achieve statistical significance by chance alone). There was evidence, however, that something other than random chance was operative here for the two high-validity positive trials: (a) one failed to blind the therapist (failure to do so has been demonstrated to elicit a placebo effect [Gracely, Dubner, Deeter, & Wolskee, 1985]) and (b) the second was funded, conducted, *and* reported by employees or consultants of the same herbal company that marketed the product.

A CAVEAT: VIGILANCE, NOT CYNICISM

While admittedly discouraging, the subject matter of this chapter should be framed in the larger context of society itself. No human activity is perfect, and no group of humans operates completely homogeneously within the same ethical framework (nor do they respond in exactly the same manner to available incentives).

The purpose of this chapter, therefore, was not to discourage prospective scientists or research consumers, nor was it to breed cynics or critics. Instead, the motivation was to raise readers' consciousness concerning the *possibility* that everything they read within the scientific literature was not written by charter subscribers to our first experimental principle.

Unfortunately, no magic bullet exists to identify fraudulent data, although the best evidence we have indicates that the vast majority of experiments are conducted as written and produced the results as published. It may well be, in fact, that science is among the most honest of professions practiced by our species. No one knows for sure, but this happens to be an *opinion* subscribed to by the present author.

Fortunately, we all have more experience than we would have wished in recognizing hype, and hopefully this book has provided some insight into the types of conclusions that can and cannot be defensively drawn from an experiment involving human participants. Fortunately, too, science has some long-term self-correctional mechanisms for bias, the two most important being (a) independent replication and (b) plausibility based on a successful theory. Failing that, we have William of Occam's 13th-century parsimony advice. Collated, and resorting to the vernacular, this means that (a) if a finding doesn't make sense, it probably is neither sensible or real, and (b) if there is a simpler explanation for any given finding—that's probably the real explanation. But in the end, it's an exciting, wondrous time in those rare occasions when we find something we didn't expect, doesn't make sense, but *is* real.

SUMMARY

The most important points for future investigators and research consumers to take from this chapter are as follows:

1. To date, no completely satisfactory method of detecting bias has been developed or (in the present author's opinion) is likely to be developed anytime soon. There have been promising developments relying on the quality of study design (e.g., Bausell, 2009; Jadad, Moore, Carroll, et al., 1996), but these techniques are imperfect and almost certainly discipline specific (as witnessed by Lipsey & Wilson, 1993).

2. None of these techniques are capable of detecting outright fraud since investigators who alter their data would also probably have no qualms about misrepresenting their experimental procedures (if indeed they knew the difference between acceptable and unacceptable methodologies).

3. When evaluating experiments relevant to one's area of concentration, investigators should take the time to review the methodologies employed closely and give more credence to those employing sound designs (i.e., using randomization, appropriate control groups, adequate sample sizes, blinding when relevant, and low attrition rates).

4. In evaluating experiments directly relevant to their work, investigators should also take the reputation of the journal (e.g., its impact rating) into account because more desirable journals generally attract higher quality (and more stringent) reviewers (and possibly more experienced researchers). Whether this advice will be relevant in the future is questionable, however, since more and more journals (even high-quality ones) allow (or require) authors to nominate their own reviewers (which greatly increases the probability of cronyism). Also, in evaluating the journal's susceptibility to publication bias, a quick survey of recent issues should be conducted to see if it appears to completely avoid publishing negative results.

5. Being constantly cognizant of the omnipresence of all types of bias, that up to 5% of previous trials may have achieved statistical significance by chance alone, and considering that an unknown (hopefully small) percentage may be fraudulent.

6. Being especially suspicious of all forms of hype, exaggeration, or the absence of sensible disclaimers in the discussion or conclusion sections.

7. Concentrating on the methodology and the actual results rather than on the authors' conclusions, since journal editors allow far more subjectivity in this section. (It is, after all, the results and the methods used to produce those results that are more scientifically relevant than someone's *opinion* about their meaning.)

8. Beginning the process of evaluating a published experiment with a jaundiced, critical mindset.

9. When bias is encountered or suspected, not bothering to attempt to determine whether it is conscious or accidental. (Individual motivations are almost impossible to ascertain and are basically irrelevant anyway.)

10. At the end of the day, realizing that all we can do as scientists is to avoid bias in our own work, eschew the conduct of seeding trials, and attempt to reduce the prevalence of bias in our disciplines by providing the best training, mentorship, and acculturating experiences for prospective scientists as possible.

11. And finally, always keeping our very first experimental principle in mind: performing all aspects of the scientific process in an absolutely, uncompromisingly, unfashionably honest manner.

REFERENCES

Amanzio, M., Pollo, A., Maggi, G., & Benedetti, F. (2001). Response variability to analgesics: A role for non-specific activation of endogenous opioids. *Pain*, *90*, 205–15.

Angell, M. (2004). *The truth about the drug companies: How they deceive us and what to do about it.* New York: Random House.

Associated Press. (2006). Disgraced Korean cloning scientist indicted. *New York Times*, May, 12. Retrieved from http://www.nytimes.com/2006/05/12/world/asia/12korea.html?_r=0

Atkinson, D.R., Furlong, M. J., & Wampold, B.E. (1982). Statistical significance reviewer evaluations, and the scientific process: Is there a statistically significant relationship? *Journal of Counseling Psychology*, *29*, 189–94.

Barnes, P. M., Powell-Griner, E., McFann, K., & Nahin, R. L. (2004, May). *Advance data from vital and health statistics.* Hyattsville, MD: Centers for Disease Control and Prevention.

Bausell, R.B. (2007). *Snake oil science: The truth about complementary and alternative medicine.* New York: Oxford University Press.

Bausell, R.B. (2009). Are positive alternative medical therapy trials credible? Evidence from four high-impact medical journals. *Evaluation & the Health Professions*, *32*, 349–69.

Bausell, R.B., & Li, Y.F. (2002). *Power analysis for experimental research: A practical guide for the biological, medical, and social sciences.* Cambridge, UK: Cambridge University Press.

Begg, C., Cho M., Eastwood S., et al. (1996). Improving the quality of reporting of randomized controlled trials. The CONSORT statement. *Journal of the American Medical Association*, *276*, 637–9.

Broad, W., & Wade, N. (1982). *Betrayers of the truth.* New York: Simon & Schuster.

Chalmers, T.C., Celano, P., Sacks, H.S., & Smith, H.J. (1983), Bias in treatment assignment in controlled clinical trials. *New England Journal of Medicine*, *309*, 1358–61.

Chalmers, T.C., Matta, R.J., Smith, H., Jr., & Kunzler, A.M. (1977). Evidence favoring the use of anticoagulants in the hospital phase of acute myocardial infarction. *New England Journal of Medicine*, *297*, 1091–6.

Concato, J., Shah, N., & Horwitz, R.I. (2000). Randomized, controlled trials, observational studies, and the hierarchy of research designs. *New England Journal of Medicine*, *342*, 1887–92.

Cooper, H.M., DeNeve, K.M., & Charlton, K. (1997). Finding the missing science: The fate of studies submitted for review by a human subjects committee. *Psychological Methods*, *2*, 447–52.

Deardorff, J., & King, K. (2014). Chicago doctor's research fails federal smell test. *Chicago Tribune*, January 19. Retrieved from http://www.chicagotribune.com/health/ct-met-sensa-weight-loss-hirsch-20140119,0,7412554.story

Easterbrook, P.J., Gopalan, R., Berlin, J.A., & Matthews, D.R. (1991) Publication bias in clinical research. *Lancet, 337,* 867–72.

Elliot, C. (2011). Useless studies, real harm. *New York Times,* July 28.

Emerson, J.D., Burdick, E., Hoaglin, D.C., et al. (1990). An empirical study of the possible relation of treatment differences to quality scores in controlled randomized clinical trials. *Control Clinical Trials, 11,* 339–52.

Ferguson, C.J., & Brannick, M.T. (2012). Publication bias in Psychological Science: Prevalence, methods for identifying and controlling, and implications for the use of meta-analysis. *Psychological Science, 17,* 120–8.

Goldacre, B. (2008). *Bad science.* London: Harper Perennial.

Gracely, R.H., Dubner, R. Deeter, W.R., & Wolskee, P.J. (1985). Clinicians' expectations influence placebo analgesia. *Lancet 1,* 8419, 43.

Greenwald, A.G. (1975). Consequences of prejudice against the null hypothesis. *Psychological Bulletin, 82,* 1–20.

Greggie, D. (2001). A survey of newly appointed consultants' attitudes towards research fraud. *Journal of Medical Ethics, 27,* 344–6.

Hattie, J. (2009). *Visible learning: a synthesis of over 800 meta-analyses relating to achievement.* London: Routledge.

Hayashino, Y., Noguchi, Y. & Fukui, T. (2005). Systematic evaluation and comparison of statistical tests for publication bias. *Journal of Epidemiology, 15,* 235–43.

Hill, K.P., Ross, J.S., Egilman, D.S., & Krumholz, H.M. (2008). The ADVANTAGE seeding trial: A review of internal documents. *Annals of Internal Medicine, 149,* 251–8.

Hirsch, A.R. Use of gustatory stimuli to facilitate weight loss. Retrieved from http://www.trysensa.com/media/pdf/Abstract_Poster_Use_of_Stimuli_for_Weight_Loss.pdf

Hirsch, A.R., & Gomez, R. (1995). Weight reduction through inhalation of odorants. *Journal of Neurological and Orthopedic Medical Surgery, 16,* 28–31.

Hixson, J.R. (1976). *The patchwork mouse.* Boston: Anchor Press.

Jadad, A.R., Moore, R.A., Carroll, D., et al. (1996). Assessing the quality of reports of randomized clinical trials: Is blinding necessary? *Control Clinical Trials, 17,* 1–12.

Juni, P., Witschi, A., Bloch, R., & Egger, M. (1999). The hazards of scoring the quality of clinical trials for meta-analysis. *Journal of the American Medical Association, 282,* 1054–60.

Kessler, D.A., Rose, J.L., Temple, R.J., et al. (1994). Therapeutic-class wars: Drug promotion in a competitive marketplace. *New England Journal of Medicine, 331,* 1350–3.

Krumholz, S.D., Egilman, D.S., Ross, J.S., et al. (2011). Study of neurontin: Titrate to Effect, Profile of Safety (STEPS) trial: A narrative account of a gabapentin seeding trial. *Archives Internal Medicine, 171,* 1100–7.

Laine, C., Goodman, S.N., Griswold, M. E., & Sox, H.C. (2007). Reproducible research: Moving toward research the public can trust. *Annals of Internal Medicine, 146,* 450–3.

Lexchin J., Bero, L.A., Djulbegovic, B., & Clark, O. (2003). Pharmaceutical industry sponsorship and research outcome and quality: A systematic review. *British Medical Journal, 326,* 1167–70.

Light, R.J., Singer, J.D., & Willett, J.B. (1994). The visual presentation and interpretation of meta-analysis. In H.M. Cooper & L.V. Hedges (Eds.), *The handbook of research synthesis.* New York: Russell Sage Foundation.

Lipsey, M.W., & Wilson, D.B. (1993). Educational and behavioral treatment: Confirmation from meta-analysis. *American Psychologist, 48,* 1181–209.

Martinson, B.C., Anderson, M.S., & de Vries, R. (2005). Scientists behaving badly. *Nature, 435,* 737–8.

Miller, J.N., Colditz, G.A., & Mosteller, F. (1989). How study design affects outcomes in comparisons of therapy. II: surgical. *Statistics in Medicine, 8*, 455–66.

Moher, D., Jadad, A.R., Nichol, G., et al. (1995). Assessing the quality of randomized controlled trials. *Control Clinical Trials, 16*, 62–73.

Office of Science and Technology Policy. (2005). *Federal policy on research misconduct.* Retrieved from http://www.ostp.gov/html/001207_3.html

Park, R. (2001). *Voodoo science: The road from foolishness to fraud.* New York: Oxford University Press.

Ranstam, J., Buyse, M., George, S.L., et al. (2001). Fraud in medical research: An international survey of biostatisticians. *Controlled Clinical Trials, 21*, 415–27.

Reed, D.A., Cook, D.A., Beckman, T.J., Levine, R.B., & Kerns, D.E., & Wright, S.M. (2007). Association between funding and quality of published medical education research. *Journal of the American Medical Association, 298*, 1002–9.

Sacks, H., Chalmers, T.C., & Smith, H.J. (1982). Randomized versus historical controls for clinical trials. *American Journal of Medicine, 72*, 233–40.

Smith, L.A., Oldman, A.D., McQuay, H.J., & Moore, R.A. (2000). Teasing apart quality and validity in systematic reviews: An example from acupuncture trials in chronic neck and back pain. *Pain, 86*, 119–32.

Steen, R.G. (2010). Retractions in the scientific literature: Is the incidence of research fraud increasing? *Journal of Medical Ethics, 38*, 228–32.

Stern, J.M., & Simes, R.J. (1997). Publication bias: Evidence of delayed publication in a cohort study of clinical research projects, *British Medical Journal, 315*, 640–5.

Turner, E.H., Matthews, A.M., Linardatos, E., et al. (2008) Selective publication of antidepressant trials and its influence on apparent efficacy. *New England Journal of Medicine, 358*, 252–60.

Vickers, A., Goyal, N., Harland, R., & Rees, R. (1988). Do certain countries produce only positive results? A systematic review of controlled trials. *Controlled Clinical Trials, 19*(2), 159–66.

Wade, N. (1976). IQ and heredity: Suspicion of fraud beclouds classic experiment. *Science, 194*, 916–9.

Weissmann, G. (2006). Scientific fraud: From patchwork mouse to patchwork data. *FASEB Journal, 20*, 587–90.

Wikipedia. (2014). Cold fusion. Retrieved from http://en.wikipedia.org/wiki/Cold_fusion#CITEREFBroad1989a

Zhang, Y. (2010). Chinese journal finds 31% of submissions plagiarized. *Nature, 467*, 153.

Zubieta, J-K., Bueller, J.A., Jackson, L.R., et al. (2005). Placebo effects mediated by endogenous opioid activity on μ-opioid receptors. *Journal of Neuroscience, 25*, 7754–62.

CHAPTER 14

EPILOGUE AND REVIEW

To anyone who has persevered to this point, the good news is that the book's final chapter will be mercifully brief. Your author sincerely hopes that his advice will prove helpful and that his discussion of design issues has been understandable and nontechnical. And, of course, he hopes that you will have the opportunity to design and conduct many meaningful experiments in the future if the idea appeals to you. For anyone not choosing this path, hopefully the book has contributed to a critical understanding and appreciation of the logic of scientific experimentation.

For those who do become scientists, there is obviously a great deal more to engaging in a meaningful scientific career than can appear between the covers of any single text, two of which have not been covered previously. These involve the importance of (a) publishing your work, and (b) always considering the advancement of your science as a personal career *obligation*. For these topics I offer the following brief observations:

1. An unpublished experiment is like a tree falling unheard in a forest, with one important difference. The tree contributed to its ecosystem during its lifetime and continues to do so after its demise. Failing to publish one's work, on the other hand, contributes to nothing or no one and is basically unethical since (a) it may require another scientist to expend valuable resources repeating an experiment that has already been conducted, and (b) it also constitutes a violation of the trust of those who volunteered their time to engage in what was surely sold to them as a societally meaningful and altruistic contribution on their part. It is true that many otherwise talented researchers find writing a journal article extremely onerous, but like most other tasks, its commission is less aversive than its procrastination. Writing a scientific article is also an activity that becomes easier each time it is accomplished. Its commission is greatly facilitated by the fact that a significant proportion (e.g., the introduction, literature review, methods, and references) can be completed before the experimental data are collected and analyzed. In fact, many of these sections will most likely already have been written in an abridged format in the IRB or funding proposals. Quoting an admittedly secondary source (but an individual

who definitely knows something about publishing [Vener, 2007]), John Hall Gladstone (1872) is reputed to have said in his biography of Michael Faraday: "It is on record that when a young aspirant asked Faraday the secret of his success as a scientific investigator, he replied, 'The secret is comprised in three words— *Work, Finish, Publish.*'"

2. As far as furthering your discipline's development, the greatest contribution most of us can make is to engage in a *program* of research (it is a rare experiment that stands alone and generates no new questions) that has the potential of leading to (a) a meaningful theoretical epiphany or (b) a clinical finding with the potential of leading to an improvement in someone's quality of life. Or, even if we fail in these regards, perhaps the record of our best attempts can facilitate others to accomplish what we did not. But obviously none of this will occur without perseverance, so just as you can begin the process of writing the final report of your study before it is completed, you should definitely begin designing your next experiment before the present one is completed. (There are, after all, only three possible outcomes for your primary hypothesis.)

Three additional points have been mentioned briefly, but bear repeating. First, keep in mind that experimentation of the genre discussed in this book constitutes only a small—and perhaps not even the most important—slice of the scientific enterprise. So don't limit yourself to conducting randomized experiments but always be vigilant for opportunities to engage in other empirical genres of research as well—remembering that many of the 25 principles and 18 experimental artifacts will apply to *any* scientific endeavor.

Second, continue to expand your empirical repertoire by engaging in other types of research when the opportunity presents itself and by keeping current with methodological and statistical advances. Some may not be superior to what they replace, but you would be well advised to be conversant with them.

Finally, and most importantly, keep abreast of both the scientific literature in general and especially in your area(s) of interest throughout your career. There have never been more continuing education opportunities available than the present, and it has never been easier to access published literature. There is simply more of it, the vast majority of which unfortunately is repetitive and trivial.

Skepticism without cynicism is a trait worth nurturing, so always keep the renowned scientific philosopher Yogi Berra edict in mind: "It's tough to make predictions, especially about the future." And obviously, advice such as being proffered here involves predicting what the future will be like.

And while that cynical remark should end this stream of advice, surely you didn't expect to get off that easily. Here are five additional and *brief* (and definitely final) pieces of it: the first four your author wishes someone had given him long ago, the fifth he discovered on his own:

- Make and retain as many professional contacts and networks throughout your careers as possible,
- Work in a team whenever possible, possibly in different teams for different purposes,
- Discuss research with colleagues and other scientists, since many good research ideas surface during such conversations (Joseph Jenkins, personal communication).
- Don't be arrogant, and
- Engage William of Occam as your clandestine scientific mentor. He will not refuse, works cheap, and couldn't care less whether you attribute anything to him or not. (However, the man can be exceedingly irritating at times.)

Now, I've surely long outstayed my welcome, so thank you for allowing me the opportunity to share the knowledge, love, and respect I have for this small but crucial aspect of the scientific process. And, in closing, I'll make two requests of you. First, please review the 25 principles introduced during the course of the book that enable the design and conduct of *meaningful* principled experiments involving human participants:

Principle #1: Do not contemplate a scientific career if you are not prepared to be absolutely, uncompromisingly, unfashionably honest and transparent.

Principle #2: Always be skeptical, but attempt to personally cultivate being open- minded.

Principle #3: Do not contemplate independently conducting an experiment until you have mastered your general field and its experimental underpinnings.

Principle #4: Do not contemplate conducting research whose primary purpose is to change the way clinicians practice their professions unless you are an experienced clinician yourself or have an active co-investigator who is.

Principle #5: Conduct your first research forays under the tutelage of an experienced, principled mentor.

Principle #6: Always translate a proposed experiment into one or more formal, written hypotheses.

Principle #7: Once the hypothesis is formulated, delineate all of the possible experimental outcomes, attempt to assess the probability of each of their occurrences, and *attempt to visualize the actual numerical outcome likely to accrue if the hypothesis is supported.*

Principle #8: Always solicit as much professional feedback on your hypothesis, design, and rationale as possible prior to conducting an experiment.

Principle #9: Always explicitly designate nonhypothesized subgroup analyses and secondary analyses employing outcome variables other than the primary outcome as such when reporting the results of an experiment. (When reading a published report, put little or no credence in a nonreplicated subgroup analysis or experimental effects involving multiple secondary outcome variables.)

Principle #10: Once a final hypothesis has been decided on, attempt to honestly assess your primary motivations (or aspirations) for conducting the experiment.

Principle #11: Avoid interventions whose relationship to self-reported (or reactive observational) outcome variables are potentially obvious to participants.

Principle #12: To the extent permitted ethically and scientifically, communicate as little as possible to participants and research staff about the specific purpose and hypothesized results of an experiment.

Principle #13: When conducting an experiment, always use at least one control or comparison group and (for designs using different participants in the study groups) always randomly assign participants to all experimental conditions.

Principle #14: Whenever possible conduct a post experimental "exit" interview to ascertain information on undetected protocol violations, guesses regarding group assignment (when applicable), reactions to experimental procedures (e.g., noncompliance therewith), and reasons for withdrawal.

Principle #15: In the presence of any significant degree of experimental attrition (differential or otherwise), conduct post hoc intent-to-treat and data imputation analyses in order to ascertain the degree to which attrition (and/or noncompliance with the protocol) potentially affected the final study results.

Principle #16: Choose the experiment's control or comparison group with exceeding care in order to match what the study actually assesses with its scientific objective or hypothesis.

Principle #17: Prior to conducting an experiment, always (a) identify all potential confounds, (b) eliminate those which are plausibly related to the study outcome by standardizing and/or counterbalancing procedures across experimental conditions to the maximum extent possible, and (c) monitor the effects of those confounds that cannot be eliminated or counterbalanced.

Principle #18: All scientifically meaningful interaction effects expected to reach statistical significance should be hypothesized a priori along with their direction, based on the presence of a theoretical or clinical rationale.

Principle #19: Regardless of who analyzes the experiment's final data, ensure that all sources of systematic variation (e.g., covariates, factors, nested and blocking variables, counterbalanced procedural elements) are included (or at least modeled to ascertain if they should be included).

Principle #20: In addition to randomly assigning participants, counterbalance all procedural components employed in an experiment via the use of blocks and then randomly assign participants to those blocks to avoid confounding.

Principle #21: Always conduct a power/sample size analysis as part of the design process and ensure that the experiment has sufficient power to detect the hypothesized effect size.

Principle #22: Do not subvert the power/sample size analytic process by making it a process for justifying a convenient, feasible, or easily available sample size.

Principle #23: Always conduct at least one pilot study prior to initiating the final experiment.

Principle #24: When conducting (or planning) an experiment, schedule regular meetings with all staff and collaborators to discuss problems, solutions to those problems, and suggestions for improvement of the experimental process.

Principle #25: Develop sufficient data-analytic expertise to either analyze your own data or to evaluate what has been analyzed for you by someone else.

My second request is to either commit to memory or create an accessible list of the 18 experimental artifacts sprinkled over the first 10 chapters and be cognizant of their nefarious potential in both the design of your own experiments and the evaluation of others'. In their order of presentation, they were:

1. Natural history or maturation
2. The placebo effect
3. Regression to the mean
4. The repeated testing artifact
5. Instrumentation changes
6. Volunteerism
7. Extraneous external events (aka history)
8. Demand characteristics (or the "good-subject" phenomenon)
9. Hawthorne-like effects
10. Experimental attrition
11. Selection
12. Differential attrition

13. Other experimental confounds
14. Treatment diffusion
15. Resentful demoralization
16. Compensatory rivalry
17. Underpowered experiments
18. Sloppily conducted experiments

REFERENCES

Gladstone, J.H. (1872). *Michael Faraday*. New York: Harper & Brothers.

Venter, J.C. (2007). *A life decoded: My genome: My life*. New York: Viking.

AUTHOR INDEX

SUBJECT INDEX

CPSIA information can be obtained
at www.ICGtesting.com
Printed in the USA
BVHW010152190320
575381BV00005B/42